Empire of Sin

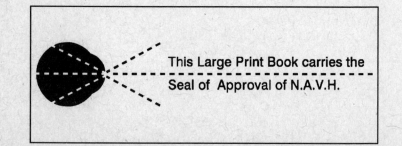

This Large Print Book carries the
Seal of Approval of N.A.V.H.

EMPIRE OF SIN

A STORY OF SEX, JAZZ, MURDER, AND THE BATTLE FOR MODERN NEW ORLEANS

GARY KRIST

THORNDIKE PRESS

A part of Gale, Cengage Learning

GALE
CENGAGE Learning·

Farmington Hills, Mich • San Francisco • New York • Waterville, Maine
Meriden, Conn • Mason, Ohio • Chicago

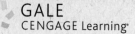
GALE
CENGAGE Learning®

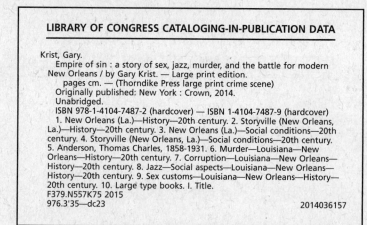

LIBRARY OF CONGRESS CATALOGING-IN-PUBLICATION DATA

Krist, Gary.
    Empire of sin : a story of sex, jazz, murder, and the battle for modern
New Orleans / by Gary Krist. — Large print edition.
        pages cm. — (Thorndike Press large print crime scene)
    Originally published: New York : Crown, 2014.
    Unabridged.
    ISBN 978-1-4104-7487-2 (hardcover) — ISBN 1-4104-7487-9 (hardcover)
    1. New Orleans (La.)—History—20th century. 2. Storyville (New Orleans,
La.)—History—20th century. 3. New Orleans (La.)—Social conditions—20th
century. 4. Storyville (New Orleans, La.)—Social conditions—20th century.
5. Anderson, Thomas Charles, 1858-1931. 6. Murder—Louisiana—New
Orleans—History—20th century. 7. Corruption—Louisiana—New Orleans—
History—20th century. 8. Jazz—Social aspects—Louisiana—New Orleans—
History—20th century. 9. Sex customs—Louisiana—New Orleans—History—
20th century. 10. Large type books. I. Title.
    F379.N557K75 2015
    976.3'35—dc23   2014036157

Published in 2015 by arrangement with Crown Publishers, a division of Random House LLC, a Penguin Random House Company

Printed in the United States of America
1 2 3 4 5 6 7 19 18 17 16 15

CONTENTS

AUTHOR'S NOTE

Empire of Sin is a work of nonfiction, adhering strictly to the historical record and incorporating no invented dialogue or other undocumented re-creations. Unless otherwise attributed, anything between quotation marks is either actual dialogue (as reported by a witness or in a newspaper) or else a citation from a memoir, book, letter, police report, court transcript, or other document, as cited in the endnotes. In some quotations I have, for clarity's sake, corrected the original spelling, syntax, word order, or punctuation. Names and certain other nouns were often spelled in various ways in various sources (for example, "axeman/axman"); in these cases, I've chosen the spelling that seems best or most plausible and used it consistently throughout the book, even in direct quotes.

It is no easy matter to go to heaven by way of New Orleans.
— REVEREND J. CHANDLER GREGG

■ ■ ■ ■

Prologue:
May 23, 1918

■ ■ ■ ■

A street in the Vieux Carré **Library of Congress**

"The crime," as detectives would later tell the newspapers, was "one of the most gruesome in the annals of the New Orleans police."

At five A.M. on the sultry morning of May 23, 1918, the bodies of Joseph and Catherine Maggio, Italian immigrants who ran a small grocery store in a remote section of the city, were found sprawled across the disordered bedroom of the living quarters behind their store. Both had been savagely attacked, apparently while they slept. Joseph Maggio lay face-up on the blood-sodden bed, his skull split by a deep, jagged gash several inches long; Catherine Maggio, her own skull nearly hewn in two, was stretched out on the floor beneath him. Each victim's throat had been slashed with a sharp instrument.

A blood-smeared ax and shaving razor — obviously the murder weapons — had been found on the floor nearby.

Police Superintendent Frank T. Mooney

11

stood among the dozen or so detectives and patrolmen working over the grocery for clues. Summoned from his bed before dawn, the superintendent had immediately rushed out to the crime scene, located at the corner of Magnolia and Upperline Streets. It was a godforsaken neighborhood on the outskirts of Uptown New Orleans, a place where a few single-story pineboard shacks stood amid a sea of weed-choked empty lots. Until recent years, this area had been little more than a fetid swamp, populated by alligators and slender-necked herons. But now people actually lived here — Italians, mostly, along with an assortment of other recent immigrants and a few blacks too poor to live anywhere else. Like much of the part of New Orleans set far back from the river and its natural levee, it was an inadequate place for human habitation, a breeding ground for all kinds of disease and squalor. And now it had become a breeding ground for crime as well: street lighting was still unheard-of out here, and even the slightest rain could transform the low-lying, unpaved streets into stagnant rivers of muck, impossible for even the sturdiest of police vehicles to navigate.

Frank Mooney, forty-eight years old and still new to his job, understood that he had to oversee the investigation of this case very closely. It would be the first high-profile homicide of his tenure as police superinten-

12

dent, and a crime so strange and sensational was bound to attract all kinds of unwanted publicity. In some ways, the case seemed straightforward enough. The intruder had clearly taken the Maggios' own ax from the backyard shed and used it to chisel out a panel of the kitchen door and pry off the lock. He had then entered the kitchen, carried the ax down the short hallway to the bedroom, and used it, and perhaps the shaving razor, to butcher the sleeping Maggios. He'd apparently made no attempt to hide the murder weapons or otherwise obscure any evidence of the brutal crime that had occurred in that tiny, airless bedroom.

The question of motive, though, was more problematic. Robbery seemed the most obvious explanation, but there was little proof that anything had actually been taken from the house. True, the grocer's bedside safe had been found open and empty. But there were no signs that the safe had been forced, and right beneath it sat a tin box, wrapped in a woman's stocking, containing several hundred dollars' worth of jewelry. Mooney's officers also found $100 in cash secreted under Joseph Maggio's pillow. No professional thief could have overlooked such easy booty.

Chief of Detectives George Long, the experienced investigator whom Mooney had put in charge of the case, had a different theory — one that implicated Andrew Maggio, Joseph's younger brother, who lived in the other half of the grocery building on Magnolia Street. Andrew had been the first person to discover the bodies, after allegedly hearing a scuffle in his brother's apartment and going next door to investigate. He was a barber by profession, and several days earlier had been seen taking a straight razor from his shop "to have a nick honed from the blade." Based on this evidence alone, Andrew Maggio — along with another younger Maggio brother — had been detained for questioning.

But there was one incongruous piece of evidence that seemed to exonerate the brothers — and to point to another kind of perpetrator entirely: Shortly before noon, two detectives canvassing the neighborhood had stumbled across a clue just a block away from the murder scene. Right at the corner of Robertson and Upperline, scrawled across the planks of a wooden banquette (as sidewalks are called in New Orleans), they'd found a chalk message written in a crude, childish hand:

MRS JOSEPH MAGGIO IS GOING TO SIT UP TONIGHT JUST LIKE MRS TONEY

It was baffling: Why would Andrew Maggio — or anyone else in his right mind — leave behind such a gratuitous clue to the murders?

14

A couple of Mooney's more senior detectives raised an unsettling possibility. They told the superintendent about a series of unsolved attacks on Italian grocers that had occurred in the city some years ago; at least three of those attacks had been committed with a hatchet. One victim, who like Maggio had been slain in bed with his wife, was named Tony Schiambra. Could Mrs. Schiambra be the "Mrs. Toney" in the chalk scrawl? And if so, what did it mean? At the time of the earlier attacks, police had attributed the crimes to the local Black Hand, a loosely knit organization of Italian extortionists that New Orleanians commonly (though not accurately) called "the Mafia." But the Black Hand had supposedly been eliminated in the city some time ago. The New Orleans police had waged a long and bitter fight against the shadowy organization to root out its members and end what had been a virtual epidemic of blackmail and murder in the city's Italian community. By 1918, it was widely believed that the battle had been won.

But now Frank Mooney had his own pair of murdered Italian grocers to deal with, and it was certain that everyone in New Orleans would be watching to see how their rookie superintendent handled the case. Ten months earlier, when he was first named to the position, the *Times-Picayune* had questioned the wisdom of Mooney's selection. Was it a good idea, the paper had asked, to trust command of the entire police department to a former railroad executive whose law enforcement experience amounted to little more than a short stint as a rail-yard cop many years ago? The new superintendent was clearly a police outsider, appointed by a mayor well known for bestowing city jobs on his political allies. Mooney didn't even *look* like a cop — with his gold-rimmed spectacles, brushy mustache, and stout, well-banqueted physique, he looked more like an insurance executive on his way to an industry convention in Omaha. And even though the *Times-Picayune* had praised Mooney's sterling qualities as a manager, the paper pointed out that these credentials did not guarantee success as commander of the New Orleans police: "As police superintendent, he will be judged not by his [past] record, however creditable . . . but by the record he has yet to make."

For Mooney, then, there was strong incentive to see Andrew Maggio as the perpetrator of these two murders, and to write them off as isolated revenge killings or a domestic crime of passion — the kind of easily explicable incident that was all too common in New Orleans' poorer neighborhoods. Far better this explanation than attributing the attack to a return of Black Hand terrorism, long after the police had supposedly eliminated that threat. The campaign against the

Italian underworld — part of a larger effort by the so-called respectable white establishment to wrest control of their city from the forces of vice, crime, and corruption — had roiled New Orleans for the better part of three decades, eventually degenerating into something like all-out class warfare. A generation-long ordeal of lynchings, riots, and large-scale police raids had taken a harsh toll on the entire city. So for an untested police superintendent trying to convince his constituents that New Orleans' bad old days were indeed over, a resurrection of the "Dago Evil," as it was called, would be an ominous development indeed.

But not, perhaps, the worst possible development. That would come a few months later. For, by the end of that summer of 1918 — with three more similar ax murders terrorizing the city and the *Times-Picayune* openly speculating about a crazed serial killer on the loose — it would be clear that a very different kind of evil was at large in the squalid backstreets of New Orleans.

■ ■ ■ ■

PART ONE:
THE WAR BEGINS

1890–1891

■ ■ ■ ■

■ ■ ■ ■

CHAPTER 1
GOING RESPECTABLE

■ ■ ■ ■

Josie Lobrano (aka Arlington), ca. 1890
Earl K. Long Library, University of New Orleans

Shortly after eleven o'clock on a bright November morning, a handsome middle-aged man dashed up to the front door of the brothel at 172 Customhouse Street in the French Quarter and let himself in with a key. It was still early for any kind of business at a New Orleans house of prostitution, so no one except the servants was up and about. But the man — Phillip Lobrano — didn't have to be formally shown in. He was well known in the house; the front ground-floor bedroom was where he regularly consorted with the madam of the place, a woman who called herself Josie Lobrano. The two had been lovers and business partners for almost a decade — ever since Josie was sixteen and the much-older Lobrano had offered her his protection. And while she was technically and legally still Miss Mary Deubler, she used Phillip's surname for professional purposes — though few people were apparently deceived.

This was, after all, New Orleans in 1890 —

the Crescent City of the Gilded Age, where aliases of convenience and unconventional living arrangements were anything but out of the ordinary, at least in certain parts of town. Identities were fluid here, and names and appearances weren't always the best guide to telling who was who. Dressed in knee-length frock coats, pinstriped trousers, and suavely cocked felt derbies, men who may or may not have been gentlemen strolled the gaslit avenues with fashionable young women who may or may not have been their wives. Clerks in the department stores on busy Canal Street were careful to ask their female customers that all-important question — "And where do we send the bill, madam?" — in a hushed, confidential, knowing tone of voice. Newsboys of uncertain parentage hawked papers on street corners, and one could only wonder who was bankrolling the rakish ne'er-do-wells dropping hundreds at the Fair Grounds Racetrack or in one of the back-room gambling dens in saloons all around town.

And so Phillip Lobrano — aging but dapper, well dressed but not conspicuously employed — entered the brothel of the woman known by some as his wife. He found Josie still in bed, sleeping late after the strain of a busy Friday night. Clearly in a state of some agitation, Lobrano told her to get up immediately and get dressed. He said that he had just seen one of her brothers — Peter Deubler, who worked sporadically as a street-car motorman — in a bar on Royal Street, supremely drunk and apparently hungry for trouble. Peter was on his way over to the brothel, and when he arrived, Josie was to send the maid to the door to say they weren't home. If she let Peter in, Lobrano warned, she would have to take responsibility for the consequences.

As Josie dressed, Lobrano recounted what had happened on Royal Street. He had been sitting in Louis George's saloon, quietly reading the newspaper, when an obviously intoxicated Peter Deubler wandered in. Seeing Lobrano, the young man ordered a bottle from the bartender and carried it over to his table. Phillip wasn't particularly welcoming. He'd always disliked Josie's family, whom he considered little more than a "flock of vultures," forever borrowing money and monopolizing too much of her time and attention. Even so, he tried at first to be civil. But Peter was still reeling from an all-night spree and was in a foul, abusive mood. In sarcastic tones, he invited Lobrano to have a drink with him, and when Lobrano declined, Peter became angry.

"You bastard, come take a drink," he insisted, filling a glass and shoving it across the table.

The bartender tried to intervene. "It looks

25

as if you want to raise hell," he observed warily. Peter, a large, muscular man who had once singlehandedly knocked down six men in a street fight, agreed that this was indeed his intention. Then, for reasons that would remain obscure, he began to deride Lobrano in a loud, menacing voice. Intimidated, Lobrano quickly finished his drink and got up to leave.

"I know where to find you," Peter said ominously as Lobrano turned away.

A few minutes later, as Lobrano was hurrying over to Josie's, a friend who had been in the bar caught up with him on Canal Street. Peter, the friend warned, had begun to make threats against Lobrano just after the two had parted. "I am going to kill that bastard Lobrano," Peter had said explicitly — in front of several witnesses — before stumbling out of the saloon.

Lobrano had barely finished telling this story to Josie when the brothel's front doorbell rang. That was Peter now, Lobrano warned, and he urged her again not to let him in. But Josie seemed unconcerned. Twenty-six years old, sturdily built like her brother, with attractive, somewhat hardened features accentuated by striking black eyebrows, she was hardly the timid, fearful type. Driven into prostitution as an eleven-year-old orphan, Josie had been forced to fend for herself and her two younger brothers from the beginning. Years of struggling to survive on the streets of New Orleans had turned her into a tough and often combative woman. She had in fact been arrested for disorderly conduct several times, once for horsewhipping a young man on Palmyra Street, and again for brawling with a fellow prostitute named Beulah Ripley (who allegedly "staggered from the scene of combat missing part of her lower lip and half an ear"). So Josie was not one to shy away from a confrontation, especially not with a member of her own family. Calling the maid, Josie instructed her to answer the door and see her brother in. She would talk to him alone in the parlor and see what was the matter.

Peter, however, turned out to be "too drunk to take to the parlor." Apparently worried that he might make a scene and upset the other occupants of the house, Josie decided instead to bring him back to her bedroom. "Are *you* here?" Peter sneered when he saw his sister's paramour in the room. Lobrano asked him what he wanted, but Peter informed him that it was none of his business. Lobrano then insisted that Peter leave immediately, and when the intoxicated young man claimed he had a right to enter his sister's bedroom whenever he wished, Josie actually took her brother's side. She pointed out that the house belonged to her and that

Lobrano had no right to order anyone out of it.

What happened next would be a matter of dispute for years to come. According to Phillip Lobrano, after a few more angry words, he decided he'd had enough. He was just stepping to the door to leave when Peter suddenly lunged at him, punched him on the side of the face, and then made a gesture as if to pull a gun. According to Josie Lobrano, however, there was no lunge, no punch, and no threatening gesture. But the Lobranos did agree about Phillip's next move: spitting out a "vile epithet," he reached into his coat for his own .32-caliber revolver, pointed it at Peter Deubler, and pulled the trigger.

His aim was perhaps truer than he expected. The bullet struck Josie's brother squarely in the nose, tore through the base of his brain, and lodged in the back wall of his skull. Peter collapsed onto the bedroom floor, his face awash in blood.

Josie screamed and fell to her knees beside her brother's fallen body. Amazingly, Peter still seemed to be conscious. "You've done it, Phil!" he allegedly cried through his shattered face. But Lobrano, standing amid the coiling smoke from the barrel of his pistol, didn't linger to see what it was he'd done. Pushing past the maid, who now stood horrified just outside the doorway, he ran out of the bedroom, hurried down the hallway, and exited by a side door into an alley off Burgundy Street.

Drawn by the sound of gunfire, a crowd soon gathered on Customhouse Street outside. The Lobranos' neighbors in the French Quarter — or the Vieux Carré, as it was more commonly called — had been expecting trouble at the brothel for some time. Phillip and Josie had never lived peaceably together, and their domestic quarrels had brought police to the door more than once over the years. But in recent weeks, the discord between the two had become even fiercer than usual. As several members of the crowd later told a reporter, they'd all "expected a tragedy to take place at almost any time" in that house.

Within minutes, Cpl. Thomas Duffy of the New Orleans Police arrived on the scene and shoved his way through the crowd. He entered the brothel and found Josie standing over her brother's blood-drenched form, surrounded by a half dozen of her prostitutes in various states of undress.

Duffy quickly summoned an ambulance and then tried to question the witnesses about the incident. But he didn't get very far. Josie, tough as she was, was apparently too upset to make much sense, and the other women professed to know nothing about the shooting; at the time it occurred, they

29

claimed, they'd all been upstairs in their bedrooms, waiting for breakfast to be served.

Convinced that they were not telling everything they knew, Duffy threatened to take the whole lot of them down to the station in a paddy wagon. This caused something of an uproar among the women. *They* had done nothing wrong, they argued, and certainly didn't deserve to be carted away like common criminals. Some said they wouldn't go unless they could walk to the station; others insisted on traveling in cabs.

But Duffy's patience had by now been exhausted. When the horse-drawn paddy wagon arrived, he and several other policemen herded the quarrelsome young women into the vehicle. Then he rode with them through the roiling streets of the Vieux Carré to the Third Precinct Station, where they were questioned and, amid much complaint about the cruel treatment they had received, released.

In the meantime, Phillip Lobrano had apparently thought better of leaving the scene of the shooting. Shortly after noon, he walked into the Central Police Station on Basin Street and surrendered himself to the officer in charge, Capt. John Journée. The latest word from the Hôtel-Dieu Hospital was that Peter Deubler's wound was "very dangerous," perhaps even fatal. So Journée immediately took Lobrano into custody. He

30

threw the prisoner into one of the station's holding cells, where he sat for a few hours before being transferred to the Second Recorder's Court. There he was arraigned on a charge of "shooting with intent to murder." Pleading not guilty, he was remanded to the Orleans Parish Prison in the Tremé district, to be held without bail.

Peter Deubler underwent surgery that afternoon and was moved to one of the Hôtel-Dieu's recovery wards, where doctors refused to allow anyone, even Josie, to see him. His condition stabilized and then improved over the next few days; at one point he even seemed well enough to be sent home. But his recovery was short-lived. Within a week he was back at the Hôtel-Dieu, "sinking rapidly" with a raging fever. He died there on December 9 at 2:15 in the afternoon, ten days after being shot.

The incident at Josie Lobrano's brothel became the talk of the Vieux Carré for some time thereafter. Murder, of course, was no novelty in the city's vice districts in 1890. But the Lobranos were well-known characters in that world, and so the shooting took on all the allure of celebrity scandal among the city's demimondaines. However, like many crimes in nineteenth-century New Orleans, it ultimately had few dire consequences for the perpetrator. Phillip Lobrano went on to be tried — twice — for the murder of Peter Deubler. Both times the defense successfully convinced a majority of jurors that the shooting had been committed in self-defense. The initial trial, after many delays and false starts, ended in a hung jury; the second, however, brought an actual acquittal, and on March 31, 1892, Lobrano was released from prison, after fourteen months of incarceration.

But Lobrano's easy life as the kept man of a successful New Orleans madam was over. Long before his release, Josie Lobrano, devastated by her brother's death and determined to be rid of her longtime paramour, had abruptly cut all business and romantic ties to him. At the same time, she also resolved to change a few other aspects of her life. For the previous fifteen years as a prostitute and madam, Josie had been living a violent, dissolute existence among society's most debauched elements. But the pointless killing of her brother had altered something in her. She'd apparently done some soul-searching, and now claimed that she was ready to "turn over a new leaf." Josie wouldn't close the brothel, of course; the business was too lucrative, and sex work was the only thing she knew. But she was determined to change the way she lived — to end her old low-life associations, get rid of her current roster of fractious girls, and cater to a new and better class of customer. She would also find herself a more agreeable inamorato and perhaps even a wealthy patron to partner with. It might take some time and more than a little money, but Josie Lobrano — until now known as one of the rudest and roughest madams in the Vieux Carré — had decided to become respectable.

CHAPTER 2
THE SODOM OF THE SOUTH

A PLAGUE OF PROSTITUTES.

An 1892 issue of the Mascot *reports on the vice problem.*
Louisiana Research Collection, Tulane University

Respectability. Josie Lobrano was not alone in her pursuit of it in Gilded Age New Orleans. The concept of respectability was very much in the air in the city of the 1880s and '90s, championed in newspaper editorials, debated in clubs and parlors, and trumpeted from church pulpits all over town. This was, after all, the era of high Victorianism, and even a place like the Crescent City was not impervious to the stringent ideals of the day. Granted, "respectability" might have meant one thing to a French Quarter madam, involving not much more than an enthusiastic embrace of the trappings of wealth, exclusivity, and a certain faux high-class refinement. But for members of what was optimistically called "polite society," the standards were somewhat higher. Keeping brawls and gunfire out of one's home was the least of it.

In nineteenth-century New Orleans, however, respectability was arguably more difficult to achieve and maintain than in almost any other place on the continent. Threats to decency were everywhere, and the city's lax cosmopolitan ethos hardly conformed to mainstream American norms of behavior. Thanks to its unique history, in fact, New Orleans scarcely seemed American at all. Founded as a French outpost in the early 1700s, the city had come of age under Spanish rule in the latter half of the eighteenth century, giving the place a distinctive Franco-Latin character that still manifested itself in everything from its architecture to its municipal administration. And although the 1803 Louisiana Purchase had forcibly thrust the city into the rapidly growing United States, several decades as capital of the American South had done only so much to make it seem less foreign. "I doubt if there is a city in the world," Frederick Law Olmsted said of New Orleans in 1856, "where the resident population has been so divided in its origin, or where there is such a variety in the tastes, habits, manners, and moral codes of the citizens." And this extraordinary multiplicity — augmented by successive waves of immigration from Europe and the Caribbean — had only grown more pronounced as the century progressed. "What a mingling of peoples!" another visitor marveled in 1880: "Americans and Brazilians; West Indians, Spanish and French; Germans, Creoles, quadroons, mulattoes, Chinese, and Negroes."

The urban culture that developed around this confluence of races and ethnicities was something that the rest of the country soon came to regard with a combination of wonder, suspicion, and often abhorrence. Worldly New Orleans was emphatically unlike, say, Lutheran Minneapolis, or even the Baptist cities in the rest of the South. For one thing, New Orleans wasn't even Protestant, at least not much beyond the handful of uptown neighborhoods containing the enclaves of Anglo-American privilege; it was still a largely Latin, Catholic city, with entrenched attitudes and mores that could seem — to anyone aspiring to conservative Protestant standards of rectitude — distressingly exotic. As such, it was a strange and disturbing place to many — a place where married white men attended "Quadroon Balls" to find mixed-race concubines, where macabre voodoo rituals occurred in shanties and back alleys, and where even prominent politicians might meet in City Park to duel with pistols or épées at dawn. In the city's notorious tenderloin districts, brothels specialized in all manner of interracial mixing and arcane sexual practices, while narcotics, alcohol, and loud, degenerate kinds of music filled the saloons and dance halls, promoting deviant behavior of all kinds.

The Crescent City was also a place cursed with a deep-rooted culture of violence and crime: colorful miscreants stalked the streets; warring vice lords shot up their rivals' saloons and gambling dens; and mysterious Italians, purportedly members of the murky organization called "the Mafia" or "the Black Hand," assassinated one another for obscure and sinister reasons. For visitors from other parts of the country — and for the city's growing ranks of white Protestant elites — the opportunities for moral contamination were legion. As one Victorian minister put it in 1868, "It is no easy matter to go to heaven by way of New Orleans."

Even so, it wasn't until the last decades of the nineteenth century that respectability had become such a burning preoccupation among the "better element" in New Orleans — or crime and indecency the source of such widespread outrage. True, gambling, prostitution, street violence, and bawdy entertainment had been a prominent feature of the city's life for its entire history. But up till this point they had been confined to certain well-defined zones along the waterfront and in several lower-class neighborhoods — places that could easily be avoided in the course of the average upstanding citizen's day. Ensconced in the Garden District around St. Charles Avenue, decent men and (especially) women could insulate themselves from the goings-on "back of town" or in the mixed neighborhoods downriver from Canal Street. But in the decades after Reconstruction, these goings-on had begun to spread from the traditional vice areas into reputable residential and commercial districts all over town, endangering the morals of anyone who rode a streetcar, dined at a restaurant, or shopped in one of the city's markets or department stores.

The assaults on respectability, in fact, had become all but ubiquitous in New Orleans. The rise of "concert saloons" — raucous theaters where patrons could drink while watching erotically suggestive stage performances — had brought crime and high-profile immorality to some of the busiest shopping avenues in the city. Establishments offering so-called coon music, considered a dangerous inducement to lewd dancing and cross-racial fraternization, were also making inroads; once confined to the black clubs and dance halls of poorer neighborhoods, the music could now assail the ears of bankers and merchants on Canal Street itself — the main artery of the business district. And perhaps most scandalous of all, brothels and assignation houses had become impossible to avoid, cropping up in many places where decent middle-class families lived. Many felt that a man could no longer feel comfortable in his own home, never knowing when the house next door might be sold and turned into a disorderly house, forcing his wife and children to bear witness to scenes of the utmost wickedness and depravity.

"The social evil is rampant in our midst," wrote the *Mascot,* the city's major crusading weekly, in 1892. "Houses of assignation and ill-fame . . . are springing up all over the city . . . Many a man has purchased a house and lot on a quiet street . . . but has woke up some morning to find the house next door occupied by disreputable people who carouse, receive visitors, hammer the piano all night, use obscene language, and convert his paradise into a hell."

The effects of this expansion of vice and crime were now plain to see throughout the city. Stories abounded of honest, job-seeking women being ruined by unscrupulous concert-saloon proprietors; of agents steering underage girls to bordello keepers for a commission; and of dressmakers' assistants and messenger boys being seduced into the "sporting life" while making deliveries to brothels, saloons, and gambling houses. By the late 1880s, criminality of all types in the city seemed virtually out of control: "At no time since the war . . . has crime been so rampant or criminals so free as at present," observed the *Mascot* in 1888. "Within [the past] two months, several brutal and deliberate murders have been planned and perpetrated. Young girls have been outraged, homes have been burglarized, citizens have been maltreated by officers of the law, poor little newborn babes have been pitilessly slaughtered, and any number of men have taken their own lives for real or fancied causes, but as yet there has been no stop to the era of blood and degradation."

Blacks and immigrants — especially Italians — were of course scapegoated for much of the lawlessness and moral corruption. Complaints about the debased behavior at "Negro dives" were a frequent feature of local newspaper coverage, which became especially virulent when that behavior crossed the color line. Meanwhile, the violence and crime endemic to the city's "Little Palermo" (the ramshackle downriver end of the Vieux Carré) was the cause of even greater editorial spleen in the press. "If given our choice between the Negro and the 'Dago,' " one writer fulminated in 1889, "we are inclined to believe that we would take the wooly son of Africa in preference to the greezy, filthy son of Italy. . . . The Dagos are a curse to New Orleans." The fact that both groups were considered a "disruptive element" in local politics only deepened the antagonism of the city's native-born Anglo-American elite. Black votes were widely regarded as for sale to the highest bidder, while Italians and other immigrants provided a reliable base of support for "the Ring" — the powerful and corrupt Democratic machine that had controlled city government for much of its recent history.

For so-called respectable New Orleans, then, the situation had become dire indeed. The lawlessness, municipal dysfunction, flagrant sexuality, and increasing visibility of vice posed a threat not just to individual reputations but also to the reputation of the city as a whole. And all of this was happening at a time when New Orleans desperately needed to project an image of competence and stability to the world. The city's antebellum glory days — when booming business in sugar, cotton, and slaves made it the Queen City of the South, indispensable to world trade — were long past. Decades of civil war and federal occupation had been hard on the local economy, while competition from newer railroad centers and other, faster-growing ports had eaten away at the city's commercial supremacy. Formerly the fourth-largest city in the country, New Orleans had since dropped to ninth place. And while business was still growing in absolute numbers, the city government had taken on a level of debt that severely limited its ability to remain competitive.

The result was a city that had become hopelessly backward, at least in terms of urban development. Other major cities —

New York, Chicago, St. Louis — had surged ahead with electrified streetcars, modern sanitation facilities, and miles and miles of well-paved streets. But New Orleans seemed stuck in an earlier era: streetcars were still pulled by dusty, overworked mules; sewage ran through open gutters at the edges of dirt-paved or otherwise primitive streets; few residents had running water; and the city's main arteries — except for the recently electrified main drag of Canal Street — were still illuminated by old-fashioned gas lamps. (New Orleans, it was often observed, was the first American metropolis to build an opera house, but the last to build a sewerage system.) By the late 1880s, then, the city desperately needed to rebuild its port and overhaul its increasingly antiquated infrastructure. To do all of that, it urgently needed to attract Northern capital investment. But as one local businessman wrote, "The reputation of our city has been fearful and it has been utterly impossible to interest capital in any enterprise in New Orleans."

Faced with this rapidly deteriorating situation, the Crescent City's self-anointed leading citizens had by 1888 concluded that drastic measures were necessary to halt the city's moral and economic slide. In that year, a well-heeled young lawyer named William S. Parkerson formed a new political party, the Young Men's Democratic Association, with the explicit purpose of taking on the Ring machine that had allowed such conditions to flourish in the city. Other similar parties, of course, had risen up with that same goal in the past, only to falter after a few years of limited electoral success. But Parkerson's YMDA had some very powerful supporters. "Its campaign committee," as one historian put it, "read like a blue book of the city's commercial elite," and they were all determined to put the city on the road to long-desired reform. Rejecting the candidates put up by Democratic Party regulars in the spring city elections ("a ticket which is an insult to the intelligence of this community and a menace to its progress and integrity"), the YMDA instead rallied around its own slate of higher-toned hopefuls. Led by mayoral candidate Joseph A. Shakspeare, the YMDA ticket promised the voters a war on vice and corruption, a total revamping of the city's inept and venal police department, and a large-scale effort to revitalize the crumbling infrastructure through honest tax collection and other sound business practices. And the reformers backed these heady promises with a threat that their opponents could understand: the association was gathering an arsenal, and would ensure that the election was conducted properly "if need be at the point of the bayonet."

The strong-arm tactics worked. Though

Ring operatives attempted "countless questionable devices and election legerdemain" to steal the vote, armed contingents of YMDA men at every polling station kept the usual hired thugs and vote buyers in check. And when the votes were counted, Shakspeare had won a commanding victory, with the rest of the reform slate taking all but two of the city's seventeen wards. The triumphant Parkerson, offered the position of city attorney in Shakspeare's new administration, ultimately declined to serve. But he — along with his gun-toting private militia — would remain a potent force backing the new mayor in all of his endeavors to come.

For the cream of New Orleans society, this was a hopeful beginning. At least for the time being, the so-called better half — the city's clergymen and newspaper editors, its upright lawyers and businessmen, its social reformers and club women — would control city government, with a popular mandate for change that few could gainsay. But the job before them was clear: in order to survive and thrive in the coming new century, the city of New Orleans — like brothel madam Josie Lobrano — was going to have to remake itself along more respectable lines. The city would have to normalize its scandalous sex life, isolate and regulate its notorious entertainment districts, and take control of the infamous crime on its streets. The task would be formi-

47

dable, requiring direct confrontation with the forces of the city's demimonde, its entrenched vice industries, and its black and immigrant underworlds. To win their city back, in other words, the self-styled champions of respectability and order were going to have to launch the equivalent of an all-out civil war.

That the first major casualty in this war was the city's popular police chief — David Hennessy, gunned down in front of his own home — was an early indication of just how bitterly the conflict was going to be fought.

CHAPTER 3
THE FIRST
CASUALTY

Chief of Police David C. Hennessy
Louisiana Research Collection, Tulane University
sity

The war began quietly enough, on a chilly, wet evening in October of 1890.

At the weekly police board meeting at City Hall, New Orleans mayor Joseph A. Shakspeare was presiding over the disciplinary hearing of two police officers accused of blackmail. Beside him at the examiner's table sat the other four members of the police board, along with several clerks and Superintendent and Chief of Police David C. Hennessy. Rain pattered the tall windows of the boardroom as the last of the early-evening light faded away.

Sgt. James Lynch and Stableman H. Thibodaux — both officers from the Eighth Precinct, just across the river in Algiers — stood in front of the board, listening to the charges against them. The pair had been accused of extorting bribes from several grocery-saloons on a Sunday evening ten days earlier. The officers had allegedly gone from one establishment to another in Algiers, demanding drinks; then, when they were served, they would turn around and threaten to charge the owners with a violation of the city's putatively faith-based Sunday Closing Law unless they paid an adequate bribe. Four of their victims had felt outraged enough to file complaints with the police department.

Sergeant Lynch, asked to respond to the charges, pled not guilty, and requested that the hearing be postponed to allow him and Thibodaux to prepare a defense.

But Shakspeare wouldn't hear of it. The mayor pointed out that the witnesses had been put to substantial trouble coming over on the ferry from Algiers on such a rainy evening. The board would therefore hear their testimony that night. The accused could answer the charges at a later date.

Shakspeare, now more than two years into his term, was doubtless feeling somewhat outraged himself. The law forbidding Sunday liquor sales was one of his own pet initiatives, and to see it abused by the city's own police must have been particularly galling. Reforming the police department, after all, had been one of the major planks in the platform on which he'd been elected back in 1888. Virtually his first act as mayor had been to appoint his friend Hennessy as chief, instructing him to reorganize the entire department and get rid of the corrupt elements that had plagued it for decades. The accusations against Lynch and Thibodaux, unfortunately, showed just how much remained to be done.

Not that anyone was blaming the chief of police for the lingering problems. David C. Hennessy — tall, lean, and dourly handsome, sporting the ubiquitous shapely mustache of 1890s fashion — was one of the most popular and admired figures in the Crescent City. Hired as a police messenger while still a boy — after his father, a longtime metro policeman, was killed in a barroom gunfight — he'd been a lawman all his life. His selection as the country's youngest police chief had been widely applauded at the time, particularly by the reform-minded element that had swept Shakspeare and his allies into office. True, Hennessy had detractors. As a young man, he had once shot and killed a rival detective on the street, and there were some who still claimed that the shooting was unprovoked. But the incident had ultimately been ruled a killing in self-defense and all charges against Hennessy had subsequently been dropped. Now, at thirty-two years of age, he was regarded by many as the straightest of straight arrows. According to the local papers, Hennessy didn't drink, he didn't gamble, and he even avoided fraternizing with women — except for his widowed mother, with whom he lived in a modest cottage on Girod Street. He was also a deeply religious man, stopping at the Jesuit church every evening at six to pray. He was seen by most reformers, in short, as a man of unimpeachable honesty and character — just the person they needed to reinvigorate the police department and start cleaning up the vice- and crime-ridden place their city had become.

But as the testimony of the four witnesses was making painfully obvious, progress had been slow. One of the alleged victims, an Italian grocer named Philip Geraci, described the two officers entering his shop at seven P.M. and demanding cash from the till. Apparently, this was not the first confrontation between them. "You had threatened me before," Geraci said, addressing Officer Thibodaux. "[You] had cursed me and called me a 'dirty Dago.' Everybody knows you are a bulldozer and a tough, and I was never in trouble until you forced me into it!"

Shakspeare clearly found this story plausible enough, and when the other witnesses' testimony proved just as damning, the mayor decided that he'd heard all he needed to hear. He, Hennessy, and the rest of the board agreed that the evidence of extortion was irrefutable. And so — with the self-righteous peremptoriness that was to characterize the reformers' efforts for decades to come — they decided to dismiss the two officers on the spot, without waiting to hear their defense. Why bother with the niceties of judicial process, after all, when there was an entire city to clean up?

After the police board meeting adjourned, the chief and another officer — Capt. William "Billy" O'Connor of the Boylan private detective agency — sat in Hennessy's office at the Central Police Station, chatting idly for an hour before heading home for the night. O'Connor was the chief's old friend, a former colleague who could often be found in Hennessy's company around town. But tonight he was accompanying his friend on a semiofficial basis: O'Connor was acting as the chief's bodyguard for the evening. After several anonymous threats to Hennessy's life over the past few months, the city had arranged with the Boylan agency to provide the chief with round-the-clock protection. And though Hennessy himself regarded this precaution as unnecessary, Mayor Shakspeare had insisted upon it. The fact that the job had gone to the private Boylan agency indicated how much confidence the mayor put in his own police department.

The death threats had stemmed from an ongoing investigation that the chief was conducting into the city's Italian underworld. For some time now, New Orleans' Italian community had been roiled by a struggle between two rival families for the lucrative dockworker contracts on the city's downriver wharves. The Provenzanos, who originally had the contracts with the city's fruit importers, and the Matrangas, who eventually wrested them away, forcing the Provenzanos out of business, had been feuding violently. The resulting wave of back-alley shootings and stabbings had outraged the city's business community, who cited it as just the kind of nonsense that was scaring away investment from Northern capitalists. After several violent murders of alleged Provenzano and Matranga associates in late 1888 and early 1889, Hennessy had decided to take action. Inviting representatives of both clans to the Red Light Club on Customhouse Street, he all but forced them to shake hands in truce, warning them that the city would no longer tolerate their feuds. The perpetrator of any crime in the Italian community, Hennessy warned, would henceforth be hunted down and prosecuted to the full extent of the law.

But the truce ended up lasting for less than a year. On the night of May 5, 1890, the Matranga brothers and five of their workers were returning home after a long day's work on the docks when their horse-drawn wagon was ambushed by gunmen on Esplanade Avenue. Several men were injured, including family patriarch Antonio Matranga himself, who eventually lost a leg as a result of his injuries. Six Provenzano men were accused of the attack and subsequently tried. And although the six were convicted, Chief Hennessy was dissatisfied with the verdict. Convinced that the shooting victims had perjured themselves at the trial, he launched an investigation into the Matranga organization, even sending to Italy for information that might tie the family to alleged Mafia crime figures in Sicily. Exactly what Hennessy had turned up in his research was never made public, but it was apparently damning enough to convince a judge to vacate the Provenzano convictions and order a new trial — and to mark the chief himself, scheduled to testify in the retrial, as a rumored target for assassination.

But on this rainy Wednesday night in October, just two days before the scheduled start of the Provenzano retrial, Hennessy seemed anything but worried about his safety. "The chief was in the best of spirits," O'Connor would later recall to reporters. And as the two men left the police station at a few minutes after eleven, the chief was even feeling sociable enough to invite his bodyguard into Dominic Verget's saloon to share a dozen oysters (which Hennessy, the famous teetotaler, washed down with a small glass of milk).

The driving rain had all but stopped by the time they left Verget's. A drizzly mist now crept along the gleaming streets, muffling the men's footsteps as they walked up Rampart. At the corner of Girod, just a few blocks from the chief's house, they stopped.

"Don't come any further with me now," Hennessy told his friend. "You go on and look after your business."

O'Connor was reluctant at first, but he knew that several other Boylan officers were stationed near the chief's house on Girod, watching over the neighborhood. And there were still many other people abroad in the streets, despite the late hour and rainy weather. So O'Connor decided that his friend would be safe enough. The two men bade each other good night and headed off in opposite directions into the gloom.

Chief Hennessy began walking the remaining two blocks to his house. This part of Girod Street was hardly a fashionable neighborhood in 1890, its motley collection of cottages, rooming houses, and cobbler shops inhabited by a variety of working-class blacks and immigrants. But old Mrs. Hennessy had lived there for many years and was reluctant to move. And so the chief — deeply devoted as he was to his mother — still lived there too, though he could certainly have afforded a home in the more prosperous neighborhoods farther uptown. Besides, the house was just a few minutes by foot from his office at the Central Police Station — always an advantage when a late-night emergency cropped up.

Shortly before the chief reached the end of the first block, a young boy emerged from a doorway ahead of him. The boy began whistling a tune, then raced ahead and turned the corner onto Basin Street. The chief apparently thought nothing suspicious in this, and he continued up Girod Street without pause. But after a few more steps, just as he was passing the shut-up secondhand store at number 269, a volley of gunshots erupted from an alley directly across the street. Before the chief could react, shotgun pellets tore through his umbrella and overcoat, searing his chest, wrist, and legs. Knocked sideways into the wall of the building, he instinctively reached for his pearl-handled Colt revolver and managed to get off a few wild rounds. But his bullets apparently missed their mark. Pistols began firing from another location on the street. Then, according to several witnesses roused by the initial burst of gunfire, two or three men with sawed-off shotguns emerged from the alley, firing again as they stepped into the street. The chief was hit repeatedly as he fell to the sidewalk, blood soaking his vest and white-checked trousers. Finally, with a shout, the gunmen were gone, scattering in several directions through the puddle-streaked streets.

William O'Connor, after parting from the chief, had not even reached the next intersection when he heard the initial gunfire. He turned in time to see the flash of more shots coming from a small, two-story frame house a block and a half away, then heard the four shots from Hennessy's revolver. He immediately started running back up Girod Street. On the way, he encountered Officer M. Kotter, one of the Boylan men assigned to patrol the neighborhood.

"Which way did they run?" O'Connor asked.

"I believe it was uptown."

O'Connor sent the man in pursuit of the gunmen. Then he continued running up Girod in search of Hennessy. The chief seemed to have disappeared, but when O'Connor had nearly reached Basin Street, he heard a call coming from around the corner: "Oh, Billy . . . Billy . . ." O'Connor turned the corner and saw his friend slumped in a doorway down the street.

"They have given it to me," the chief said as O'Connor rushed up to him. "I gave them back the best I could."

Hennessy was bleeding profusely from his face, arms, and legs; his bloodied overcoat was shredded up and down the left side; the spent revolver hung from his right hand.

"Who gave it to you, Dave?" O'Connor asked.

Hennessy told him to come closer. And then, as O'Connor bent over him, the chief allegedly uttered a single word: "Dagos."

By now, numerous neighbors and uniformed police were on the street, gathering

60

around the chief's hunched form in the doorway. Several men helped carry the wounded Hennessy into the house — the Gillis residence at 189 Basin — while O'Connor ran to a grocery across the street to telephone for an ambulance and notify the Central Police Station. When he returned, he found Hennessy propped up on pillows on the floor of the Gillises' parlor, being tended by Auguste Gillis and her mother. They untied the chief's cravat and loosened his bloody collar and cuffs. Hennessy was obviously in great pain, but said very little. When one of the women offered to go and get his mother, however, he roused himself to speak. "No! For God's sake, don't do that," he said, ". . . my poor mother . . ."

Soon the horse-drawn ambulance arrived on Basin Street. The chief was wrapped in a heavy blanket and carried out to the waiting vehicle. The ambulance then rushed him to nearby Charity Hospital, with O'Connor following in a police patrol wagon.

A half mile downriver on Basin Street, the Central Police Station was in an uproar. Mayor Shakspeare, summoned from his home by news of the shooting, was meeting with police department officials to orchestrate the investigation. No one seemed to doubt who was responsible for the ambush. Scores of police were out in the streets, gathering

61

evidence and searching for Italian suspects. Already one weapon — a double-barreled, muzzle-loading shotgun with a collapsible stock, allegedly a "Mafia weapon" — had been found in a gutter on Franklin Street, dropped by one of the fleeing gunmen. But now day officers, roused from sleep, were at the station waiting to be deployed. George Vandervoort, Chief Hennessy's secretary, asked Mayor Shakspeare for instructions.

The mayor was in no mood for subtlety. "Scour the whole neighborhood," he said. "Arrest every Italian you come across, if necessary. And scour it again tomorrow morning as soon as there is light enough. Get all the men you need."

At Charity Hospital, Chief Hennessy was now lying on the table in the operating amphitheater, which by this time was filled with anxious friends, colleagues, and reporters. The chief's bloodstained shirt and undershirt had been cut away, and he was being examined by assistant house surgeon J. D. Bloom and several student physicians. What they found was not encouraging. Hennessy had received multiple bullet wounds — one in his right leg, another in his left forearm. But the most serious wounds were the four ugly, gaping holes that cratered the left side of his torso. One of these seemed especially dangerous; a bullet, after entering the chest just below the left nipple, had apparently grazed the pericardium (or heart sac), perforated the right lung, and lodged under the skin near the eighth rib. In Bloom's opinion, the wound was inoperable. And though it was not necessarily fatal, the surgeon thought it best, after bandaging all of the wounds, to call in a priest to administer last rites.

Shortly after one o'clock, old Mrs. Hennessy was finally brought to the amphitheater, clinging to the arm of Thomas C. Anderson, one of her son's closest friends. Hennessy was still conscious and spoke in consoling tones to her, assuring her that she needn't worry about him. "Now go home, Mother," he said after a few minutes with her. "I am all right." Reluctantly, the old woman let herself be led away.

Assistant recorder David Hollander then approached the wounded man. "Chief, you know who I am," he whispered. "Do you wish to make a declaration?"

The question was veiled but unambiguous. If the chief had recognized or could give a description of any of his assailants, now was the time to make a statement — a dying declaration that would be admissible evidence in court. But Hennessy stubbornly refused. "No, I don't think I am that bad off," he said. Then he asked for a glass of milk — a request that was gently refused by his doctor.

Over the next few hours, between periodic

examinations by Dr. Bloom, several of Hennessy's friends and colleagues attempted to elicit a statement from him. But the chief, who was now resting more comfortably under a heavy dose of opiates, continued to insist that he would recover. Toward dawn, however, Hennessy's condition worsened noticeably. Messengers were again sent to fetch his mother. Before she arrived, Captain Beanham tried a last time to coax a statement from the dying man. "Captain, I tell you I am going to get well," the chief insisted, and when Beanham persisted, Hennessy bluntly dismissed his concerns: "Your alarm is unnecessary," he said. "These people can't kill me."

This bit of bravado, however, proved empty. After spending a few more minutes with his mother, going over his financial affairs, the chief began to sink rapidly. He held on for a few more hours as friends gathered around his sickbed to pay their last respects. By now, he was incapable of making a declaration even if he wanted to. He died at ten minutes past nine on Thursday morning.

By midday, virtually everyone in the city had heard about the "dastardly deed" perpetrated on Girod Street the night before. Evidence that the murder had in fact been the work of Italians was hardly conclusive, but the shocked citizens of New Orleans were fully prepared to think the worst of a group they had long regarded as threatening and undesirable. And so outrage against the city's Sicilian population was growing by the hour. A quickly composed editorial in the *Daily States* echoed the opinion of many New Orleanians in condemning "a class of foreigners who infest this city, known as Dagos" — a term that no one seemed shy about using, even in print. "Heretofore these people have confined themselves to murdering each other," the paper observed, "and hence, except that these terrible deeds reflect upon the good name of New Orleans, there has not been much for us to complain of." But now that the city had finally begun taking them to task for their outrages, they had struck back in a manner that was utterly intolerable: "They have had the audacity to murder the Chief of Police," the *States* wrote, "because [he] had ferreted out some of their crimes and had become a lion in their path."

Several notices, signed by prominent members of the community, appeared in the late editions of the morning newspapers, urging citizens to attend mass meetings and form committees "to assist the officers of the law in driving the murderous Mafia from our midst." Forty-two Italians had already been arrested, many on the flimsiest of evidence, and more were being rounded up every hour. Police were ransacking homes in the Italian quarter and elsewhere. Anyone remotely associated with the Matranga family was considered a suspect, no matter what the person's alibi. Many residents kept to their houses all day, knowing that they might be stopped on the street and arrested on the mere suspicion of being Italian.

At the Central Police Station, a shrouded portrait of Chief Hennessy now stood in a window overlooking Common Street. Telegrams expressing sympathy and outrage were pouring into the station from all over the country. The city's commercial exchanges were closed, as were many government offices and private businesses. Makeshift memorials to the chief were being put up everywhere — at the Grand Opera House, in the department-store windows on Canal Street, and at police stations and firehouses all over the city.

At four o'clock that afternoon, a contingent of uniformed police assembled at Francis Johnson & Sons undertakers to carry Hennessy's coffin to his house on Girod Street. Crowds were already surrounding the little shotgun cottage as the officers carried the silk-lined mahogany casket into the front parlor, which was filled with floral arrangements that had been arriving all day. While the grief-stricken Mrs. Hennessy looked on, the casket was opened and its lid replaced with a pane of glass to allow visitors to see the chief's face, which had been heavily made-up to conceal his wounds. Over the next hours, hundreds of people came through the house to view the body. More were still waiting outside at ten o'clock when, seeing Mrs. Hennessy's exhaustion, a group of Boylan men closed up the house and asked the bystanders to leave. Only the mother and a small number of intimate friends remained inside, keeping vigil overnight — until six A.M., when the doors would be opened again to allow the flow of mourners to resume.

Friday dawned sunny and bright, with only a few high clouds lingering as reminders of the midweek rain. A detail of police arrived at the Girod Street cottage at ten A.M. to carry the chief's coffin on to City Hall. A hearse had been provided by the funeral home, but the pallbearers insisted on carrying the chief the entire way to Lafayette Square, through streets lined with grieving spectators. At the broad marble stairway leading into City Hall, the procession was met by a company of city officials; they took the coffin and carried it into the bright, flower-strewn main council chamber. Here the pallbearers lifted it onto a bier draped with a large black bearskin in the center of the hall, a few feet from where the remains of another honored son of New Orleans — Jefferson Davis — had lain just a year earlier. The chief's hat, truncheon, and belt were placed on the lid of the coffin. An honor guard of police was stationed at its foot. Only then did police allow the crowds of waiting New Orleanians to enter and pay their last respects, twenty-five at a time.

The solemnities went on all day. At three, after the singing of a De Profundis in the council chamber, the coffin was carried out to the street again. There it was placed in a hearse, which then joined a mile-long procession to the cemetery, led by the chief's riderless jet-black horse. After a stop at St. Joseph's Church, where Rev. Patrick O'Neill led a funeral service to overflowing pews, the procession continued up Canal Street. Twilight had just set in when the hearse crossed the bridge and passed under the stone arches of the Metairie Cemetery. Here Hennessy's casket was set down inside a white-painted brick vault luxuriantly entwined with honeysuckle vines.

Father O'Neill said a few last words of benediction. As a tribute to their slain chief, scores of New Orleans policemen came forward to throw their badges into the vault. And then a single man stepped up to close the tomb with a makeshift wooden tablet — a temporary marker that would eventually be replaced by a carved marble slab. The man was Thomas C. Anderson, described by the *Daily Picayune* as David Hennessy's "bosom friend," a short but powerfully built figure with penetrating blue eyes and a lush, reddish-blond mustache. No one present could possibly realize it at that moment, but this young man honoring the first victim of New Orleans' war against its underworlds would someday find himself at the very center of that war. Over the next thirty years, in fact, Tom Anderson would come to be regarded as *the* principal symbol of lawlessness in New Orleans — the enemy of the city's better half, the nemesis to all of their aims, and the main target of their efforts to reform and control the city. Nor could Anderson himself have known that his next act would in a sense mark the beginning of that era of turmoil in New Orleans, a time that would see his own star as leader of the city's underworlds rise and fall precipitously. For now, he was just memorializing his old friend Dave Hennessy, a symbol of law and order cut down too soon in the line of duty.

Anderson stepped up to the wooden tablet, took a pencil from his vest pocket, and wrote out the chief's simple epitaph: "David Hennessy, died Oct. 16, 1890" — the date that would mark the beginning of New Orleans' civil war.

Friday — the day of Chief Hennessy's funeral — had been the time for mourning the dead. Saturday was the time to act, and city officials were ready for battle. The man chosen by

69

respectable New Orleans to lead their crusade had been killed before he'd even had a chance to strike the first blow. Now others would have to take command.

At 12:35 on Saturday afternoon, a still-irate Mayor Shakspeare strode into a special council session at City Hall. The room was filled to capacity with the city's aldermen, members of the police board, and other city officials. Reading from a prepared text, the mayor formally announced the death of David C. Hennessy "by the hands of despicable assassins." Four of the five supposed gunmen were already in custody, and police were reportedly closing in on the fifth. But these five men represented just a small fraction of the enemy they were facing. "It is clear to me," the mayor stated, "that the wretches who committed this foul deed are the mere hirelings and instruments of others higher and more powerful than they. These instigators are the men we must find at any cost." Then, pointing out that he himself had received death threats in the days since Hennessy's shooting, he called upon the assembled aldermen to take action. "The people look to you to take the initiative in this matter," he said. "Act promptly, without fear or favor."

The council responded with a standing ovation as well as a plan. The time had come, Alderman Brittin said, for the city to call upon her best citizens to rise to her aid. He proposed the formation of a "Committee of Fifty," its members to be selected by the mayor. The committee would investigate the matter of secret Italian murder societies and to devise "the most effectual and speedy measures for the uprooting and total annihilation of such hell-born associations."

The resolution passed unanimously, and Mayor Shakspeare promptly announced the eighty-three names he had selected in advance for the so-called Committee of Fifty. They amounted to a collection of New Orleans' wealthiest, most prominent, and most powerful men — a clear sign that what was to come would be, at root, a class war on behalf of the city's native-born elite. The real crime to be avenged here was not just a brutal assassination, but the assassination of a representative of that elite, by a class of citizen considered beneath their notice. "A shining mark have they selected on which to write . . . their contempt for the civilization of the new world," the mayor said in conclusion. "We owe it to ourselves, and to everything that we hold sacred in this life, to see that this blow is the last. We must teach these people a lesson that they will not forget for all time."

■ ■ ■ ■

CHAPTER 4
RETRIBUTION

■ ■ ■ ■

An engraving depicting the Parish Prison lynching **Louisiana Research Collection, Tulane University**

It was hard to imagine what was causing the delay. In the main courtroom at St. Patrick's Hall, all eyes were on the door to the upstairs deliberation room, where the jury in the Hennessy murder trial had been sequestered for over eighteen hours. Most of the spectators who'd crammed into the courtroom's gallery at ten A.M. had expected an immediate verdict. According to that morning's *Picayune,* the jury had supposedly reached its decision very quickly last night, before retiring to bed. But even now, two hours after the scheduled start of the morning session, the door to the jury room remained stubbornly closed.

For many in New Orleans, it had already been far too long a wait for justice. The lesson that Mayor Shakspeare had promised to teach the enemies of law and order had ultimately taken almost five months to unfold — five months of late-night raids, wild accusations of citizens against citizens, and blanket arrests of Italians of all stripes. The morning after the Hennessy outrage, there had been talk of immediate violent action to punish the alleged assassins already in custody. But ultimately the law — such as it was in New Orleans — was allowed to run its course. The Committee of Fifty, led by YMDA leader W. S. Parkerson — who served as liaison between the committee and the mayor's office — had conducted a vigorous investigation of the alleged conspiracy. Under the committee's often heavy-handed "guidance," the police had ultimately arrested more than a hundred Italians. Most had subsequently been released for lack of evidence, but the grand jury did end up indicting nineteen defendants. Nine had been charged with direct involvement in the shooting; the rest — including prominent Italians like Joseph P. Macheca and Charles Matranga — were held as accessories before the fact. Did these nineteen men constitute the entire extent of the conspiracy against Chief Hennessy and the city of New Orleans itself? Few believed that to be so, but bringing this group to justice would at least be a start.

Once the trial began on the morning of February 16, 1891, however, it became immediately obvious just how difficult it would be to secure even this small measure of justice. For one thing, this trial would be only the first of two court proceedings for the

Hennessy murder. District Attorney Charles Luzenberg, worried about the unwieldiness of a prosecution against nineteen defendants at once, had asked for and been granted a severance; thus only nine of the defendants would be tried now, leaving the other ten for a future action.

And even this first trial soon proved to be maddeningly complicated and drawn-out. More than 1,300 potential jurors had to be examined simply to find 12 who did not have a "fixed opinion" about the case, either from local gossip, newspaper reports, or else their own prejudice against Italians. Once a jury was finally impaneled, it had to hear evidence from more than 140 witnesses — over 60 for the prosecution and over 80 for the defense — much of which was contradictory and of dubious reliability. Two key police witnesses — including Capt. William O'Connor himself, who had said good night to the chief just moments before the first shot — were for unknown reasons not even called to testify. And arguably the most important witness for the state (a painter named M. L. Peeler) was, according to some convincing defense testimony, quite likely drunk when he supposedly recognized the shooters.

Not that the defense witnesses had been any stronger. Many were called merely as character witnesses, attesting to the "good name" of one or the other defendant; others provided alibis that were difficult if not impossible to corroborate. One defense witness seemed particularly befuddled. He claimed that he saw one of the accused men at the Poydras Market, blocks away from the crime scene, at the exact time of the ambush. When asked how he could be so certain of the hour, he insisted that he had made sure to check the market clock, knowing that he would be asked about it in court (this at a time when he wouldn't even have known that a crime had occurred).

And there had been plenty of other distractions to muddy the process of justice. One morning, prizefighter John L. Sullivan showed up to watch the proceedings, which were being closely followed in newspapers worldwide. He was given a seat of honor right next to the jury box, so that the great Irish boxer could ensure that the great Irish policeman would be properly avenged. Meanwhile, rumors began circulating that some of the jurors had been bribed by agents for the defense; private detective Dominick O'Malley, a known associate of defendant Charles Matranga, was soon arrested and accused of offering money to jurors in exchange for a not-guilty verdict. And as if all of this weren't enough, one of the defendants — a non-English-speaking fruit peddler named Emmanuele Polizzi — had continually disrupted the proceedings with fits of real or feigned madness, stomping his feet, throwing himself on the floor, and even trying to bite anyone who came near him.

What the jury had made of these courtroom antics — and of the ocean of confused and inconclusive evidence — was impossible to say. But for many of the spectators in court on that wet afternoon of March 13, 1891 — and for the "immense throng" of New Orleanians crowded on the street outside St. Patrick's Hall — there was no doubt at all: at least some of the nine defendants had to be guilty. And though the judge had given a directed verdict of not guilty for two of the defendants for lack of evidence, the rest simply *must* be punished; no other outcome — according to the newspapers, at least — was acceptable.

At one thirty P.M., a knock was finally heard at the door of the deliberation room. Sheriff Gabriel Villere hurried through the door and went upstairs to consult with the jurors. After a few minutes, as nervous murmurs swept through the courtroom, Villere reappeared and crossed the room to the private office of Judge Joshua G. Baker. And when the judge himself came out into the courtroom, ordering Villere to ring up the parish prison and have the prisoners delivered to court, there was no longer any room for doubt: The wait was over. After nearly a full day of deliberations, the jury had finally reached a verdict.

Judge Baker ordered the courtroom cleared of everyone except members of the bar and the press; all others had to join the unruly crowds waiting outside. The excitement on the street was even greater than it had been on the morning of the chief's death. Police Secretary Vandervoort, anticipating trouble, telephoned the Central Station for an extra detail of police to control the multitudes. The police, after all, didn't want any harm to come to the defendants — at least, not until a proper verdict had been delivered.

At around two thirty P.M., the jury filed into the courtroom. Most of the twelve members were averting their eyes. Although this is usually a bad sign for defendants (few jurors like to meet the gaze of men they are condemning), this was not necessarily the case here. The accusations of jury tampering had created an atmosphere of suspicion in the courtroom, and the jurors knew that their judgments would be met with skepticism no matter what the outcome.

The jury foreman, Jacob Seligman, handed the written verdict to the clerk, who passed it on to Judge Baker. After instructing the defendants to rise, the judge opened the folded paper and read the contents. He stared at the note for nearly a full minute — in what some reporters later interpreted as disapproval. Then he announced the jury's findings to the room.

The verdict came as a shock to nearly everyone. With regard to three of the defendants, including the apparently deranged Polizzi, the jury had been deadlocked; a mistrial was declared, meaning that all three would have to be retried. As for the other six — everyone from the wealthy shipper Macheca to Asperi Marchesi, the young boy accused of whistling to alert the assassins to the chief's approach — the decision was unanimous: all were found not guilty.

This outcome caused the spectators in the courtroom "to turn and look at one another in mute amazement." But then the shouting began — both inside and outside the courthouse. Reporters rushed the dismissed jurors as they gathered up their belongings to leave. Besieged with questions, they refused to reveal anything about their decision. Sheriff Villere, knowing the reception they were likely to get outside, advised them to exit the building by the side door. But after some discussion, the jurors decided to brave the judgment of their fellow citizens. They left by the main courthouse door. And although the mob outside was unruly and belligerent, the jurors were able to push through the milling throngs unmolested. A boy in the crowd, apparently convinced that the bribery rumors were true, shouted to one juror: "Say, how much did you get?"

The nine defendants, on the other hand,

were met with more overt hostility. Though six of them had been acquitted of the murder charges, all had to be returned to prison until certain lesser charges against them could be formally withdrawn. They were thus again returned to the Black Marias waiting outside. A detail of police tried to hold back the jeering mob to clear a path. Despite some scuffling as spectators pushed against police lines, the prisoners were loaded into the vans without incident. Even so, a howl of frustrated rage rose up in their wake as they departed.

The afternoon newspaper editorials about the outcome were blistering: "Red-handed murder . . . struck at the Law itself," the *Daily Item* proclaimed, "and the agencies of the law were found impotent to punish the foul deed." The writer for the *Daily States* was utterly apoplectic: "Alien hands of oath-bound assassins have set the blot of a martyr's blood upon your vaunted civilization." And yet the spillers of that blood were now to be set free. Such a verdict, according to the paper, was an affront to justice, a grievous injury that admitted only one possible solution: "Rise, people of New Orleans!"

It was a suggestion that some "people of New Orleans" were already seriously contemplating.

When William S. Parkerson stepped into his second-floor law office at 7 Commercial

Place that evening, he found several dozen agitated men waiting for him, with more arriving at the office door every minute. Parkerson had been in another courtroom all afternoon, but by now he had heard about the outcome of the Hennessy trial. So he knew why these men were here: incensed by the verdicts, they were looking to him for guidance on how to right what they all regarded as a blatant miscarriage of justice.

That the men in his office — some of them much older and more prominent than he — should now turn to Parkerson for leadership was not surprising. Balding, bespectacled, and somewhat portly, the thirty-five-year-old lawyer may not have looked the part of the dynamic leader of men, but his intensity in the courtroom was legendary. A powerful natural orator, he had been a political force in the Young Men's Democratic Association for some time already. But it was his position as alleged leader of the YMDA's unofficial militia that explained why these men were at his office. Described by one historian as a "Southern 'special gentlemen's police,' " Parkerson's so-called Regulators included many of the city's most prominent citizens. These were the men who had brought Mayor Shakspeare and his reform government into office, and who now felt it their job to correct the "mistake" the jurors had made that day.

After fifteen minutes, Parkerson broke up the meeting, instructing the men in his office to assemble again later that night. They would meet at the home of Franklin Brevard Hayne, a young cotton merchant who was also a leader of the Regulators militia. And when they reconvened in the parlor of Hayne's home — at the corner of Royal and Bienville Streets in the Vieux Carré — their ire was, if anything, stoked even higher than before. Many had heard stories of raucous demonstrations in the Italian colony that day; one report even had some Italians spitting on an American flag in joyous defiance. To the 150 men present, the meaning of this was obvious. The Mafia society was flaunting its power, celebrating its victory over the forces of law and order in New Orleans.

Many at the meeting wanted to march to the parish prison at that very moment to exact their revenge. But Parkerson dissuaded them. Convinced that any such vigilante action needed a popular mandate behind it, he argued instead for a mass meeting to be held the next morning — a gathering that would attract a large number of participants. And so together they composed an announcement to be printed in all of the morning papers. Signed by sixty-one men, it read:

> **MASS MEETING!**
> ALL GOOD CITIZENS ARE INVITED TO ATTEND A
> MASS MEETING ON SATURDAY, MARCH 14,
> AT 10 O'CLOCK A.M., AT CLAY STATUE, TO
> TAKE STEPS TO REMEDY THE FAILURE OF
> JUSTICE IN THE HENNESSY CASE.
>
> **COME PREPARED FOR ACTION.**

The announcement did not specify what action was meant, but Parkerson's intentions were clearly telegraphed by what he did next: After adjourning the meeting at Hayne's house, he and a select group of trusted friends rode a horse-drawn wagon to a hardware store across town. There they loaded it up with an ample supply of rope, plenty of ammunition, and 150 Winchester rifles and shotguns. Then they carried this arsenal back to Hayne's, where they loaded it into several large trunks, to be easily available the next day.

When Sheriff Gabriel Villere read the newspapers the next morning, he was under no illusions about the probable result of the announced mass meeting, and he wanted to be ready for it. Whatever his own sympathies, he was responsible for the safety of the nineteen prisoners in his charge. So at eight thirty A.M.

he left his office at the parish prison and headed toward City Hall to find Mayor Shakspeare. If the crowds at the mass meeting turned into an unruly mob, he wanted the mayor to give him more men, or maybe even help from the state militia.

At roughly the same time of the morning, Pasquale Corte, Italy's consul to New Orleans, was heading through the streets in the same direction. The announcement in the papers had distressed the consul considerably. At least two of the defendants in the trial were Italian nationals, and Corte saw it as his responsibility to make certain of their safety. So he, too, was going to see the mayor, hoping to persuade him to protect the acquitted men.

Sheriff Villere was already at City Hall when Corte arrived, but both were to be disappointed. Neither Mayor Shakspeare nor his secretary were in their offices, and no one seemed to know where they were. Chief of Police Dexter Gaster, Hennessy's successor, was present, but the neophyte chief seemed reluctant to do more than send a few extra patrolmen over to the parish prison. If Corte and Villere wanted any greater precaution than that, they would have to speak to the mayor, who — conveniently, some would later say — wasn't due in City Hall before noon.

Frustrated, and in a state of rising alarm,

Corte and Villere hurried over to consult with Louisiana governor Francis T. Nicholls, who was known to be in town at his lawyer's office. But here they got no help either. Nicholls, a white-haired former Confederate general, seemed sympathetic to their concerns, but he claimed that there was nothing he could do to aid them. To deploy the militia in any city, he would have to receive an official written request from its mayor. Without such a document, he said, he was powerless. But Nicholls at least knew where Shakspeare could be found: the mayor was breakfasting at the Pickwick Club. If the gentlemen would simply have a seat, he would send a message over to the club and ask Mayor Shakspeare to come to the office.

By this time, crowds were already gathering at the foot of the Henry Clay statue, which in 1891 still stood on the neutral ground (the median) of Canal Street at the intersection of Royal. At ten o'clock, when Parkerson and his self-styled "Vigilance Committee" arrived on the scene, approximately six to eight thousand citizens already thronged the avenue. Intersections were blocked to traffic and the Canal Street trolleys were so swamped that they could barely move.

Amid shouts and cheering, Parkerson and the other leaders of the committee got the meeting started. They marched three times around the monument to give the other leaders a chance to fall in behind them. Then Parkerson climbed the steps to the foot of the statue. He took off his hat as another cheer rose up from the crowd.

"People of New Orleans, once before I stood before you for public duty," he began, referring to his role in the 1888 elections. "I now appear before you again, actuated by no desire for fame or prominence. Affairs have reached such a crisis that men living in an organized and civilized community, finding their laws fruitless and ineffective, are forced to protect themselves. When courts fail, the people must act!"

Again the crowd roared its approval. By now, spectators had climbed to the roofs of the paralyzed streetcars to get a better view. Others looked on with opera glasses from nearby windows and balconies.

"What protection is there left us," Parkerson went on, "when the very head of our police department — our Chief of Police — is assassinated in our very midst by the Mafia Society, and his assassins [are] again turned loose on the community? The time has come for the people of New Orleans to say whether they are going to stand [for] these outrages. . . . I ask you to consider this fairly: Are you going to let it continue? Will every man here follow me, and see the murder of D.C. Hennessy vindicated? Are there men enough here to set aside the verdict of that infamous jury, every one of whom is a perjurer and a scoundrel?"

The roar of the spectators left no doubt about their answer. And after a few other men had made speeches from the foot of the Great Pacificator, the crowd, excited to a frenzied pitch, heeded Parkerson's final words: "Men and citizens of New Orleans, follow me! I will be your leader!"

The crowd parted as Parkerson and the other leaders made their way down Royal Street. At Hayne's house on the corner of Bienville, a previously selected group of men armed themselves with the shotguns, Winchester rifles, and rope that they had cached there the night before. Then they returned to Canal Street and began their march toward the parish prison. "The crowd accordingly fell in line, three and four abreast," the *Daily Item* would later report. "The vanguard was composed of the most wealthy and respected citizens of New Orleans. They were followed by honest, hard-working mechanics, tradesmen, and laborers . . . Here was a body of men on their way to do what the law had failed to do."

The mob moved "like a mighty roaring stream" along Canal and then turned right up Rampart toward Congo Square. Along the way, crying women waved handkerchiefs from galleries; shouting men climbed on beer and grocery wagons, on awnings and rooftops, encouraging the marchers forward. Some began chanting, "Who killa de Chief? Who killa de Chief?" — a hateful ethnic taunt that would be flung at the Italians of New Orleans for decades to come. The few policemen in the crowd were driven out of the path under a salvo of stones and clumps of mud.

The armed men at the head of the procession marched on with almost military discipline. "It was the most terrible thing I ever saw," Parkerson would later boast to the newspapers, "the quiet determination of the crowd. There was no disorder." With a Winchester rifle in one hand and a revolver tucked into his pocket, Parkerson led his followers to Congo Square, just one block from the prison. Here he stopped and addressed them again about the grave duty they were about to perform.

Two municipal detectives left the park and ran ahead to the parish prison to alert Warden Lemuel Davis of the approaching mob. The warden realized that it was too late to move the inmates to another location; he and his men would just have to hold off the mob as best they could. Moving quickly, he ordered that the doors to the prison be barred from the inside. After calling the Central Station with an urgent request for reinforcements, he went to see the prisoners in their cell on the second floor — a large, low-security area called the Star Chamber — where they were waiting for their release. When told of the approaching mob, Joseph Macheca, the most prominent of the prisoners, asked the warden that they all be given arms to defend themselves. Davis refused, but did agree to release them from the cell for their own safety. He sent a guard over to the women's section of the prison, ordering that the female inmates be moved to allow the Italians to hide there. Then he turned a set of keys over to the prisoners and allowed them to scatter throughout the cavernous building.

By this time, the mob had reached the front gate of the prison. Officers from the Fourth Precinct station, which shared the same building as the prison, made futile attempts to keep the banquette clear in front of the entrance. One deputy sheriff pushed a man away from the gate, only to have the man silently raise a pistol to his head. "I've done all I can," the officer declared, backing away from the gate with his hands raised.

Eventually, Parkerson himself stepped up to the iron gate and called out to Warden Davis. He asked that the keys to the gate be turned over, on the authority of the people of New Orleans. Davis refused, and refused again after Parkerson threatened to break down the gate. Frustrated, the lawyer ordered that gunpowder and some stout pieces of wood be found to batter through the gate. He also sent a contingent around to the side of the massive prison, where a far less imposing wooden doorway led from the street to the warden's private office.

It was the side door that eventually gave way. Though prison guards had nailed wooden boards across the inside of the door, Parkerson's men were able to batter it in with cobblestones and railroad ties taken from a nearby construction site. Parkerson stationed several guards at the splintered door while his handpicked squad of executioners entered, leaving everyone else outside. A locked gate still stood between the armed men and their prey inside the prison, but this proved to be just a temporary hindrance. The men quickly broke the padlock and threw the gate back on its hinges.

The armed vigilantes now fanned out through the enormous building as other inmates of the prison — among them Phillip Lobrano, still incarcerated while awaiting trial for the murder of Peter Deubler — looked on. According to some reports, Parkerson had beforehand made up a list of the prisoners to be executed and those to be spared. The boy Asperi Marchesi, for one, was to be left alone, presumably because of his age; so, too, were the two defendants given a directed not-guilty verdict by the judge. But the others were to be captured and marched outside, there to be judged and executed with great solemnity. "The intention had been not to shoot any of them," Parkerson would later tell an interviewer. But that's not how it happened. "When my men were inside — there were about fifty of them — they got very furious, and after the first taste of blood, it was impossible to keep them back."

Several of the executioners ran into the now-deserted prison yard. One of them saw a face at a window on the second floor. "There's Scaffidi!" he yelled, identifying one of the defendants, and he raised his revolver and fired. This was all the encouragement the others needed. Breaking discipline, they also fired at the window, shredding its white-washed frame and sending down a shower of white dust and shards of wood. Warden Davis rushed into the yard, urging calm and restraint, but the men merely pushed past him toward the stairway to the second floor.

Now the killing began in earnest. Egged on by the crowds outside, which began cheering and screaming at the first sound of gunfire, the executioners set off after their quarry. Macheca was the first to be found. Spotted from below, he and two others were in a third-floor gallery, where they had run — against the warden's advice — to find a route out of the prison. Macheca was trying key after key to open a locked door that would have led into the Fourth Precinct police station. As his pursuers rushed up the stairs, he gave up on the keys and began hammering the padlock with an Indian club. But the lock would not give. Macheca spun around as the gate from the stairs to the gallery burst open — and was immediately shot in the face. The two men with him were also killed, one shot long-range from the floor below. The other — the father of Asperi Marchesi — had been thrown back against a wall when the gate flew open. As he stood there, dazed by the blow to his head, two men with shotguns approached and triumphantly discharged them into his chest.

Others were being routed elsewhere in the prison. Seven of the Italians had fled as instructed to the women's section of the prison, but they were soon found by one of the execution squads. Flushed from their hiding places, the prisoners huddled together at one corner of the women's yard. They were begging for mercy, but the vigilantes had by this time lost all restraint. They lifted their weapons and fired indiscriminately into the gaggle of men. Five were killed instantly, and a sixth was shot again when he lifted a trembling arm from the pile of bodies.

One of the prisoners in the pile, Antonio Bagnetto, was found still alive. He was unceremoniously dragged from the yard and carried out to the front of the prison. Emmanuele Polizzi, the supposed madman, had also been found alive and was likewise pulled outside. And there — amid cheers and shouts from the crowd — both men were strung up on ropes. Bagnetto was hanged from a tree just outside the prison, Polizzi from a lamppost at the corner of Tremé and St. Anne Streets. As the bodies of the two men dangled above, they were riddled with bullets before a crowd of thousands.

When all was finished, Parkerson emerged from the parish prison to resounding cheers. He himself had not fired a single shot, but he took full responsibility for the results. "Bagnetto, Scaffidi, Polizzi, Joe Macheca, Monastero, and Marchesi are dead," he announced to the crowd from atop an overturned streetcar. "I have performed the most painful duty of my life today. . . . If you have confidence in me and in the gentlemen associated with me, I ask you to disperse and go quietly to your homes. You have acted like men. Now, go home like men."

But some in the crowd were not ready to disperse. In triumph, they marched back to the Clay statue on Canal Street, carrying Parkerson on their shoulders. There the lawyer made another speech — "You have today wiped the stain from your city's name!" — and then asked them again to disperse, promising that more would be done to address those accused of bribing the jury. For that day, at least, their mission was complete.

Back at the parish prison, some of Parkerson's associates had arranged a gruesome tableau, so that all New Orleanians could bear witness to what had been done for their welfare. The two hanged men were left swinging outside for all to see, while several other bodies were lined up in a large room inside the prison for more convenient viewing. For five hours, thousands of men, women, and children filed past to see them. Some of the women allegedly dipped lace handkerchiefs into pools of blood to keep as mementos of the day, while others took away bits of the victims' clothing and shoelaces. One enterprising man even began peeling strips of bark from the tree on which Bagnetto had been strung up, to bring home as a souvenir.

Eleven men in all were killed at the Orleans Parish Prison that day. Three of the slain had been tried and acquitted; a jury had failed to agree on three others; five more belonged to the second group of defendants that had not even been tried yet. Asked later whether he regretted what had happened in the prison, Parkerson was adamant. "Of course, it is not a courageous thing to attack a man who is not armed," he admitted. "But we looked upon these [men] as so many reptiles. . . . This was a great emergency, greater than has ever happened in New York, Cincinnati, or Chicago . . . Hennessy's killing struck at the very root of American institutions. The intimidation of the Mafia and the corruption of our juries are to be met only with strong measures. I recognize no power above the people."

Parkerson was not alone in this judgment. Many in New Orleans were soon hailing the lawyer and his followers as heroes. The city's business community was virtually unanimous in its approval; the Board of Trade and the Cotton, Sugar, Produce, Lumberman's, and Stock Exchanges all passed resolutions praising the vigilante action. The local newspapers also came to the mob's defense: "Government powers are delegated by the people," the *Daily Picayune* opined, "and [the people] can reclaim them if they feel that the power is not being executed properly." The *Item* agreed: "When the ordinary means of justice fail, extraordinary means are resorted to. This is a characteristic of the American people, and has today been illustrated once more in a most impressive fashion."

Emboldened by this definitive blow for order and self-defense, Parkerson and his Vigilance Committee promised further extralegal means to ensure the submission of the so-called Mafia threat. Vowing to burn down the Italian quarter if revenge were taken on the lynchers, Parkerson proceeded to investigate claims of jury bribery (even as an official grand jury was doing likewise). Evidence was eventually found that certain members of the jury pool had indeed been promised money, but apparently no actual jurors were bribed. That didn't help the twelve men who had delivered the unpopular verdict. Many were forced to leave town, including jury foreman Jacob M. Seligman, who was summarily expelled from the Stock Exchange and the Young Men's Gymnastics Club. Eventually, finding life in New Orleans untenable, he moved to Cincinnati.

As for the lynchers themselves, the grand jury, citing its inability to fix guilt on "the entire people of the parish and city of New Orleans," indicted precisely no one, calling the incident "a spontaneous uprising of the people." Those people themselves, however, were in no doubt as to who their leaders were. Parkerson, universally identified as the head of the lynch mob, became something of a national celebrity, and was soon being invited to give speeches in places as distant as Boston and Bloomington, Indiana. Over the next few years, he would receive threatening letters, many of them in Italian, and his home in New Orleans would twice suffer minor damage by arsonists' fires. But neither he nor any of the others would ever suffer serious consequences — legal or otherwise — for their actions.

For "respectable" New Orleans, then, the lynching was a triumph. Though opinion throughout the rest of the country was deeply divided, many prominent figures came out in favor of the action. Even a young Theodore Roosevelt, then a Civil Service commissioner in Washington, DC, approved of it; the future president called the lynching "a rather good thing," and said so at a party attended by what he described as "various Dago diplomats." Those diplomats, of course — as well as their fellow Italians both here and in Europe — had a very different perspective. In fact, the incident — regarded as the largest mass lynching in American history — caused something of a political crisis between Italy and the United States, at one point bringing the two countries dangerously close to a declaration of war. But eventually, with the payment of a $25,000 indemnity divided among the victims' families, the crisis passed. In the minds of many "law-abiding citizens," both in New Orleans and in the rest of the country, Parkerson and his band had accomplished an important and worthy goal: they had taught the Crescent City's lawless Italians the harsh lesson that the city council had called for back in October.

Mayor Shakspeare could not have been more pleased at the outcome. After receiving laudatory letters from all over the country (one of them praising "the able manner in which 'you stayed at home and attended to your own private business' " while the prison was under siege), he was inclined to thank his friend and former campaign manager for a much-needed cleansing of the Italian community. Asked by a newspaper reporter about the position of the Mafia in New Orleans after the lynching, the mayor was upbeat. "They are quiet, quieter than they have been for years," he said. "The lesson taught them at the parish prison has had a most excellent effect and I do not anticipate we will have any more trouble with them. You may announce that the reign of the Mafia in New Orleans is over."

That utterance, of course, would eventually prove to be far too optimistic. But for the time being, the city's Italian underworld — "Mafia" or not — was subdued. The Italian colony would in fact remain relatively quiet through the rest of the 1890s.

But the reformers' efforts to clean up the city would not end with the killings at the Orleans Parish Prison. There were still other lessons to be taught, other threats to be neutralized. The war for control of New Orleans had actually just begun.

■ ■ ■ ■

PART TWO:
DRAWING
BOUNDARIES

1890s–1907

■ ■ ■ ■

CHAPTER 5
A SPORTING MAN

Tom Anderson **Louisiana Division, New Orleans Public Library**

Tom Anderson was a man on the rise. In mid-1890s New Orleans, this was already a well-known fact. Now in his thirties — dapper and always well groomed with his pomaded reddish-brown hair and carefully waxed mustache — the young Scots-Irishman had already established himself as a shrewd businessman with a hand in many different ventures around town. In the few short years since his friend David Hennessy's unfortunate death, Tom had come far — making a name in sporting circles as a boxing manager, a horseracing entrepreneur, and a saloon- and restaurant-owner with an unstinting sense of hospitality. He'd also had success in more "legitimate" endeavors, as proprietor of a small but growing oil business — the Record Oil Company (the "Only Independent Oil Company Not Controlled by Trusts or Monopolies"), dispensing everything from axle grease to salad oils from a warehouse in the Central Business District. Some said Tom

Anderson was extraordinarily lucky. But luck, as he well knew, was something that had to be made; luck was hard work and handshakes; it was cultivating influential friends from all walks of life, both high and low, and making sure they were happy. And now, flush with this early success, he was even contemplating that inevitable next step — into politics, the game that in New Orleans was so often the key to greater prosperity.

Tom Anderson, in short, was a man who so far had made very few mistakes in his life. Except one: namely, *Mrs.* Tom Anderson, the former Catherine Turnbull, Tom's second wife. On January 24, 1894 — in what must have been a weak moment — he'd married the pretty but combative young prostitute, and had regretted it almost immediately. Their marriage had been a disaster from the beginning — a nonstop melodrama of bickering, histrionics, and recriminations. Less than a year after the wedding, Anderson was already desperate to call it quits. He sued his wife for a separation of bed and board, hoping eventually to divorce (without alimony or division of joint property) and just move on as if the whole thing had never happened. But Kate was not about to let him off so easily. She was Mrs. Anderson now; there was no way she was just going to disappear with nothing to show for their association. So she was willing to fight him in court to prevent it.

That their brief marriage had come to this impasse was somewhat out of character for the genial young businessman. Tom Anderson, after all, was well known for being accommodating to everyone, willing to go along to get along, forever the man eager to do a favor that would, in the natural course of things, eventually be repaid. It was the law of the streets he grew up on — reciprocity, mutual protection. As the product of a bloody-fisted childhood in the neighborhood known as the Irish Channel, Tom had learned early in life that those who escaped the rough Channel streets were those who hustled, made friends, avoided trouble, and kept an eye out for the main chance. When, as a young boy peddling the *Daily Picayune* on street corners, he happened to witness a petty theft on Basin Street, he did not, as so many other boys would have done, clam up when a patrolman asked him about it. Instead, he pointed out the thief's hiding place, and even agreed to testify in court about everything he'd seen. For this service he received a small monetary reward; more important, the deed also earned him a reputation among the local constabulary as a boy who could be relied upon. Most likely, it had been a calculation on Tom's part: a sneak thief could do nothing for him, but a beat cop . . . well, you never knew. . . .

But Tom liked to make himself useful to others in the neighborhood as well. He wasn't overly fussy about his associates, and he was soon helping out at the local brothels, running to the corner pharmacy to fetch the ladies their regular doses of opium and cocaine. When someone told the boy that those drugs, while easy to obtain in New Orleans, were actually illegal, he obligingly agreed to forgo the deliveries — at least while his police friends were watching.

Though his career at school had been undistinguished and brief, Tom's mathematical abilities had nonetheless been sharp enough to land him a job early on as a bookkeeper and shipping clerk for the Insurance Oil Company. Here he did everything right — working hard, ingratiating himself with his coworkers, and saving as much of his salary as possible. After just a few years of apprenticeship, he was ready for bigger things. One day in 1879, when he was just nineteen or twenty years old, he breezed into the office and made an announcement to his colleagues: "Well, boys, I am going to leave you. I got married to a young woman uptown, [and] I am going into business for myself."

The young woman in question was his childhood sweetheart, Emma Schwartz, the daughter of Dutch immigrants living in his old neighborhood. The newlyweds set up house downtown on St. Louis Street. And within a year, Emma gave birth to a daughter, Irene. Young as he was, Tom was apparently very happy to be a family man. ("William," he told one of his old coworkers from Insurance Oil, "I got a fine little baby girl up home.") But it was not to last long. In November of 1881, Emma succumbed to typhoid fever. ("William," Tom told the same colleague when next they met on the street, "my wife is dead.") Clearly unprepared to raise an eighteen-month-old child alone, he turned Irene over to the St. Vincent's Infant Asylum. There the child lived until she turned five, at which point he enrolled her in the St. Mary's Convent School in nearby Carrollton. It was hardly an ideal arrangement, but Tom apparently felt he had no choice. His own mother was working full-time as a domestic and couldn't care for the child, and Emma's family was apparently in similar circumstances. This way, at least, the baby would be close enough for him to visit when he could.

The 1880s proved to be a profitable decade for the young widower. He did not, as he had told his friends, go into business for himself, at least not yet. Instead, he worked as a bookkeeper for a number of other enterprises, including the Louisiana State Lottery Company. For an ambitious young man seeking to find his way in New Orleans' semi-legitimate economy, there could have been no better training ground. Long the nemesis of Louisiana's good-government reformers (W. S. Parkerson was a major foe), the Lottery was a boondoggle of impressive proportions. Run as a private corporation, it was chartered by the state government to hold regular drawings and distribute cash prizes to the lucky winners. In exchange, the company donated the small sum of $40,000 annually to the Charity Hospital; the rest of the profits went to shareholders in the corporation. Of course, keeping such a government-sanctioned swindle in operation required copious incentives in high places, and the company's attentive bookkeeper was sure to take note of exactly how these were provided. In this way, he learned the important lesson that you had to spend money to make money. And he was careful to do likewise in his own endeavors. Tom saved where he could, but also generously contributed to political campaigns, police department benefits, and charity drives sponsored by the men's clubs he made sure to join. Soon the young lottery clerk was on intimate terms with some of the most prominent businessmen and political figures in town. These, of course, did not include the blue-blooded elites of the Boston and Pickwick Clubs; they never would have looked twice at an Irish Channel man. Instead, Tom's new associates were the more down-to-earth sorts: the ward politicians and tavern owners, the newspaper reporters and fire department chiefs. These were the people a man could deal with, even if his forebears hadn't had generations in which to wipe the soil of the potato fields from the family escutcheon. And although reformers were eventually successful in getting rid of the Lottery in 1893 (when the company's charter expired and it was forced to move its operations to Honduras), Tom Anderson had by then gotten what he needed from the venture, having made connections in many of the significant places of power in the city.

He cultivated those connections with all the care of a St. Charles Avenue yardman. When he scraped together enough money to open his first restaurant — at No. 110–112 North Rampart Street, in collaboration with a friend named David Heller — he played the generous host to all of his police, politico, and demimonde friends. At Tom Anderson's convivial establishment, such men could always find plenty of good food and fine liquor; perhaps most helpfully, they could also find private rooms where deals, payoffs, and rendezvous could be made, far from the prying eyes of strict constructionists of the law. In fact, Anderson's soon became known as a kind of "neutral ground," a place where representatives from different spheres could meet and hammer out their mutually beneficial understandings. And whenever such parties came together, Tom Anderson was always right there — to make introductions, arbitrate disputes, and keep everyone's beer mugs full to the brim.

His hospitality ("My motto," he always claimed in advertisements, "[is] 'The Best of Everything' ") was soon the stuff of urban lore. When he branched out into the boxing game — as manager of Andy Bowen, the lightweight champion of the South — there were always free tickets to distribute to his friends and associates. When the horse owned by his oil company ran a race at the City Park or Fair Grounds Racetrack, choice grandstand seats were available to anyone who might look kindly on one of his future projects. Yes, the prickly reform types might be immune to such blandishments, and they were not above harassing him in small ways, seeing that he was fined or even briefly arrested on minor charges of illegal gambling or serving liquor on a Sunday. But these petty annoyances could always be made to go away, particularly for a man with so many friends who happened to be cops or judges.

Sometime in the early 1880s, while he was still in his twenties, Anderson and another friend, Frank Lamothe, had begun sponsoring an annual Mardi Gras fete, a so-called French ball to which ladies of a certain type were admitted free of charge. Advertised as

112

"The Ball of the Two Well Known Gentlemen," it soon became one of the most sought-after tickets of the season. To many, it was a welcome corrective to the stuffy, formal affairs sponsored by the more established Carnival krewes. Anderson's fete was a kind of parody of those other celebrations, which had grown up in the decades after Reconstruction. Elite krewes like Comus, Momus, and the Twelfth Night Revelers had been created expressly to bring order and hierarchy to Mardi Gras; their elaborate programs of balls and processions were designed to be exclusive — in order to keep undesirables out, to push disrespectable riffraff off to the sidelines.

The Ball of the Two Well Known Gentlemen, on the other hand, was the regular New Orleanian's answer to this high-handed appropriation of Mardi Gras. Like the elite krewes' balls, Tom Anderson's affair featured a royal court and a series of costumed tableaux. But "the queen and her court were prostitutes, not virgins from prominent families. Women in tights, not men in costumes, performed the tableaux." The result was an alternative Mardi Gras, a Carnival for the city's other half. And for a man on the rise like Tom Anderson, being co-host of an event like this was priceless publicity, an excellent means of raising his profile and setting himself up as a mover and shaker in the city's semi-legitimate economy.

It was at this point in his life, in the early 1890s, that he decided to give marriage a second chance. Little is known about Catherine Turnbull, the twenty-nine-year-old woman from St. Louis he married in early 1894. Apparently, she was a widow who had fallen into prostitution after the premature death of her first husband, a man named M. L. Roder. But her profession made little difference to Tom Anderson. Having grown up as a messenger boy for Irish Channel brothels, he held little truck with the hypocrisies of Victorian moral ideals, and seemed to truly enjoy the company of prostitutes. But Kate soon became an exception. Within months of his bringing her into the Prytania Street home that he shared with his widowed mother, Honora, the battle was on. The elder Mrs. Anderson developed a vehement dislike of her new daughter-in-law, and Tom, like the dutiful Irish son he was, always took his mother's side. The three Andersons argued bitterly and frequently, sometimes even in public, until matters came to a head in August of 1894. Catherine demanded that Mrs. Anderson leave the premises. Tom obliged, moving his mother — and himself — to a new house on Canal Street. He instantly filed suit for a separation from his wife, prefatory to a divorce.

It was to be one of the few times in his life

that Tom Anderson did not get his way in the local justice system. Appearing before a judge in Civil District Court, Anderson accused his wife of "excesses of cruel treatment and outrages" and of threatening to shoot him with a loaded pistol. Contesting the suit, Catherine denied ever threatening her husband, and in turn cited a few transgressions of his, among them "compelling her at times to perform various duties such as scrubbing, washing, and cooking, refusing to permit a servant to perform said duties." She further accused him of using "the most profane and vulgar language" toward her, of "humiliating her in the presence of his employees," and of "treating her in an outrageous manner, for which she could never forgive him." And as if this weren't enough, she rounded off her case with a whopping revelation: Catherine Anderson alleged that she was now pregnant with child. As a mother-to-be, then, she was entitled to support in the amount of $100 per month in perpetuity, along with a fair portion of Tom's existing assets.

Whether Catherine's alleged pregnancy was real or merely a ploy to earn the judge's sympathy (there appears to be no record of any child ever being born), it got the job done. The court ultimately ruled in the wife's favor, refusing the divorce and holding the husband responsible for his wife's continued upkeep. Anderson began an appeal, but meanwhile he had to suffer the indignity of having court assessors rummage through his home and businesses, inventorying all of his assets — right down to the two-dollar keg of pickles in the cellar of his restaurant.

It's possible that one point of contention in his marriage was Anderson's growing association with the brothel madam Josie Lobrano — now calling herself Josie Arlington. Rumors of a romantic relationship between the two would persist for decades, but there's no real evidence that they were ever anything more than close friends and business partners. Most likely Tom recognized in Josie a kindred spirit — another no-nonsense pragmatist with a determination to succeed in one of the few ways available in 1890s New Orleans to persons not born to wealth and privilege.

For Josie, too, was now a businessperson on the rise. The four or five years since the killing of her brother had been transformative for her. She'd successfully shed the taint of her former rough life and started out anew, just as she had vowed to do back in 1891. She'd taken up with a new paramour, John Thomas "Tom" Brady, an easygoing, mild-mannered clerk in the City Treasurer's Office, much closer to her own age than Phillip Lobrano had been. Several months after the shooting, she and Brady had gone off on an extended vacation to Hot Springs, Arkansas.

There they'd witnessed firsthand the lush life offered by the city's celebrated Arlington Hotel, a luxurious spa where the well heeled could take a water cure amid the trappings of Gilded Age opulence.

For a former orphaned child once forced by her aunt to sell apples on street corners (only to be beaten unmercifully if she didn't bring back $1.50 a day), this was a revelation, a potent vision of a very different and desirable kind of life. Josie came back to New Orleans resolved to re-create a bit of that elegance at her Customhouse Street brothel. She changed the name of her establishment to the "Chateau Lobrano d'Arlington" and proceeded to fill it with "gracious, amiable foreign girls who would be at home only to gentlemen of taste and refinement." She even began advertising her high-toned new offerings in the newspapers: "Society is graced by the presence of a bona-fide baroness, direct from the Court of St. Petersburg," ran one announcement in the *Mascot*. "The baroness is at present residing incog. at the Chateau Lobrano d'Arlington, and is known as La Belle Stewart." True, the alleged baroness was soon exposed as nothing more than "a hoochy-koochy dancer and circus specialist," but the tone that Josie was striving for was evident nonetheless.

Perhaps in part to finance her wholesale image renovation, Josie Arlington sold an interest in the Chateau to her friend Tom Anderson, whose Rampart Street restaurant stood just around the corner. Whether this was Anderson's first foray into the brothel business is uncertain, but it would not be his last. The saloon and brothel businesses, after all, were natural complements. And it wasn't long before the bar at 112 Rampart Street became a popular stopping-off place for clients heading to or from the Chateau at 142 Customhouse. To cement the association in the mind of the public, Tom eventually renamed his restaurant the Arlington. Soon both establishments were prospering mightily, enriching both principals and even allowing the genial Tom Brady (a friend of Anderson's in addition to being Arlington's kept man) to quit his job at the City Treasurer's Office and invest in a local pool hall.

So for Tom Anderson, Josie Arlington, and their associates in vice, things weren't going too badly in the New Orleans of the mid-1890s. Business was good, despite a nationwide depression, and harassments from police were minimal. But the forces of reform had not been idle, and the outlook for the city's vice industries was about to change significantly. A new and more energetic reform administration had been elected to office in 1896, and they were ready to ratchet up the battle to clean up the city. Under the leadership of Mayor Walter C. Flower, this new administration set its sights in particular on the spread of vice and crime into respectable neighborhoods all around the city. And their proposed solution to the problem was a uniquely practical one. Recognizing that any attempt to abolish vice entirely was doomed to failure (at least in New Orleans), they hoped instead to regulate and isolate the trade. And they would do it by moving vice out of the central city and the better residential neighborhoods, into a part of town where few respectable people would come into contact with it. Drawing boundaries to isolate vice and crime was the new progressive answer of the day, and it would ultimately change the culture of New Orleans in ways that no one could anticipate.

For a place with such a deeply entrenched culture of prostitution, of course, any scheme to segregate the practice would not be easy to implement. New Orleans' reputation as a center of sin and perdition had dogged the city virtually since its founding in 1718. Established in that year under a temporary charter to the private Company of the West, La Nouvelle-Orléans was from the beginning a community filled with rough, ungovernable men and women of dubious morality. John Law, the notorious Scottish adventurer who had contracted with France "to establish, thirty leagues up the river, a burg which should be called New Orleans," needed to populate his new town as quickly as possible, and he wasn't overly fastidious about how he accomplished the task. According to one early historian, "Disorderly soldiers, black sheep of distinguished families, paupers, prostitutes, political suspects, friendless strangers, unsophisticated peasants straying into Paris — all were kidnapped, herded, and shipped under guard to fill the emptiness of Louisiana." French jails and hospitals were ransacked for potential colonists, while men with an opportunistic bent were enticed with promises of free transportation, free land, and the prospect of fabulous riches derived from a region of unimaginable abundance. To deal with a chronic shortage of women, prospective wives were also imported from the Old Country, among them eighty-eight inmates from a Parisian house of correction known as La Salpêtrière. As a result, the town was — within a decade of its birth — already famous as a den of iniquity, a place "without religion, without justice, without discipline, without order, and without police."

By the latter half of the eighteenth century, New Orleans had polished away some of its rougher frontier edges, and had even attained a patina of French refinement in parts. But the city retained its notoriety for vice and lawlessness. Subsequent political upheavals did little to change this. In 1762, to avoid surrendering New Orleans and western Louisiana to Britain after the Seven Years' War (known in North America as the French and Indian War), King Louis XV secretly ceded these territories to his Spanish cousin, King Carlos III. But although Spain took political and military control of Louisiana for the rest of the century, the Spaniards sent over few additional colonists; as a result, New Orleans remained distinctly French — and libertine — in character. (Spain did, however, rebuild much of the central city after two devastating fires, which is why the architecture of the "French Quarter" is actually Spanish.) In 1800, the whole territory reverted to France, but by then the mother country's ardor for its unruly American colony had cooled. Three years later, Napoleon sold New Orleans and the whole Louisiana territory to the United States for the sum of $15 million. Residents had no say in this matter, and were not at all pleased, but nothing could be done. And so, in 1803, the old Gallic metropolis became American — at least politically.

The population explosion set off by the Louisiana Purchase took New Orleans vice to new levels of visibility. Tenderloin districts grew up along the busy waterfront, where rowdy flatboatmen from the American interior, carrying cargoes downriver to the newly unrestricted port, indulged in sprees of gambling, drinking, and "wholehearted wallowing in the fleshpots." Soon the rise of the Mississippi steamboat culture was bringing a somewhat higher class of scalawag to the Crescent City — in the form of confidence men and professional riverboat gamblers. Gambling, in fact, became something of an obsession for New Orleanians of every class. And although the Louisiana State legislature, occasionally dominated by conservative elements from the state's Anglo-Protestant north, passed various anti-gambling laws over the years, they were — in New Orleans, at least — widely ignored.

Efforts to control prostitution were likewise ineffectual. By the mid-1800s, prosperous Anglo-American planters and merchants had built entire neighborhoods of capacious, colonnaded mansions in the "American" part of the city — the Garden District, upriver from Canal Street. Here they hoped to set themselves apart from the neighborhoods of downtown "Creoles" (a term that at this point meant the offspring — white, black, or mixed-race — of French or other foreign-born parents). To keep their enclaves free of sin, efforts were made to regulate prostitution by city statute. But thanks to lax enforcement over the years, the problem of "vice contamination" in respectable neighborhoods did not go away, and in fact by 1890 seemed worse than ever.

But now, with the election of the new reform government of 1896, city officials were determined to make vice segregation work. Just after the election, a newly installed alderman named Sidney Story took it on himself to devise a way to protect "the pure and noble womanhood" of New Orleans from this unwanted contamination. "That vice should be allowed to flaunt its scarlet drapery in the face of virtue," as he would later opine to the *Item,* "was not only a blotch upon our escutcheon, but a constant menace to the moral health of the community." So Story developed a plan that would make prostitution illegal everywhere in the city *except* in a certain eighteen-block area, a neighborhood that was already rife with vice establishments. In this way, sin would be drawn out of prominent and respectable parts of town and relegated to places where, he believed, it would do the least harm to decent sensibilities.

This was not an entirely new idea. Story had seen similar schemes in several European cities during a tour of the Continent some years earlier. And even some American cities had experimented with officially tolerated vice districts. What made Story's plan unique, however, was the explicitness of the toleration and the specificity of its geographical limits. And since the proposed ordinance did not actually legalize prostitution within this area (but merely made it illegal everywhere else), it would be able to survive the inevitable court challenges it was bound to inspire.

Story's innovative new idea was widely applauded by the city's business reformers in particular; they hoped that isolating vice in this way would improve New Orleans' reputation and thus make it easier to attract Northern capital investment. Even the conservative *Daily Picayune* lauded the proposal, looking forward to a time when the perpetrators of vice and immorality would operate only in "obscure neighborhoods, where decent people will not constantly be offended by their open and shameless flaunting." The city's so-called moral reformers — the clergymen, bluestockings, and others who would rather have outlawed prostitution entirely — were naturally less pleased. But even they seemed willing at least to give the new proposal a chance.

The area designated as the so-called restricted district (though it soon would be known as Storyville, much to the alderman's annoyance) was located behind the Vieux Carré, downriver of Canal Street. This was a mixed-race working-class neighborhood that contained only one church — the Union Chapel, a Methodist Episcopal establishment with an exclusively African American congregation that lacked any political clout. A second, much smaller area uptown of Canal

Street (eventually known as Black Storyville) was also designated, though unofficially, in order to forestall a wholesale exodus of black prostitutes already entrenched there. Known prostitutes in all other parts of town would be ordered to move to the restricted districts by a certain deadline; if they did not comply, notices of eviction — signed by Mayor Flower himself — would be sent and acted upon if necessary.

On January 29, 1897, Alderman Story's ordinance was passed by the city council (an amended version would be passed again in July). And so, on the first day of 1898, Storyville would officially be born.

Long before that date, of course, brothel landlords and other vice entrepreneurs scrambled to establish beachheads within the confines of the new district. And one of the first among them was Tom Anderson. Always well connected to sources of insider information, he moved quickly to acquire a choice property in Storyville-to-be. He bought the Fair Play Saloon, a large restaurant located on the corner of Basin Street and Customhouse, right at the point where most visitors would be entering the district, and made plans to renovate it into a showplace. Josie Arlington, too, acquired a lavish property on Basin Street, just a few doors down from Anderson's. The vast commercial potential of operating within a legally tolerated vice district was not lost on either of the two entrepreneurs, and they were determined to take full advantage of the opportunity.

Anderson in particular saw the coming change as propitious. Until now, he'd had to operate his more questionable enterprises on the gray margins of the law, subject to the whim of any overzealous police captain or city politician eager to make a show of cracking down on vice and petty crime. Now Anderson would be able to operate with the explicit blessing of the authorities. To him, it seemed like an ideal arrangement. Maybe this new crop of reformers wasn't so bad. With enemies like this, who needed friends?

And so Anderson began to lay his plans. He could set up shop in a bigger way in the new district. He could call in some political favors from his friends at the Choctaw Club — where the Ring political organization held court — and get himself elected to some position that might prove useful. And maybe he could even find some way of getting rid of his unwanted second spouse. For a man with an entrepreneurial streak and a flexible sense of propriety, the possibilities in this new scheme were virtually endless.

As for Alderman Story, Mayor Flower, and the other reformers, they too had good reason to expect that their segregated vice district would be a success, lending a semblance of order to a chaotic aspect of the city's life that had resisted all previous attempts at regulation. What they did not anticipate, however, was quite how wildly successful their well-meaning social experiment would become.

■ ■ ■ ■

Chapter 6
New Sounds

■ ■ ■ ■

The only existing photograph of the Buddy Bolden Band
Hogan Jazz Archive, Tulane University

But there was another phenomenon brewing in those areas soon to be set aside by the city fathers as enclaves of sin. At first, no one — certainly not those city fathers themselves — would recognize it as anything significant or worthy of notice. But for the one-quarter of New Orleanians designated in the census as "Negro," the phenomenon would come to be very important indeed — a way of coping with the changes around them, a way of holding their own, of asserting their identity in a time of adversity.

The new sound was born sometime in the mid-1890s, in the working-class black clubs and honky-tonks near the poor Uptown neighborhood soon to be known as Black Storyville. You could hear it in the venues on and around South Rampart Street — at Dago Tony's, the Red Onion, Odd Fellows Hall — or farther afield in the "Negro dives" on the other side of Canal. For a time, the music was known only to those who flocked to such places, the so-called ratty people — "the good-time, earthy people," as one musician of the day defined them. But before too long, the new sound was also being heard in parks, on street corners, in dance halls, and in places well beyond the confines of the city's destitute black neighborhoods. And that, naturally, was when the trouble started.

No one ever recorded the New Orleans musicians of the 1890s, so it's difficult to say for sure that it was a young Uptown cornetist named Buddy Bolden who first played the music later known as jazz. Certainly many others — black, mixed-race, and even white — would eventually lay claim to the distinction. But many of his contemporary musicians believed that Bolden was the man who started it all, and to hear them tell the story, he was extraordinary: "That boy could make women jump out the window," one of his early listeners said. "He had a moan in his cornet that went all through you." For many people in New Orleans, accustomed to the straighter, more schooled styles of music that preceded it, the Bolden sound was a revelation: "I'd never heard anything like that before," one convert would later say. "I'd played 'legitimate' stuff. But this, it was something that pulled me in. They got me up on the [band]stand and I played with them. After that I didn't play legitimate so much."

Charles Joseph "Buddy" Bolden, like so

many of the jazzmen who would follow him, grew up poor and without much in the way of material prospects. The grandson of slaves, he was born on September 6, 1877, in a small house on Howard Street in Uptown New Orleans. As neighborhoods go, it was not a very healthy place to live, perched on the edge of a fetid and foul-smelling canal. By the time Buddy was six years old, he had lost his father, one sister, and his grandmother to various illnesses. Buddy and his sister Cora moved around with their mother, Alice, for the next few years, probably staying with relatives and friends, then finally settling in a small shotgun cottage at 385 First Street. This was a tough but integrated area (not unusual in the New Orleans of the time), populated mostly by German and Irish laborers who seemed to have little trouble getting along with their black neighbors. Mrs. Bolden made a modest living there as a laundress, earning enough to allow her two young children to stay in school without working themselves.

For a ten-year-old boy with a yet-unrealized musical gift, working-class New Orleans in the 1880s was an auspicious place to grow up. Music was everywhere around him, and thanks to the cosmopolitan nature of the city's population, it was as varied as it was ubiquitous. Peddlers in the alleys advertised their wares by blowing riffs on old tin horns;

"spasm bands" of children, wielding cigar-box banjos and soapbox basses, played tunes for handouts on street corners; Latin and Caribbean songs spilled from the decks of ships at anchor on the wharves. In that age before radio, events like parades and picnics were the everyday diversions, and each one came with its own performing brass bands. Churches, meanwhile, reverberated with hymns and spirituals, dockworkers sang work songs and blues, and even funerals were held with a complete musical accompaniment.

"The city was full of the sounds of music," one old-time New Orleanian remembered. "It was like a phenomenon, like the Aurora Borealis. . . . The sound of men playing would be so clear, but we wouldn't be sure where [it was] coming from. So we'd start trotting, start moving — 'It's this way!' 'It's that way!' . . . Music could come on you anytime like that."

Despite being surrounded by this feast of sounds, however, young Bolden apparently had no musical training until about 1894, at the age of sixteen or seventeen. That was when his mother allowed him to take cornet lessons from a neighbor named Manuel Hall, a short-order cook who was keeping company with her at the time. It was a late start for a musician, but Buddy learned quickly. He also had plenty of opportunities to play: The city's established brass bands — groups like the

Excelsior, Onward, and Eureka bands — would sometimes work long days, playing funerals or association affairs that stretched from early morning to very late at night. The older musicians would need a break now and then to have a beer or simply to rest their chops, and teenagers like Buddy would fill in for them. By 1897, though, he was already playing with his own regular band at parades and picnics. And despite (or maybe because of) his lack of formal training, he was soon attracting attention by "ragging the hymns, street songs, and dance tunes to create a musical sound that people were unfamiliar with."

The Bolden sound, to hear witnesses describe it, was hot, wide-open, low-down, and — like his most ardent fans — "ratty." It was bluesy and folksy, "music that [made] you want to dance." Like many Uptown black musicians, Buddy couldn't read music very well, but that didn't matter much, since he could pick up anything he needed by ear. "He could go and hear a band playing in the theater," one old friend recalled, "and he come on out and practice in between dances, and that morning, before the ball was over, he play that piece and play it well." And it wasn't only other bands he borrowed from. According to another contemporary, Bolden got ideas from everywhere — from what he heard in the "Holy Roller" churches he sometimes attended with his mother and sister, or even from the man peddling rags with his tin horn: "Buddy, he stole lots of things from the rag man," one friend confessed. But each time, he'd "put his own feeling to it," and thus make it his own.

And the music he made was electric. It was showy, improvisational, sometimes raunchy, and always very, very loud: "Bolden would blow so hard," one musician claimed, "he actually blew the tuning slide out of his cornet and it would land twenty feet away."

This, of course, is a physical impossibility, but it was only one of the legends that eventually grew up around the Bolden persona. Young Buddy did not, for instance, publish a scandal sheet called *The Cricket,* and he was not a barber. He did, however, spend a lot of time in barbershops, as did many of the early jazzmen, since the shops were common rendezvous points for musicians assembling personnel for upcoming gigs. At Charlie Galloway's barbershop on South Rampart Street in the late '90s, Bolden — still in his teens — got many of his earliest jobs. Working by day as a laborer and occasional plasterer, he would play by night in the neighborhood halls and honky-tonks. And the Bolden Band was soon attracting plenty of attention — and spawning a raft of imitators.

Even some of the older musicians took

notice. Bandleaders like Galloway, Edward Clem, and Henry Peyton had already been making some innovative music when Bolden came up, but Buddy took the music in new directions. "Buddy was the first to play blues for dancing," one fellow musician said, summing it up. Bolden was also one of the first New Orleans musicians to perform improvised solos, or "rides." "With all those notes he'd throw in and out of nowhere," another musician said, "you never heard anything like it." But it was the younger musicians in particular who were picking up the new sound. Not just other cornetists, but clarinetists, trombone and bass players, drummers, and guitarists. Musicians like Freddie Keppard, Bunk Johnson, George Baquet, Pops Foster, "Big Eye" Louis Nelson, Willie Cornish, Frankie Dusen, even a young Creole pianist (something of an outsider among the Uptowners) named Jelly Roll Morton . . . all were soon doing their own innovations, taking old tunes — or making up new ones — and stamping them with their own personalities.

What exactly were they all playing? Critics would argue for decades about what the new music actually was. They traced its lineage to African, Caribbean, French, and/or Spanish roots, to ragtime, to various religious forms, and to secular traditions like the blues. But in a way, it was utterly new — music created by largely untrained musicians without much experience in any formal tradition: "That's where jazz came from — from the routine men, ya understand — the men that didn't know nothin' about music. They just make up their own ideas."

Perhaps guitarist Danny Barker summed it up best: "Who cared if you read music? You were free: free to take liberties, free to express yourself from deep inside. The public was clamoring for it!"

Many who heard him claimed that Bolden actually wasn't a very skilled player technically. "He wasn't really a musician," trombonist Kid Ory once said of him. "He didn't study. I mean, he was gifted, playing with effect, but no tone. He just played loud." But that loud, piercing horn helped him break the music free from the more reined-in style of his predecessors, bringing the soloist — that is, himself — to the fore.

And people began noticing, especially women. Bolden — an attractive, "light brown-skin boy" with reddish-black hair, a round face, and a "sort of Maori look about him" — was soon a local celebrity in black Uptown, traveling around with a harem of female admirers who would fight one another to hold his hat, his coat, even his handkerchief (but never his cornet, which he allegedly didn't let out of his sight). And he appreciated the attention. "Oh, he was crazy about womens," a friend would later say. One of those "womens" — an older neighbor named Hattie Oliver — even bore him a baby son before his twentieth birthday. Buddy took care of both mother and child, at least for a while.

Eventually, though, the new sound played by Bolden and his emulators became so popular — among working-class audiences both black and white — that it began to draw attention from some unwanted quarters as well. Police would show up at so-called cutting contests (where two bands would meet and try to outplay each other) and begin "whipping heads" to restore order. And eventually the city's reformers began to take notice, and they did not like what they heard. To their ears, the new sound was dangerous, an affront to their notions of respectability, restraint, temperance, and civil order. This new black music represented excess and licentiousness, a direct flouting of traditional moral values. Perhaps most perniciously, it promoted contact — much of it of the most scandalous type — across the color line, and in a context of social equality that was simply intolerable to most Southern whites.

Even before Bolden began to make his mark, reformers had already started protesting about the detrimental effects of so-called coon music. In 1890, the *Mascot* had railed against a "nigger band" then playing in one

139

of the city's more notorious venues: "Here male and female, black and yellow, and even white, meet on terms of equality and abandon themselves to the extreme limit of obscenity and lasciviousness." Soon the *Daily Picayune* was also taking up arms against the new sound, calling it "demoralizing and degrading" — something "wholly forced and unnatural."

And now, with the rising popularity of Bolden and his peers, black music in New Orleans had taken an ominous new turn. "Jazz," as one historian would later put it, represented the equivalent of "musical miscegenation." In the context of the city's ongoing crusade for order, racial purity, and respectability, that meant it had to be suppressed.

For black New Orleanians — particularly for those old enough to remember the days of Reconstruction — the last few years of the nineteenth century had seen some dismaying changes in the city. The New Orleans of their youth had been a relatively accommodating place for people of color. In the Louisiana of the early 1870s, black citizens could vote and serve on juries. Schools were desegregated, and interracial marriage was legal. Blacks and whites rode on the same streetcars, frequented the same parks and lakeside beaches, and often lived side by side in the same neighborhoods. Of course, racial prejudice did exist — as it always had, in New Orleans as in most places both North and South — and some of these freedoms were often denied in the day-to-day conduct of life. But as one historian observed, "For at least two decades after the war, many residents from the rank and file of both races played and worked together on amicable, harmonious, even equalitarian terms."

In fact, New Orleans had had a long tradition of interracial fraternity extending back into its French and Spanish days. Relatively liberal manumission laws under the old colonial slave codes, combined with substantial immigration from Haiti, Cuba, and Martinique, had given the pre-American city a large and often prosperous community of free people of color. They often intermarried with their white French and Spanish neighbors, giving rise to a significant population of mixed-race children and grandchildren. These so-called Creoles of Color, most of them French-speaking Catholics, came to occupy a position in the city's social hierarchy somewhere between whites and their African American slaves; Creoles of Color often took up trades like cigar making, carpentry, ironwork, and shoemaking (some of them even owned slaves of their own).

In the cosmopolitan atmosphere of nineteenth-century New Orleans, social and sexual relations between these people of color and white New Orleanians were not unusual, even engendering a widely accepted system known as *placage,* in which a married white man would establish his mixed-race mistress in a separate household of her own. So-called quadroon balls — widely anticipated and often quite formal and luxurious — would bring these couples together, providing a context in which white men and young mixed-race women (and usually the women's mothers) could meet and come to mutually agreeable terms for a relationship. Such liaisons continued to occur well beyond the end of the Civil War, and were regarded, at least in some circles, as perfectly normal and acceptable.

After Emancipation, of course, a steady migration to New Orleans of rural ex-slaves complicated the racial dynamics of the city. The newly arrived African Americans — far less educated and predominantly Protestant and English-speaking — tended to cluster in Uptown neighborhoods, while Creoles of Color remained mostly in their old neighborhoods on the other, downriver side of Canal Street. But although tensions and competition existed between the two groups, they often worked together for Reconstruction-era legislation granting rights to all people of color, whether black or mixed-race, African American or Afro-Creole.

All of this had begun to change in the late 1870s, when the Compromise of 1876 brought the end of Reconstruction. With the removal of federal troops from the South, white "Redeemers" had acted quickly to assert political control over New Orleans and the rest of Louisiana. A new state constitution in 1879 removed many of the equal-rights provisions put in place right after the war. But even so, the Redeemers (many of whom eventually wound up on the Committee of Fifty that played such an important role in the Hennessy affair) were reluctant to do too much too soon. Fearing a return of federal military intervention, they did not begin to codify white supremacy (a term that in nineteenth-century Louisiana carried no pejorative connotation among most whites) for some time. Even as late as 1884–85, when New Orleans hosted the World's Industrial and Cotton Centennial Exposition, inter-racial contact was still relatively free. One prominent visitor of the day, writer Charles Dudley Warner, was pleasantly surprised by what he saw at the fair. "White and colored people mingled freely," he reported. "On 'Louisiana Day' . . . the colored citizens took their full share of the parade and honors. Their societies marched with the others, and the races mingled on the grounds in unconscious equality of privileges."

But starting in 1890 — just around the time

that Mayor Shakspeare and his allies had begun their campaign against the Italian underworld — Louisiana whites decided it was time to reassert old racial hierarchies as well. And in this task the white elites had the full support of the white working class, now feeling the pinch of job competition from black workers. New steps were taken to assert an inviolable color line in everyday life, and at the same time to systematically erase the "middle-caste" distinction enjoyed by the city's Creoles of Color. The most ominous of these efforts was a movement to institute a railroad segregation law. Naturally, political opposition to the proposed measure — Section 2 of the 1890 Louisiana Legislature's Act 111 — was fierce. But by the summer of 1890, Act 111 had been passed by the legislature, becoming the state's first official Jim Crow law. Unfortunately, it would not be the last.

The story of how this pernicious new law was tested by a young man named Homer Plessy, a light-skinned Creole from the Faubourg Tremé, is well known. Less well known is the fact that Plessy's arrest on June 7, 1892, was entirely orchestrated by an organization of well-heeled Creoles of Color known as the Comité des Citoyens. Even the train conductor and arresting policeman were in on the plot, calmly apprehending the young shoemaker when he refused to leave the whites-only carriage of an East Louisiana Railroad train. But although Plessy's court challenge would take years to work its way to the Supreme Court, the onslaught of Jim Crow in Louisiana just continued. Over the next few years, other new laws were passed to suppress the status and freedom of the state's black population. Interracial marriage was banned again, and even interracial boxing was prohibited (after a match in which a black featherweight fighter convincingly dismantled his white opponent in the ring). Worst of all, a movement arose for yet another new state constitution, the effect of which would be to deprive virtually all of the state's black residents of their right to vote. And when *Plessy v. Ferguson* was finally decided by the Supreme Court in 1896, it was yet another blow: the court upheld the Separate Car Act, institutionalizing the concept of "separate but equal" accommodations for whites and blacks (both African American *and* Creole) for decades to come. Jim Crow had arrived in Louisiana to stay.

And now, in the late '90s, the self-styled forces of white supremacy began to target yet another arena of black aspiration — the new music being played by Buddy Bolden and the other proto-jazzmen. For many whites in the city, the music challenged the spirit of Jim Crow in a literal way, by bringing white and black audiences together, but also symbolically as well. Jazz was, in a very real sense, an expression of defiance, a projection of black male power that rebelled against the increasing efforts to marginalize and suppress the race. As such, it was viewed as a threat not just to respectability but to the entire social order that was being reasserted in the post-Reconstruction South.

Even so, an organized effort to quash this less tangible form of black self-assertion would come only gradually over the next years. In the meantime, there were just sporadic and unorganized acts of intimidation — a band at a "Negro fish fry" broken up here, a racially mixed street concert raided by police there. In 1896, during one of the city's occasional small-pox epidemics, an effort would be made to close the notorious "Negro dives" of Franklin Street, ostensibly for health reasons; the effort did not succeed. But with the opening of the two Storyvilles in 1898, it was hoped that the black jazz culture could similarly be segregated and contained, moved out of the sight of respectable New Orleanians. In this first phase of the city's war of reform, all that was disrespectable and disruptive, if it could not be stamped out, would at least be kept within boundaries.

But jazz, like prostitution, would not be so easy to control. A few months after the opening of Storyville, after the start of the Spanish-

American War, Buddy Bolden and his band were playing at the wharf at the end of St. Louis Street, sending off a Negro regiment bound for Cuba. The band was playing "Home, Sweet Home" — in their own expressive way — as the ship moved away from the dock. But then many of the soldiers on board, overcome by a nostalgia evoked by the music, began jumping off the ship with their own musical instruments and swimming back to shore. "I'm telling you, that was it," one musician said, recalling the incident. "Over the side the boys went; they just couldn't take it. [We] had banjos and violins floating on that river for a week."

Of course, this story may be at least partly apocryphal, but it hints at the power of Bolden's music as the kind of disruptive force unwelcome to the city's powers-that-be. In fact, according to some reports, military bands in New Orleans were forever-after forbidden to play "Home, Sweet Home" — in a jazzy style or otherwise. The song's message, after all, was hardly conducive to persuading men to go off and be killed for their country.

But in those final years of the nineteenth century, another young black man — somewhat older than Bolden — had come to New Orleans with some subversive new ideas of his own. He was not a loud and flashy musician; most who knew him even described him as quiet, scholarly, and unassuming. But Robert Charles, a former railroad maintenance worker from Mississippi, was not one to passively accept the city's new racial strictures without a fight. And he was soon to challenge the city's white establishment in a much more overt way — with an act of defiance that would end up altering the racial dynamics of the Crescent City for many years to come.

■ ■ ■ ■

Chapter 7
Desperado

■ ■ ■ ■

Robert Charles **Jean Stone, Louisiana State University Press**

On a dark, tropical Monday evening in July of 1900, two black men sat quietly on the front steps of a house on Dryades Street in Uptown New Orleans. It was nearly eleven o'clock, and they had been waiting there for some time. The two were hoping to visit some female friends who lived down the block, but since the friends were renting the back room of a white woman's house, they all had to be somewhat discreet. The landlady would certainly not allow a late-night visit, especially not by two black suitors of her tenants. So the men were biding their time, waiting for the lights to go out in the front room of the house.

The two men — Robert Charles, thirty-four years old, and his much younger friend, Lenard Pierce — were roommates, living in a single room of a cottage on Fourth Street, just a few blocks away. They had known each other for years, and in fact may have been cousins, though it was only recently that they had moved in together. Charles had just lost his job at a lumberyard the month before, and after moving around for a while to ever-cheaper lodgings, he had eventually convinced his friend to share the room on Fourth so that they could split their living expenses. Pierce, also unemployed, had been more than willing to agree, eager to vacate the house where he had lived with his now-separated parents. Besides, Charles was an agreeable roommate, very easy to get along with. Intelligent and bookish, he carried himself with an "air of elegance" accentuated by his well-tailored clothes and ever-present black bowler hat. But although Charles seemed peaceable enough to most people who knew him, some friends noted an underlying resentment beneath his surface good nature. The plight of the black man in the New Orleans of 1900 did not sit well with Robert Charles, and he had become increasingly angry at the growing injustices he saw all around him.

Certainly he had concrete reasons for feeling resentful. No black man in that era was a stranger to intimidation and bigotry, but Charles had seen more than his share. Born just after the Civil War into a family of share-croppers in rural Pine Bluff, Mississippi, he had witnessed firsthand the violent reassertion of white supremacy that had followed the collapse of Reconstruction in the South. During the 1883 elections in his native Copiah County, young Robert and his family had been forced to flee their home and hide in the woods for days on end to avoid marauding gangs of whites determined to control the election by terrorizing any blacks who might have the audacity to try to vote. One African American church was burned to the ground, and numerous black leaders were dragged from their homes and threatened with lynching if they dared to intervene.

After that fraudulent and violent election, many demoralized blacks migrated out of Copiah County — and Robert Charles was one of them. He moved to Vicksburg, some thirty miles away, and found employment on the Louisville, New Orleans, and Texas Railroad. But things didn't go well for him there, either. In May of 1892, during a dispute about a stolen pistol, Charles got involved in a shootout with a white railroad flagman. No one was hurt in the incident, but by then Charles knew that a black man could not shoot a gun at a white man without dire consequences in Mississippi, no matter what the provocation. And so he became something of a fugitive, traveling around the state for months under the alias Curtis Robinson.

By late 1894, he had found his way to New Orleans. Still living under his assumed name, he worked on and off as a manual laborer and a seasonal contractor, hiring black New Orleanians to work as extra hands on sugar plantations outside the city. He also earned some money distributing literature for the International Migration Society, an organization for American blacks who wanted to migrate to Africa. Charles had joined the society in May of 1896, and had even paid a deposit on a voyage to Liberia for himself.

What caused the thirty-year-old to contemplate such a drastic step is not known for sure, but it likely had to do with the evolving racial attitudes in New Orleans in the 1890s. Having escaped the malignant bigotry of the rural Mississippi of his childhood, he had arrived in the Crescent City just at the time when it was playing catch-up with the rest of the South on issues of white supremacy. By the late '90s — as Homer Plessy, Buddy Bolden, and every other black New Orleanian could attest — Jim Crow was making the formerly tolerant city far more similar to the rigidly segregated cities in the rest of the South. And the timing of Charles's application to the migration society was especially significant, having come just one month after the Louisiana election of April 1896 — an election that had brought race relations in New Orleans to a new low. It was then that he began distributing migration literature and making plans for his escape to Liberia. It was also then that he began carrying a concealed pistol in his pocket whenever he left his home. And that pistol was with him now, as he and Lenard Pierce sat on the steps of the Dryades house on the night of July 23, 1900, waiting for that light to go out.

But their presence in the neighborhood had not gone unnoticed. Police sergeant Jules C. Aucoin was making his nightly rounds when, at about eleven P.M., a passerby told him of "two suspicious-looking Negroes" sitting in front of a house on the next block. Aucoin gathered up two more patrolmen — August T. Mora and Joseph D. Cantrelle — and enlisted them to help him investigate. They found Charles and Pierce on the steps of 2815 Dryades and demanded to know what they were doing there. According to later testimony by Patrolman Mora, the men gave a vague answer about "waiting for a friend." Then Charles, for whatever reason, stood up. Mora apparently interpreted this as an aggressive move. "I grabbed him," the patrolman said. "The Negro pulled, but I held fast, and he finally pulled me into the street. Here I began using my billet and the Negro jerked from my grasp and ran."

Mora seemed confused about exactly what happened next. In one interview, he claimed that Charles pulled out his pistol first; in later testimony, he said that he himself was the first to draw his gun. Either way, the two were soon shooting at each other, with Patrolman Cantrelle also taking several shots at the retreating black man.

155

It was over very quickly. Charles, who had been hit in the thigh, was nonetheless able to sprint down the street, with Cantrelle on his heels. Mora lay in the street, bleeding from a wound to the hip. Lenard Pierce, meanwhile, sat frozen on the steps, staring at Aucoin's "big Colt revolver" aimed straight at his head.

One of the most violent weeks in New Orleans history had just begun.

An hour later, Lenard Pierce was sitting in the Sixth Precinct station, charged with shooting at Sergeant Aucoin. The charge was bogus, of course — even Aucoin himself denied it — but it was intended to frighten the terrified youth into telling what he knew about the man who did shoot at the police. And Pierce was forthcoming — to a degree. He told Capt. John T. Day that his companion was named "Robinson" (he knew Charles's real name but chose to reveal only his alias) and that he was from Mississippi. Pierce claimed to know little about him other than that.

Captain Day had in the meantime assigned several patrolmen to return to the scene and try to follow the trail of blood from the wounded man's leg. This, however, proved fruitless; the trail petered out after a few hundred feet, and the patrolmen eventually had to return to the station empty-handed. But by then Captain Day had learned the assailant's real name and home address — either from Pierce or by some other means. When he met the search party at the door of the station, he was smiling. "I know where I can get that nigger now," he said.

The captain's instinct was right. Charles, after shrewdly running in the opposite direction from his home for a few blocks, had doubled back and headed toward his room at the Fourth Street cottage. Once there, he had wrapped his leg wound in green gauze and armed himself with a .38-caliber Winchester rifle that he'd borrowed from his brother some time before. Charles may have intended to move on from there to a different hiding place, but he was still home when, at about three A.M., Captain Day and six police officers pulled up at the yellow cottage in a police wagon.

Day instructed three of the officers to remain with the wagon. Then he took the other three — including Sergeant Aucoin, from the earlier incident — to the gate at the side of the house. By the light of kerosene lanterns, they could see that the gate led to a dark, covered alleyway running past six separate doors, each one the entrance to a one-room apartment in the cottage.

Captain Day opened the gate. He and the other officers — along with a civilian bystander who had volunteered to go with them — then stepped along the alley's plank walkway to the first door and knocked. A woman, apparently roused from sleep, came to the door. Day demanded to know which door belonged to the room shared by "those men," and the woman seemed to realize immediately whom they meant. "In Room Number Four," she told them. The five men continued down the walkway to the fourth door in the line. They noticed that it was already slightly ajar.

"Open up there!" one of the officers shouted.

The door swung open to reveal Robert Charles standing in the dim light. He was holding the rifle, aimed directly at Captain Day.

Without any hesitation, Charles fired. The bullet struck Day in the chest; according to later testimony, the captain spun around, gave "an awful moaning cry," and collapsed dead onto the plank walkway.

For almost fifteen seconds after the shot, no one moved, all — including Charles himself — apparently incredulous at what had just happened. Then the civilian bolted down the alley and back to the street. "My God," he shouted, "I think they have killed Captain Day!" But the other patrolmen remained standing in the alley as if paralyzed by disbelief — until Charles fired a few more bullets into Captain Day's sprawled body, lifted the rifle, and fired another shot that virtually shattered a second policeman's skull.

At this, Aucoin and the other surviving patrolman — Cpl. Ernest J. Trenchard — came to their senses and began to return fire. But Charles had by now slammed his door shut and was reloading the Winchester. During the lull in gunfire, the door to the second room on the alley opened. A young black woman — later identified as Annie Cryder — beckoned to the men in the alley. "Come in, Officers! Come in here!" she hissed at them. Aucoin and Trenchard gladly complied. They rushed to the offered refuge just as Charles reopened the door to his room and stepped into the alley. Annie Cryder slammed her own door shut and then blew out her lamp, plunging the room into darkness.

For several minutes, nothing happened. Charles began pacing the plank walkway outside, his measured footsteps clearly audible on the creaking boards. He was muttering curses under his breath, ridiculing the policemen through the closed door and daring them to leave their hiding place. But Aucoin and Trenchard didn't move.

Out on the street, meanwhile, the three policemen stationed there by Captain Day — incredibly — did nothing. After hearing the shots and the shout of the fleeing civilian volunteer, one of them — Cpl. Honore Perrier — told the other two to run around the block to the back of the building to cut off any escape Charles might attempt. But when nothing else happened after many minutes, they returned and consulted with Perrier. Finally, at about three thirty A.M. — a full half hour after the first shots had been heard — one of them walked up to the cottage gate and called out: "Do you need any assistance in there?" But there was no answer, so he returned to his place. And there the officers just waited.

About an hour later, they saw a dark figure come up to the end of the alley. It was Charles, and as they watched, he lifted his rifle and took a potshot at Corporal Perrier; the bullet narrowly missed his head and embedded itself in a pole behind him. At this, the three officers ran away — ostensibly, they later claimed, to find a telephone to call for assistance. Why this had not occurred to them earlier is a mystery. In any case, one of them rang up the station from a nearby pharmacy and reported "considerable firing" at the Fourth Street cottage. Reinforcements were immediately dispatched. Then the three policemen returned to the scene of the shooting — though they maintained a safe distance from the gate at the side of the cottage.

At five A.M., just as dawn was breaking, Aucoin and Trenchard carefully opened the door to Room Two and peered out into the murkily lit alley. They had heard no movement out there for some time, and when they saw no sign of the gunman, they piled out of the doorway and ran down the alley to the street. Several units of police had by now gathered on the scene. Aucoin and Trenchard told them what had happened, and when they felt they had enough men, they all cautiously approached the gate. Eventually, they felt it was safe to enter the alley. The two dead officers lay just where they had fallen hours earlier. But Charles was nowhere to be seen. And though the police now conducted an extensive search of the cottage and the surrounding neighborhood, they were obviously too late. Robert Charles — with his Winchester rifle and his pistol — was already long gone.

By seven A.M., nearly every police officer in the city of New Orleans was on the scene, along with scores of armed would-be vigilantes from the neighborhood. Police and several white civilians were ransacking the room of the man they now knew as Robert Charles, looking for evidence. Others were scouring the neighborhood for any sign of the man. The scene was chaotic — and volatile. When one witness claimed to have seen Charles ducking into a backyard privy, the reaction was swift. "In a moment, a hundred or more infuriated men had run into the yard," the *Item* reported. "Quicker than work could tell, they had torn up the floor of the vault and a veritable hail of lead . . . was being poured

161

into the dark hole." The outhouse was then pushed off its foundation and the pit below it was dragged, but the hole yielded only human waste and soiled paper.

Meanwhile, the discovery of Charles's cache of migration literature was fueling speculation that he was some kind of fanatical race agitator intent on "evil toward the white man." This revelation only stoked the anger of the crowd and hardened its determination to find him. Soon alleged sightings of the gunman were sending mobs of vigilantes out into an ever-widening area of the city. According to rumors, Superintendent of Police Gaster "wanted that man badly," and had allegedly told searchers "not to hesitate in shooting the villain if he showed the slightest attempt to fight."

By midday, the largest manhunt in the history of New Orleans was turning the city upside down. Trains and ferries were stopped; citizen volunteers watched all major roads in the parish. Police were conducting floor-by-floor searches in public and private buildings throughout the city, as well as in Kenner, Gretna, and even as far away as Natchez and Vicksburg, Mississippi, where it was said some of Charles's relatives lived. The hunt for the man the *Times-Democrat* was now calling "one of the most formidable monsters that has ever been loose upon the community" went on for hours — and ultimately for days — but without success.

The ease with which Charles had eluded them caused considerable consternation among his would-be captors, and it wasn't long before this frustration was being vented on a more available target — namely, the city's black population. On Tuesday, the first day of the fruitless search, a few skirmishes broke out between groups of whites and blacks, mostly in the vicinity of the Fourth Street cottage. Police arrested many blacks who appeared to be sympathetic to the missing man — and even one white visitor from New York who merely suggested that Charles may have shot the three policemen in self-defense. At the Sixth Precinct station house, threats to lynch Charles's "accomplice" forced Superintendent Gaster to move Lenard Pierce to the relative safety of Orleans Parish Prison. But white crowds became increasingly belligerent over the course of the day, until rumors that Charles had been captured in suburban Kenner calmed some of their ire. Even so, by midnight there were numerous reports of black men and even women being beaten by the roving mobs.

By morning, when word spread that Charles had not been captured after all, the violence escalated again. Encouraged by inflammatory editorials in the morning newspapers — in particular a *Times-Democrat* piece that essentially blamed the black race "as a class"

for the crimes of its individual members —
gangs of openly armed men raced through
the streets of New Orleans, terrorizing any
black person they could find. The atmosphere
only worsened when the first edition of the
afternoon *States* appeared. An editorial
entitled NEGRO MURDERERS — written by
the newspaper's notoriously racist editor,
Henry J. Hearsey — all but called upon the
city's white male population to retaliate in
kind for what amounted to a secret and
widespread black insurrection: "We know
not, it seems, what hellish dreams are arising
underneath; we know not what schemes of
hate, or arson, or murder and rape are being
hatched in the dark depths," Hearsey warned.
"We are, and we should realize it, under the
regime of the free Negro, in the midst of a
dangerous element of servile uprising, not for
any real cause, but from the native race
hatred of the Negro."

Not that many white New Orleanians —
frustrated by increasing job competition with
blacks — needed much encouragement. On
Wednesday night, violence spread throughout
the city. A mob of some two thousand whites
formed in Lee Circle, at the foot of the tower-
ing monument to the Confederate general. In
a scene hauntingly reminiscent of W. S. Parkerson's rally against the Hennessy acquittals
just nine years earlier, several orators spoke
to the throng, inciting them to outrage, urg-

ing them to save the good name of New Orleans by punishing a black population that was clearly sheltering the murderous fiend in their midst. And so again an armed mob surged through the streets of New Orleans, with spectators cheering them on from the sidelines. Again "justice" was going to be served — only this time the victims were to be innocent blacks rather than innocent Italians.

The mob was, if anything, even more indiscriminate than the one of 1891. "Unable to vent its vindictiveness and bloodthirsty vengeance upon Charles," journalist Ida B. Wells later wrote, "the mob turned its attention to other colored men who happened to get in the path of its fury." Streetcars were stopped and overturned; black passengers were taken out and beaten or shot. "Negroes fled terror-stricken before the mob like sparrows before a picnic party," the *Times-Democrat* reported. "The progress of the mob was like a torchlight procession all the way to Washington Avenue. . . . On every side cries of 'Kill the Negroes,' 'shoot them down,' and like expressions were freely used."

By nine thirty, the mob — now numbering some three thousand men and boys — had reached the new parish prison in the central business district, where Lenard Pierce was being held. But they found the doors barricaded and the building protected by a double cordon of armed policemen and sheriff's deputies. The throngs tried to rush the doors, and there were several altercations between rioters and police — and even a few shots fired — but this time the line of blue held fast. "The angry men swayed this way and that," the *Times-Democrat* reported, "and their utter impatience in getting at the Negro Pierce . . . seemed to drive them into a state of madness."

By ten P.M., the frustrated crowd had moved on from the prison, breaking into smaller groups that roamed the city in search of prey. One group crossed Canal Street and entered the new Storyville District. "The red-light district was all excitement," a reporter for the *Picayune* later wrote. "Women — that is, the white women — were out on their stoops and peering over their galleries and through their windows and doors, shouting to the crowd to go on with their work, and kill Negroes for them." Saloons, dance halls, and houses of ill fame — at least those catering to a black clientele — were by this time largely shut up tight, but the mob assailed them anyway. "Out went the lights in the honky-tonks," the *Picayune* reported. "The music stopped in the dance houses, and the blacks, who were dancing, singing, and gambling, ran in the dark. Some hid under the houses . . . [others] sought refuge in outhouses and under cisterns."

At the club called Big 25 on Franklin Street, Buddy Bolden was sitting in with Big Bill Peyton's band, playing with Peyton on accordion, "Big Eye" Louis Nelson on clarinet and bass, Jib Gibbson on guitar, and a few others. According to Nelson, a woman ran in and warned them that a mob was heading into "the District," as Storyville had also come to be known. Nelson was tempted to leave that minute, but Peyton calmed him down. "Aah, we never had nothing like that in New Orleans yet," Peyton said, "and it won't happen tonight." He told the band to just keep playing. But then they started to hear some shooting nearby, and everyone panicked. "Me, I was sitting at the inside end of the bandstand, playing bass," Nelson later recalled. "All them boys flung themselves on me in getting away from the door and out toward the back. The bass was bust to kindling, and I sailed clear across the back of the room, so many of them hit me so hard all at once."

The musicians and customers climbed out a back window into the alley behind the club — only to find that it was already filling with white rioters. So they ran in the other direction. "Me and Bolden and Gibbson was together," Nelson continued. "We thought Josie Arlington might let us through her house in Basin Street. [But] when she saw who we was, she slammed the door, locked it, and start[ed] to scream. So we cut on through the lot next door, made it over the fence and on down Basin. Not one of us had a shirt on him by then, and Bolden had left his watch hanging on the wall near the bandstand. We might have been assassinated, but we was lucky enough to get to a friend's house. We locked ourselves in and barred the doors."

The rampage went on all night — in the District, the Vieux Carré, and any other neighborhoods where blacks might be found. It was clear that the rioters had one simple, ugly intent: "The supreme sentiment was to kill Negroes," as the *Picayune* put it. "Every darky they met was ill-treated and shot." And through all of this, the New Orleans Police Department arrested no one.

By morning, three blacks had been brutally killed, with six more critically wounded. Around fifty others had received lesser injuries — including five whites, two of them shot by mistake and three others beaten or shot for merely objecting to the senseless violence. Fearing a second day of mayhem, then-mayor Paul Capdevielle, who had been out of town recovering from an illness, returned to the city. He ordered every saloon in the city closed, and called for the formation of a force of five hundred special volunteer police to quell the violence. By afternoon, he had three times that many, including hundreds of the city's most prominent citizens. Business in New Orleans, after all, had come to a virtual halt by now, as huge numbers of workers — black *and* white — stayed away from their jobs; the riot was even having a negative effect on the city's securities market. Something had to be done. "The better element of the white citizens," according to Ida Wells, "began to realize that New Orleans in the hands of a mob would not prove a promising investment for Eastern capital, so the better element began to stir itself, not for the purpose of punishing the brutality against the Negroes who had been beaten . . . but for the purpose of saving the city's credit."

Whatever their motivation, the citizens' force did make progress in heading off the violence. By Thursday night, when the special police were supplemented by an influx of state militiamen, the city seemed more or less under control — but not before two more blacks had been killed and fifteen others nonfatally shot or beaten. And although a semblance of order now reigned, no one forgot the fact that Robert Charles was still at large, and there was no telling what might happen when that "bloodthirsty champion of African supremacy" was finally caught.

In a small room in the rear annex of 1208 Saratoga Street, just fourteen blocks from his home on Fourth, Robert Charles was waiting. He had been there — holed up in the single room that constituted the structure's entire second story — for three days now, having come directly from the scene of the shootings early Tuesday morning. It was not, perhaps, the best place for him to find refuge. He was known in the neighborhood as a friend of the Jacksons, the family who rented most of the densely occupied duplex building from its white owner; any police investigator checking out the gunman's friends and associates would hear about the Jacksons eventually. But Charles's mobility was still limited by his leg wound. And as the owner of the most famous black face in the city of New Orleans, now emblazoned across the front page of every daily newspaper, he didn't have many other options. Nor could he have had any illusions about how this adventure was likely to end. A black man who killed two white policemen in the New Orleans of 1900, no matter what the circumstances, would never be allowed to explain himself in court.

And so Robert Charles was preparing to defend himself. He still had his Winchester rifle, and in a first-floor closet under the building's narrow staircase he had set up a small charcoal furnace. Here he was melting bits of lead pipe to make bullets. His intent was clear: if he was to die at the hand of a mob or the New Orleans police, he was going to take as many people with him as he could.

Charles's vigil came to an end on Friday afternoon, when he saw a police patrol wagon pulling slowly into Saratoga Street. Superintendent Gaster had received a tip shortly before noon that day. A black informant had claimed that a family by the name of Jackson — thought to be relatives of the fugitive — was harboring him in their home. A few quiet inquiries had revealed the location of that home as 1208 Saratoga Street. And although this was only one of numerous leads Gaster had received in the days since the shootings, it was a plausible one. So he'd sent one of his best officers — Sgt. Gabriel Porteus, who had been instrumental in turning away the mob at the parish prison on Wednesday — to check it out, accompanied by three other men from the Second Precinct.

When he saw the police wagon at about three P.M., Charles collected his weapons and retreated into the closet under the stairs on the first floor. With the closet door slightly ajar, he had a clear view of the front door of the annex, which opened onto a courtyard separating the front and back portions of the building. Charles sat there — on the chair he had been using when making bullets — with the loaded Winchester on his lap.

In the courtyard outside, Sergeant Porteus and one of his men, Cpl. John Lally, were now questioning the main tenant of the place, a black laborer named Silas Jackson. Without preamble, Porteus asked him where "his brother Robert Charles" was. Jackson, who had just woken from an after-work nap, replied that he did have a brother named Charles *Jackson,* but that "Robert Charles was no relation of his." Porteus, hoping to intimidate the man into revealing what he knew (and Jackson almost certainly had to be aware that the fugitive was hiding in his back annex), insisted again that Charles was his brother and placed him under arrest. The sergeant then demanded that Jackson let them search the premises. Jackson could do little but agree, and he led them to the door of the annex.

Once inside, Porteus caught sight of a water bucket standing on a little table across the room, just outside the closet where Robert Charles was hiding. Claiming to be thirsty, Porteus stepped over to the bucket and grabbed the dipper. Charles didn't hesitate. He thrust the barrel of his rifle through the crack of the open closet door and fired a shot point-blank into Porteus's chest. Then he turned the rifle on Lally and shot the corporal in the gut. Both officers fell to the floor with fatal wounds.

As Silas Jackson ran in a panic from the room, Charles gathered up his supply of homemade bullets and carried them, along with the rifle and his Colt revolver, up the stairs to the second-floor room. Once there, he began to kick at the wood-and-plaster wall that separated the room from its counterpart in the other half of the duplex building. He managed to pound a large hole in the flimsy wall, which he then crawled through into the empty room next door. Now, with access to both sides of the duplex, he would be able to watch the courtyard in front of the annex and the alleyways on either side of it. Clearly he was preparing to make a last stand, and he was going to make his capture as difficult for the police as possible.

Within minutes, scores of white neighbors and passersby were filling the street in front of the building. The other two policemen who had come with Sergeant Porteus had by now called in the shooting and were awaiting backup. But others were not so cautious. Dozens of white neighbors, apparently thinking that Charles had decamped, were soon flooding into the alleys and courtyard around the back annex. One off-duty police officer — Patrolman Peter Fenny, who lived down the block — entered the ground-floor room and saw Porteus dead and Lally sinking fast. The latter, sitting upright on the floor in a slowly expanding puddle of blood, requested a priest. Feeny ran out to the street to find one, and before long was leading a Father Fitzgerald from a nearby church through the

173

milling crowds and into the ground-floor room.

At this point, Robert Charles decided it was time to make his continued presence known. Scanning the crowds in the yard below, he selected a white youth standing near the fence, aimed his Winchester out the back window, and fired. The young man — nineteen-year-old Arthur Brumfield — was hit in the hip and fell to the ground amid panicked mayhem. While others scrambled to exit the closed yard, Brumfield began crawling toward a stairway leading into the front building. He looked back and apparently saw Charles in the second-story window, still aiming the rifle. "For God's sake, don't shoot!" he allegedly cried. But Charles fired again, this time sending a bullet into the youth's chest that killed him instantly.

By now, word of the discovery of Charles's hideout was spreading through the entire city. Police from stations all over Uptown New Orleans were arriving on the scene, along with hundreds of armed white civilians drawn from their homes and workplaces. The special citizens' police force was mustered again and quickly dispatched to the scene. Mayor Capdevielle, notified of the situation as he enjoyed a Turkish bath at the St. Charles Hotel, realized instantly the great danger the situation posed to the city. He called on the state militia to hurry to Saratoga Street with their two Gatling guns — allegedly with orders to fire into the white mob if their fury degenerated again into widespread violence against innocent blacks.

Utter chaos now reigned in the streets around 1208 Saratoga. An estimated ten to twenty thousand people were thronging the neighborhood. Hundreds of men had climbed onto rooftops surrounding the house and were now taking potshots at the second-story windows of the back annex. Charles, moving back and forth through the hole he'd kicked in the wall, would occasionally appear at one window or another to fire back. Each time, his shot would be met by dozens of answering reports, the bullets shattering the glass panes and shredding the wooden façade of the annex. How many times Charles himself was hit would never be known, but he was taking a heavy toll on his attackers. Seven of them — police and citizens alike — were seriously wounded in these exchanges, with a dozen or more others sustaining lesser wounds. Whatever else they thought they knew about Robert Charles, they now knew for sure that he was an excellent shot.

But the standoff was not to go on indefinitely. Capt. William King of the Julia Street fire patrol, along with a few other men — apparently acting without permission — had managed to sneak into the ground-floor room of the annex of 1208 (from which the bodies of Porteus and Lally had been removed sometime earlier). They found an old horsehair mattress in the room and carried it over to the foot of the stairway leading up to the second floor. Then, while Charles paced across the two rooms above their heads, they poured kerosene on the mattress and set it afire. King doused the flames with water, so that the fire would smolder and produce copious amounts of smoke. Then he and the other men retreated from the room.

For five minutes, the crowds looked on expectantly as black smoke filled first one side and then the other of the two-story annex. But Charles seemed unfazed, still pacing the two rooms and firing from the windows. Finally, however, the stairway of 1208 caught fire. The heat generated by the mounting flames must have been intense, and when fire and smoke began penetrating the roof, many of the spectators wondered if Charles would be burned alive. But then the fugitive appeared at the front door of the far side of the annex, the Winchester leveled at shoulder height, his derby hat pulled low over his eyes. Taken by surprise, no one got off a shot at him as he raced across the courtyard to the front section of the building. Still aiming the rifle ahead of him, he rushed into the ground-floor room of 1210 — only to find several men lying in wait inside. One of them — a medical student named Charles Noiret, a member of the special citizens' police — was the first to react; he fired at Robert Charles just as he stepped into the room. Charles fell face-first to the floor, and was just rolling over to shoot back when Noiret and every other man in the room began emptying their firearms into Charles's body. The gunfire didn't stop, as dozens of other men, howling in triumph, raced toward the room and discharged their own weapons into the corpse. The orgy of shooting let up only when the last man's last bullet thudded uselessly into the lifeless body.

Eager to show their quarry to the crowds outside, several men lifted Charles's corpse and carried it to the front door. They dumped it on the stoop, and then, when it was understood what had happened, a cheer ran through the crowd outside. Several men ran up to the porch and dragged the body into the street. A few fired their own weapons into the corpse; others kicked or spat at it. Then a policeman carrying a double-barreled shotgun pushed his way through the crowd. It was Corporal Trenchard, the lavishly mustached patrolman who had humiliated himself during the incident at the yellow cottage, cowering in a darkened room long after Charles had fled the scene. He had borne the brunt of much scornful criticism since then, but here he felt he could redeem himself. "Now who says I am a coward?" he crowed.

Then he put the muzzle of his shotgun to Charles's chest and fired both barrels.

Content at first to let the mob vent its rage on the corpse, police stepped in when someone brought up a container of kerosene to burn the body. They forced the would-be arsonists back and made room for the patrol wagon to be pulled up. Two officers lifted the body by the arms and legs and flung it roughly into the back of the wagon. The frustrated mob attempted to get at the body again, but police held them off. The patrol wagon pulled away then, Charles's head hanging precariously over the edge of the wagon's bed, as hundreds of screaming, rock-throwing citizens followed in its wake.

And so the "hideous monster" had been punished, but unfortunately black New Orleans still had to endure one more night of terror before it was all over. Dissatisfied with the fact that Charles had endured so little physical retribution before he died, white New Orleanians went on another ugly rampage that night. Again the mobs ran through the streets, ostensibly looking for "accomplices" but actually attacking any black person they found on the street. Two more bystanders were killed, and the Lafon School for black children — regarded as "the best Negro schoolhouse in Louisiana" — was burned to the ground. Throughout the night, there were other threats of arson and attempted massacres of black citizens. But thanks to the intervention of the special volunteer police, the bloodshed was not nearly as bad as it had been on Wednesday night. By the time dawn broke on Saturday, the mobs' anger was all but spent, and the city was relatively quiet.

The weekend papers generally expressed satisfaction at the quick resolution of the Saratoga Street standoff, and relief over the end of mob violence in the city. Surprisingly, they also admitted to a certain amount of grudging respect for the bravery of the gunman who had sold his life so dearly. "Robert Charles was the boldest, most desperate and dangerous Negro ever known in Louisiana," the *Picayune* wrote. Even Henry Hearsey of the *States* seemed impressed. "Never before was such a display of desperate courage on the part of one man witnessed," he wrote. "[I] cannot help feeling for him a sort of admiration, prompted by his wild and ferocious courage." But all of the papers made sure that the proper lesson was drawn from the Robert Charles affair — namely, that any future challenge to white supremacy in Louisiana would be met with the harshest retribution. The days of even moderate racial tolerance in New Orleans were officially over.

This new low point in the city's racial atmosphere became increasingly palpable to blacks in the aftermath of the riot. For when

the incident had finally played itself out —
after the mutilated body of Robert Charles
had been buried in an unmarked plot in the
city's potter's field, and after the post-riot
investigations had led to the inevitable conviction of absolutely no one (except for five
police officers who were convicted of coward-
ice and dismissed from the force) — the city
emerged as an even harsher and more hostile
place for its black citizens. Political disenfranchisement and social segregation were now
reinforced by a hardened resolve among
whites to actively "keep the black man down"
in the century just beginning. This new attitude was perhaps best expressed by one
white city official in 1902: "The nigger's all
right in his place," the man explained to a
reporter for the magazine *Outlook,* "[but]
when he tries to get out of it, hit him on the
head, and next time he'll come in with his
hat off."

For the musicians in New Orleans' nascent
jazz culture, the changing environment would
mean more outright suppression of their
livelihood — more reform campaigns against
the dance halls they played in, more police
disruption of their parades and picnics. Most
of them had escaped physical harm, but the
psychological effects of the riot were to linger
on. And at least one musician had lost his life
in the violence. "Big Eye" Louis Nelson's
father — a butcher and occasional accordion-

ist — had been killed by a mob in the Vieux Carré on the first night of the major rioting. His body, battered and shot-up, was found in a gutter on Decatur Street and was carried to the hospital in the early morning hours of July 26.

"Nobody knew him," Nelson later recalled, "[but] when they showed him to *me,* I knew him. It was my daddy. They had snatched him off his meat wagon down at the French Market and killed him. . . . Was I angry about it? Well, sure, I was. But what could I do? It just wash away. It all just wash away. Couple of days later, I was back there at 25s playing harder than ever." That's when Nelson learned that to play the new music right, you had to "shove in *crying* wherever you get the chance."

But it was one thing to suppress the spirit of self-assertion represented by Robert Charles — and, for that matter, by jazz itself; destroying it would be something else entirely. In the years after 1900, in fact, Charles became something of a folk hero among the black citizens of New Orleans. Legends soon grew up around his name — that he had killed thirty-two policemen, for instance; that he'd shot one officer at a funeral, killing the cop but leaving the priest standing beside him unharmed. Some people even said that Charles had never died in that house on Saratoga Street, that somehow he'd escaped and lived to a ripe old age in hiding. And, of course, this last legend was in a sense true. Robert Charles did live on — in a song about his exploits, composed by an unknown hand in the days after his apotheosis. It was played in private all-black gatherings for years thereafter, though rarely in public. According to Jelly Roll Morton, who was just fifteen years old at the time, "This song was squashed very easily by the [police] department, and not only by the department but by anyone else who heard it, because it was a trouble-breeder. So that song never did get very far. I once knew the Robert Charles song. But I found out it was best for me to forget it."

Others in the city's black neighborhoods, however, would not forget the song so easily.

■ ■ ■ ■

Chapter 8
Storyville Rising

■ ■ ■ ■

Basin Street **Hogan Jazz Archive, Tulane University**

The lights were what amazed everyone. There were a hundred of them, suspended from the ornate tin ceiling like the bright-burning stars in Tom Anderson's own private galaxy. "We didn't have no sunglasses in them days," one habitué of the place would later claim, "but you needed 'em in Anderson's . . . Hurt my eyes [just] to walk *past* at night."

It was 1901, opening night of Tom Anderson's monumental new Annex in Storyville. Sprawled over the corner of Basin and Customhouse Streets, the Annex was a palace for the appetites — the "most modernly equipped and brilliant bar in the South," and reportedly the first in the nation illuminated entirely by electric lights. Its half-block-long cherrywood bar, punctuated by polished brass cuspidors and decorated with gilt bas-reliefs in Neo-Empire style, ran the length of the building, backed by five huge arched mirrors that multiplied those hundred lights to create a dazzling glow. Twelve bartenders manned this ocean liner of a fixture, this virtual bowling alley of beer and whiskey, serving customers who stood four deep on the brown-and-white tiled floor.

"Opening night was a thing to marvel at," the bar's intrepid manager, Billy Struve, would later recall. "Hundreds of people were there, representatives of the big breweries and the wine companies from all over the country. More than one hundred cases of Champagne were sold, the patrons outbidding each other for their favorite vintages. Before the night was over, everyone was walking in Champagne."

And there was ample reason for celebration. Storyville, technically open for business since 1898, finally had its linchpin, its headquarters. For patrons approaching the new Tenderloin from the Central Business District or the Vieux Carré, Anderson's Annex would be the first stop they'd come to — the District's gatehouse, as it were, perched tantalizingly aglow on the neighborhood's leading edge. From here, over a bracing glass or two, a sporting man could plan out his entire evening's entertainment, asking advice of the knowledgeable bartenders or even consulting a Blue Book, the uncensored, ubiquitously available Baedekers to the District's countless offerings. These guides, helpfully published by Anderson and Struve (a former reporter for the *Daily Item* who had begun working for Anderson in 1900), were aimed at "the man who wants to be a thoroughbred bounder." They contained ads, photos, and descriptions of every one of the better brothels and prostitutes in the eighteen-block area of Storyville, with each practitioner conveniently identified by "race" — for example, *w* for white, *c* for colored, *J* for Jewish, and *oct.* for octoroon. To own a Blue Book was to have the District at one's fingertips. "Go through this little book," the preface assured readers, "and when you go on a 'lark' you will know the best places to spend time and money. . . . It puts the stranger on a proper grade or path as to where to go and be secure from holdups, brace games, or other illegal practices usually worked on the unwise in Red Light districts." In short: "Anyone who knows today from yesterday will say that the Blue Book is the right book for the right people."

And the right people were in the right place at Anderson's Annex. The big electric sign over the door, spelling out the proprietor's name in bright white letters, told them as much. After all, Tom Anderson — the former Irish Channel snitch, the erstwhile office clerk with the easy manner and the open hand — had already become the dominant figure of the nascent District. Resplendent in a fine suit with an emerald-encrusted pocket-watch and diamond-topped cravat pin, he looked like anything but a common saloonkeeper.

"Mr. Anderson had a little white, waxed mustache and looked rather like a banker," one patron admitted. "He always wore a white flower in his buttonhole, and kept his pants pressed like a boulevardier." And from his command center amid the glittering lights of Basin Street, he could look out on the new centerpiece of an ever-growing domain — one that besides the Annex now included his original Arlington Restaurant on Rampart Street, another Rampart Street club for black patrons called the Astoria Club, and a soon-to-be-opened restaurant on Gravier Street called the Stag (whose elegance, the *Daily Item* would say, was such "that Nero himself, in all the attempts he made to make his palaces the finest in the world, never imagined"). In addition to these drinking and eating establishments, he also had his interests in Josie Arlington's brothel and in a number of other similar places in the District. The forty-three-year-old Anderson, in fact, was already being identified in the newspapers as the unofficial "mayor of Storyville" — a moniker that would stay with him through the rest of his life.

But by now Tom had an official title as well — Representative Anderson. Early in 1900, thanks to his numerous friends in the local Ring, Anderson had successfully gotten himself nominated for a seat in the Louisiana General Assembly, representing New Orleans'

Fourth Ward — the one that encompassed most of the new district. Opposition to his candidacy had been fierce, particularly from the always-conservative *Daily Picayune.* "Mr. Anderson," the paper opined when his nomination became public, "is the owner or conductor of a place on North Rampart Street that bears perhaps the worst reputation of any drinking house in the city."

For this reason, the *Picayune* viewed his nomination with distinct disapproval: "The lawless classes have no right to participate in the making of laws," the paper went on, "for if that responsible duty were turned over to them, they would reverse the positions of good and evil and trample right, justice, virtue, and industry underfoot." If the Fourth Ward had to be represented by a saloon-keeper (as the Ring claimed when nominating Anderson), "it is certain that one could have been found who at least conducted an orderly and decent place, patronized by a respectable class of people."

But despite this full-throated opposition from the forces of respectability — and an attempt by the State Democratic Committee to disown the candidate — Anderson went on to win his seat. Sworn in on May 14, Anderson took office claiming to owe allegiance to no one, not even the Ring, and he vowed to support civil-service legislation and other reform efforts. But few people took these protestations seriously. By June, the papers were already taking note of the new representative's chumminess with "certain saloon influences in Baton Rouge." When in November he made his petition to open up the palatial new establishment on Basin Street, the application sailed through without a hitch. And although he was still having occasional trouble with the more conscientious elements in the police department (including a pesky arrest in March of 1901 for violating the Sunday Closing Law — a law that he had been elected, some said, expressly to overturn), he was generally prospering in the new open environment of legalized vice.

And why should he not prosper? For an entrepreneur like Anderson, the business model of the vice industry was all but failure-proof. In his bars and brothels he was supplying high-priced, high-margin goods and services to a market where demand was virtually unlimited. And unlike his oil-supply business, where he constantly had to suffer the depredations of bigger fish like the Standard Oil Company, his drinking, gambling, and prostitution establishments had no larger players to compete with. Storyville, in short, was a small businessman's dream, and Tom Anderson was doing everything in his power to take advantage of it.

So, too, were many others in New Orleans' sporting world, for there was plenty of business in Storyville to go around. Vice had always been lucrative in New Orleans, but in this new era of official tolerance, the profits to be made were growing. Yes, beat cops still had to be paid off for their genial blindness to minor infractions, but the weekly *douceurs* (left discreetly in the boxes gracing every brothel's front porch) were not nearly as onerous as they once were. Now able to operate with impunity on the sunny side of the law, scores of vice entrepreneurs — both male and female — were turning Storyville into a virtual supermarket of sin, catering to appetites and pocketbooks at all points on the socioeconomic scale.

The new District, in fact, was laid out almost as rationally as the D. H. Holmes department store on nearby Canal Street. Each of the six major cross-streets of Storyville specialized in its own portion of the market. Basin Street, the broad avenue that anchored the foot of the District (closest to the Vieux Carré and the river), was the place for the luxury trade. Here was the already-famous row of large mansions hosting the so-called Five-Dollar Houses. These brothels, elaborately decorated and aspiring to an air of opulent exclusivity, were the ones specializing in the white and octoroon beauties most relentlessly touted in the Blue Books; they were the "refined sporting houses" aimed at a white clientele of certain means. One block behind Basin was Franklin Street, a decidedly less high-toned thoroughfare of smaller brothels, along with many of the dance halls, honky-tonks, and saloons that would soon give the District its reputation as a center for music as well as for sex. Extending back from there — in roughly descending order of refinement and expense — were Liberty, Marais, Villere, and finally Robertson Street, home of countless saloons, cafés, and brothels of low and lower repute. On these streets — and on the four intersecting thoroughfares of Customhouse, Bienville, Conti, and St. Louis — were also the notorious lines of "cribs," tawdry one-room shacks rented by the day by the Tenderloin's rougher class of prostitutes. Standing half-clothed (or sometimes even naked) in doorways, the mostly white women of Liberty and Marais and the mostly black women of Villere and Robertson would advertise their wares in the most forthright way imaginable, for whatever price the market would bear. These backstreets of Storyville were also the home of a few black brothels — the only sex establishments available to African American patrons outside of those in the unofficial Black Storyville located on the other side of Canal Street.

And so here, within the boundaries delineated by "respectable" New Orleans, disreputable New Orleans flourished. Of course, prostitution and vice did not cease to exist beyond the borders of Storyville; in fact, in 1902 the *Daily Item* would launch a campaign to eliminate the vice establishments that doggedly continued to operate elsewhere in the city. Nor did the geographic containment do much to mitigate the inherent noxious and abusive elements of that way of life — the rampant drunkenness and violence, the dissipation, the corruption of underage girls (and sometimes boys) forced into a way of life they cannot have chosen freely. The exchange of loveless sex for money, after all, carries with it an ethos that no amount of velvet, Champagne, and gold leaf can make any less degrading. But Storyville was an attempt, at least, to forge a compromise between human ideals and human nature, to rationalize the inevitable and alleviate the harm of activities that realistically could not be abolished. Or so the city's progressive reformers believed, at least for a time.

Meanwhile, until that time passed, there were many who took full advantage of the opportunity to make a lucrative living off the experiment — not just worldly men like Tom Anderson, but many women as well. Prostitution had traditionally been one of the few alternatives for working-class and lower-middle-class women to a life of drudgery in factories or domestic service. In the permissive environment of Storyville, these women could now make real money without actually breaking the law. And make money they did, particularly the elite corps of Basin Street madams.

Josie Arlington, for instance, was doing very well indeed at her new brothel at 225 Basin Street, just a few doors down from her business partner Anderson's Annex. Having purchased the large and spacious mansion back when the boundaries of Storyville were first decided, she had allowed her consort Tom Brady to oversee its renovation into a showpiece of late-Victorian opulence. With its domed cupola and canopied balconies, the four-story façade exuded just the kind of ostentatious respectability she had begun aspiring to in the '90s, after her split with Phillip Lobrano. The interior, decorated with leather furniture, ornate tapestries, and "oriental statuary," was a perfect expression of Gilded Age excess, featuring one hall (the Mirror Maze Room) paneled entirely in mirrors, a music room, and individual parlors done up in Turkish, Japanese, Viennese, and American styles. Upstairs were sixteen bedrooms, each dominated by a large brass bed where Arlington's exclusive roster of beautiful women could entertain their customers. It was, according to the Blue Book, "absolutely and unquestionably the most decorative and costly fitted-out sporting palace ever placed before the American public." And as a generator of revenue, Josie Arlington's was nonpareil. The take from those sixteen bedrooms, combined with wine and liquor sales in the parlors and the percentage from the house's gambling business, amounted to a substantial weekly profit for the establishment's two principals. And all of this now came with little threat of the kind of arbitrary police raids that had previously cut so heavily into vice-industry earnings.

But Anderson and Arlington were hardly the only entrepreneurs making good on Basin Street. The two blocks between Customhouse and the edge of the St. Louis Cemetery No. 1 on Conti were teeming with similar establishments, all operating under the aegis of a female entrepreneur and all competing for the higher-end segment of the market. "These places were really something to see," pianist Clarence Williams would later say of the Basin Street houses. "They had the *most* beautiful parlors, with cut glass and draperies, and rugs, and expensive furniture. They were just like millionaires' houses." And the women on offer in these palaces were — at least to impressionable eyes — as elegant and refined as the furnishings. "The girls would come down dressed in the finest of evening gowns, just like they were going to the opera. They were just beautiful. Their hairdos were just-so, and I'm telling you that Ziegfeld didn't have any more beautiful women than those. Some of them looked Spanish, and some were Creoles, some brownskins, some chocolate brown. But they all had to have that figure."

That so many of the prostitutes on Basin Street were mixed-race was one of the District's great paradoxes. The rest of New Orleans may have been subject to the hardening Jim Crow regimen of strict black-white separation, but in Storyville, for the right price, white men could relive the fantasy of the city's more racially fluid past. No blacks were allowed into the Basin Street brothels as customers, and darker-skinned black prostitutes were largely confined to the backstreets of the District. But sexual contact across the color line was not only tolerated here, it was actively promoted, at least in the District's first years. Early Storyville, in fact, was arguably the most racially integrated square mile in the entire American South.

Two of the finest houses on Basin Street made a particular specialty of interracial sex. Mahogany Hall — an elaborate, iron-balconied mansion at 235 Basin, just two doors down from Josie Arlington's — was the fiefdom of Lulu White, a legendary madam whose so-called "stable of octoroon beauties" soon became one of the Tenderloin's biggest attractions. Lulu White herself — who advertised as an octoroon but who was, by most reports, substantially darker-skinned than the label would imply — came from mysterious origins. Depending on the source of the story, she was born in 1864 or 1868, either in Cuba, Jamaica, or (most likely) on a plantation in rural Alabama. What's known for sure is that she was already well established in the New Orleans vice world by the late 1880s. Often in trouble with the law, she was arrested frequently through the '80s and '90s but somehow rarely served time in jail, thanks to the influence of some wealthy patrons. It was those same wealthy patrons (connected with the local Democratic Ring) who assisted her financially when, shortly after the creation of Storyville, she sought to build a brand-new establishment on Basin Street. White razed the existing structure on the site and spent a small fortune creating a showpiece — a four-story brick palace with five parlors (one of them, like Josie Arlington's, paneled entirely in mirrors), numerous boudoirs (each with a private bath), cut-glass chandeliers, and an ornate elevator built for two. The furniture alone was said to cost over $2,000. And here at Mahogany Hall, Miss Lulu White held court, always bedecked in a formal gown, a bright-red wig, and so many diamonds that she was said to rival "the lights of the St. Louis Exposition." A figure of exaggerated flamboyance (White was supposedly a model for the screen persona of actress Mae West), she insisted that no luxury was too great for the patrons of her house, where, as

Louis Armstrong later recalled, "the Champagne would flow like water." Given the treatment afforded most people of color in 1900s New Orleans, Lulu White's success and status within the confines of the District was nothing less than astonishing.

Nor was it unique. Faux refinement may have been the stock-in-trade of all the Basin Street madams — their genteel, high-society affectations offered up with an ironic wink and a knowing leer — but the madam who played the role most convincingly was Willie V. Piazza. Also self-described as an octoroon, Piazza was one who by general consensus could credibly *"passe pour blanc."* Though she called herself a countess, Piazza was apparently the daughter of an illiterate woman of color (possibly a former slave) and a first-generation Italian hotelkeeper from Copiah County, Mississippi — the place where Robert Charles had grown up. The countess, according to popular lore, was a sophisticated, well-read woman who spoke several languages fluently, smoked Russian cigarettes in a long, jewel-studded holder, and wore a monocle offset by an expensive diamond choker. How she had acquired her education (her brothel at 317 Basin boasted an extensive library of literature in several languages) remains a mystery, but one that her patrons were apparently disinclined to look into very closely. A woman of discerning musical tastes, she reportedly slept on a mattress embedded with a music box; she also furnished her brothel's parlor with a perfectly tuned white grand piano, on which only the finest musicians were allowed to play. She was something of a fashion icon too. Her finely styled outfits — and those of her house's ladies, reportedly "the most handsome and intelligent octoroons in the United States" — were carefully studied by local dressmakers, allegedly to be copied for the ensembles of customers belonging to the city's "better half."

But luxury houses like those of Piazza, Lulu White, and Josie Arlington accounted for only a portion of the new economy brought about by the creation of Storyville. By the time Tom Anderson's Annex opened in 1901, there were already an estimated 1,500 prostitutes of all kinds operating in the District, with perhaps 500 more imported seasonally for the high tourist traffic in winter. These 2,000 women, and the subsidiary businesses that their activities supported — the bars, gambling houses, dance halls, restaurants, honkytonks, and other entertainment establishments of the District — provided work and profits to a large and varied population of New Orleanians, from pimps to chambermaids, from musicians to cab-drivers and bartenders. In the eyes of the progressive reformers who had created Storyville, then, the experiment seemed to be working. The city's ineradicable vice industry had, to an extent, been isolated and rationalized. And while the reformers did not exactly approve of the goings-on in Storyville (though some of them profited from it, as landlords of property in the District), they could at least content themselves that a framework had been built by which respectable and disrespectable New Orleans could peacefully coexist. While not entirely out of sight *or* mind, sin in the Crescent City was at least on the way to being contained.

From the perspective of those who did business in the District, on the other hand, the experiment was a smashing success. Big money was being made — not just by corporations or old-money elites but by individual entrepreneurs of a lesser class. And for Tom Anderson in particular, who was now in a position — if not to "reverse the positions of good and evil" — at least to ensure that the denizens of Storyville had a voice in the state legislature, the future was bright indeed. Even the Storyville mayor's personal life had taken a turn for the better. Sometime before the advent of the District in 1898, Tom had taken up with a lovely young woman from Kansas named Olive Noble. She, too, was a prostitute (working under the professional name Ollie Russell), but she was soon styling herself as "Mrs. Anderson" and setting up housekeeping in the apartment above her "husband's" Arlington Restaurant on Rampart.

Of course, there were difficulties, not least of which was the *other* Mrs. Anderson, whom Tom had not yet been able to divorce. And while apparently quite enamored of his new concubine (who was seventeen years his junior), the mayor of Storyville was not above straying occasionally with his other constituents. Ironically, these two problems managed to work each other out. One night, after hearing that Anderson had been consorting with another woman, Ollie confronted him in the bar of the Arlington Restaurant. She ended up taking a shot at him with a small pistol, though somehow managed only to shoot herself in the foot. Even so, the misadventure ultimately redounded to her favor. The foot wound turned out to be minor, and the incident apparently gave the real Mrs. Anderson the solid grounds she needed for a favorable divorce settlement. Naming Ollie Russell as co-respondent, and citing the shooting episode as evidence of infidelity, Kate Anderson proceeded to launch her own divorce suit. This time, the divorce was granted, on highly favorable terms to her. And when it became official in 1899, Tom Anderson, though somewhat poorer, became free to marry his true love — that is, Ollie herself, eager to become the third Mrs. Anderson.

It didn't happen — at least not for a while.

The death of Tom's beloved mother intervened in January 1900. Anderson was left
with the problem of what to do with his now
twenty-year-old daughter, Irene, who had
come to live with him and his mother four
years earlier, after her graduation from the
convent school. Tom couldn't leave Irene
alone in the house on Canal Street; nor could
he, with good conscience, expect her to live
with him and his ex-prostitute "wife." But
here again, a fortuitous solution presented
itself. In late 1900, he introduced Irene to
George Delsa, a bartender at his Arlington
Restaurant. The two apparently liked each
other immediately and were soon engaged to
be married. When that wedding occurred in
1902 — with Tom dressed in his best tuxedo
to give away the bride — the difficulties with
his personal life seemed to be past. He and
Ollie could finally live what he himself called
a life of "ideal bliss," free of complications.
After the heartbreak of losing the beloved
wife of his twenties and the anguish of disas-
sociating himself from the hated wife of his
thirties, he was apparently entering his forties
in a state of domestic *and* professional
hopefulness. And the fact that his brand of
respectability was not identical with that of
the *Daily Picayune* or the denizens of the
Pickwick and Boston Clubs — that seemed
not to trouble him at all.

But to at least one member of the Storyville

aristocracy, the Basin Street version of respectability was not enough. For Josie Arlington, the so-called queen of the demimonde, the yearnings for legitimacy and Victorian standards of propriety had, if anything, grown even more acute since the creation of Storyville. Granted, she was making money on Basin Street — lots of money — and it was said that she, unlike many other madams, had at least some rules about what kind of behavior could take place in her house. ("I'll never have a girl ruined under my roof," she once allegedly said, explaining why she would never hire a virgin as a prostitute.) But she still had designs on a more "normal" life as a wife and mother. And she was determined to realize those designs, in one form or another, in the person of Anna Deubler, her brother Henry's young daughter.

By all accounts, Josie's relationship to Anna was one of complete devotion. Josie was "in love with Anna," one friend later said. In conversation, "there was hardly any other topic but Anna"; Anna was "her whole pleasure in life." The girl was seventeen years old in 1901, yet somehow Josie and Tom Brady — known to her as "Aunt Mary and Uncle Tom" — had kept her entirely in the dark about the family's source of income. Josie, who lived mainly at the Basin Street brothel, paid rent for her brother and his family to occupy a home in Carrollton, safely distant from Storyville. In this way, she hoped — like the reformers — to draw a boundary around her life of sin, keeping her dear Anna safely on the other side. But now that the girl was getting older, her aunt feared that Anna might eventually discover the true identity of Aunt Mary. And so Josie arranged for Anna to go to a convent school a thousand miles from Basin Street — at St. Joseph's Academy in Emmetsburg, Maryland. Her motive was plain; according to one friend, "She didn't want her niece to know what life [Mary] Deubler was leading." So, while Arlington herself may have been ineradicably sullied by the life of Storyville, she was determined to keep her beloved niece pure and untouched by it. Anna, it seems, was to be Josie's surrogate in the respectable world to which she herself could never truly belong.

The arrangement proved satisfactory for about a year. Anna happily pursued her studies at St. Joseph's, and during the summer holiday, Aunt Mary and Uncle Tom rented a vacation cottage for the whole family in Pass Christian, a gulfside resort in Mississippi. Here they could pretend to be the respectable family that Josie yearned for. But when the Bradys traveled up to Emmetsburg to take Anna for her second year at the academy, they encountered trouble. They telephoned the school from their hotel and spoke to the Mother Superior, who coldly informed them that Anna was no longer welcome at the school. Do not come, the nun said, "or you will hear more than you want to hear." Apparently, the father of another pupil from New Orleans had told the Mother Superior about Mrs. Brady's true identity. Now Anna was being unceremoniously expelled.

What Josie told her remarkably naïve niece is not known, but evidently she found some way of explaining the necessity of returning immediately to New Orleans. And once there, her aunt went to work finding an alternative plan that would ensure that Anna remained comfortably ignorant of the source of her upkeep. The solution Josie ultimately found was extreme: If Maryland was not distant enough to keep Anna free of the taint of Storyville, maybe a different continent would be. And so Josie Arlington, aka Mary Brady, made arrangements for a surrogate to run the brothel for a few months. She and her "husband" were going to take Anna Deubler to Europe.

■ ■ ■ ■

CHAPTER 9
JAZZMEN

■ ■ ■ ■

Jelly Roll Morton as a young man **Hogan Jazz Archive, Tulane University**

The years immediately following the Robert Charles riot were not easy ones for black New Orleans. Bitterness over the four days of rampant violence did not pass quickly, and the twin insults of disenfranchisement and increasing segregation only grew more intolerable as the months passed. But despite the worsening situation — or perhaps partly because of it — the new music of the ghetto seemed to be thriving. By 1903, in fact, the "raggedy" sound was making inroads all over the city, often in some surprising venues:

THE KNIGHTS OF PLEASURE CLUB

REQUESTS THE PRESENCE OF YOUR COMPANY AT THEIR

FIRST GRAND SOIREE

AT THE LADIES PROVIDENCE HALL, COR. OF PHILLIP AND LIBERTY STS, WEDNESDAY EVENING FEBY 18, 03

209

MUSIC BY PROF. BOLDEN'S ORCHESTRA

DANCING FROM 8PM TO 2:30AM
SUBSC. 15C

This advertisement — the only written notice of a Buddy Bolden performance surviving in the historical record — would seem to promise a somewhat staid and genteel event. After all, a "Grand Soiree" at something called the "Ladies Providence Hall," with music by one "Professor" Bolden, sounds like an eminently respectable gathering. And perhaps it was; Bolden's mother, Alice, was a member of the Ladies' Providence Society, and the city's instrumental ensembles were by necessity flexible, playing music appropriate to whatever audience had hired them. But given that a Bolden performance the very next month was raided by police, this advertisement may be unrepresentative. A more typical Bolden venue was the Odd Fellows Hall on Perdido Street near Black Storyville, where a Labor Day ball that same year was promoted in a very different way: "Tell all yo' friends!" Bolden allegedly told a crowd some days before the event. "If you likes raggedy music, come one, come all! You all can dance any kind of way! And don't forget, there's a prize for the bitch who'll shake it hardest — an' I don't mean her snoot!"

So life was hardly all doom and gloom in the black neighborhoods of New Orleans, and the new music both reflected and contributed to that fact. Audiences were clamoring for it, and musicians like Bolden were fast becoming celebrities. "The main topic of talk with the people around [town] was music — like, who was a famous trumpet player," one New Orleanian remembered. "They spoke of these great musicians . . . they were idolized." Any event would become an excuse to hear jazz, and often the music itself was the excuse to hold an event. "All over New Orleans on Saturday night there'd be fish fries," according to bassist Pops Foster. "To advertise, you'd get a carriage with the horses all dressed up, a bunch of pretty girls, and then the musicians would get on, and you'd go all over, advertising for that night. . . . The fish fry that had the best band was the one that would have the best crowd."

Out on the shores of nearby Lake Pontchartrain were three resorts — Spanish Fort, West End, and Milneburg — that were popular destinations for weekend outings. Each camp or pavilion would have its own band playing — all within earshot of the others, allowing for some fruitful cross-pollination of styles. "The picnics at the lake were the ideal place for the younger people to hear the different bands and musicians," guitarist Johnny St. Cyr explained. "We could hear them all at different camps and picnic grounds, and, needless to say, we all had our favorites."

Storyville, too, soon became an important venue for the new music. At first, the establishments of the District were reluctant to hire bands — if customers were busy dancing, after all, they couldn't be buying drinks (or women). But eventually the music proved too popular to ignore. Bolden's band and other "hot" ensembles were soon playing regularly at Storyville clubs like Nancy Hank's Saloon and Big 25. Tom Anderson's Annex began by hiring a string trio (with piano, guitar, and violin) but eventually became a place for larger bands as well. Even the brothels wanted the new music — usually in the form of a single piano "professor" playing in the parlor while clients chose their partners for the night. According to some reports, Countess Willie Piazza was the first madam to bring music into her house, hiring a legendary pianist known as John the Baptist to play on her famous white grand. Pianists such as Tony Jackson, Clarence Williams, and Jelly Roll Morton eventually found their own regular gigs in the District — at Lulu White's, Gipsy Schaeffer's, Hilma Burt's, and the other Basin Street brothels. And while Storyville can in no way be considered *the* birthplace of jazz, as has sometimes been claimed, the various District venues did provide many early jazzmen with vital employment and helped to bring their music to a wider — and often non-black — audience.

Two of the most important settings for the development of early jazz opened in 1902. Lincoln and Johnson Parks, located right across the street from each other just off South Carrollton Avenue, quickly became popular gathering places for the city's black population. They were much closer to the central city than the lake resorts, and therefore were more accessible locales for picnics, prizefights, and other entertainments throughout the week. Lincoln Park, the larger and more developed of the two, hosted a skating rink, a theater, and a performance "barn" where large dances and sporting events could be held. Lincoln was also the site of one of black New Orleans' most storied events — the weekly hot-air-balloon ascensions of Buddy Bartley, the park's manager, who was also known to New Orleans police as a pimp and small-time criminal. The heavily advertised ascensions would feature the aerialist Bartley going up in the balloon (to a full orchestral accompaniment, of course) and flying around for a time before dramatically jumping from the basket and parachuting to the ground. How the balloon itself was brought to earth after its pilot had decamped is unclear — one hard-to-credit story holds that it was actually brought down with a rifle shot — but the spectacle was one of the most memorable entertainments of the era for many New Orleanians. Bartley's regular ascensions, in fact, came to an end only after a mishap left him seriously injured. According to a witness: "One Sunday, he drifted too far because of the high winds and when it was time for his parachute jump back to earth from the balloon, instead of landing in the park as usual, he wound up in the chimney of one of the houses fairly close to Lincoln Park — and what a mess he was."

The attractions offered at Johnson Park across the street were usually less elaborate. The place was principally a baseball park, though it was also used for picnics and open-air concerts, and typically attracted a somewhat rougher crowd than its neighbor. It was in Johnson Park that Buddy Bolden normally played, often to the chagrin of those playing in the neighboring Lincoln Park. The regular band at Lincoln was the Excelsior, led by John Robichaux, a well-regarded Creole entrepreneur who had dominated the black music scene in the 1890s. On more than a few Sundays, Robichaux's band would be packing them in at the Lincoln performance barn when Bolden and his crew were preparing to play at Johnson. But Bolden wouldn't be worried, because he had a secret weapon — his cornet. According to his friend Louis

Jones, "That's where Buddy used to say to [trombonist Willie] Cornish and them, say, 'Cornish, come on, put your hands through the window. Put your trombone out there. I'm going to call my children home. . . .' Buddy would start to play and all the people out of Lincoln Park would come on over where Buddy was."

The crowds came not just because Bolden played loud — though he did do that — but because he played "hot" and "down-low." Robichaux and his band of highly polished, academically trained musicians played "sweet" — that is, the straighter, more traditional and refined music beloved of the city's educated Creoles of Color. But as one musician put it, "Old King Bolden played the music the *Negro* public liked." It was bluesier, more spontaneous, and at times downright raunchy. One crowd-pleaser that soon became Bolden's signature number was "Funky Butt," aka "Buddy Bolden's Blues," a barrelhouse blues with ever-changing lyrics that could range from the light and comic to the low and coarse:

I thought I heard Buddy Bolden say,
Funky butt, funky butt, take it away . . .
You're nasty, you're dirty, take it away . . .
I thought I heard Buddy Bolden shout,
Open up that window and let the bad air
out.

To Creoles like Robichaux and the other "dicty" people, as they were called, this kind of vulgarity was distasteful. As one musician put it, "When the settled Creole folks first heard this jazz, they passed the opinion that it sounded like the rough Negro element." But in the racially polarizing atmosphere of turn-of-the-century New Orleans, they often couldn't avoid it. A lot of the skilled trades traditionally pursued by Creoles were now being closed off to them in the new world of Jim Crow. Many were forced to turn to music as a profession rather than just a hobby, which meant playing the newer style of music pioneered by Bolden and the other early jazzmen.

Even an establishment figure like Robichaux soon found defectors in his own ranks. George Baquet, a Creole clarinetist who played "sweet" with Robichaux for many years, found himself attracted to the new style and would sometimes sit in with Bolden on an occasional gig. One evening, the Bolden and Robichaux bands were playing in two rival saloons not far from each other. The two groups decided to have one of the cutting contests so beloved among black audiences of the day, the winner to be determined by the response of the audience. At first, Bolden's band seemed to dominate, but then Baquet came to the rescue of the Robichaux group. He played a wild stunt routine in which he would gradually throw away various parts of his clarinet, while continuing to play it as if it were still whole. By the end, he was playing the mouthpiece alone — to the roaring approval of the crowd, who granted the win to Robichaux hands-down. What the Creole maestro himself thought of the performance is unknown — it was just the kind of low gimmick he likely would have disapproved of. But the rare win against Bolden must have been at least somewhat gratifying. As for Buddy himself, he was reportedly furious. "George, why did you do it?" he hissed to Baquet afterward, apparently stung by being defeated at his own game.

Bolden's music was particularly influential among younger downtown Creoles, who were less likely than their elders to cling to their sense of separateness from the Uptown African Americans. Jim Crow was forcibly pushing the two groups together, and it was the young who adapted most readily to the change — both socially and musically. "Bolden cause all that," one Creole musician admitted. "He caused these younger Creoles . . . to have a different style from the old heads." But the young Creole musicians who began to play "hot" brought with them the greater reading skills and more polished technique of downtown, changing the new style even as it was changing them.

Bolden's influence, in fact, was soon being

felt well beyond the borders of New Orleans. The Bolden band and other groups often traveled out into the hinterlands, playing at harvest festivals, payday parties, parish fairs, and other events. And they spread the gospel of jazz wherever they went. "I came to New Orleans in 1906, when I was fourteen years old," pianist Clarence Williams explained. "It was after I heard Buddy Bolden, when he came through my hometown, Plaquemine, Louisiana, on an excursion, and his trumpet playin' excited me so that I said, 'I'm goin' to New Orleans.' I had never heard anything like that before in my life."

A man who was to become one of the most important figures in the second generation of New Orleans jazzmen — Edward "Kid" Ory — had a similar story to tell. Growing up in the sugar-mill town of LaPlace, some twenty-five miles upriver from New Orleans, young Ory would hear bands like Bolden's, Edward Clem's, and Charlie Galloway's playing a banquet or other event and be intrigued. "Sometimes," he later wrote, "the guys would put the horns down and be drinking beer. I'd slip in and get one of the horns and try and blow it. I noticed how they were putting it into their mouth and I'd just [keep] on till I got a tone. We were all self taught."

The son of a white father of Alsatian ancestry and a mixed-race mother, Ory had the straight hair, light skin, and Anglo features to pass for white. But since he was black by law, he had to contend with the diminished job expectations allowed to members of that race. Becoming a musician seemed to be an excellent route out of the drudgery of a life of sugar production. So Ory soon formed a band with a few like-minded friends. At first, since none of them could afford instruments, they styled themselves as a "humming" group, harmonizing tunes on a nearby bridge at night. "It was dark and no one could see us," Ory recalled, "but people could hear us singing and they'd bring us a few ginger cakes and some water. We hummed and when we knowed the tune itself, the melody, the others would put a three- or four-part harmony to it. It was good ear training."

Eventually, Ory's group made their own musical instruments, constructing a five-string dinner-pail banjo, a cigar-box guitar, and a soapbox bass. "After finishing the three instruments, we started practicing in the daytime, but evenings would find us drifting to our favorite spot . . . the bridge . . . and the people, especially the youngsters, found us there and would hang around listening to us play, and they would start dancing there in the dusty road. It made us feel wonderful. . . ."

In 1900, when Ory was just thirteen, his mother died, followed less than a year later by his father. The boy had to move in with his older sister's family on the sugar plantation. But he was already making plans to leave, pinning his hopes on a fine new banjo his father had bought for him two weeks before his death. Ory worked a series of hard-labor jobs for the next few years — first at a lumberyard, and then for a bricklaying crew (where his drunken, abusive overseer would sometimes rouse the boy from sleep to play him some blues on the banjo). All along, though, he was honing his musical skills, branching out from the banjo to the instrument that would later make him famous — the trombone. When he was about sixteen or seventeen, he bought himself "an old beat-up valve trombone" for $7.50 and started practicing with it. The instrument was so riddled with holes that he had to stuff them with soap to get a decent tone. This worked all right at first, but after playing for a while he'd find himself blowing bubbles. Finally, he borrowed $100 to buy real instruments for the rest of his band. "Then we had some real rehearsing with the honest-to-God instruments," Ory wrote, "and decided we were good enough to play at the [local] ball games."

The ultimate goal, of course, was to move to New Orleans and make a living there, but Ory had promised his mother before she died that he wouldn't leave LaPlace until he was twenty-one. In the meantime, though, he and his friends took weekend trips into the city to hear the bands they emulated. On one such trip in 1905, Ory went to Werlein's Music Store on Canal Street and bought a new trombone. Later, as he was trying out the new instrument at his older sister's house on South Robertson Street, a passerby heard him and knocked on the door.

"Young man, are you blowing the trombone?" the man asked.

Ory told him he was.

"Well," the man continued, "you know who I am?"

Ory didn't.

The man said: "I'm the King." It was King Bolden himself, and he was apparently quite impressed by Ory's playing.

"I'd like to have you work for me," Bolden said. "You sound very good."

Ory was thrilled, but since he was still only eighteen years old, his sister put an end to all such talk. "Oh, no, he has to go back home [to LaPlace]," she insisted. "He can't leave home now till he's twenty-one years old."

But Ory did keep in touch with Bolden. Whenever the young trombonist and his friends came to town, they'd seek out the members of the Bolden Band wherever they were playing — at Johnson Park, Odd Fellows Hall, or the dance hall on Perdido Street (also used as a Baptist church) where Bolden played so often that it was soon better known

221

as "Funky Butt Hall." And although Ory did admire many of the other bands in town — including that of Robichaux, from whom Ory learned the more polished manner of playing that was later to characterize his own mature style — Bolden was his first and arguably his most influential favorite.

So many of the young players around New Orleans at this time cited their first taste of Bolden's music as a seminal experience. Sidney Bechet, who would become perhaps the greatest jazz clarinetist of all time, first heard Bolden playing on the street when he was seven or eight. He was never the same afterward. As the youngest child of a traditional Creole family, he had often been taken by his mother to the French Opera House on Bourbon Street to hear some of the great soloists of the day (Enrico Caruso was an early favorite). But Sidney seemed more inspired by the syncopated music he heard on the streets of New Orleans. When he was barely six, his mother found him trying to blow the nozzle of her douche like a horn. Mortified but amused, she responded by giving the boy a small fife to play with. He practiced on it for hours at a time and soon mastered it. Then he started playing his brother Leonard's clarinet on the sly. One day his mother heard him secretly practicing under the porch. She was about to scold him for fooling with his brother's possessions —

but then she heard what the boy could do with the instrument. She immediately arranged to get him his own clarinet and sign him up for formal lessons.

Sidney proved to be a disobedient student. A series of old-school Creole teachers wanted him to practice scales and classical marches, but the boy had his own ideas. Then came the day he heard Bolden. It was during a street parade when Bolden and his band got into a cutting contest with the more traditional Imperial Band. Sidney was mesmerized — at least until a stick-wielding cop came along and spoiled the fun. "[It] was down there around Canal Street somewheres," Bechet would later recall. "I was awful little then — and a policeman come along and he looked at my head and he looked at my ass, and he smacked me good with that stick he was carrying. I ran home then and I was really hurting some, I couldn't even sit down for dinner that night; and my mother, she took one look at me and she knew right away where I'd been."

His parents and teachers, and even his older brother, Leonard, didn't approve of Bolden's brand of ratty music. ("Us Creole musicians always did hold up a nice prestige," Leonard Bechet insisted.) But that's the kind of music Sidney wanted to play — "all of those interpreting moans and groans and happy sounds," as he later put it. And his musical taste sometimes got him into trouble. "No, no, no," his teacher Luis "Papa" Tio would tell him. "We do not bark like a dog or meow like a cat!" The admonition fell on deaf ears. Bechet began to model his clarinet playing on the rough Uptown style of "Big Eye" Louis Nelson, from whom he even took a few lessons. These were much more to his taste: "Some musicians played the tune prettily," he later said, "but I like the playing that makes me want to dance."

At his brother's twenty-first birthday party in April 1907, ten-year-old Sidney had a chance to show off what he'd learned. His mother had booked the band of cornetist Manuel Perez to play for the party. But at the last minute Perez had sent a replacement band, led by the young Creole cornet player Freddie Keppard (whose style of music may have been a bit earthy for the proper Mrs. Bechet). Keppard's clarinetist — the ubiquitous George Baquet — was late for the gig, so the band started playing without him. Sidney saw his chance. "I knew I was too young for them," he later recalled, "but I sure wanted to play along with them all the same." So he began improvising a quiet clarinet accompaniment to Keppard's lead. But he did it from another room, not wanting to risk being publicly reprimanded by the older musicians.

As the story goes, Keppard heard Sidney's

clarinet and thought it was Baquet warming up in the other room. But then Baquet himself showed up, and the identity of the phantom clarinetist was revealed. Baquet was impressed, and (despite taking some hearty ribbing from the other band members) he sat little Sidney down right next to him. "He kept me there all evening, playing right along beside him," Bechet remembered. "That night, I guess I was the richest kid in New Orleans. You couldn't have bought me for a sky full of new moons."

To hear his contemporaries tell it, Bechet was — in a city full of great musicians — a phenomenon, a natural who could play virtually any instrument he touched. "I used to see Sidney around [violinist Armand] Piron's barbershop," one musician recalled.

Now, Piron had a house full of every kind of instrument. So this little boy, he come in one day and pick up the flute. "What is that?" he ask Piron. "That is a flute, Sidney," Piron tell him. So Sidney start right in playing it. Show Piron what *is* a flute. Put that down. Walk over and pick up a saxophone and say, "What is *that*?" "That's a new something they call a saxophone, son." "Well, it look like a pipe to me, I see if this pipe will make a tune." And be damn if he didn't start making the thing just talk!

225

The boy soon became so accomplished that Baquet himself would sometimes employ him as a substitute. According to Sidney's brother, Leonard, "When Baquet wanted to lay off, he used to come and speak to my mother and ask could he take Sidney to play in his place for the evening." Mrs. Bechet, the old-school Creole lady, was reluctant. "We didn't want to jeopardize our family by mixing with the rough element," Leonard explained. "We worried a lot about Sidney, when he'd be out playing. So, when Baquet would come for Sidney, Mother would insist that he be sure to bring the boy back and not lose him. Baquet would promise, and he'd generally bring him back about two in the morning. Sidney would bring money home to Mother and tell her don't worry, he was all right."

Mrs. Bechet may not have been happy about her son playing in saloons and dance halls, but it was the type of compromise that Creoles of Color increasingly were forced to make in 1900s New Orleans. Any difference between Creoles — often educated, urban, and middle-class — and African Americans — the children of slaves more recently arrived from the countryside — was gone now, at least in the eyes of whites. "Negro" and "disreputable" had become functionally synonymous, and many younger Creoles, in response, began rejecting their parents' now-outdated scruples. In any case, Mrs. Bechet's strong-willed and irrepressible son had made his choice of lifestyle, and there was little she could have done to keep him "respectable," even if she had tried.

But not every young Creole musician was pulled into the orbit of Bolden and the other Uptown jazzmen. Jelly Roll Morton — né Ferdinand Joseph La Menthe on October 20, 1890 — was a Creole pianist who affected a casual disdain for the music of what he called "Uptown Negroes." A musician of stunning originality himself, he was busily developing his own unique blend of piano-based ragtime, dance music, and blues — a "Spanish-tinged" style that would eventually have its own claim as the prototype for the kind of music still a decade away from being known as "jazz."

Like many Creoles of the era, Morton (who changed his name from La Menthe because he "didn't want to be called Frenchy") grew up in an atmosphere saturated with music. His godmother paid for guitar lessons for the boy when he was very young; by the time he was seven he was already an accomplished musician, playing in a three-piece string band that performed late-night serenades for their neighbors in the Seventh Ward. One day at a party, he heard a man playing "a very good piece of ragtime" on the piano and decided that this was the instrument for him. He began studying with a series of teachers — some better than others — and was soon proficient enough to have something of a reputation around town. One Saturday night, he and his friends were on a wild jaunt through the Tenderloin when they were approached by someone looking for a pianist to fill in at one of the District's houses of ill fame. Young Morton (he was about fifteen at the time) agreed to go along, but insisted that his friends come too for moral support. As he later told the story:

> I was so frightened when I first touched the piano [that] the girls decided to let me go immediately. One of my friends spoke up, "Go ahead and show these people you can play." That encouraged me greatly and I pulled myself together and started playing with the confidence of being in my own circle. "That boy is marvelous" — this was the remarks of the inmates. Money was plentiful and they tipped me about $20. . . .

At the end of the night, Morton was offered a job as the brothel's regular "professor." He hesitated at first, worried what his proper Creole family might think. But eventually he took the position and merely told his family that he had switched to the night shift at his regular job at a barrel-making factory. He soon became a denizen of the District, and one of its most evocative chroniclers: "The streets were crowded with men," he would later recall. "Lights of all colors were glittering and glaring. Music was pouring into the streets from every house. Women were standing in the doorways, singing or chanting some kind of blues — some very happy, some very sad, some with the desire to end it all by poison, some planning a big outing, a dance, or some other kind of enjoyment. Some were real ladies in spite of their downfall and some were habitual drunkards and some were dope fiends. . . ."

The young Creole professor became a favorite among the brothel women, who often wheedled big tips for him from their customers. Soon Morton had "more money than I ever heard of in my life." He eventually had a diamond implanted in one of his front teeth and bought a loud new suit with a Stetson hat and a pair of St. Louis Flats shoes with toes that turned up almost to his ankles. He was wearing those clothes when he ran into his great-grandmother on the street one Sunday morning. She was just returning from church, and it was quite obvious to her that the same was not true of her great-grandson. It was to be a life-changing encounter for Morton. When she heard about it, his grandmother, whom he had been living with since his mother's death the year before, kicked him out of the house. At the age of sixteen, he was now on his own. And although his Creole pride would keep him somewhat aloof from the mainstream of the Uptown African American music scene — unlike Bechet, Keppard, and some of the other younger Creoles — he soon became an important force in the development of New Orleans jazz (though, as Louis Armstrong would later remark, "no matter how much his Diamond Sparkled, he still had to eat in the Kitchen, the same as we Blacks").

Creoles weren't the only players succumbing to the attraction of the new sound. By 1905 or so, the music had become popular enough in saloons and dance halls to start making an impression on the city's young, working-class white musicians. Some of the best bands in New Orleans during this era were those of "Papa" Jack Laine, a white bandleader and entrepreneur who often had several groups playing around town at once. Laine's Reliance bands generally played sweet, reading from music with little of the improvisation or "bending" of notes so characteristic of the Uptown black bands. But Laine had a few musicians in his fold who took an avid interest in the hotter style. Cornetist Nick LaRocca, trombonist Tom Brown, clarinetist Larry Shields, and several others who played with Laine's groups were soon blowing their own version of the new sound. And although LaRocca in particular would deny the influence (in fact, he, like Jelly Roll Morton, would later claim to have invented jazz himself), reports of white musicians listening in on performances of the black bands are too numerous to be ignored.

Like many of the early white jazzmen, LaRocca was Sicilian (as was, for that matter, Jack Laine, whose real surname was Vitale); as such, he was already considered ipso facto disreputable by the likes of the Garden District elite. Playing jazz just reinforced that impression. "Whites who played jazz altered their racial identity," as one historian has put it, "becoming less white in the eyes of 'respectable' Caucasians." And LaRocca, again like many of the Creoles, had to face the disapproval of his family when his interest in music went beyond the acceptable weekend-hobby stage. When Giarolamo LaRocca discovered that his young son Nick had taught himself to play his (Giarolamo's) own cornet, the father took the instrument out to the yard and destroyed it with an ax. Fortunately, this didn't discourage the boy for long, and he soon had saved up enough money to buy his own cornet. But when his father found out about it, he grabbed his ax and smashed the new cornet as well.

Despite such discouragements, the new music was soon attracting white audiences as well — and not only among the working classes. Edmond Souchon, a doctor who grew up in New Orleans in what he called "the citadel of white caste privileges," described stealing off to the District when he was still a boy in short pants in order to hear his idol, Joe Oliver, playing at Big 25. (When challenged by police, Souchon would claim to be a newsboy delivering a paper that Oliver had ordered from him — which worked, for a time.) Bassist Pops Foster remembered lots of whites listening to jazz in the early years, even in allegedly all-black venues: "Most saloons had two sides, one for whites and one for colored. The colored had so much fun on their side dancing, singing, and guitar playing, that you couldn't get in for the whites. It was the same way at Lincoln Park for the colored; you couldn't tell *who* it was for, there were so many whites there."

Still, given its association with sex, alcohol, a rise in cocaine use among blacks, and interracial mixing, the music was developing a major image problem in the early years of the 20th century. The entire culture of jazz seemed an affront to decency for many people in New Orleans, including many middle-class blacks. Describing the scene at a Negro dance hall in 1902, the *Item* could barely contain its abhorrence: "The orchestra consisted of a clarinet, a guitar, and a bass fiddle. The guitar was plucked by a bullet-headed Negro with a far-away look in his eyes, and a molasses-colored musician that blew the clarinet had to brace his feet against the railing of the players' stand to prevent himself from being hurled backward by the strength of his breath, which at each blast into the instrument had the effect of making the player kick back like a shotgun. . . . Even the music had an indecent ring about it that was disgusting."

The bad image of jazz and jazzmen was also not helped by the growing number of violent incidents occurring in places where the music was played. Jelly Roll Morton described one incident at a Bolden performance — probably in early 1905 — at Jackson Hall. A short, ill-tempered man was standing at the bar, listening to the music, when a "great big husky guy" stepped on his foot. An argument erupted between the two (with Morton standing right between them), during which the small man pulled out a very large gun and shot the other man at close range, just barely missing the pianist. "This big guy laid there on the floor, dead," Morton recalled, "and, my goodness, Buddy Bolden — he was up on the balcony with the band — started blazing away with his trumpet, trying to keep the crowd together. Many of us realized it was a killing and we started breaking out windows and through doors and just run over the police they had there."

Bolden himself was arrested in the incident — much to Morton's puzzlement ("I've often wondered why they would put Mr. Bolden in the patrol [wagon] when he was up there blowing high notes to keep everyone quiet"). But King Bolden in particular seemed to be regarded by the white establishment — when they became aware of him — as a threat. Sidney Bechet recalled the reaction when his own band would play "Funky Butt": "When we started off playing Buddy's theme song, 'I Thought I Heard Buddy Bolden Say,' the police put you in jail if they heard you singing that song." Like the Robert Charles song, Buddy Bolden's song had political connotations that the police tried hard to discourage. As one historian has noted, both were "manifestations of cultural resistance within African American circles; each made the white power structure nervous."

Even the way these black men dressed was considered a provocation: "These guys wouldn't wear anything but a blue coat and some kind of stripe in their trousers," Jelly Roll Morton recalled, "and those trousers had to be very, very tight. They'd fit um like a sausage. I'm telling you, it was very seldom you could button the top button of a person's trousers those days in New Orleans." One of Bolden's suspenders would always be hanging down, and his shirt would be "busted open so that you could discern his red flannel undershirt." And all of this was carried off with a kind of strut or "mosey walk" — commonly known as "walking the agate" — that allegedly made the women wild.

But Bolden's days as leader of this defiant subculture were to be tragically brief. The year 1905 marked the peak of his popularity. At that point, as one witness put it, "just the sight of the famous cornetist was enough to satisfy some of his fans." Whenever he practiced on his front steps, neighborhood children would gather around him on the sidewalks, shouting "King Bolden! King Bolden!" And his effect on women was legendary. In 1902, he had met and married one of his neighbors, Nora Bass, a twenty-two-year-old mixed-race woman from a religious family, and had had a daughter by her sometime the next year. But the attention he received from his young female fans didn't end. "Sometimes," according to one of his friends, "he would have to run away from the women."

But this kind of celebrity eventually took its toll. In March of 1906, Bolden began to experience severe headaches. Other symptoms appeared: He seemed disoriented at times, failed to recognize his friends, and would walk the streets talking incoherently to strangers. Sometimes his mother and sister would have to send Buddy's friend Louis Jones to find him and bring him home. He even developed what seemed to be a fear of his own cornet.

No one really knows what caused Bolden to begin losing his grip on reality. Some said he drank too much and slept too little; others said he simply succumbed to the pressure of having to keep innovating to avoid becoming yesterday's sensation; Louis Jones thought it might have something to do with an untreated ear infection. But the mother of drummer Paul Barbarin had the simplest explanation — she'd always told her son that Bolden would blow his brains out someday because he just played too loud.

Whatever the cause, his deterioration was rapid. He eventually was even kicked out of his own band. After Buddy had failed to pay his band members once too often, they began arranging their own gigs without him. At the start of one of these engagements — at Odd Fellows Hall on Perdido — Bolden arrived late, only to find that his band had replaced him with his old rival Edward Clem.

"You can go back home," Frankie Dusen, his second cornetist, told him.

"You mean to tell me you're gonna put me out of my own band?" Bolden asked. He reminded Dusen that he had hired the younger man "when nobody would have you."

"That makes no difference," Dusen replied. "I'm the King now."

In the spring of 1906 — while bedridden and being tended by his mother and his mother-in-law, Ida Bass — Bolden turned violent. Convinced that he was being poisoned, he jumped out of bed and attacked

Mrs. Bass with a water pitcher. She suffered only a minor head wound, and Bolden was soon calmed down again. But the two women, concerned that more violence might follow, had him arrested on a charge of insanity. He was held in jail for a few days and released. But there were more incidents and arrests to come. According to one uncorroborated story, Bolden even threw a neighbor's baby out of a window. Soon parents and older siblings were warning kids away from him. "He's nuts, you know," one neighbor explained to his younger brother.

Bolden's last gig was playing for the Labor Day parade in New Orleans later that year. It was a huge parade, and virtually every musician in town would have been playing in it. But sometime before the marching was over, Bolden had to drop out. He spent a troubled week at home, and by Saturday his mental state was bad enough for his mother to have him incarcerated again on an insanity charge. Again he was released after a few days, but he was by now too far-gone for help. He spent the winter drinking heavily and doing little else. Then, on March 13, 1907, Alice Bolden had her son arrested for a third — and final — time.

Bolden sat in the House of Detention for several weeks before finally being transferred to the State Insane Asylum in Jackson, Louisiana. The commitment document read, in part, as follows: "Character of Disease: Insanity. Cause of Insanity: Alcohol. Is Patient Dangerous to Himself or Others? To others."

Bolden would remain at Jackson for the rest of his life. But though the first "King" of jazz was gone, there were many musicians in New Orleans who would carry on — and expand upon — his legacy. One of them was just a small boy when Bolden was put away. He would later tell conflicting stories about whether he really remembered hearing Bolden play, but it was actually likely that he did. He lived quite near Funky Butt Hall on Perdido, and recalled listening — when he was a boy of four or five, just when Bolden would have been at his peak — to a band playing to advertise Saturday-night dances at the hall. "Before the dance," the boy would later write, "the band would play out front about a half hour. And us little kids would all do little dances. If I ever heard Buddy Bolden play the cornet, I figure that's when."

The boy was named Louis Armstrong, and he would eventually do more than anyone in history to spread Bolden's new sound beyond the confines of the ghettos of New Orleans and out into the world.

■ ■ ■ ■

CHAPTER 10
THE SIN FACTORY

■ ■ ■ ■

A Bellocq portrait of a Storyville prostitute
Hogan Jazz Archive, Tulane University

ARE WE TO HAVE A "WIDE-OPEN" CITY?

Representative Anderson of the Fourth Ward of the city, but commonly known as the mayor of Storyville, has succeeded in passing through the House of Representatives a bill allowing prize fights up to twenty-five rounds in regularly organized clubs in New Orleans, without asking the consent of the mayor.

Doubtless the classes whom Mr. Anderson specially represents desire a "wide-open" city, and so far there has been nothing to prevent [it]. It will be astonishing if the General Assembly of Louisiana shall permit the purveyors of vice and the habitués of the purlieus of New Orleans to set the legal and official standard of the morals of the city.

— *New Orleans Daily Picayune,*
June 20, 1902

By 1905, the city of New Orleans — or at least that part of it known to an increasing portion of the world as Storyville — was just about as "wide-open" as the poor *Daily Picayune* had feared. In the seven or eight years that the District had been open, it had developed into a vast, well-functioning factory of sin, as lucrative and efficient as any lumber mill or city gasworks in the country. Its 230 brothels, 60 assignation houses, and scores of one-room cribs could by now process the raw materials of male sexual desire at an astonishing rate of speed. "I'll tell you, five minutes was a long time to spend in one of those rooms," one customer said of a typical brothel visit. "In fact, from the time you'd come in the front door of the house until you'd be back on the banquette [sidewalk] hardly ever took more than fifteen minutes. And there you'd be, standing on the banquette without a cent in your pocket, and no place to go but maybe home. And that would be the last place in the world you'd want to go."

Like the factories of other American industries, moreover, the vice mills of Storyville were kept churning day and night, rotating workers as needed. "This Tenderloin District was like something that nobody has ever seen before or since," Jelly Roll Morton insisted. "The doors were taken off the saloons from one year to the next." Why bother with doors, after all, if your establishment never closed? Even the crib women marched to and from their shifts like factory workers. "A lot of the prostitutes lived in different sections of the city and would come down to Storyville just like they had a job," Louis Armstrong remembered. "There were different shifts for them. . . . Sometimes — two prostitutes would share the rent in the same crib together. . . . One would work in the day and the other would beat out that night shift."

The high-toned houses of Basin Street, despite their pretensions, were likewise operated with an eye to a maximally efficient revenue stream. And the smaller brothels could be virtual assembly lines of sex. "Those places were organized to take *all* your money," one customer explained. "Let's say you went into a so-called two-dollar house. Well, you couldn't very well sit down in the parlor without buying a little wine or at least putting some change in the player piano. It would cost you usually a couple of dollars before you even got around to the business you came for. Clever girls, once they got you in a boudoir, would always offer little 'extra' services, for 'extra' prices, naturally — and you'd *pay*! Things are not easy to resist at such times." And lest the laborers of the District waste their time trying to exploit an already-spent resource, customers were typically sent on their way with a lagniappe — a little bonus, like a rose for their button-hole or a feather for their hat, "so that the hustlers in the bars and nightclubs would know you'd already had it for the night."

If Storyville was indeed an industry, then its chief industrialist — the Andrew Carnegie of the carnal — was none other than Thomas C. Anderson. According to at least some reports, there was no transaction that occurred in the District of which he did not get a cut. Anderson was, according to Jelly Roll Morton, "the king of the district." And like a king, he took tribute from all of his subjects. When Lulu White, for instance, had a free-spending group of celebrants in her house, she would send someone down Basin Street to the Annex for a quick delivery of the really good Champagne. White would charge her customers $5 per bottle — a hefty sum in 1905 currency — but Anderson would get no less than $4 of that. It was easy money for very little effort, but Anderson was the man with connections to the liquor distributors, and so it was paid.

Given his political connections, his commercial dominance, and his considerable personal magnetism, he was now arguably one of the most powerful men in New Orleans, dispensing advice, protection, charity, and patronage wherever they were needed. And to those who dwelled in his eighteen-square-block realm — now called Anderson

County by newspaper wags — his word was law. "From time to time," one Storyville memoirist explained, "the highly honored and respected Tom Anderson would send forth an order: 'Close all the houses 'til the heat's off!' [or] 'No gambling, the police's gonna raid all the joints!' " Compliance was instant. "Doors would be locked and all lights put out. The joints would be abandoned and deserted . . . until Anderson sent word that the heat was off and they could resume business."

Soon his establishment on the corner of Basin and Iberville (the new name for Customhouse Street after 1904) was becoming nationally, if not world, famous. When a writer for *Collier's* magazine visited New Orleans, he wrote about the reigning vice lord with barely concealed incredulity:

Tom Anderson overtops the restricted district; He is its law-giver and its king. In his shadow flourish the unblushing street-open shame of Iberville and Conti and St. Louis Streets; the saloons with their wide-open poker and crap games; the dives where Negroes buy, for fifty cents, five cents'-worth of cocaine. He is, too, the [buffer] between the poor, foolish, awkward law written in the books and the people who dwell under his kindlier law. For example, when a woman of "Anderson County" commits robbery, and when the victim complains so loudly that she has to be arrested, Tom Anderson comes down and gets her out. He does not even have to give cash bail. . . .

But the bad publicity — that eternal oxymoron — merely brought more and more people to the District. Many of them were celebrities. When the actress Sarah Bernhardt visited New Orleans, she took the obligatory tour of the Storyville District. She showed particular interest in a street-corner performance by Emile "Stalebread" Lacoume and his Razzy Dazzy Spasm Band of youngsters playing on homemade instruments (though her tip to the band was, according to one witness, "below whore scale"). At the Annex, Anderson would play host to some of the greatest sports figures of the era, including boxer "Gentleman Jim" Corbett and baseball legends Babe Ruth, Frank Chance, and Ty Cobb. When George M. Cohan showed up at the bar one night, he amused everyone by performing tricks with his derby hat, rolling it up and down his arms in time to the music of the resident jazz combo. And Anderson was nothing if not a considerate host. When boxer John L. Sullivan, late in his career, came to town for an exhibition bout and got too drunk to walk straight, it was the mayor of Storyville who escorted the aging warrior home from the Annex to his boardinghouse on Rampart Street.

But this was the way of Tom Anderson, who, as despots go, tended toward the benevolent. According to those who knew him, he was always "immaculate, cool-headed, and calm," no matter what the situation. He was especially polite to women, even those who were drunk. "He listened to their love problems, when their men were there and when these women came in alone," one friend said. And Tom's advice was always palliative and reasonable: "Take it easy," he'd say. "Everything will turn out for the better. Don't do nothing drastic; you may regret it."

No wonder, then, that he was such a popular figure — not only among the denizens of the Tenderloin, but also in the halls of the state legislature in Baton Rouge. Anderson had an easy amiability and wry sense of humor that could disarm even his most rabid political enemies. When making a long argument against a proposed coal bill in 1904, his speech — even in the opinion of the usually hostile *Picayune* — was "characteristically humorous, and provided much merriment in the chamber." It also succeeded in getting the measure quashed.

For although the papers would rarely admit it, Tom Anderson was actually a fairly effective representative, and one who espoused some unquestionably noble causes. He was a member of the Ways and Means Committee and took a special interest in improving the atrocious conditions at many state institutions, especially the Louisiana State Insane Asylum at Jackson (where Buddy Bolden was incarcerated, though there's no evidence that the two actually ever met). In 1905, when Louisiana faced one of its periodic epidemics of yellow fever, Anderson, as proprietor of the Record Oil Company, generously donated a large supply of oil to the city. (Oil was used to kill mosquito larvae that bred in the city's ubiquitous water cisterns.) And later that year, when President Theodore Roosevelt came to New Orleans as a gesture of solidarity with the fever-stricken city, the Democratic mayor of Storyville was named to the honorary committee that welcomed the staunchly Republican president. A picture of the two of them shaking hands would adorn a wall behind the Annex bar for many years to come.

Not that some of his pet causes couldn't be viewed as somewhat self-serving. When Representative Anderson sponsored bills to raise the salaries of New Orleans police and court stenographers, he was surely implementing the lesson he had learned early in his career — namely, that favors produced friends, and that friends in turn produced favors. Naturally, it didn't always work. The New Orleans Police Department in this era was still too fractured by rivalries and competing factions for any politician to be friends with *everyone* on the force. And although Anderson was chummy enough with Chief John Journée to invite him to his daughter's wedding, he still faced occasional police harassment. Even then, however, Anderson had ways of appeasing his antagonists. When, during one of the police department's occasional grandstanding efforts to enforce the widely ignored Sunday Closing Law, Anderson was arrested, tried, and convicted (by one Judge Skinner), the amiable saloonkeeper did not hold a grudge. After the case was appealed and overturned in a higher court, he made sure to send over a large supply of liquor and cigars to Judge Skinner, to be shared among all members of the lower court. After all, why let something like a little misdemeanor conviction come between two men of the world just doing their jobs?

Prospects for Anderson — and for Storyville in general — improved significantly with the results of the municipal election of 1904. That year a Ring stalwart named Martin Behrman, from the Algiers district just across the river, was elected mayor, and his attitude toward the city's vice industry was as accommodating as any sporting man could ask for. The ultimate anti–silk stocking, Behrman had little use for the high-minded moralizing of the Garden District elites, and he scoffed at their attempts to meddle in the serious business of running a big city. To Behrman, the typical silk stocking was the kind of citizen who "always knew what [had] led to the fall of the Roman Empire, but did not seem to know that the bulk of the voters were more interested in schools, police, firemen, the charity hospital, the parks and squares, and labor troubles than the Roman Empire." And while Behrman admitted that he might be — as the *Times-Democrat* called him — somewhat "uncouth," he at least knew what the common people of New Orleans wanted.

Virtually all of the city's newspapers had opposed the election of such an unpolished machine politician. "Mr. Behrman does not rise to the standards [of public office]," the *Times-Democrat* wrote during the campaign, "but represents the very elements that would assure misgovernment of the city and seriously hinder and check its prosperity." But Behrman's most vociferous detractor was none other than W. S. Parkerson, the blue-blooded paragon who had led the parish prison lynching back in 1891. Still active in reform politics, Parkerson accused Behrman of all kinds of malfeasance, including "grafting" for the Edison Electric Company and making illegal use of a railroad pass. The campaign turned out to be one of the bitterest in recent memory ("I would rather be a maggot in the suppurating carcass of an insane mule than [be] that man Parkerson," one Behrman operative announced at a rally). But Behrman ultimately emerged triumphant. And in this new mayor, Storyville and its people could not have found a better friend.

Meanwhile, the District was maturing, so to speak, into a full-fledged subculture, as colorful as it was profitable. A list of the neighborhood's extensive cast of characters — including prostitutes, pimps, gamblers, and various hustlers — would include such names as Steel Arm Johnny, Mary Meathouse, Gold Tooth Gussie, Bird Leg Nora, Titanic, Coke-Eyed Laura, Scratch, Bull Frog Sonny, Snaggle Mouf Mary, Stack O. Dollars, Charlie Bow Wow, Good Lord the Lifter, and many more. The exploits of most of these notorious individuals have been lost to history, though a few — like Boxcar Shorty and Boar Hog — were later immortalized in the lyrics of jazz recordings. And although some historians claim that the rate of violent crime was actually relatively low in Storyville (at least by the standards of New Orleans as a whole, which from 1900 to 1910 had a per-capita murder rate three times that of Chicago), this was hardly a peaceable bunch of men and women. According to Jelly Roll Morton, one Storyville tough by the name of Aaron Harris ("no doubt the most heartless man I've ever heard of or seen") had no fewer than eleven murders to his credit.

Even some of the Basin Street madams were known for their readiness to resort to guns or knives to settle their disputes. In 1904, Lulu White was arrested on a weapons charge after firing two shots at her white lover, George Lambert, who apparently had left her for another woman. Unable to contain her jealousy, White had gone to her lover's home to confront him as he was playing poker with some friends. According to the *Daily Picayune*, "Lulu dashed into the room where the poker players were. Seeing Lambert, she began abusing him and fired two shots at him." The shots missed — as perhaps they were intended to — and one of the other poker players pulled the pistol from her hand before she could fire again. White ultimately was charged, but with nothing more than carrying a concealed weapon, a crime that in New Orleans rarely led to any serious consequences.

Such colorful episodes were relatively harmless and easy to dismiss, but there were increasing signs in recent years that the debauched goings-on in Storyville might be getting too outré for even the most open-minded New Orleanians. Of course, some of the wilder stories told about the District are surely more folklore than history. The fact that they were told at all, however, indicates a growing disgust in the city at large regarding the monster that had been created some ten years before. One story held that Lulu White began offering her customers a discount book of fifteen tickets, each depicting a different lewd act — said act to be provided to the bearer simply upon presentation of the ticket. And there were other, more lurid tales: of de-flowering auctions, mother-daughter harlot teams, erotic animal acts, and one so-called dancer — Olivia the Oyster Queen — who allegedly could shimmy a shelled, glistening bivalve over her entire naked body without ever touching it with her hands. Many of these reports centered on one brothel: Emma Johnson's House of All Nations at 331 Basin Street. Johnson herself — described as a tall, rangy, and very masculine Cajun lesbian — was getting on in years by the first decade of the twentieth century, but her house offered some of the youngest (the very youngest) prostitutes in the District. They purportedly gave nightly "sex circuses" in which every form of fetishism, voyeurism, and sadomas-ochism was engaged in.

"They did a lot of things that probably couldn't be mentioned . . . right before the eyes of everybody," reported Jelly Roll Morton, who often played piano at Johnson's house. "A screen was put up between me and the tricks they were doing for the guests. But I cut a slit in the screen, as I had come to be a sport now myself, and wanted to see what everybody else was seeing." But Morton's breezy knowingness aside, this was where the Storyville pretense of harmless racy fun showed its depraved underbelly. To most sensibilities of the day, pedophilia, bestiality, and sodomy were outrages that even isolation in a restricted district could not make tolerable.

Certainly the District's excesses were becoming increasingly intolerable to Josie Arlington. Although she was by all reports making prodigious amounts of money at her palace on Basin Street, she still could not get past her persistent discomfort with her life — and her growing desperation to keep that knowledge from her adored niece Anna. According to one friend, Arlington "was in dread fear continually that this girl would find out who she was." In 1903, faced with the quandary that Anna would soon be returning home from convent school in Paris, Arlington used some of her brothel profits to buy a house in Covington, Louisiana, safely away from New Orleans, near Abita Springs on the other side of Lake Pontchartrain. She named the place Anna's Villa, and when the girl returned from Europe in July of 1904, she was sent directly there to spend the summer. Arlington then enrolled the girl in another convent school — this one in Clifton, Ohio — where she could be sheltered for another two years. But this could only be a stopgap measure; after those two years, Anna would be finished with her schooling, and she would want to come home to her family in New Orleans.

Then, on the morning of December 1, 1905, some workmen painting the Arlington brothel's top floor accidentally set fire to the building. It was eleven A.M., and the residents of the place were all still asleep, but they were quickly roused and evacuated. According to the *Daily Picayune,* the panicky women ran down Basin Street carrying bedsheets stuffed with whatever possessions they could grab. They then assembled — "scantily clad" — in the saloon of Tom Anderson's Annex. Fortunately, the brothel fire burned slowly, and had only destroyed the attic and two upper floors before it was put out. But although the place was adequately insured, Josie Arlington had lost many of the beautiful paintings and furniture she had bought when traveling in Europe.

A reporter for the *Picayune* took the opportunity to engage in a bit of sermonizing. He described the overdramatic women weeping and moaning — "some of them more for the purpose of exciting sympathy and attention than for [any] actual loss." But then he saw one woman, legitimately grief-stricken, crying in a hallway. When asked why she was so upset, she said that, in the excitement of her escape, she had forgotten to rescue a picture of her mother. It was this loss that caused the young woman such pain. "Surely there was some good left in the heart of the little woman," the reporter oozed, "who, amidst the vices by which she was surrounded, and in her degradation, yet remembered her mother, valuing the picture far above all the diamonds, jewels, and fine dresses which she was possessed of."

This scene from Victorian melodrama notwithstanding, Arlington and her employees were unwilling to be out of business for long, so while the house at 225 Basin Street was being repaired, they set up shop in the upper rooms of Anderson's Annex (which henceforth became known as the "Arlington Annex"). But while the brothel's proprietress had come through the fire physically and financially unscathed, the close call only reinforced her conviction to somehow live a more respectable kind of life. According to some reports, after the fire she began to speak gloomily to her prostitutes of the fire and brimstone that awaited all sinners after death. And her desire to keep Anna free of the taint of Storyville just grew stronger.

By 1906, she had become prosperous enough to pull off this feat. In that year, Arlington purchased an imposing white mansion on Esplanade Avenue, in an ultra-respectable part of town out toward the City Park. This, she decided, was where she would undertake to live her second life of sober propriety. Until this point, she and Tom Brady had lived separately, she in the brothel and he in his mother's house (though they did also have a room at the home of Arlington's cousin where they could rendezvous whenever necessary). This was her choice, not his. Brady had actually asked her to marry him several years earlier, but she'd refused. According to Brady, she told him that since they'd gone along this far without doing the deed, they might as well go along as they were for "the balance." But now they would live together as ostensible man and wife for all the world to see. Josie arranged for her brother Henry Deubler's family (including his wife and three sons, Anna's brothers) to move in with them, and of course Anna herself would join them after leaving school. In preparation, Arlington instructed everyone they knew — everyone that her niece might have any contact with — to start addressing her not as Josie or Miss Arlington or even as Mary Deubler, but as "Mrs. Brady." If the masquerade was to work, there could be no mistakes.

And so the Deublers and the Bradys lived the life of a normal extended family in the large house on Esplanade. Arlington put more and more of the responsibility for running the brothel on one of her surrogates, but she still enjoyed the revenue stream that made her new life possible. Some of her more presentable Storyville associates, including Tom Anderson, would occasionally be invited to family dinners and birthday parties — at the house or at Anna's Villa. But Anna (who apparently was not a careful reader of the New Orleans newspapers) never suspected that these people were anything other than upstanding friends of her aunt Mary and uncle Tom. The young woman would in fact live for years in the house on Esplanade in blissful ignorance of the source of her family's prosperity on Basin Street, just a few short miles away.

But others in New Orleans did not have the luxury of being so insulated from the spectacle of Storyville. Local business reformers may still have been satisfied with the results of their 1898 experiment, but moral reformers, emboldened by the rise of organizations like the Anti-Saloon League and the Social Hygiene movement, were becoming increasingly vocal in their opposition to the goings-on in the city's tenderloin. Drawing boundaries around sin had clearly not worked, and the impulse toward outright prohibition — of prostitution, alcohol, gambling, and other vices — was gaining ground all over the nation in the first decade of the twentieth century. In the Louisiana state legislature, support was growing (despite Representative Thomas C. Anderson's strenuous efforts) for stronger legislative measures to put the lid on sin. Already in 1904 they had passed a law to close the state's pool-rooms. Another proposed measure would prohibit horse-track betting throughout the state. And now, as the 1908 elections approached, there was talk of an even more comprehensive anti-vice law, one that would totally revamp the way alcohol could be sold in Louisiana, at the same time placing onerous new restrictions on the ability of women and blacks to work in and patronize the establishments that served it.

For the members of New Orleans' demi-monde — the madams, pimps, saloon and dance-hall proprietors, and the prostitutes and musicians they employed — there were to be some tough times ahead. In its first ten years of existence, the city's segregated vice districts on both sides of Canal Street had largely been left alone, and they had thrived — far too well for the comfort of many. But now there were to be some changes in New Orleans. The city's self-styled champions of virtue and purity were finally ready to strike back.

■ ■ ■ ■

PART THREE:
BATTLEGROUNDS OF SIN

1907–1917

■ ■ ■ ■

■ ■ ■ ■

CHAPTER 11
THE BLACK HAND

■ ■ ■ ■

A fanciful newspaper engraving of a secret Mafia meeting
Louisiana Research Collection, Tulane University

On a warm June evening in 1907, a small, fair-haired boy named Walter Lamana was playing outside his father's undertaking business on St. Philip Street in the French Quarter. The boy was alone, amusing himself quietly in the alley beside the building. It was nearly eight P.M. and the amber evening light was waning — the time of day when the Quarter's characteristic smells of garlic and horse dung and sweetly rotting fruit seemed momentarily to intensify in the dusk.

As Walter played under the arches, one of the establishment's horse-drawn hearses, returning from a late Saturday funeral, turned into the alley. The driver stopped and said a few words to the boy. Then he continued down the alley to the courtyard beyond, where he busied himself unhitching the wagon and settling the horses into their stables for the night.

After a few minutes, another man — in his early forties, with sparse graying hair and a small mustache — approached Walter in the alley. Exactly what he said to the eight-year-old boy is unknown. But he produced two nickels from his pocket and offered to treat the boy to ice cream from a candy store down the street. Walter apparently saw nothing amiss in the offer. He got up from the pavement, took the man's offered hand, and walked with him up St. Philip Street toward the store.

When they reached Bourbon Street, they came upon a covered wagon stopped at the corner. A tall man stood beside the wagon, as if waiting for them. This man took Walter's hand and then, before the boy could protest, lifted him up to the driver, who quickly pushed Walter into the covered space behind him. The tall man then climbed into the back of the wagon and pulled the tarp closed after him. The driver spurred the horse, and the wagon began moving noisily down the poorly paved street. The first man remained standing on the banquette, watching them go in the faltering light. Then he turned away and disappeared into the warren of tenements, outbuildings, taverns, and warehouses of the lower French Quarter.

When Walter did not come back into the family's living quarters after nightfall, his parents were at first unconcerned. The boy often liked to hide in various places around the courtyard, hayloft, and livery stables;

sometimes he'd even fall asleep in his hiding place. But as the evening wore on, the Lamanas became worried. Peter Lamana, Walter's father, searched the premises and the surrounding neighborhood, but the boy was nowhere to be found. Finally, it occurred to the father that Walter might have stowed away on the tallyho his older brother John had driven that evening to West End, the lakeside resort some six or seven miles from the city. Lamana had one of his horses saddled up and rode out to the resort in the moonlight. But when he returned, hours later, he had nothing to report. John had not seen his younger brother.

For the rest of that night and throughout the day on Sunday, Peter Lamana searched the French Quarter for his son, enlisting friends, employees, and neighborhood children in the hunt. They talked to neighbors, shopkeepers, and anyone else they encountered, but no one seemed to have any idea what had happened to the boy. By Sunday evening, Lamana decided to go to the police. That he had waited even this long to report the disappearance was not unusual. Members of the city's Italian community typically preferred to deal with their own problems. Besides, the police did not always respond energetically to cases involving Italians, since investigations of crimes in Italian neighborhoods were often met with a wall of mistrustful silence. But Peter Lamana's case was an exception. As the owner of a prosperous undertaking business and the largest livery stable in the Vieux Carré — and as a member of the city's powerful Progressive Union, a civic organization composed of the most prominent local businessmen — he was considered a very important man, worthy of the best efforts of the police. And so they responded to the report with a greater determination than they would have if the missing boy had been the son of a downtown grocer or banana handler. The search was expanded to the riverfront, the lakeside district, and throughout the "sewers, dark alleys, back yards, and hidden courtyards" of the Quarter.

But then, on Monday morning, an anonymous letter was delivered to the Lamana residence. Written in Italian in a crude, barely legible hand, it read: "Your boy is comfortably housed, clothed, and fed. He is well and no harm will be done him, but we will not be responsible for the consequences should you fail to comply with our demands." What followed was a demand for a ransom of $6,000 — a huge sum in 1907 dollars — to be delivered by Lamana himself. According to the instructions in the note (which Lamana kept secret from everyone except the police), the undertaker was to raise the money in gold and then take it — alone, on horseback — out along the road toward Bogalusa, a small

268

town about seventy miles north of the city. Somewhere on the way, he would be approached by a person who would accept the money from him and tell him where his boy could be found. Unless he wanted Walter sent back to him "cut up in pieces," Lamana was to follow these instructions to the letter.

The note was signed with a small skull and crossbones at the bottom — a sure indication, it was said, that it came from the organization known to all Italians as the Black Hand.

For more than a decade following the Orleans Parish Prison lynching of 1891, New Orleans' Italian underworld had been relatively quiet. "Some twelve years ago we discovered our mistake in tolerating the vendetta here," the *Times-Democrat* observed in 1902. "[But] we were aroused from our mistake . . . by a shock of thunder that shook the whole city and, indeed, the whole Union." That shock — the assassination of David Hennessy — had of course been met with "corrective" violent action by many of the city's leading citizens. "The lesson then given was salutary," the paper continued, "and for twelve years New Orleans was almost free from the vendetta. The general peace and order of the community were better because of it, and the Sicilians themselves secured the best results from the improvement."

Whether "the Sicilians themselves" would have agreed with this assessment is perhaps doubtful. But the fact remains that the city had been more or less free of assassination-style murders for the rest of the 1890s. That changed in 1902, however, with the arrival in New Orleans of a man calling himself Francesco Genova. Under his real name, Francesco Matesi, he had allegedly fled his native Sicily after being indicted for the slaughter of an entire family named Seina. Coming to Louisiana by way of London and New York (where he apparently became associated with legendary mafioso Giuseppe Morello), he quickly established himself as a leader in New Orleans' Italian community, which reportedly knew all about his activities in Sicily and was appropriately cowed. Genova and his supposed accomplice in the Seina murders, Paolo Di Christina (real name: Paolo Marchese), attempted to take control of the local pasta-making business. But they met with some resistance. Two brothers who owned a macaroni factory in nearby Donaldsville — Antonio and Salvatore Luciano — refused to stand for Genova's attempts to force them out of business. One day in early May 1902, Salvatore Luciano caught sight of Genova and Di Christina in a buggy near the Lucianos' boardinghouse on Poydras Street in New Orleans. Thinking that the two men had come to make good on their various threats to harm the brothers, Salvatore ran inside to grab his shotgun, rushed up to the buggy, and fired at Genova.

The shot missed, and although Genova and Di Christina both suffered painful powder burns, police arrived before anything more serious could occur. But the incident set in motion a brutal interfamily mob war that ended up appalling a city that had hoped its Italian crime problems were over. One night, about a month after the original incident, Antonio Luciano was hosting a poker game at the Poydras Street boardinghouse while Salvatore sat in an adjacent room, writing a letter to their mother in Italy. Four men walked in off the street and, without much preamble, fell upon Salvatore Luciano with knives and clubs. Antonio, hearing the disturbance, grabbed his shotgun and started firing. The ensuing melee left Salvatore and one of the poker players dead and two more men seriously wounded.

The next day, after being released from jail under a plea of self-defense, Antonio Luciano was overseeing his brother's wake at the boardinghouse. Friends of the family were milling around Salvatore's body, which had been laid out on a table in one of the larger rooms. Antonio looked on in amazement as a man named Ferrara, whom he recognized as one of his brother's murderers, stepped up to the corpse, pushed aside the gauzy shroud, and planted a kiss on the dead man's lips. Enraged and incredulous, Antonio beckoned to Ferrara to follow him into the courtyard of the boardinghouse. Ferrara, apparently unaware that he'd been recognized, complied — and was met with both barrels of a loaded shotgun. Antonio discharged the weapon into Ferrara's chest and then, while the horrified guests looked on, proceeded to beat the man's head to a pulp with the broken stock of the shotgun. "I am satisfied," Antonio crowed as he was arrested. "I have killed the man who slew my brother!"

Francesco Genova, on the other hand, was emphatically *not* satisfied. But he was patient. When Antonio Luciano was again released from jail after a quick acquittal for the killing of Ferrara, Genova sent for a gunman from New York — one Espare, a stranger to New Orleans who befriended Luciano and, over the next few weeks, slowly earned his trust. One day in August 1902, the genial Espare accompanied his new friend to a photographer's shop on Canal Street to fetch some newly developed photos. After they had retrieved the prints — as they were descending the outdoor stairwell back to Canal Street — Espare calmly took a revolver from his belt and fired six shots into Antonio Luciano's back. Luciano attempted to shoot back, but lost his footing and tumbled down the stairway into the street. Espare raced up to the roof, jumped to the roof of the adjoining building (which happened to be Tom Anderson's Arlington Restaurant on Rampart Street), and disappeared into the open skylight.

Fortunately for the cause of New Orleans justice, the fatal shooting had been witnessed by several members of the city's exclusive Pickwick Club, which stood just across Canal Street from the photographer's shop. When Espare was brought up on murder charges, these worthies — unlike the Italian witnesses to so many other vendetta murders — actually testified to what they had seen. Espare was quickly convicted of the crime. And when he was hanged for it in 1905, it allegedly marked the first time in the city's history that an Italian was executed for the murder of another Italian. But the conclusion to be drawn from this six-month back-and-forth killing spree was inescapable: as the newspapers put it, the city's Italian underworld was reawakening from its decadelong slumber.

And the Luciano affair did indeed herald a marked increase in so-called Mafia activity in New Orleans. In particular, the extortion gangs known collectively as the Black Hand began again to make their presence felt in the city. Crime historians today generally make a clear distinction between the Black Hand (essentially a blackmail technique that all but disappeared after the 1920s) and the Mafia (a much longer-lived syndicate of organized crime families), whose members often engaged in Black Hand activity. But to the general public of the early 1900s, they were essentially the same threat, perpetrated by the same population of immigrants. And when merchants in the Italian community began to receive anonymous extortion letters in the aftermath of the Luciano incident, the police and the newspapers had their suspicions about who was responsible. For many, the uptick in Mafia activity followed too closely upon the arrival of Francesco Genova to be coincidence. A new *capo* had apparently come to New Orleans, and the lesson of the Orleans Parish Prison lynching was one he'd never learned.

Even so, the ire of the city's "better element" was not fully raised again until, as in the Hennessy case, one of its own was affected. This is what happened on that June evening of 1907. Peter Lamana, a "prosperous and worthy" stalwart of the Progressive Union, had had his beloved son stolen from the threshold of his own home. The lesson of 1891, it seemed, would have to be taught again.

A crowd of four to five thousand people packed the main auditorium of the Union Française Hall on the evening of Wednesday,

June 12. Four days had passed since the disappearance of Walter Lamana, and no trace of the boy had yet been found. The night before, following the instructions of the Black Hand letter, Peter Lamana had ridden out on the road to Bogalusa with a sack containing $6,000 in gold; contrary to those instructions, he'd been followed by a contingent of New Orleans police. But either the police had been detected or something else had gone wrong, because no kidnapper met the father to take his offered ransom. Now the police were left with few concrete leads to work with.

Wednesday night's mass meeting — called by the city's Progressive Union and several Italian leaders — was intended to produce some clues by urging members of the Italian community to abandon their customary silence on Mafia matters. The Lamana kidnapping was the type of outrage that could not be allowed to stand. "The people of New Orleans are easy-going and overlook many things," the *Daily Picayune* observed, "but now and then malefactors, emboldened by immunity for years, strike a blow which threatens the very foundation of society or the home. Then they are given an exhibition of the power of a people aroused in their wrath."

But that wrath had to be properly channeled, and so this meeting had been called.

Speaker after speaker pleaded with the residents of the Italian quarter to come forward with information about the Lamana case or about any other Mafia-like activity they might know about. Judge Philip Patorno, one of the leaders of the community, announced the formation of an Italian Vigilance Committee to handle the problem of crime in the neighborhood. "From now on, the Italians will be resolved to act," he vowed. "Any Italian who henceforth receives a threatening letter will be compelled to lay it before the committee."

Patorno's speech was met with enthusiastic cheering and applause, as were the similar declamations of many other speakers that night. But the greatest ovation — at least if the *Daily Picayune* is to be believed — was reserved for Col. John C. Wickliffe, one of the leaders, with W. S. Parkerson, of the 1891 lynching. ("There were also loud calls for Parkerson," the paper noted, "but Mr. Parkerson was not present.") Wickliffe urged the crowd to cooperate with Judge Patorno. "There has been too much of a disposition on the part of Italian people to fight their own battles alone, and to fear asking aid," he said. "But they ought to be made to know that they are living in a land of liberty and that they can get the support of every citizen. . . . Is it possible that a handful of criminals can defy a city of three hundred thousand inhabitants? Is it possible that these men can remain undetected? On behalf of your own little ones, strive [in] every way possible to stop such an infamous business!"

After the meeting was adjourned, excited crowds poured out into the streets of the Vieux Carré. Too impatient to wait for voluntary offers of information, one vigilante mob gathered near the site of the old parish prison, threatening to "make more history for Congo Square" — a not-so-veiled reference to the Italian lynchings of 1891. Others flooded into the streets around the Lamana residence. Defying police, they stormed through the surrounding neighborhood, pounding on doors and demanding to be admitted to search the premises. The terrified residents could do little but comply. "True, [the vigilantes] were after blood," the *Daily Picayune* admitted the next day, "but only the blood of the guilty."

These intimidation tactics produced results. In one overcrowded rooming house, the vigilantes found two schoolboys who admitted having seen Walter Lamana walking on Saturday with a man named Tony Costa. Reinvigorated by this breakthrough, the mob proceeded immediately to Costa's home on the corner of St. Philip and Chartres. They entered the premises and ransacked the house from top to bottom. And although they found no one fitting Costa's description, another resident of the house told them that

Costa did indeed live there, that he was a notorious gambler and ex-con, and that he had been missing since Saturday.

The police had in the meantime met with some investigative success of their own. Rumors that a strange Italian had recently purchased a covered wagon in the neighborhood proved to be accurate. Detectives following a lead out in Jefferson Parish, west of the city, turned up a witness who saw a covered wagon late on Saturday night, pulling into the yard of a St. Rose Plantation farm owned by one Ignazio Campisciano. This was another name, at least.

Then, on Thursday morning, Peter Lamana received another unsigned letter: "With tears in my eyes, I send you these few lines for your comfort," the letter began in flowery Italian. "Therefore, be a man and accept my confidence. I do so for the love of your son." The letter writer went on to tell Lamana how to find the boy: "Go to Harvey Canal and call on a man named Macorio Morti. He knows all. When you get him, ask him about the barber who was living at Harvey Canal. . . . The barber is the chief of all. I have no doubt that he has your son."

Following up on these and several other leads, police had by Friday arrested ten suspects, most notably Tony Costa, who had been found holed up in a house on Clouet Street. Also in custody were the farmer

Campisciano, the Harvey Canal informant mentioned in the anonymous letter, the owner of the ice-cream store near the Lamana home, and — at the special request of the Italian Vigilance Committee — Francesco Genova, the alleged capo who had been involved in the Luciano shootings five years earlier. Genova was by this time a wealthy businessman, allegedly feared by all Italians of New Orleans. What evidence, if any, the committee had of Genova's involvement in the case is unclear. But since he was the leading figure in what passed for the local "Mafia Society," police seemed certain that he was in some way implicated.

At this point, Capt. Thomas Capo, the inconveniently named officer in charge of the investigation, had some justification for believing that he was making progress. But virtually all of the evidence on which these men were held was circumstantial. After the intervention of lawyers, police were forced to release all except Tony Costa, who nonetheless still protested his innocence in the most vehement terms possible. Even so, police were careful to keep the released suspects under constant surveillance, and to keep pursuing tips and other leads, which were being brought to the Vigilance Committee in increasing numbers.

By now, more than a week had passed since Walter Lamana disappeared, and hopes that the boy would be found alive were fading. Acting on persistent rumors that the boy had been killed and concealed in the bayou behind the Campisciano farm, police on June 21 hired a special train and transported a twenty-five-man search party to the site. But the swamp in this area was one of the densest and most forbidding in Louisiana. Although the men searched with a team of blood-hounds for an entire day — often knee-deep in muck and tormented by mosquitoes — they found nothing. At dusk the exhausted searchers emerged empty-handed from the swamp, as the tight-lipped Campisciano, ostensibly working his land, looked on.

As more and more days passed without any further progress in the case, tensions began to surface among the frustrated investigators. The police began accusing the Italian Vigilance Committee of meeting in secret and withholding important information. Peter Lamana, meanwhile, had all but cut off communication with the official investigators, choosing to follow his own lines of inquiry. Apparently, he felt that a heavy-handed police presence did more harm than good, interfering with the willingness of potential witnesses to tell what they knew.

Finally, some two weeks after the disappearance, another key name emerged from the cacophony of innuendoes and accusations. For days, Judge Patorno had been hearing from various Italian businessmen who had received extortion letters over the past weeks. But one of them actually claimed to know who wrote the letter he'd received. Taking the judge to the window of his own office, the merchant pointed to a man standing on the corner just outside. "That is the man who wrote it," the merchant said. "Tony Gendusa!"

Judge Patorno did not act immediately on this revelation. It was, after all, only one of numerous accusations he was hearing every day. But when he eventually compared the merchant's note with the original letter sent to Peter Lamana, he noticed that the handwriting was suspiciously similar. And when he went to Tony Gendusa's home, he discovered that the man was now missing. Patorno sent some detectives out to Pecan Grove, a town near the Campisciano farm in St. Rose, where — according to Tony Gendusa's brother Frank — the missing man's sweetheart lived, but they found nothing.

Patorno, however, kept digging, and he soon began to turn up some suggestive connections between Tony Gendusa and a few of the other suspects in the crime. Gendusa, he learned, had been seen with prime suspect Tony Costa several times in the weeks before the kidnapping, often accompanied by another man, Francisco Luchesi. Now Luchesi was also missing. And so, apparently, was another known associate named Leonardo Gebbia, who lived with his sister and parents in a house just a few doors away from the Lamana residence. According to neighborhood gossip, the Gebbias knew more about Walter Lamana's disappearance than they had revealed to the police. Mrs. Gebbia, Leonardo's mother, had allegedly visited Mrs. Lamana several times since the kidnapping, assuring her that little Walter was safe and encouraging the Lamanas to pay the ransom to get him back. At the time, her words had been dismissed as the well-meant reassurances of an aging neighbor. But now they were beginning to seem rather more sinister.

Very early one morning, police staged a raid on the Gebbia home. Leonardo Gebbia was in the house, still in bed, and he was apprehended without incident. And his arrest proved to be the break that ultimately unraveled the entire conspiracy. Professing his own innocence in the plot, he nonetheless confessed to know all about it. He had seen Tony Costa leading the boy away from the undertaking parlor, he said. He'd seen Costa turn the boy over to a man named Stefano Monfre, who had been waiting at the corner of Bourbon and St. Philip with a covered wagon, driven by Francisco Luchesi. Gebbia also confirmed that Tony Gendusa had written the Black Hand letter demanding $6,000.

This was sufficient information for Judge Patorno to start making new arrests. He had the entire Gebbia family locked up, along with Tony Gendusa's brother Frank, Stefano Monfre's wife, and even the couple who, with the Gebbias, ran the rooming house on St. Philip.

But the most important revelation came in the confession of Gebbia's sister, Nicolina, who verified what Patorno had long suspected — that the boy had been taken to the Campisciano farm in St. Rose. Ignazio Campisciano, of course, had been arrested and released some days earlier for lack of evidence. Now Patorno had the corroboration he needed to proceed more aggressively against the farmer. He arranged with the Illinois Central Railroad for a special train to St. Rose and assembled a posse to head out there that evening. Among the posse members was a trainmaster for the railroad named Frank T. Mooney — the same man who ten years later would become Superintendent of Police. Mooney, apparently interested in police work even then, involved himself closely in the Campisciano arrest, and even provided the *Daily Picayune* with a sensational account of it.

After the special train arrived at Pecan Grove at around midnight, Mooney explained, "We put out the headlight of the engine and all the lights in the coach, and

[then] walked the tracks for one and a half miles to Campisciano's houses." Patorno put a guard around both buildings — Campisciano's home and a shed about fifty yards away, where it was believed Walter Lamana might be held. Then they pounded on Campisciano's door until they had roused him from sleep. The farmer finally came to the door in his underclothes.

"Our party pushed the door open and stepped inside," Mooney told the *Picayune:*

Judge Patorno spoke out sharply: "Give us the boy. We came for the child."

Campisciano stood without a word.

"Where is the Lamana boy?" demanded Judge Patorno, without a quiver.

The Italian only shrugged his shoulders in the Roman style, pleading ignorance. He declared he knew nothing of the matter and stoutly maintained that position.

[But] the party had come there determined. It was not to be put off as it had been once before. Campisciano was quickly seized and bound hand and foot. His hands were pinioned behind his back and his legs were bound with ropes. He was carried outside and a rope [was] quickly fastened around his neck.

Intimidated by this somewhat less-than-legal interrogation technique, Campisciano relented and indicated that he would speak. The noose around his neck was loosened, and he proceeded to tell how Monfre, Luchesi, and two other men, one of whom he knew as Angelo Incarcaterra, had brought the boy to his house in a covered wagon. But when Patorno asked the farmer where the boy was now, the man turned stonily silent. Again the rope was tightened around his neck, and he was threatened with hanging from a nearby tree. Finally, he gave in. When the rope was again loosened, Campisciano made the admission that everyone had feared: "The boy is dead."

"He went on to relate every detail of the heinous crime," Mooney continued. "He took us over to the other house and showed us the very spot and the position the child was lying [in] when he was murdered, choked to death. He pleaded that he had nothing whatsoever to do with it and that the others had committed the deed."

Judge Patorno demanded that Campisciano lead them to the boy's body. The farmer wanted to wait until morning, since the place was deep in the swamps behind his house and the moon had already set. But Patorno insisted. And so they set off, several men holding lanterns as they picked their way through the marshy wilderness. Campisciano begged his captors to untie his hands, so he could at least push aside the reeds as he walked. Patorno agreed, but they kept a rope around his neck and another around his shoulders, each held by one of the posse, to ensure that the farmer didn't slip away in the gloom.

"You can imagine the situation," Mooney told the *Picayune,* "this Italian leading a party through the swamp, wading in water to their waists and through brush and briars. None of us felt sure that he had told us the truth, and who knew that this leader of the Black Hand was not leading us into a death trap." But finally, several miles into the fetid swamp, Campisciano stopped and pointed to a spot under some willow branches. "There," he said.

"And he told the truth," Mooney reported. "Upon lifting the heavy boughs, we saw this gray-colored bundle. It was resting on some wild cane reeds. The odor was terrible, and as the bundle was picked up and the blanket unwrapped, the head dropped from the shoulders."

This last macabre detail — of the boy's head detaching from the torso, apparently as a result of advanced decomposition — would be picked up and headlined in newspapers all around the country over the next few days. In New Orleans, it raised the level of mob hysteria to a new and feverish pitch. When the body was brought back to the city and laid out in the morgue, thousands of people assailed the building. The *Daily Picayune* described the scene:

> The mob thronged the yard and jammed through the narrow door of the dead house. There, the insane desire to possess some gruesome souvenir of the most horrible crime to shock New Orleans since the Hennessy assassination took hold of the people, and they fought and fell over each other in an effort to tear off pieces of the clothes in which the body had been found, and which still lay, reeking with maggots and shreds of rotting flesh, on the slab.

Meanwhile, other information was emerging from interrogations with the incarcerated suspects. According to Campisciano, Walter Lamana had actually been killed on the Wednesday following the kidnapping, meaning that the child had been dead for ten days already. Apparently, the kidnappers had been frightened by news of the mob actions in New Orleans that evening and had decided to abort the kidnapping. So Angelo Incarcaterra — allegedly on the order of Leonardo Gebbia, the leader of the group — had seized the boy and unceremoniously strangled him to death. Then they had wrapped the body in a blanket and carried it out to a remote corner of the swamp, where they hoped it would never be found.

The extent of the conspiracy involved in this ugly piece of business was difficult for officials to assess. Police had six of the principal suspects in custody — Campisciano and his wife, Tony Costa, Frank Gendusa, and Leonardo and Nicolina Gebbia. At least four were still at large, including Luchesi the wagon driver; Tony Gendusa the letter writer; Stefano Monfre, who owned the covered wagon; and Angelo Incarcaterra, who had actually strangled the boy. But there were several other conspirators mentioned in various bits of testimony who remained unaccounted-for — a "tall man named Joe," whom Campisciano had seen with Stefano Monfre on the morning after the kidnapping; a mysterious man with a pockmarked face who had come to Monfre's house several times before the kidnapping; and — perhaps most tellingly — a "wronged man" named "Mr. Cristina." Could this have been Paolo Di Christina, the associate of capo Francisco Genova who had been involved in the 1902 Luciano incident? Whatever the connections, it was clear that the kidnapping cabal was large and complex. That such an elaborate conspiracy could have flourished in the festering alleys of the lower French Quarter — apparently known to so many residents, none of whom saw fit to report it to the police — was appalling. So much for the so-called lesson of the Hennessy lynching.

Still, at least some members of the community had come forward with information, and so the Italian Vigilance Committee tried to put as good a face on the situation as they could. "The reign of the Black Hand is over in New Orleans," they told the *Times-Democrat* — though it was clearly a declaration more hopeful than justified.

Police continued to pursue the missing suspects, even sending detectives to Kansas to check out a tip that Stefano Monfre might be hiding out with relatives there. But it soon became apparent that Monfre and the other absent conspirators were gone for good. The six suspects in custody, meanwhile, were indicted and sent to the prison in Hahnville, the seat of St. Charles Parish (where the case would be tried, since the murder had occurred in that parish).

The trial of the first four defendants began at the courthouse in Hahnville on July 15. Nicolina and Leonardo Gebbia would be tried at a later date, but the Campiscianos, Tony Costa, and Frank Gendusa would face a jury first. Autopsy results had indicated that Walter Lamana had been killed by a hatchet blow to the forehead; this had only increased the public's rage at the perpetrators, and the trial attracted huge, hostile crowds to the little county seat. Security was heavy, with scores of sheriff's deputies and other police on hand to keep order.

The trial lasted four days. During their testimony, the defendants predictably professed their own innocence of any active role in the affair, casting themselves as merely frightened witnesses to acts perpetrated by the five men and one woman still at large or not yet on trial. But in this case, unlike in the Hennessy case sixteen years earlier, the evidence against the accused was persuasive. The police work had been far more careful this time, and no one but the defense attorney seemed at all discomfited by the fact that Campisciano had been forced to confess with a rope around his neck. Even so, the jury, after deliberating for less than an hour, came back to the courtroom with a qualified verdict. "Guilty," the foreman announced, but "without capital punishment." The evidence, as one juror later explained, was simply not conclusive enough to justify hanging.

It took three companies of the state militia, bayonets drawn, to prevent the enraged crowds outside the courtroom from administering their own form of justice — on the defendants *and* on the jurors. One confrontation nearly erupted into bloody violence when a train commandeered by an irate mob from New Orleans was turned back at gunpoint from the tiny Hahnville station. Back in New Orleans, Mayor Martin Behrman was forced to order the closing of all saloons, hotel bars, and private clubs in the city, and to send a force of special police into the Italian quarter to keep order and defend the Lamanas' neighbors. These precautions proved effective. Despite the all-too-predictable mob cries of "We want the Dagos!" the widespread violence that had characterized the Hennessy and Robert Charles affairs never materialized.

Meanwhile, the *Daily Item* was almost wistful in its editorial regrets over what it — and virtually every other paper in New Orleans — considered a ridiculous outcome. "A real verdict, a verdict with a capital punishment attachment in this Lamana case, would have gone far to make them [i.e., 'lower-class Sicilians'] recognize that American law was a vital and mighty thing — a thing to fear. . . . So much of good would surely have resulted from a legal execution in the premises. . . ."

In the end, the people of New Orleans did get that legal execution. The trial of Leonardo and Nicolina Gebbia — much delayed because of the high feeling provoked by the earlier trial — ended with both brother and sister being found guilty and sentenced to hang. Nicolina's sentence was later commuted to life in prison (the prospect of executing a woman was still repugnant to many, no matter what the crime). But on Friday, July 16, 1909, Leonardo Gebbia was led to a scaffold in the Hahnville prison yard and hanged by the neck until he was dead. Afterward, the noose was presented to Peter Lamana, who expressed his gratitude that at least one of the perpetrators had gotten his "just deserts."

Ultimately, something tangible did come out of the Lamana tragedy. The year after Gebbia's execution, the Louisiana state legislature passed a law mandating a death sentence for anyone convicted of kidnapping a child. It was — for some, at least — a satisfying outcome. But any notion that the Black Hand had been routed for good in the Crescent City would eventually be dispelled, and much sooner than even the most pessimistic New Orleanian might have expected.

■ ■ ■ ■

CHAPTER 12
A REAWAKENING

■ ■ ■ ■

Philip Werlein **Louisiana Division, New
Orleans Public Library**

The second wave of reform arrived in 1907 — in the shape of a woman wielding an ax.

A few days before Christmas, a Northeastern Railroad train from Mississippi pulled into New Orleans bearing one of the iconic reform figures of the age. Carrie Nation, the hatchet-swinging firebrand from Garrard County, Kentucky — famous nationwide for her saloon-smashing campaign to stamp out "Demon Rum" and all of its attendant vices — had come to the city as part of a speaking tour throughout the American South. Armed with a Bible and an ample supply of miniature gold-plated hatchets to distribute as souvenirs, she had planned out a full program of lectures and prayer meetings in some of the town's most notorious dens of iniquity. She knew that she'd face plenty of opposition, but Carrie Nation was determined to save the Crescent City's soul.

Initially, the white-haired, lantern-jawed reformer had been reluctant to bring her message to the so-called Great Southern Babylon. "New Orleans is too tough a place for me to tackle," she'd told reporters in Birmingham in mid-December. "It is a very, very bad place . . . and I am getting too old."

But somehow she had thought better of her decision. "I believe in being everlastingly on the warpath," she announced a few days later, explaining her change of heart. "We must fight the devil. And there *are* real devils." Nowhere was that truer, apparently, than in New Orleans, and so she had come after all.

Trailing an entourage of newsmen, admirers, and gawkers, Nation went straight from the train station to City Hall to meet with Mayor Martin Behrman. His Honor the Mayor, no slouch himself when it came to deviltry, seemed somewhat amused by the compact but passionate old woman who appeared at his office door in her trademark widow's weeds. Speaking before reporters, Behrman welcomed her to the city but insisted that she refrain from any saloon-smashing while she was there.

But Nation could make no promises. "I am nothing but a lump of mud in the hands of God," she said. "Would the mayor be so audacious as to refuse the Lord his right to smash?"

Behrman thought about this for a moment before responding that "he would not attempt to prevent the Lord, but he certainly would have his officers prevent her." Thus they parted on good if somewhat uneasy terms, with a promise to meet again before she left town.

Over the next three days, Mrs. Nation made a thorough tour of the city's hotels, taverns, and barrelhouses, preaching her message of temperance to all who would listen. The time had come, she insisted, for the total prohibition of alcohol — not just in New Orleans but in the nation at large. "President [Theodore] Roosevelt is a bag of wind," she told one crowd at the St. Charles Hotel. "Roosevelt, Busch, Schlitz, Pabst, and Muerlein are the quintet which is doing America much harm. The first is a beer-guzzling Dutchman, and the others are making it [the beer] for him and his loyal subjects. The country should be ashamed of the people ruling it!"

But alcohol was only one of the targets of Mrs. Nation's wrath. Gambling, smoking, foul language, "sexual impurity," and, of course, prostitution were also on her prohibition agenda, so she made sure to investigate Storyville itself. She first accepted an invitation from Emma Johnson to visit the House of All Nations, perhaps the most flagrantly depraved of all the Storyville brothels. Invited into the parlor with the madam and her charges, the fiery orator ended up doing more listening than preaching. One by one, the women of the place explained to her how they had come to prostitution not as a result of coercion or entrapment by an evil seducer — the tendentious "white slavery" explanation put forth by many reformers of the day — but rather by their own free will. Forced to fend for themselves in a world where female workers made pennies a day in so-called legitimate jobs, they had instead chosen their current profession. All who spoke to Mrs. Nation, in fact, professed to be content with their lives and saw very little wrong in them. Madam Johnson herself even claimed that she prayed regularly, and fully expected to end up in heaven.

This last may have been the most shocking thing Mrs. Nation heard in Storyville on that Saturday night. But she found a more suitably repentant audience at her second stop in the District — at Josie Arlington's palace on Basin Street. Here the ladies of the house listened respectfully as Nation roundly rebuked them and urged them to repent their ways, falling onto her knees at one point to pray for their salvation. Josie Arlington, whose thoughts of late had been turning in precisely this direction, proved to be a particularly receptive auditor. With some emotion, the queen of the demimonde promised the great reformer that she would heed the call to return to a more respectable way of life. Josie claimed that she would retire soon and use her fortune — now totaling some $60,000, as she pointedly confided — to build a home for fallen women, so that they would not have to turn to prostitution to survive. She would do this, Josie said, just "as soon as [I get] a little richer."

Perhaps frustrated by the conspicuous lack of any instant converts to her cause in Storyville, Nation arrived at her last stop of the night, Tom Anderson's Annex, with her usual pugnacity — and her ax, apparently — on full display. According to one story, Anderson had heard beforehand that she was on her way, and so had cleared the long bar of all but the cheapest whiskey. When Nation and her entourage entered the Annex, Anderson was there to greet her, dressed in his finest evening clothes. "Welcome, Mrs. Nation," he said, giving her a deferential bow. "I've been expecting you."

She was not impressed. After snatching a cigarette from the mouth of one of the customers hovering around her, she allegedly walked over to the bar with her ax and smashed several of the whiskey glasses standing on it. Then she turned to Anderson and said, "Want to make something of it?"

Unruffled as always, Anderson bowed again. "Mrs. Nation," he oozed, "the pleasure is all mine."

It was to be her toughest audience of the night. Provided with a crate to stand on, Nation addressed the crowd of men in the bar, urging them to shun the saloons, the gambling houses, and the brothels and instead to "be men." Numerous times she was interrupted by drunken hecklers, but she was undeterred. She talked, in fact, for almost a full hour — until manager Billy Struve, concerned about the Sunday Closing Law, forcefully brought the proceedings to a close at a few minutes before twelve. By the stroke of midnight, Nation and her audience were all out on the banquette in front of the Annex. She then rode home from her evening of slumming in Storyville, according to the *Daily Picayune,* "none the worse for her lively experience."

By the time Mrs. Nation left the city the next day, however, she was looking noticeably pale and worn out. After giving a lecture to an audience of eight hundred at the local YMCA (a lecture that reportedly included such lurid descriptions of the goings-on in Storyville that even the *Picayune* was scandalized on behalf of the women present), she returned to City Hall to pay her respects to the mayor. At their meeting, she asked Behrman to promise that he would stamp out the horrible practices she had witnessed in the District. The mayor's response is unrecorded, but most likely he demurred. And with that, Carrie Nation moved on. She was, by her own admission, old and tired now, and maybe New Orleans really was too tough a place for her. That evening, after three days in the belly of the beast, she quietly boarded a ship bound for Florida, where, one can presume, the resident sinners weren't quite so recalcitrant.

To say that Carrie Nation's visit in late 1907 galvanized the city's slumbering moral reformers would perhaps be an exaggeration. But her appearance did coincide with the beginning of renewed efforts to take control of New Orleans' persistent sin problem, and to do so in a rather less accommodative way. Tolerance and segregation of vice had been tried, and this is what had resulted — rich madams, contented whores, booming business in saloons and gambling halls, and a nightly tableau of debauchery in the District that was all too reminiscent of a painting by Brueghel the Younger. The sheer complacency and matter-of-factness of sin in the Crescent City — captured vividly in a series of Storyville portraits executed around this time by a white Creole photographer named E. J. Bellocq — indicated to many that a different approach was needed, and that the whole idea of Storyville had outlived its usefulness. In any case, Victorian attitudes toward prostitution were changing. No longer was it viewed as a distasteful but necessary safeguard for respectable women — as a safety valve of sorts for the release of male sexual energy.

With the rise of the Social Hygiene and other Progressive Era movements, prostitution was increasingly being seen as a threat, a conduit by which ills like syphilis and gonorrhea could invade the sanctity of the home. As such, it was not enough just to tuck it away in its own district. Rather, it had to be stamped out entirely. And as Carrie Nation's sermons had made clear, the new spirit of prohibition was nothing if not comprehensive, targeting not just prostitution and alcohol but gambling, dancing, tobacco use, and — in New Orleans, at least — the lingering affront to decency of interracial fraternization, represented most visibly by the so-called octoroon houses of Basin Street.

One big new problem with Storyville — in the reformers' eyes — was that the supposedly isolated vice district was no longer so isolated. On June 1, 1908, a new union railroad terminal opened for business right at the intersection of Basin Street and Canal. This new "Frisco depot," designed by Chicago architect Daniel Burnham, was a gorgeous neoclassical pile with high ceilings and sweeping architectural lines that would have been a credit to any city. But the terminal's location forced arriving trains to come directly down the middle of Basin Street, passing every one of that street's luxury brothels on the way. Within weeks of the station's opening, reports were already flooding in —

of naked prostitutes waving to passengers from brothel windows, of so-called light-houses (usually young boys) waiting in the terminal to lead willing male arrivals to the nearby District, and even of unsuspecting young women wandering off into the streets of Storyville in search of their hotels. For those trying to improve the city's reputation as a serious center for business and commerce, the situation was a disaster.

First to respond to this new embarrassment was the Travelers Aid Society, a women's organization founded by New Orleans' reformist ERA Club to prevent young girls from being recruited by the city's brothels. By August of 1908, they were already agitating to move the Basin Street houses from their current location and convert the buildings to workers' housing. "We have no doubt that every person and organization of good moral and civic principles in the city will join us in what we have undertaken," the society's spokesperson, Mary Werlein, told reporters. "The restricted district was already unfortunately located, on almost every ground imaginable, but now that several railroads are emptying thousands of new people at its very doors, it seems to us [that] we can not properly allow such an entry into our city to be maintained. First impressions are the strongest, and we can imagine no more undesirable first impression of New Orleans than this."

But the true leader of this new offensive against Storyville was Mary Werlein's nephew Philip, scion of the venerable Werlein family that had been doing business in New Orleans since 1853. The Werlein Music Store on Canal Street — founded by Philip's grandfather, a Bavarian pianist and composer — had been the local bastion of traditional music for decades. True, the store was the source of many of the instruments played by the city's jazzmen (it's where Kid Ory bought the trombone that led to his 1905 encounter with Buddy Bolden), but the company was proudest of its distinction as the original publisher of the classic Southern anthem "Dixie."

Like Joseph Shakspeare, W. S. Parkerson, Sidney Story, and many of the other reform leaders who preceded him, Philip Werlein was a blue-blood through and through. President of the Pickwick, Boston, *and* New Orleans Country Clubs; director of the Interstate Bank; sponsor of the French Opera House; and now president of the New Orleans Progressive Union, he was the perfect embodiment of the wealthy white establishment that had been actively trying to reform the city for two decades now. In 1909, Werlein and the Progressive Union proposed an alternative solution to the problem of the Basin Street depot. Instead of moving the street's brothels as his aunt suggested, Werlein proposed to erect a wooden screen that would essentially put a wall between the depot and the Storyville side of Basin Street. This proposal, silly as it sounds, actually got as far as the city council, but the aldermen ended up defeating it soundly, seeing it as entirely impracticable. Undeterred, both Werleins vowed to fight on.

Other reform efforts on the state level were making better progress. In 1908, the Louisiana legislature passed the so-called Gay-Shattuck Bill. Pushed through mainly by conservative elements in the northern parishes of the state, the measure was a comprehensive law that attacked the vice problem on virtually every front — addressing the issues of wine, women, *and* song. Besides dramatically raising the license fees for selling alcohol statewide, it banned women from patronizing or working in any place where liquor was sold. The law also prohibited the serving of blacks and whites in the same establishment, and made musical performances illegal in all saloons. The only exception to these rules was one made for restaurants and hotels where meals were served. But for the vast majority of businesses in Storyville, the law's implications were dire: No more jazz combos at the Arlington Annex (which had no kitchen), no more Champagne at Lulu White's Mahogany Hall, no more interracial fraternization at the dance halls on Franklin Street if alcohol was being served. In fact, the *Daily Item* predicted that fully one-half of the barrooms in New Orleans would be forced into bankruptcy once the law took effect in early 1909.

And indeed, Gay-Shattuck did "put the lid down in the Tenderloin," as the newspapers liked to say — at least at first. In January, when the new rules were implemented, the *Daily Picayune* noted with satisfaction that "the saloon-men and divekeepers raised a howl which vibrated from one end of the District to the other. The old familiar blast of the trombone and cornet, and the accompanying shriek of the clarionet [*sic*], were not among the attractions to lure the slummer into the saloons and dance halls."

But the denizens of Storyville were nothing if not resourceful. Noting the exception in the law for places serving meals, the establishments of the District were soon styling themselves as restaurants. One saloon set up a makeshift tamale stand next to its front door, while many another club owner or saloonkeeper unearthed some "antique sandwich" that could be passed around the room indefinitely as proof of the establishment's culinary bona fides. Exploitation of this loophole — combined with a general lack of enforcement by Mayor Behrman's eminently persuadable police force — meant that it was soon business-as-usual for most places in the District, at least while no one in authority was watching.

For the mayor of Storyville, now in his early fifties and graying into an ever-more distinguished-looking middle age, the depredations of the city's reformers were still taking a relatively minor toll on the operations of his empire of sin. The first decade of the District's existence had proved lucrative indeed for him, and Tom Anderson now found himself a very rich man. Growing profits from his various Tenderloin businesses were only part of the bounty; his legitimate oil interests had also thrived, allowing him to sell his old Record Oil Company and start a new enterprise — Liberty Oil — that promised to be an even greater success. Vice and hydrocarbons had proved to be the twin engines of New Orleans' prosperity, and Tom Anderson had a hand in both.

But there were indications that Anderson's charmed life might be entering a more difficult phase. It had begun with a personal tragedy. Sometime in mid-1907, Olive Anderson had become sick. The exact nature of her illness remains unclear, but she probably developed some form of cancer. She underwent two surgeries that fall, and although her doctors were at first optimistic, complications had set in. By December, it was clear that she would not survive. Tom would later claim that he and Ollie had married in June of 1898 (which seems unlikely, given that his divorce from Catherine Turnbull did not become official until the following year), but they had another ceremony performed at her deathbed in the Hôtel-Dieu Hospital. Ollie, the former prostitute, had recently converted to Catholicism and wanted a priest to officiate. But since the Church did not recognize Anderson's divorce from his second wife, this proved impossible. And so a judge had done the deed — in Ollie's hospital room, with a nurse as witness — a few days before Christmas. Ollie died on December 26. Two days later, the funeral was held at the home of Tom's daughter, Irene — now Mrs. George Delsa. Attending were some of the Andersons' closest friends, including Mayor Behrman, former police chief John Journée, Billy Struve, W. J. O'Connor (the man who had been with David Hennessy on the night of his assassination), and, of course, Josie Arlington, aka Mrs. Tom Brady.

His wife's death seemed to change Tom Anderson's luck. It was just a few months later that reformers began their assault on sin in the Crescent City, and much of the onslaught seemed to be targeted primarily at the mayor of Storyville himself. In March of 1908, the reverends E. L. Collins and S. A. Smith, superintendents of the Kentucky and

Louisiana Anti-Saloon Leagues, came to New Orleans to carry out an investigation of conditions in Storyville. What they found was — predictably — shocking: "If an absolutely truthful man had sworn on the witness stand that things were as bad as they are, I would never have believed them," Reverend Collins told the press. "For shame to flaunt itself so openly and brazenly right on the streets is something that I have never seen in my life." Dr. Smith, however, offered some hope: "Tom Anderson and such cattle," he said, "want everything stopped but dirtiness and evil. But public opinion is rising against them, bless your hearts, and their course will be stayed."

Largely in response to appeals like this, the Gay-Shattuck Law was passed shortly thereafter. But since Anderson and the other proprietors of the District proved so adept at getting around its provisions, the most effective attacks on Anderson County came via Tom's old nemesis — the Sunday Closing Law. Anderson had already been inconvenienced several times on this issue, but in the renewed spirit of reform heralded by Gay-Shattuck, the attempts at Sabbath-day entrapment became more frequent. One case against Anderson in September of 1909 actually came to trial. The charges were eventually dropped, however, when it was discovered that the two arresting officers — intentionally or otherwise — had failed to secure any evidence of the violation.

But Anderson soon found a more formidable foe in the person of Rev. J. Benjamin Lawrence, pastor of the First Baptist Church. Lawrence, a leader of the city's temperance movement, began conducting his own undercover investigation of the city's demimonde in June of 1910. He, along with a young man named Alvin Callendar and a third man, entered the Arlington Restaurant on a Sunday. Lawrence ordered a bottle of whiskey, Callendar ordered a beer, and the third man requested a pack of cigarettes. All were served — and this time, the evidence was retained and turned over to the police waiting outside. Tom Anderson and his bartender were promptly arrested and charged with three counts of violating the Sunday Closing Law and one count of selling alcohol to a minor (since Callendar turned out to be just seventeen years old).

The case, which took months to work its way through the courts, created a furor in the city far out of proportion to the relatively minor transgressions that had generated it. Reformers were determined to punish Tom Anderson, while the mayor of Storyville himself, backed by powerful wholesale alcohol interests, was equally determined to make the case go away. And so Anderson's lawyers made prosecution of the case as difficult for officials as possible. At first, no judge or prosecutor — for reasons known only to themselves — seemed willing to try the case at all. After repeated continuances, the matter was finally brought to court, only to be thrown out on a technicality: no proof could be obtained that Tom Anderson even owned the Arlington Restaurant on Rampart Street (despite the fact — pointed out by the exasperated *Daily Item* — that a large sign outside the establishment had prominently displayed his name as proprietor for more than fifteen years). When the district attorney ordered a new trial, the proceedings were again delayed when the new affidavits drawn up for trial proved defective, lacking a valid address for the saloon in which the infractions had allegedly taken place. Outraged, the *Item* insisted that this nonsense be stopped and that the case be resolved. "No good excuse can be offered for permitting this case to lie in the files until the witnesses die or move to Montana," the paper fulminated in an editorial. "The defendant may need a vacation, the weather may be uncomfortably warm, or the barroom cat may have the mumps — but the case of the State of Louisiana against Thomas C. Anderson should be prosecuted promptly."

Ultimately, the unstoppable force and the immovable object came to terms. Anderson agreed to plead guilty to one count of selling whiskey on a Sunday if the other charges were dropped. The prosecution agreed, and so Tom Anderson paid a $25 fine (plus another $50 for selling to a minor — a matter resolved separately in Juvenile Court). Reverend Lawrence, of course, claimed victory. But Tom Anderson knew better. The $75 was just a minor cost of doing business. And although he and his backers had probably paid far more than that in legal fees, their point had been made: you could fight the mayor of Storyville and perhaps even win a round or two, but the price would be exceedingly high.

And so the vice mills of Storyville rolled on more or less unchecked. Lulu White, Emma Johnson, and Willie Piazza continued to do business on Basin Street, within plain sight of the passengers arriving at the Frisco depot. In the dives and dance halls of Franklin Street, Freddie Keppard, "Big Eye" Louis Nelson, and the young wunderkind Sidney Bechet continued to play their new music to mixed audiences, provided there was an old ham sandwich on the premises. But for one Storyville icon, life had changed. A few years after her evening with Carrie Nation, Josie Arlington had retired and left the profession as promised. She leased the Basin Street brothel to her former housekeeper, Anna Casey, but retained ownership, thereby ensuring an ample revenue stream to support the family's luxurious new life on Esplanade Avenue. And though her plans to build a home for wayward girls were apparently on hold (and would in fact never come to fruition), she was now at least free of the taint of Basin Street in all ways but financial. She and her beloved niece Anna could spend all of their time together now, shopping, gardening, making excursions to Anna's Villa in Covington, and generally living the life of just the kind of respectable upper-class family that Anna still believed she belonged to.

For the woman now known to the world as Mrs. John Thomas Brady, this transformation must have come with overtones of revenge. Her yearnings for respectability had always seemed shaded by a certain contempt for those born into the condition naturally, and this contempt had erupted memorably on at least one occasion late in her career. According to hoary Storyville legend, the queen of the demimonde had by 1906 come to resent the daring young persons of socially prominent families who would show up incognito at Tom Anderson's annual Mardi Gras fete, the Ball of the Two Well Known Gentlemen. Masked in Carnival regalia, these slumming voyeurs would gape condescendingly at the colorful revels of fallen women and their sporting men, all while remaining safely anonymous behind their masks. "Josie Arlington solved the problem," one Storyville chronicler explained, "by arranging for the police to raid the affair and to arrest any woman who did not carry a card registering her as a prostitute in good standing. The stratagem caused great embarrassment to the large number of ladies of New Orleans 'high society' who were summarily carted off to the police station, unmasked, and sent home." But now, in 1909, Arlington had an even sweeter revenge: those society ladies who enjoyed masquerading as prostitutes for a night would now have to tolerate a prostitute masquerading as a society lady for the rest of her life.

But Mrs. Brady seemed capable of extracting only so much pleasure from her new life of respectability. According to reports from friends and associates, the retired madam became increasingly morbid and religious over the next few years. Eventually, she spent $8,000 on an elaborate red-marble tomb in Metairie Cemetery. Flanked by two imposing stone flambeaux, the miniature temple featured elegant carvings and bas-reliefs front and back. At the doors to the tomb stood a statue of a beautiful young woman carrying an armful of roses, her other hand placed against the door as if in the act of pushing it open.

Mrs. Brady had meanwhile decided to devote the rest of her life to the cultivation of her adored niece. "I am living only for Anna," she confided to a friend, and indeed, the two women were reportedly inseparable now. At one point, Mrs. Brady confessed that she would rue the day that Anna finally got married. When the girl asked why, her aunt said simply, "Because men are dogs."

For a woman who'd spent her entire life catering to the carnal desires of thousands of men, the sentiment was perhaps understandable. But Anna was now in her mid-twenties. How much longer could even the most sheltered innocent be kept in ignorance of the basic facts of her own deceptively privileged life?

By 1910, it had become clear that reformers generally — and Philip Werlein in particular — were not going to give up their campaign against Storyville. Their proposals to screen off the District and to move the Basin Street brothels had proven both unpopular and politically untenable. But now Werlein, armed with the provisions of the Gay-Shattuck Law, decided to try a new tack. And it would center on the one issue about which moral reformers, business reformers, and machine politicians were all of one mind — race: "The one thing that all Southerners agree upon is the necessity of preserving our racial purity," Werlein told reporters in early February. "The open association of white men and

Negro women on Basin Street, which is now permitted by our authorities, should fill us with shame as it fills the visitor from the North with amazement."

In the Gay-Shattuck Law, which forbade any alcohol purveyor from serving both blacks and whites in the same building, and in another 1908 law against interracial concubinage, Werlein thought he had the ammunition needed to abolish at least the so-called octoroon houses, and he was willing to use it. "I will enlist the aid of every minister in New Orleans," he vowed. "I am determined to arouse public sentiment against the awful conditions which exist. . . . It is a shame and a disgrace that Negro dives like those of Emma Johnson, Willie Piazza, and Lulu White, whose infamy is linked abroad with the fair name of New Orleans, should be allowed to exist and to boldly stare respectable people in the face." His conclusion: "These resorts should be exterminated, and the Negresses who run them driven from the city."

The war against Storyville thus entered a new and particularly ugly stage. Until now, the District had been a lone holdout in the overall movement in New Orleans toward greater repression of African Americans. Black men had never been allowed to come to Storyville proper as brothel customers (even the black crib prostitutes were available to whites only), but they had always been able to work, dance, and drink there. And certainly sexual congress between white men and black women had not only been allowed but actively encouraged and advertised. All of this, however, was to change over the next few years, as reformers attempted to move the city closer to traditional Southern norms of racial regimentation. Life in Storyville — as both blacks *and* whites had known it — was about to change.

But perhaps the greatest threat to the District would come not from those who wanted to destroy it but rather from those who wanted to exploit it. For the remarkable success of Storyville had not gone unnoticed in the criminal underworlds in the rest of the country. A number of gangsters from places like New York and Chicago had been arriving in the Crescent City in recent years, eager to win their share of the bounty. One pair of brothers from New York — Abraham and Isidore Sapir (or Shapiro), alleged white slavers looking to expand their interests — seemed especially determined to shake up the status quo of Anderson County. Changing their names to Harry and Charles Parker, respectively, they came to New Orleans in the early years of the twentieth century and opened a saloon on the corner of Liberty and Customhouse Streets. In 1910, they sold that saloon and bought a dance hall on Franklin Street called the 101 Ranch, right behind Tom Anderson's Annex. By all reports, they were not pleasant, easygoing fellows like the mayor of Storyville. And they were apparently eager to show the local vice lords just how a tenderloin was supposed to be run.

CHAPTER 13
AN INCIDENT ON
FRANKLIN STREET

Young Louis Armstrong (circled) in the Waif's Home Band
Louisiana State Museum Jazz Collection

When the Parker brothers first decided to get into the dance-hall business in Storyville, their prospects for success were bright. A dance craze had been sweeping the country, and bold new steps like the bunny hug, the grizzly bear, and the turkey trot were becoming wildly popular — in New Orleans as in the rest of the nation. Local clergymen and bluestockings may have complained, pointing to provisions of the Gay-Shattuck Law that were supposed to keep women, alcohol, and music strictly separated. But police enforcement had so far been lax. Business was good, and by 1910 numerous dance halls and cabarets had opened in Storyville, clustering mainly on and around Franklin Street, just one block behind the Basin Street brothels. The Parkers' 101 Ranch quickly became one of the liveliest and most popular venues in the District, attracting crowds to hear some of the best black bands in the city.

But the Parkers weren't satisfied. The

competition for customers on Franklin Street was keen, and the brothers from New York were determined to eliminate some of their homegrown rivals. Their first target was John "Peg" Anstedt, the popular, one-legged proprietor of Anstedt's Saloon (a place where many white musicians like Nick LaRocca came to hear the black bands). According to local gossip, in 1911, Charles Parker began spending time with Anstedt's mistress — a prostitute named May Gilbert — hoping to convince her to swear out an affidavit accusing her lover of being engaged in the white-slavery trade. When Anstedt heard about this, he was enraged, and responded as one typically did in Storyville in 1911 — by taking a potshot at Parker one evening in a Franklin Street saloon. The bullet missed its mark, as did Parker's retaliatory shot at Anstedt sometime later at another District dive. But although no one was hurt or arrested in the incident, it did make one thing clear — the power structure that had grown up in the District in its first decade of existence was about to be challenged.

In 1912, the Parkers sold the 101 Ranch to William Phillips, a local restaurateur (and friend of Peg Anstedt's). Phillips renovated the building and reopened it as the 102 Ranch, a venue that soon became a popular gathering place for the city's horse players. Tom Anderson — still very much involved in the racing world — was said to occasionally take refuge at the 102, whenever he tired of the many tourists who came to his Annex around the corner and insisted on seeing the great host.

But the Parkers had not left the dance-hall business. That same year, in fact, they opened the Tuxedo, almost directly across the street from the 102 Ranch — a move that was in direct violation of a clause in their sales agreement with Phillips. The new Tuxedo, moreover, was a large and modern entertainment complex, with a dime-a-dance section in the rear and a large bar up front that opened out directly onto Franklin Street. Soon the Parkers were directly competing with Phillips for the best of the city's musical talent.

Even so, Phillips, to the Parkers' annoyance, continued to attract a large share of the dance-hall business. The rivals argued frequently, sometimes coming to blows in the street. The resulting brawls soon created lurid newspaper headlines that ended up hurting Storyville's reputation at a particularly inopportune time, just when reformers were looking for ammunition in their campaign to close the District.

For New Orleans' jazzmen, however, the increasing competition among dance-hall and cabaret operators was a boon. Thanks to the ongoing dance craze — to which the revolutionary new sound proved especially conducive — jazz was becoming increasingly popular, not just with the denizens of poor black neighborhoods but among the city's white "sporting set" as well. Work was plentiful, and musicians were finally making enough money to give up their day jobs and play full-time. Clarinetist Alphonse Picou described a typical jazzman's schedule during these years. "I worked at my trade all week. All day Saturday I would play in a wagon to advertise the dance that night. [Then I'd] play all night. Next morning we have to be at the depot at seven to catch the train for the lake. Play for the picnic at the lake all day. Come back and play a dance all Sunday night. Monday we advertise for the Monday night ball and play *that* Monday night. Sometimes my clarinet seemed to weigh a thousand pounds. . . ."

By this time, most of the now-storied venues of early New Orleans jazz were up and running. In 1910, Italian businessman Peter Ciaccio opened the Manhattan Café on Iberville. Universally known as "Pete Lala's," the club was, according to one Storyville denizen, "a noisy, brawling barn of a place, [offering] music and dancing downstairs, heavy gambling in the back rooms, and assignations upstairs." And it wasn't long before it became central to the city's jazz scene. "Pete Lala's was the headquarters," pianist

Clarence Williams would later recall, "the place where all the bands would come when they got off work, and where the girls would come to meet their main man. . . . They would come to drink and play and have breakfast and then go to bed." Trombonist Kid Ory, who finally moved full-time to New Orleans in 1910, managed to get his group a regular gig at Pete Lala's, and soon many of the other big names were playing there as well.

Another Lala — John T. Lala — ran the Big 25 on Franklin just west of Iberville, which also became a noted hangout for musicians and gamblers. (It was where, according to Louis Armstrong, "all the big-time pimps and hustlers would congregate and play 'cotch.' ") The Frenchman's, a bit farther afield at the corner of Villere and Bienville, was a particular favorite of the District's piano professors. According to Jelly Roll Morton (who by this time was spending most of his time away from New Orleans), the Frenchman's was "the most famous nightspot after everything [else] was closed. It was only a back room, but it was where all the greatest pianists frequented after they got off from work in the sporting houses. About four A.M. . . . they would go to the Frenchman's and there would be everything in the line of hilarity there."

Storyville's reputation as the birthplace of

jazz has often been exaggerated — Black Storyville across Canal Street actually has a better claim — but the District can definitely take credit for nurturing the new music's childhood and adolescence. Keppard, Baquet, Ory, Bunk Johnson, and other members of the post-Bolden generation were now making music history nightly in the dance halls and clubs of Storyville, though few people at the time — including the musicians themselves — realized this, given the character of the venues they played in. "My first job was in Billy Phillips' place," trumpeter Mutt Carey would later recall. "We played anything we pleased in that joint; you see, there was no class in those places. All they wanted was continuous music. Man, they had some rough places in Storyville in those days. A guy would see everything in those joints, and it was all dirty. It was really a hell of a place to work."

Meanwhile, the music was changing as new star soloists rose to take up the mantle left behind by Buddy Bolden. For some years after Bolden's institutionalization, Creole trumpeter Freddie Keppard was widely regarded as his principal heir. "After Buddy died," Sidney Bechet would later write (forgetting that Bolden didn't actually *die* until much later), "Freddie Keppard was King. Freddie kind of took Buddy's way some; he played practically the same way as Buddy, but he *played,* he *really* played."

In the intensely competitive environment of New Orleans music, however, there was always someone new coming up, eager to snatch the coveted title for himself. Cornetist Joe Oliver — an Uptown African American who, like Bolden, lacked some of the downtown polish of his Creole peers — rose to prominence in these years. Though several years older than Keppard, he came to music somewhat later; he began his career around 1910 with the Eagle Brass Band, the new name for Bolden's old outfit. Soon he was also playing the better clubs of the District — 102 Ranch, Pete Lala's — and wowing audiences with his driving "freak" style, using various mutes to make his horn sound like everything from a rooster to a baby. ("How he could make it talk!" one fellow player marveled.) One famous night at Aberdeen's in the District, Oliver decided to stake his claim. To hear one version of the story:

Something got into Joe one night as he sat quietly in the corner and listened to the musicians who were praising [Freddie] Keppard and [Manuel] Perez. He was infuriated by their tiresome adulation; didn't they know that Joe Oliver could play a cornet, too? So he came forth from his silence, strode to the piano, and said, "Jones, beat it out in B flat." Jones began to beat, and Joe began to blow. The notes tore out clear as a bell, crisp and clean. He played as he never had before, filling the little dance hall with low, throbbing blues. Jones backed him with a slow, steady beat. With this rhythm behind him, Joe walked straight through the hall, out onto the sidewalk. There was no mistaking what he meant when he pointed his cornet, first towards Pete Lala's, where Keppard played, then directly across the street, to where Perez was working. A few hot blasts brought crowds out of both joints; they saw Joe Oliver on the sidewalk, playing as if he would blow down every house on the street. Soon every rathole and crib down the line was deserted by its patrons, who came running up to Joe, bewitched by his cornet. When the last joint had poured out its crew, he turned around and led the crowd into Aberdeen's, where he walked to the stand, breathless, excited, and opened his mouth wide to let out the big, important words that were boiling in his head. But all he could say was, "There! That'll show 'em!" After that night, they never called him anything but "King" Oliver.

Actually, there's no evidence that anyone called him King until he went to Chicago some years later, but Oliver's importance to New Orleans music in the teens would be difficult to exaggerate. He was especially influential among the younger generation of players just coming into their own. In this time of musical ferment, bands shuffled personnel frequently, so neophytes would eventually get the chance to play with many of the older players they admired. Sidney Bechet, for instance, was now playing with a number of different ensembles all over town, despite the fact that he was still in his mid-teens. Hoping to discipline their wild child, his conservative Creole parents would sometimes lock up his clarinet in a cabinet. But Sidney would just go to his gig anyway, asking his bandleader to get him any old pawn-shop clarinet. Often, when he was supposed to be playing with his brother's somewhat staid Silver Bells Band, Sidney would gig instead with his own band, formed with his friend Buddy Petit, called the Young Olympians. "I'd always catch hell from my brother when he'd find I was playing in [the Olympians]," Bechet would later recall. "Many a time he'd come to catch me at it and drag me off . . . I didn't care to have trouble with my brother, but it was like I couldn't help myself. There was so much more of what I was looking for in other bands, so much more of what I was needing."

Even Bechet's most admired mentors had trouble keeping the young clarinetist under control. "We could never keep our hands on that Sidney," remembered Louis Nelson, who played with his former protégé in several venues around town. "Regular little devil, always running off down the alley after them little women." So eager was Bechet to be perceived as a ladies' man that he once pretended to have VD (by pouring Musterol ointment over his crotch and then wrapping it up in a bandage). Sometime later he tried to take credit for impregnating a neighborhood girl. "I'm sure I can support a wife," he told the girl's father one night. "I earn 75 cents [or] a dollar a night in the District." The two of them drank wine and talked it over all night, until the father (who knew exactly who it was who'd made his daughter pregnant) carried the sleeping boy back to his family's house and put him to bed.

The final break with his family, though, came in 1913, when Sidney was sixteen or seventeen. Whether he was kicked out or just decided to move himself out, he left the Bechet residence for good and relocated Uptown. And that's when he really started to get into trouble. "One night we ended up in jail together," the bassist Pops Foster recalled. "[Sidney] was fooling around with a chick at a dance out at the lake. She pulled a knife and stabbed him. I grabbed a stick and started after her. When the cops came, we told them we were [just] playing. They took us to jail and then let us go. When we got back to the dance, she thanked us for not getting her in trouble. Sidney was always wanting to fight, but they [the fights] never came off."

But it was certainly not difficult for a young black man to find trouble for himself in New Orleans at this time. The perception among white New Orleanians was that the city's black residents, in the decade after the Robert Charles riot and the rise of Jim Crow, had become defiant and "more assertive than ever before." This was especially true at Mardi Gras time, when blacks who formerly celebrated in their own neighborhoods began to "invade" white residential areas in their revels. Sometimes the results were violent, as during the 1908 Carnival, when a group of Mardi Gras Indians (young members of a black krewe masking as Indians) engaged in a melee on Burgundy Street with a group of white youths. The next year, the *Times-Democrat* complained about black spectators at a parade in the central business district. "The objectionable feature was the manner in which the Negroes elbowed and shoved their way through the crowds to get in the front row," the paper observed. "Complaints were many, especially from women and children, who were powerless to hold their places. . . . The change in demeanor of the Negro crowds was strongly remarked by nearly everyone."

By 1911, the alleged problem had reached

the notice of even J. Benjamin Lawrence, the Baptist preacher who had targeted Tom Anderson the year before. Speaking to his congregation on the Sunday after Mardi Gras, he took special note of the aggressiveness of the black revelers: "I went carefully up one side and down the other of Canal Street," he told his flock, "and from St. Charles Street up I found Negroes occupying the front places almost wholly. I also noticed two or three Negroes to every white person. Big, black Negro men were pushing themselves through the crowd and pressing in upon white women in a manner to make a white man's blood boil. . . ."

Police efforts to maintain order at parades and other public events often amounted to arresting many of the black males present. And the arrests often included those who were busy providing the entertainment. Rare was the New Orleans jazzman who hadn't spent at least one night sitting up in some precinct lockup after a gig that had somehow gotten out of hand.

Louis Armstrong, still a young boy at this time, was no stranger to the volatile racial atmosphere of New Orleans in the early teens. Born on August 4, 1901, to a fifteen-year-old mother in a tough area of the city known as the Battlefield, he grew up among the "pimps, thieves, [and] prostitutes" of a neighborhood frequently targeted by police in their peace-keeping efforts. "I seen every-thing from a child, growing up," Armstrong would later remark. "*Nothin'* happen I ain't never seen before."

His was anything but a sheltered childhood. His parents separated when he was still very young. His father, Willie, had run off with another woman, leaving Louis's mother, Mayann, to fend for herself and her baby alone. Overwhelmed, Mayann, who was little more than a child herself, turned Louis over to his paternal grandmother, Josephine. May-ann then moved into the area known as Black Storyville, where quite likely she worked as a prostitute to make ends meet. Josephine, meanwhile, tried her best to keep Louis away from the criminal elements in the Battlefield, making sure he went to church and Sunday school every week. When necessary, she would discipline him with switches that she made him cut himself from a china ball tree growing in their front yard. This kind of liv-ing arrangement was not particularly unusual in the black New Orleans of the day, where grandparents often played the role of sur-rogate parents to young children. And Louis would later recall this part of his childhood in mostly positive terms. But an elderly widow could presumably do only so much to nurture an energetic young boy in such an environment.

When he was about five, Louis learned that

his parents had reunited — at least long enough to give birth to another child. But by the time he got to meet his baby sister, his father had again abandoned his family ("busy chasing chippies," as Armstrong would bitterly recall). Sometime in 1906, a friend of his mother's appeared at Josephine Armstrong's house and told the old woman that Mayann was sick and needed Louis back to care for her. Josephine packed up the boy's things and tearfully sent him off to Black Storyville with the friend. To get there, they had to ride the Tulane Avenue streetcar. That ride gave Louis his first and most vivid taste of the segregated place New Orleans had become. As he would later write:

It was my first experience with Jim Crow. I was just five, and I had never ridden on a streetcar before. Since I was the first to get on, I walked right up to the front of the car without noticing the signs on the backs of the seats on both sides, which read: FOR COLORED PASSENGERS ONLY. Thinking the woman was following me, I sat down in one of the front seats. However, she did not join me, and when I turned to see what had happened, I saw her waving to me frantically. "Come here, boy," she cried. "Sit where you belong."

Over the next years, young Louis would

learn just how "disgustingly segregated and prejudiced" his hometown truly was. But for the moment, he was just happy to be reunited with his mother and new baby sister. Mayann, still only twenty years old, tried to make amends: "I realize I have not done what I should by you," she told him when he first returned. "But son, mama will make it up to you." And she did — to the best of her ability, given the circumstances. She enrolled Louis in the nearby Fisk School, kept him and his sister fed on red beans and rice, and doctored them with the natural laxatives that Armstrong would swear by as a cure-all for the rest of his life. Louis and Mama Lucy (as his young sister came to be called) had to deal with a series of "stepfathers" who shared their mother's bed — sometimes noisily — in the small one-room house on Perdido. Some of these men were pleasanter than others; a few of them fought bitterly with Mayann, and one even struck her in the face one day and knocked her into the old Basin Canal. But even the kinder ones were no substitute for a loving father.

Left largely to his own devices, young Louis tried to help out by selling newspapers, running errands, and selling overripe produce he found on the streets. He was no angel, certainly, and before long he was also bringing home his winnings from street games of craps, "coon can," and blackjack. ("I got to be a pretty slick player," he once admitted.) But for all of his rough edges, he was a good-hearted, likable boy. Soon even the neighborhood bullies — whom he handled with a canny mixture of fearlessness, generosity, and respect — were looking out for the boy rather than beating him up.

There was, of course, no money in the household for anything like music lessons. ("In those days," he would later quip, "I did not know a horn from a comb.") But he was soon learning the basics, as Bolden and many others had, from the street peddlers, advertising wagons, and parade bands that abounded in the city in those days. Working on a junk wagon for a Jewish family who lived in the neighborhood (the Karnofskys, who would eventually become like a second family to the boy), he got a chance to blow a little tin horn for himself, summoning children to bring their old rags and bottles for purchase. And when he got a little older, he formed a vocal quartet with some friends and began singing for coins on the streets of Storyville.

"Little Louis" got his first potential break in music at the age of eleven, when Bunk Johnson heard the quartet singing in an amateur contest. The trumpeter liked their sound, and told his bandmate Sidney Bechet about them. Bechet, who was only fifteen himself at the time, went to hear the quartet and was equally impressed. "I got to like

Louis a whole lot, he was damn nice," Bechet later wrote. "One time, a little after I started going to hear this quartet, I ran into Louis on the street and I asked him home for dinner. I wanted him and the quartet to come around so my family could hear them." But Louis seemed reluctant to make the long trip downtown. "Look, Sidney," the boy said, "I don't have any shoes . . . these I got, they won't get me there." Sidney ended up giving him fifty cents to get his shoes fixed and made him promise to come. Louis took the money, but then never showed up to perform. Forty-eight years later, Bechet was still annoyed: "It's a little thing," he confessed in his 1960 autobiography, "[but] there's big things around it." Apparently, the common enemy of Jim Crow had not yet eliminated *all* of the traditional friction between downtown Creoles and uptown blacks. Then again, maybe Little Louis just forgot.

It ultimately took a brush with the law to propel Armstrong into the mainstream of New Orleans music, though at first the incident seemed like a setback. On December 31, 1912, Louis was preparing to do some New Year's celebrating. He found one of his "stepfather's" pistols in a cedar trunk, filled it with blanks, and brought it with him when his quartet set out to perform that night in Storyville. As the boys were making their way up Rampart Street, another kid from the neighborhood began shooting a cap gun at them. Knowing he could top this, Louis pulled the pistol from his belt and started shooting back. The policeman standing nearby was not amused. He grabbed the boy and dragged him to jail, where he spent what must have been the most frightening and unpleasant New Year's Eve he'd ever experienced. The next day, he was brought before a judge in the juvenile court. The verdict: incarceration in the Colored Waif's Home for Boys for an indefinite term.

It would prove to be the best piece of luck in Louis Armstrong's entire life.

When the Parker brothers first ventured into the dance-hall business on Franklin Street, they were not the only outsiders moving in on what had widely been regarded as Tom Anderson's turf. The city's Italian underworld had also seen the profit potential of business in and around Storyville, and they did not hesitate to claim a share for themselves. To state that "the Mafia moved in on Storyville" would be inaccurate; most serious crime historians doubt that the Italian crime syndicates in New Orleans at this time were organized enough to justify the Mafia title, no matter what the local newspapers might think. But it is true that many of the nightclubs, saloons, and dance halls of the city's entertainment districts were being taken over

by Italians, and many of their surnames —
Matranga, Segretta, Tonti, Ciacco — were
well known to police as prominent in the
criminal doings of the city. It was as if the
nemeses of the city's reformers were closing
ranks. Italian criminals and black musicians
were, in a sense, finding refuge in the bastion
of the vice lords — that is, in Storyville.

At the same time, the fallout of the Lamana
kidnapping of 1907 seemed to have plunged
the city's Italian underworld into disarray.
Francesco Genova, regarded by police as the
principal figure in the local Mafia, had left
town shortly after being released from jail in
the Lamana case, never to return. Some
believed that his young lieutenant Paul Di
Christina was now in charge. But this succession of leadership was apparently not satisfactory to Giuseppe Morello up in New York.
Sometime in 1908, the Boss of Bosses traveled to New Orleans for several days of meetings with local criminal leaders. The visit —
which ended with Morello parading through
the Italian quarter wearing a knotted red
handkerchief on his head, a supposed "Mafia
death sign" — had several purposes. It did
not go unnoticed in the press, for instance,
that a prominent Italian hotelier was stabbed
to death within hours of Morello's return to
New York. But the meetings also seemed to
signal a change in leadership within the local
organization. A letter from Morello (under

the pseudonym G. LaBella) to New Orleanian Vincenzo Moreci — dated November 15,
1909, and written in the flowery, ambiguous,
falsely humble style of such missives — more
than hints at the ongoing shake-up:

"Dear Friend," it began. "Am in possession
of your two letters, one that bears date of the
5th, the other on the 10th of November. I
understand the contents. In regard to being
able to reorganize the family, I advise you all
to do it, because it seems it is not right to
stay without a king nor country. But I autho-
rize you to convey to all [i.e., to everyone]
my humble prayer and my weak opinion, but
well understood, that those who are worthy
and that wish to [belong] should belong;
those that do not wish to belong, let them
go."

The recipient of this letter, Vincenzo
Moreci, was a native of Termini Imerese,
Sicily. He had emigrated to New Orleans in
1885 and was now an inspector (or "banana-
checker") for United Fruit. Regarded by the
Daily Picayune as "an Italian of the better
class," he had actually been a prominent
member of the Italian Vigilance Committee
that had investigated the Lamana affair. But
there was more to Moreci than the *Picayune*
realized at the time, and this was to become
obvious over the next several years.

Late one Saturday night in March of 1910,
Moreci was walking down Poydras Street

when he was approached by two well-dressed men who pulled pistols out of their belts and fired five shots at him. Two bullets struck Moreci in the head, and he fell to the pavement, seriously wounded, as the two men ran away in different directions. Moreci ended up surviving the attack, and when questioned by police he claimed to have no idea who his assailants were. But it was generally understood that one of the shooters was Paul Di Christina, and that the other was a member of his faction named Giuseppe Di Martini.

This apparent act of rebellion against Moreci was not to go unpunished. One month later, Di Christina was shot and killed on the street as he was entering his grocery-saloon on the corner of Calliope and Howard Streets. His neighbor, another Italian grocer named Pietro Pipitone, admitted that he had fired the shot, claiming that Di Christina owed him two months' rent. But given the victim — and the fact that the grocery trade was a favorite cover for Italian criminals — police thought there was more behind the killing. And when, two months later, Giuseppe Di Martini was also fatally shot — on Bourbon Street, by a man seen moments before in the company of Vincenzo Moreci — it was clear that this back-and-forth series of assassinations and assassination attempts bore all the earmarks of a Mafia power struggle.

Moreci was eventually acquitted of involvement in the Di Martini murder, but the killings went on, most of them involving Italian grocers who had allegedly been threatened by the Black Hand. In July of 1910, grocer Joseph Manzella, who had received several Black Hand extortion letters, was shot to death in his store by a man named Giuseppe Spannazio. In this case, there was a witness — Manzella's seventeen-year-old daughter, Josephine, who grabbed a small revolver and chased the assailant into the street, where she shot him dead on the banquette. "I'm glad I killed him," the unrepentant girl told police. "If he had been arrested, he probably would have been set free within a few months."

But then came a series of more mysterious murders that seemed fundamentally unlike those that had come before. They took place in the dead of night, for one thing, and in the privacy of the victims' bedrooms rather than on the street or in their stores. In August of 1910, grocer John Crutti was brutally beaten with a meat cleaver as he lay sleeping with his wife and children in the residence behind their Royal Street store. Some months later, another grocer, Joseph Davi, was also butchered — again with a cleaver, and again while in bed with his wife (who was injured but survived). In both cases, police had no leads and were able to make no arrests.

Then, at two A.M. on the morning of May

16, 1912, an attack left yet another Italian grocer dead. Antonio Schiambra and his pregnant wife were asleep beside their young son in the bedroom of their home on a lonely stretch of Galvez Street. An assailant climbed through an unlocked kitchen window, made his way down the hallway, and entered the bedroom. As the victims slept, he lifted the mosquito netting over their bed, pressed the barrel of a pistol against the grocer's torso, and fired five shots. Schiambra died almost instantly, and his wife, who was struck by a bullet that had passed through her husband's body, was mortally wounded. She was able to crawl to a window and scream for help, but by the time a neighbor arrived, the shooter had escaped.

Police were again baffled, but this time they at least had some clues. While moving two boxes to help him reach the kitchen window, the killer had left a clear footprint in the soft mud around the house's water cistern. The imprint was of a new shoe, and one "of the latest and most stylish shape." Perhaps more important, a neighbor told police about an incident she had witnessed in the Schiambra grocery two weeks earlier. Two Italian men, one of them tall and well dressed, had walked into the establishment. "Good morning, Mrs. Tony," the tall man said to Mrs. Schiambra (a form of address that police would later recall when the mysterious "Mrs. Toney" chalk message was found in the Maggio ax murder investigation). Mr. Schiambra asked his wife to leave, and then argued with the two men in Italian for some time. The men finally left, according to the witness, "with scowls on their faces." But when the district attorney tried to follow up on this suspicious incident, Mrs. Schiambra (who survived for some ten days before succumbing to her bullet wound) was strangely uncooperative.

"The Italians of New Orleans," the *Daily Item* reported in some dismay, "awed by the power of the Black Hand . . . fear the murderers will become more desperate. They ask, 'Who will be next?' " Assassinations of known mobsters on the street were one thing; but Schiambra, like Crutti and Davi, was apparently a legitimate businessperson, slaughtered in his bed as he lay beside his wife and child. Few in New Orleans had any hope that their police would get to the bottom of these crimes. As the *Daily States* observed a few days after the killing, "Many theories have been advanced, [but] the Schiambra outrage promises to be listed among the many mysterious cases which have never been solved."

Helpless as they were to control crime in the Italian enclaves of the city, the New Orleans police were having better luck implementing the reformers' campaign to crack down on Storyville. The passage of two new laws

344

significantly expanded the arsenal that could be brought to bear against the libertine practices of the Tenderloin. In 1910, the city council passed a bill amending the original Storyville ordinance, strengthening restrictions against lewd dances in brothels and beefing up penalties for all other infractions. State laws passed that same year toughened the prohibition against interracial concubinage and other forms of contact across the color line. Though the state legislature declined to put a strict definition on the term "colored," reformers like Philip Werlein hoped to use the new laws to put the Basin Street octoroon houses out of business for good.

Meanwhile, Gay-Shattuck was also being used more effectively as a weapon for reform. Shortly before Mardi Gras in 1911, Tom Anderson's persistent scourge — Dr. S. A. Smith, superintendent of Louisiana's Anti-Saloon League — launched a campaign against that most cherished of Storyville traditions, the French ball. On the day before Anderson's Ball of the Two Well Known Gentlemen, the district attorney, under heavy pressure from reformers, announced that the provisions of Gay-Shattuck would be strictly enforced. In other words, if women were present at the ball, no liquor could be served, and vice versa. According to the announcement, "No subterfuges [would] be tolerated."

For once, the mayor of Storyville was effectively stymied. The day after the ball, the *Daily Picayune*'s headline was triumphant: OLD CARNIVAL ORGY CURBED, WITH NOT A DRINK IN SIGHT. According to the paper's report, all attendees had been searched for contraband bottles and flasks as they entered Odd Fellows Hall. And while the ball did go on, the atmosphere had been decidedly sober — or "sadly lonesome," as the paper reported. Anderson's other bane, Rev. J. Benjamin Lawrence, could barely contain his glee. "Every lover of decency and morality," he told his congregation that Sunday, could rejoice that these "debauching revels . . . will [soon] pass out of existence."

But the hardest blow to Storyville would come two years later — in March of 1913 — with the culmination of the so-called Dance-Hall Wars on Franklin Street. The Parker brothers had been gearing up for a confrontation for months beforehand, importing various thugs and mob enforcers from New York, ostensibly to work as waiters in the Tuxedo dance hall. Most hard-bitten of the lot was one Charles Harrison, known to police departments throughout the Northeast as "Gyp the Blood." An enforcer of some reputation, Harrison was fleeing a potential murder charge in New York when he showed up in Storyville and started working at the Tuxedo. And it was soon clear that the Parkers had hired him to do more than wait tables.

In the early-morning hours of Easter Monday 1913, James Enright, a waiter at Billy Phillips's 102 Ranch, walked into the Tuxedo with two friends. Because of the Sunday Closing Law, there had been no music at the dance hall that night, but now that midnight was past, the Tuxedo's bar was apparently open for business. Enright — who resented the newly imported crop of servers at the Tuxedo, who were allegedly working for scab wages — got into an argument with the cashier. Harry Parker intervened, ejecting Enright and his friends and thrashing them soundly in the process. As he left the waiter lying in the street, Parker allegedly made some comments about his boss that were highly uncomplimentary to his character.

When Phillips heard about the fight, he immediately headed over to the Tuxedo. Unarmed and still in his shirtsleeves, he walked into the bar and began verbally abusing the Parkers, berating them for their rough handling of his employee. A heated argument followed, but before matters could get out of hand, Phillips was dragged out of the dance hall by his friend and fellow saloonkeeper Tony Battistina.

Back at the 102 Ranch, Phillips apparently calmed down over the next few hours. By four A.M. (when there was still plenty of action in Storyville, even on the morning after Easter), Phillips was feeling conciliatory. Still unarmed, he again walked across the street to the Tuxedo, with a number of friends and curious bystanders in his wake. The Parkers were still there, along with some customers and staff. Phillips stepped up to the bar and threw down a dollar bill. "Come on, give us a drink," he said. "We'll see about the fight later."

At this point, Gyp the Blood, who had slipped out the establishment's back door at Phillips's reappearance, came in the Tuxedo's front door with a nickel-plated revolver in his hand. Creeping up behind Phillips, he thrust the barrel of the gun against the saloonkeeper's ribs. "Come on, you bastard," he said. "Let's have it out." Then he fired three or four shots into Phillips's torso at point-blank range.

The ensuing melee of gunfire would prove to be impossible for police or the courts to sort out. Twenty eyewitnesses would later testify to what happened, but there would be no meaningful consensus on who shot whom in the chaotic moments after Gyp's assassination of Billy Phillips. Certainly Harry and Charles Parker had both fired some shots, but others — never identified, probably friends of the victim — had clearly been firing back. When the gunfire finally ended, Phillips and Harry Parker were dead, while

Gyp the Blood, Charles Parker, and a black porter named Willie Henderson were wounded. Ultimately, only one person — Gyp, aka Charles Harrison — would be tried for murder. But thanks to the highly contradictory nature of the eyewitness testimony, the case would end in a hung jury, allowing Harrison to go free.

For the fate of Storyville, the night of the Tuxedo shooting would prove to be a decisive turning point. Respectable New Orleans had now officially had enough. In the wake of the Easter Night melee, amid enormous public outrage, Superintendent of Police James Reynolds closed down all of Storyville on Monday. Some places would be allowed to reopen on Tuesday, but the dance halls were to remain shut indefinitely. "As long as the operators of these resorts were willing to conduct them properly," Reynolds told reporters, "the police had no objection, and the resorts were tolerated. But now that they have shown a disposition to operate outside of the law, it is evident that the public has become disgusted. I have determined to close all places where men and women of the underworld congregate in nightly orgies."

The order was likely to hit the economy of Storyville hard. But Reynolds was unequivocal. At noon on Monday, March 24, he issued an order to Captain Leroy of the Fourth Precinct: "You will at once take up all permits of dance halls in your precinct, send them to this office, and close up at once all [such establishments] in your precinct." The glory days of a wide-open and thriving Storyville, it seemed, were about to end.

■ ■ ■ ■

CHAPTER 14
HARD TIMES

■ ■ ■ ■

New Orleans in the early teens **Library of Congress**

In the months following the killings at the Tuxedo, the shuttering of the Storyville dance halls created a detrimental ripple effect that was felt throughout the District. With fewer customers coming to the Tenderloin to dance — and many others frightened away by the neighborhood's worsening reputation for crime and violence — businesses of all kinds suffered, and a much more staid and sedate atmosphere descended on Franklin Street. "New Orleans seems to have put the kibosh on the bunny hug, grizzly bear, turkey trot, Texas Tommy, and other fastidious creations," the *Daily Picayune* reported in its March 30 edition. "In the place of the dance halls which once did such tremendous business, cabarets have been effectively established, [with] tables and chairs taking up all the available space once used for dancing. Now, instead of noisy Negro bands, the low whining of half-tuned string instruments and the strumming of a piano are heard."

This dampening of spirit was exacerbated by an increased police presence in and around the District, as well as a greater tendency among police to actually enforce the restrictions of Gay-Shattuck and other laws. Sunday closing was no longer regarded as a mere suggestion, and cafés that used to employ a female singer were now forbidden to do so. Only one proprietor seemed immune to the stricter enforcements. "It is passing strange," one disgruntled competitor complained to the *Picayune,* "that Tom Anderson should be allowed to have women entertainers and we are barred from having them. He is like the rest of us, except, of course you know, he has a political pull, and they won't touch Tom. He's too strong."

But even the all-powerful mayor of Storyville couldn't do much to halt the District's slide. In the months after the Parker-Phillips shootout, the number of prostitutes working in the Tenderloin slipped to just seven hundred. Lulu White's Mahogany Hall began employing only eight women regularly, while half of the cribs on Villere and Robertson Streets became vacant. Meanwhile, prices were being cut all along Basin Street. By 1916, the cost of a fifteen-minute romp at Josie Arlington's palace had fallen to one dollar even.

The city's musicians were feeling the pinch as well. Jazz bands reduced the number of players in their rosters, replacing their guitarist, bassist, and violinist with a single pianist to back up soloists. With fewer gigs available, many jazzmen were forced to go back to their day jobs. Even after the dance halls reopened in 1914, when New Orleans caught the tango fever that had swept through much of the country, behavior in the halls was tightly controlled. In the so-called Tango Belt — a stretch of Rampart Street in the French Quarter where many of the District's dance halls had moved — Superintendent Reynolds announced strict prohibitions on all vulgar forms of the dance, insisting that there be "daylight between the dancers" and no lewd "snake-wriggling" of the shoulders and hips. Violators were promptly arrested, sometimes in droves. The effect on the city's nightlife was sobering. According to the *Item,* Reynolds "had closed down the lid so tight in the 'belt' that the music was no more than a dirge for the gaiety departed, and a lot of young men in New Orleans were keeping their money out of the beer pots and wassail bowls."

Some musicians, responding to the worsening employment picture, began to look for opportunities elsewhere. Several members of the Tuxedo dance-hall band — including Freddie Keppard and George Baquet — reorganized as the nucleus of a new group called the Original Creole Band. In August of 1914, under the leadership of bassist Bill Johnson, they left New Orleans and began touring the vaudeville circuit, ending with an extended stay in Los Angeles. Others followed their lead over the next few years. Jelly Roll Morton, for instance, who had already been spending much of his time on the road, began finding new opportunities — and more receptive audiences — in Chicago, New York, and California.

White bands also began heeding the call from other cities. In late 1914, the vaudeville dance team of Frisco and McDermott performed in New Orleans. After their show, they stopped by the Club Creole and heard a white jazz band led by trombonist Tom Brown. "Boy, listen to that music; what a band!" Loretta McDermott allegedly told her partner. "C'mon, Joe, let's go. What rhythm!" They found the band's loose, syncopated beat ideal for their style of dancing. According to jazz legend, when they returned to Chicago, they convinced the owner of Lamb's Café in the Loop to bring the band north. And although accounts differ on the details, what's known for sure is that Tom Brown's Band left New Orleans in May of 1915 with a six-week contract to play at Lamb's. They were an instant hit, and soon the exciting new music from New Orleans, which finally being referred to by the name "jass" or "jazz," was revolutionizing the sound of popular entertainment in the Second City.

Another white New Orleans band went north a few months later. In December of 1915, Nick LaRocca (the cornetist whose disapproving father had destroyed his first two instruments with an ax) was playing in one of Jack Laine's "ballyhoo bands" at the corner of Canal and Royal, advertising a prizefight. A visiting Chicago café owner named Harry James heard them and was deeply impressed by the young man "pointing his cornet skyward and blowing to the point of apoplexy." James approached Laine afterward and asked if he might be interested in taking his band north to Chicago. Laine claimed that he was too busy, but he advised James to go hear LaRocca perform that night at the Haymarket Café with another band, led by drummer Johnny Stein. The Chicagoan liked what he heard there, too, and soon "Stein's Dixie Jass Band" had a contract to open the Booster's Club in Chicago in early 1916. Word was getting out, and the diaspora of the Crescent City's musical talent was now under way.

Not that those who remained behind were entirely idle. In some cases, the emigration of talent just meant a reshuffling of personnel in existing bands. When Keppard and Baquet decamped to California, for instance, their places in the popular New Olympia band were soon filled by Joe Oliver and Sidney

Bechet. And there was always a new crop of younger jazzmen to fill the artistic vacuum. Trombonist Kid Ory, whose band was now playing full-time in the city after their move from LaPlace, was proving to be especially popular — not only among black audiences but also among many young whites, who liked their more polished style of jazz. Once, at a gig for whites at the Gymnasium, Ory's band played opposite one of John Robichaux's more established "straight" ensembles and earned a larger share of the applause. Afterward, Robichaux offered Ory a job, saying, "I like the way you play."

"I like the way you play, too," Ory replied smartly. "But I'm not going to break up my band. It's too late. You had your day."

Ory was apparently much more impressed by a certain child cornetist from the Colored Waif's Home brass band, whom everyone in town had been talking about. Ory first heard "Little Louis" Armstrong at the Labor Day parade in late 1913, and he couldn't believe that such a young boy could be so accomplished a player. "You're doing a good job," Ory told him at the parade. "You're going to be all right someday, you keep that up."

For Armstrong, this praise from one of New Orleans' top jazzmen was utterly thrilling. The boy had had no easy time of it during his stay at the Waif's Home, at least in the beginning, before he'd made the adjustment from life on the streets. The home, which housed some two hundred inmates, was run with strict military discipline, and the kid from Black Storyville was identified early on as a boy with "a bad stamp." But somehow the regimen of Army-style drilling and regular stints on cleaning and gardening crews spoke to the boy's need for structure and discipline. Soon he was thriving in the new atmosphere, where his innate good-heartedness and natural skill as a clown made him popular among the other boys.

From the beginning of his sentence, Louis had yearned to join the home's brass band. Unfortunately, this meant convincing the band's leader, Peter Davis, that he was worthy of belonging. "Davis didn't like me too much [at first]," Armstrong later admitted. But the boy was conscientious and eager to please, and eventually the bandleader softened toward him. First, Davis allowed Louis to play the tambourine with the group; from there, the boy graduated to the snare drum. Eventually, he was entrusted with an old bugle — to wake the other boys with a reveille every morning. Finally, Davis gave the boy a cornet and taught him to play "Home, Sweet Home."

Under Davis's careful tutelage, Louis picked up the cornet with amazing facility. By the summer of 1913, he was already leading the band, which frequently was hired for gigs "on the outside" — at parades, private parties, and picnics at Spanish Fort and the other lake resorts. Here Armstrong heard, and was heard by, some of the best musicians in the city. The ubiquity of music in the Crescent City began to work its magic on the boy, who would later recall lying on his bunk on Sunday evenings, smelling the honeysuckles outside and listening to a jazz band playing for "some rich white folks" about half a mile away. "Me and music got married at the home," he would later say. "I do believe that my whole success goes back to that time I was arrested as a wayward boy."

Sometime in the summer of 1914, Armstrong's father persuaded the juvenile court to release Louis into his custody. The boy didn't want to leave the Waif's Home, especially not to go live with his unloved and unloving father. And when it turned out that Willie Armstrong wanted his son around only as long as he worked more than he ate, Louis moved out. The boy took up residence again with his mother, Mayann, and sister, Mama Lucy, on Perdido Street — in "that great big room," as he later put it, "where the three of us were so happy."

Faced with the necessity of helping support the household, Louis immediately found work hauling coal on a mule-drawn coal cart for fifteen cents a load. But what he really wanted to do was play his horn. After performing for so long with "simple, pimply-faced boys" at the home, he was eager to learn something from the real pros. His first day back at Mayann's, he ran into an old friend, Cocaine Buddy, who tipped him off to a job at Henry Ponce's honky-tonk in the neighborhood. "All you have to do," Buddy explained, "is to put on your long pants and play the blues for the whores that hustle all night. . . . They will call you sweet names and buy you drinks and give you tips." Louis was hired immediately, and soon he was bringing in as much money with his cornet as he was with his coal shovel.

Early on, he found a musical mentor in the person of Joe Oliver. To Louis's mind, Oliver was the best horn player in New Orleans — "better than Bolden, better than Bunk Johnson." Louis began shadowing his idol all over, second-lining behind him in parades and sometimes holding his cornet between numbers. When delivering stone coal to a crib prostitute in the District, Louis would become entranced by the sound of Oliver's horn coming from Pete Lala's next door. "I'd just stand there in that lady's crib listening to King Oliver," he later wrote. "All of a sudden it would dawn on that lady that I was still in her crib, very silent, while she hustled those tricks, and she'd say, 'What's the matter with you, boy? . . . This is no place to daydream . . . I've got work to do!' " But Louis didn't mind the scolding. "As long as [Oliver] was blowing," he said, "that was who I wanted to hear at any chance I got."

Oliver started taking a special interest in his young disciple and began to give him cornet lessons. He also frequently invited the boy over to his house, where Mrs. Oliver would stuff him with that New Orleans staple, red beans and rice ("which I *loved,*" said Armstrong). Oliver even gave Louis one of his old horns — a beat-up York cornet that the boy accepted with unctuous gratitude. "I always knew, if I'm going to get a little break in this game," he later recalled, "it was going to be through Papa Joe, nobody else."

But Louis was already playing well enough to make his own breaks. One evening shortly after his discharge from the Waif's Home, "Black Benny" Williams, an enormous (and notoriously combative) bass drum player from the neighborhood, took him to hear Kid Ory headlining at National Park. The real star of the night, however, proved to be Armstrong himself. "Benny asked me if I would let Louis sit in with my band," Ory recalled years later. "I remembered the kid from the [Labor Day] street parade and I gladly agreed. Louis came up and played 'Ole Miss' and the blues, and everyone in the park went wild over this boy in knee trousers who could play so great." Ory was so impressed that he urged the young horn player to sit in with the band anytime he wanted to. "Louis came several times to different places where I worked and we really got to know each other," Ory said. "He always came accompanied by Benny, the drummer. In the crowded places, Benny would handcuff Louis to himself with a handkerchief so Louis wouldn't get lost."

Black Benny grew so proud of his little protégé that the drummer was soon singing his praises to anyone who'd listen. "You think you can play," he told Sidney Bechet when the two met one day. "But I know a little boy right around the corner from my place, he can play 'High Society' better than you." Intrigued (and likely a little put out, accustomed as he was to being regarded as the local wunderkind himself), Bechet said, "Well, I'd like to see that boy." So they arranged to go hear him play. "It was Louis," Bechet explained in his autobiography, "and I'll be doggone if he didn't play 'High Society' on the cornet. . . . [The tune] was very hard for *clarinet* to do, and really unthinkable for cornet to do at those times. But Louis, he did it."

Bechet had of course already heard Armstrong sing, but this was the first time he'd listened to the boy play cornet, and he was amazed at the quick progress Louis had made on the instrument. So he hired Armstrong to play with him and a drummer on a little advertising gig he'd set up to promote a show at the Ivory Theatre. The drummer and Louis were paid fifty cents each; Bechet kept a dollar for himself. But there were no hard feelings, apparently. "We went out [afterward] and bought some beer with the money and got those sandwiches — Poor Boys, they're called," Bechet recalled. "We really had good times." Even so, the two recognized each other as rivals. And as Bechet's biographer points out, "For the rest of their lives the two geniuses of early jazz treated each other with the utmost caution."

That Little Louis had Benny as a protector was fortunate, since New Orleans in the teens had become a very dangerous place, particularly for black musicians playing in low-down dives and on the increasingly perilous streets. Sometimes the problem was just low-level harassment on the parade routes. ("All the bands wanted Benny to play the bass drum in parades," Armstrong recalled. "Any time anybody give us kids trouble, Benny'd hit 'em over the head with the drum mallets.") But often the violence could be life-threatening. Despite the newly beefed-up police presence in the city's entertainment districts, shootings and knife fights between rival miscreants remained common, and musicians were often caught in the crossfire. "Our bandstand was right by the door," Armstrong wrote of one tonk he played at, "and if somebody start

shooting, I don't see how I didn't get hit."
Sometimes the calls were very close indeed.
One night in 1915 at Pete Lala's, Bechet and
Oliver were enjoying a drink at the bar when
a customer was shot dead right in front of
their eyes.

Little Louis himself had a harrowing experience on a Sunday morning at Henry Ponce's.
Armstrong was talking with the owner in the
doorway of the tonk when he noticed several
men — apparently friends of Ponce's rival,
Joe Segretta — gathering in front of the
grocery across the street. "All of a sudden I
saw one of them pull out his gun and point it
at us," Armstrong remembered. Their shots
missed Ponce, at which point the club owner
pulled out his own revolver and started
pursuing the shooters, firing as he ran. But
Armstrong just stood there in fright. "I had
not moved," he later recalled, "and the flock
of bystanders who saw me riveted to the
sidewalk rushed up to me. 'Were you hit?'
they asked. 'Are you hurt?' When they asked
me what they did, I fainted. . . . I thought the
first shot had hit me."

The racial atmosphere of the city was also
growing more volatile in the mid-teens. Often
police would have to break up parades to
prevent violent confrontations between black
and white spectators and participants. Sometimes the police themselves were the aggres-
sors. "Lots of times the both races looked

like they were going to get into a scrap, over just nothing much," Armstrong wrote about those years. "[And] even if the colored are in the right — when the cops arrive, they'll whip your head, and then ask questions."

For the city's black jazzmen, the situation in New Orleans — despite the growing popularity of their music among young whites — was becoming untenable, and the possibilities elsewhere ever more tempting. More and more of them were seriously considering the offers of jobs outside of New Orleans. "People were hearing a lot of excitement about what was happening up North," Bechet said of this time, "and I had this idea in my head that I was to see other places. . . . We'd heard all about how the North was freer, and we were wanting to go real bad."

Up on Esplanade Avenue — far from the ongoing turmoil in Black and White Storyville — retired madam Josie Arlington had fallen gravely ill. Sometime in early 1913, right around the time of the Tuxedo shootings, she had taken to her bed and had been declining ever since. By autumn, she was experiencing periods of delirium and had lost control of her bladder and her bowels. Whether this was a case of late-stage syphilis or some other disease is unknown. She was only forty-nine years old, but Josie Arlington had led a difficult and presumably unhygienic existence for much of her life, despite the luxury and ease she had more recently enjoyed as Mrs. Mary Deubler Brady.

Anna Deubler, now twenty-nine, was her aunt's principal caregiver. According to the testimony of family friends, the two were still absolutely devoted to each other. And while there were others in the house to help — Anna's mother, her aunt's cousin Margaret, a nurse named Mrs. Jackson, and a family friend named Mrs. Walker — it was Anna who was mainly responsible for looking after the invalid. Once she even injured herself while trying to lift her now rather stout aunt from her bed. It was hard work for the slender young woman, but apparently Anna felt it was the least she could do for the person solely responsible for giving her the comfortable, respectable life she had enjoyed since birth.

Sometime in November of 1913, her aunt Mary became more forthcoming about her past. "Little girl," she said one day when the two were alone, "how I have been fooling you." She explained that she wanted Anna to help her write a book about her life — "a book for the protection of young women." Anna was confused at first, but then, in a rush of confession, her aunt revealed everything. She told her all about her former life as a prostitute and then as Josie Arlington, queen of the demimonde, the famous madam of Basin Street. She also revealed that she and "Uncle Tom" had never been married, that even cousin Margaret had once been a prostitute, and that Margaret's son — Anna's own cousin Thomas — was a bastard, born in Josie's first brothel on Customhouse Street.

Anna, understandably, was appalled. She ran out of the bedroom, found her uncle Tom, and asked him whether any of this was really true. "Child," Brady said, "go back to Auntie and pay no attention. You know she is delirious." But then Anna asked Mrs. Walker, who reluctantly confirmed everything. "My God," the older woman lamented, "how much would Auntie not have given to spare you this." Frantic, Anna went back to Brady and asked again if the story was true. Brady felt he could lie no longer. "Yes," he said finally. "I'm sorry to say, it's true."

This sudden revelation was "simply horrible," Anna would later say. She seemed especially upset by the fact that the whole family had been aware of the truth and hadn't told her. "My father knew it; my brothers and my mother knew of the existing circumstances, and they countenanced it," she said. "But I didn't." In a state of high dudgeon now, she demanded that Brady turn over all of her jewelry — "because I didn't intend to live under the roof where such things existed." The irony was stark. Having taken great pains over the years to turn this day laborer's daughter into a refined young woman, the Bradys were now going to have to suffer the consequences of her impeccable middle-class scruples.

Eventually, however, the impressionable and pliable young woman was mollified. Perhaps realizing that she had absolutely nowhere else to go, she gradually allowed herself to be talked out of leaving. Her beloved aunt needed her — no matter what her history or current living situation. And all of her immediate family lived in that capacious house on Esplanade, a place where she had felt happy and cared-for. So she did not run away after all. She decided simply to continue going on as she had before, nursing her lifelong benefactor amid the comforts and luxuries she had long ago become accustomed to.

But Miss Mary Deubler — for now she could be known by her real name — just grew sicker. And when it became clear that the matriarch was not going to recover from her illness, it occurred to Anna's parents that the future of their family was hardly assured. Mary Deubler had always been secretive and rather grudging about her financial affairs — "Miss Deubler was a very tight proposition," as Tom Brady would later put it — and the contents of her will were unknown. Deubler had told several friends that she intended to leave her entire estate to Anna. But in early

1913 she had signed papers to transfer ownership of the Esplanade mansion to Brady, ostensibly in exchange for $25,000 in cash that Brady had given her "at various times during the last twenty years." Worried that the ailing woman might also have left the rest of her estate to her longtime inamorato, Anna's mother began to concoct a plan whereby the Deubler family might ensure their future prosperity. One day in late 1913 or early 1914, she broached a sensitive topic with her daughter. Wouldn't it be a "wonderful thing," she said, if Anna were to marry Tom Brady after Aunt Mary died? That way she would guarantee that everyone could continue to live together in the Esplanade house — as one extended family — the way they had been living until now.

Anna at first found the whole idea outrageous. Could it be that her mother actually wanted her to marry the man she had regarded as an uncle for her entire life? A man twenty-one years her senior? The man who had been living and sleeping with her dear aunt for well over a decade?

One can certainly understand the young woman's initial aversion to the proposal. (Tom Brady, apparently, had no objection to it.) But Anna — sheltered as she had been all her life, and perhaps intimidated by the prospect of facing the world without the bulwark of her aunt's fortune — was susceptible to persuasion. Over the next weeks, she talked with other members of the household about it. "Mrs. Jackson," Anna said to the nurse one day. "Isn't it awful? They are talking about me marrying Mr. Brady as soon as Auntie dies." Mrs. Jackson confessed to being surprised, but didn't necessarily think the idea was all that awful. "Mr. Brady can do you no good, but you can do Mr. Brady a world of good," she said. "You cannot take Mr. Brady from the sphere he has been in and raise him to your level . . . but you can do him a world of good." Mrs. Jackson also agreed with Anna's mother that the marriage would keep the family together, and make it respectable for all of them to be living together under one roof.

The two priests Anna then consulted also saw wisdom in the plan. Father Anselm Maenner and Father Philip Murphy both felt that, under the circumstances, Anna would protect herself from scandal by marrying Brady. "If you love him and he loves you," Father Murphy said, somewhat disingenuously perhaps, "I think it is the best thing to do."

Eventually, Anna was convinced that she needed a protector, and that Brady would serve admirably. "I needed someone who would guide me," she later explained, "and since Mr. Brady, all during my childhood, had shielded me and protected me, I thought he was the one most capable of doing it."

At six P.M. on February 14, 1914 (Valentine's Day, appropriately enough), Mary Deubler, aka Josie Arlington, aka Mrs. Thomas Brady, died, eight days before her fiftieth birthday. Her funeral that Sunday was an elaborate affair, with "a line of flower-freighted carriages" winding from the Esplanade house to nearby St. Boniface Church, where the service was conducted by Fathers Maenner and Murphy. In attendance were many members of New Orleans' political and sporting circles — including, of course, Tom Anderson, her longtime friend and business partner. But as the *Daily Item* pointed out, "Though her life had been spent among the women of the demimonde, none attended the funeral. The only homage received at the hands of her companions were wreaths of flowers sent to the home and laid upon the tomb."

Exactly one week after Mary Deubler's death, Anna Deubler and John Thomas Brady were married at their home on Esplanade (with Tom Anderson again in attendance). Anna's father, Henry, who later claimed that he was presented with the marriage plan as a fait accompli, was not happy, and he apparently showed up at the ceremony quite drunk. But he was eventually persuaded to give his daughter away at the appropriate time. ("Take her, Tom," he allegedly said to the groom. "You helped spoil her, now take your own medicine.")

Mary Deubler's will had been read the day before, after a locksmith broke open the safe whose combination had gone with the deceased to her grave. In that document, dated June 29, 1903, Mary Deubler left small bequests to her brother Henry, her cousin Margaret, and their children. But everything else, including the brothel on Basin Street, went to Anna — and so to Tom Brady as well.

The will, however, would not go uncontested. Three weeks later, Henry Deubler, claiming that he was "done up in this deal" between Brady and his daughter, would file suit to nullify not just the will but also the earlier transfer of the Esplanade mansion to Brady. Apparently, the prospect of having a wealthy daughter was not enough for the man; he wanted his fair share of his sister's treasure. He did not win his challenge, however, and the estate eventually went as dictated to the new Mrs. Brady. She and her aging husband went on to enjoy a seemingly happy marriage that soon produced two children. But the Bradys apparently spent through Mary Deubler's fortune quite rapidly. By 1918, they were already being sued by their old friend Tom Anderson for failure to pay back some loans he had guaranteed for them. High moral standards, it would seem, could be very expensive to uphold.

In the meantime, Storyville had lost its reluctant queen. And on the very same day as her death, the District had suffered another blow. The *Daily Item* published a pointed editorial that day under the title NO NECESSARY EVIL. In it, the paper expressed the city's growing discontent with the whole idea on which Storyville had been predicated — that prostitution and vice were necessary evils that could safely be segregated and regulated rather than prohibited. "Segregation of immoral women has always failed," the paper contended. "The result has been a worldwide awakening to the fact that the wages of sin is death, and that the welfare of the race is threatened by the widespread indulgence in vice."

The message was clear: Just "putting the lid" on vice in New Orleans was no longer enough. The campaign to abolish the segregated district entirely would now begin in earnest.

■ ■ ■ ■

CHAPTER 15
THE NEW
PROHIBITIONISTS

■ ■ ■ ■

Jean Gordon (third from right) and fellow reformers **Library of Congress**

Shortly after six P.M. on a Tuesday evening in February 1915, a stout, bespectacled man stepped down from the car of a local train at the tiny station of North Shore, Louisiana. The man had come to spend the night at the Queen and Crescent camp, a rustic country lodge owned by the exclusive New Orleans social club of the same name. The camp — located amid the marshlands and piney woods of the north shore of Lake Pontchartrain, some thirty-five miles northeast of the city — was a popular retreat for well-heeled urbanites in certain seasons. But now, mid-week in February, it was all but deserted. Aside from the caretaker of the place, Walter Santa Cruz, no one else was there.

The arriving guest was W. S. Parkerson, and he was not looking well. "I'm tired," the now fifty-seven-year-old reformer said to Santa Cruz. "I haven't slept in three nights, and I need rest." Refusing the offer of dinner, Parkerson requested nothing but a cot in the dormitory with "three or four blankets," and asked that he not be disturbed until morning. Santa Cruz quickly made up the bed and then left him alone.

At eleven the next morning, the caretaker went to the dormitory to light a fire and awaken his only guest. Parkerson was still in bed, wrapped in blankets. "Never mind about the fire," Parkerson said when the caretaker moved toward the fireplace. Asked if he would come down to the dining room for breakfast, Parkerson demurred. "I'll be off soon," he said. "I don't want breakfast."

The remark was puzzling. No train was scheduled to leave the North Shore station for several hours, so where would Parkerson be off to? But Santa Cruz said nothing. He merely left the dormitory and went about his duties.

Three hours later, however, Parkerson had still not emerged from his room. Concerned that his guest might be late for the train going back to the city, the caretaker returned to the dormitory to rouse him. He found Parkerson awake but in desperate condition. "He looked as if he was bleeding to death," Santa Cruz later told reporters. "Blood was all over the bedclothes. He was cut in the neck, and he held an ordinary two-bladed pocketknife in his right hand. I tried to take the knife away from him, but he wouldn't let it go."

"I'm full of blood," Parkerson whispered.

When Santa Cruz asked him what he had done to himself, the lawyer just repeated, "I'm full of blood."

Santa Cruz ran to the telephone and called the sheriff in nearby Slidell. Within an hour, the sheriff was at the camp with a local physician, Dr. Outlaw. As the doctor attempted to staunch the bleeding, Parkerson admitted that he had inflicted the wound himself. Several months earlier, apparently, his young daughter had died of asphyxiation when a bathroom gas fixture in their home had malfunctioned. Parkerson's grief at her loss had been unbearable. For months afterward, he'd lost interest in his job and everything else, and now he just wanted to die.

Dr. Outlaw and the sheriff rushed Parkerson to the North Shore station, where a train to the city had been delayed for his transport. They arrived in New Orleans at 4:45 P.M. and were met by an ambulance, which carried the patient to Touro Infirmary. There he was put under the care of his family physician, Dr. Parnham, who pronounced the wound "trivial," though he admitted that the lawyer had lost a good deal of blood. "Unless aggravated by unforeseen complications," the doctor announced, "I think the wound will have no bad effects."

But complications did set in. Over the next few days, Parkerson developed a lung infection, apparently as a result of the neck wound

379

being left untreated for so long. He took a turn for the worse over the weekend, and at four A.M. on the morning of Sunday, February 14 (exactly one year after Josie Arlington's demise), he died in his bed at Touro Infirmary. The cause of death, according to Dr. Parnham, was "an edema of the lungs, caused by septic broncho-pneumonia."

In one respect, the death of W. S. Parkerson at this point in New Orleans' vice war was symbolic. By the mid-teens, Parkerson and the earlier generation of reformers had all but ceded the field of battle to what might be called the new prohibitionists — the clergymen, social puritans, and club women who had risen to prominence in the wake of Carrie Nation's late-1907 visit. Unlike their predecessors of the 1890s, who were open to negotiation with the forces of the demimonde, this new crop of moral warriors were absolutely uncompromising. They demanded outright interdiction of all vices, including drugs, alcohol, prostitution, gambling, and even tobacco. As a sop to these more stubborn opponents, Mayor Behrman (now serving his third term and in full command of the Ring political machinery) had taken on a new commissioner for public safety in 1912. Harold Newman, an ex-lawyer and businessman from a prominent New Orleans family, came to the job with impeccable credentials as a reformer, so Behrman hoped that his installation as the city's chief moral watchdog would deflect some of the mounting criticism of his administration. It was a shrewd move. Politically, Newman was something of a neophyte, and whenever his insistence on strict enforcement of vice laws became too cumbersome, Behrman had ways of circumventing his orders — as when, by special permit from the mayor's office, Tom Anderson was allowed to employ a female singer when all other cabaret owners could not.

Unfortunately for the mayor, however, the city's reformers soon saw through the ruse, and their honeymoon with the new commissioner did not last long. They were soon attacking the ineffectual Newman with a vehemence — and a condescending sarcasm — usually reserved for members of the demimonde themselves. Two figures in particular proved to be consistent critics of the commissioner's feeble attempts to clean up New Orleans. Kate and Jean Gordon, irrepressible daughters of a Scottish émigré schoolmaster, had come to reform as young women in the 1880s. Born to privilege, they had given up early on the idea of marriage and motherhood and turned their substantial energies to public service — mainly, to hear Kate tell it, "because we never cared what people thought." Such defiant confidence was apparently a legacy from their mother, a teacher from a socially prominent New Orleans family. "[Our mother] believed it was all right for a lady to go up to City Hall or a newspaper office," Kate once explained. "In fact, she believed that a lady might do anything, if it were for good."

As with many self-styled moral champions of the day, however, their idea of "good" was often distorted by class and racial prejudice. So while the two sisters fought for such laudable aims as female suffrage, public-health improvements, and child-labor regulation, they also lent their support to the cause of racial purity as embodied in Jim Crow legislation and the disenfranchisement of Louisiana's black population. Worse, they held some astounding beliefs about eugenics. As heads of the Milne Asylum for Destitute Girls, they advocated for the forced sterilization of children who showed signs of a future in crime, prostitution, or alcoholism: "Took Lucille Decoux to the Women's Dispensary July 17 [for an appendectomy follow-up]," Jean once wrote in her diary. "This was an excellent opportunity to have her sterilized . . . and thus end any feeble-minded progeny coming from Lucille."

But while it would not be unfair to dwell on the sisters' monstrously callous sense of class and racial superiority (Kate once refused an invitation to the White House because Booker T. Washington was also invited — "and I declined . . . to attend any function where I would be placed on equal terms with Negroes"), they did believe they were doing God's work, and were determined to "stamp out of His world the unfit." In their minds, prostitutes, criminals, and paupers were inherently unfit, and therefore justifiably a target for social engineering of any type, no matter how high-handed.

In the battle against Storyville, "Miss Jean," as the younger sister was typically known, took a particularly prominent role. She had worked with the ERA Club in its 1908 campaign to move the Basin Street brothels away from the new railroad station. After the failure of that effort, she began to see total prohibition as the better path. And she believed that the way to accomplish this end was to give women the vote. "If you don't want the ballot for yourselves," she once told one of her women's clubs, "you should want it for the good you can do. You need it, for your 'woman's influence' is a miserable failure as long as it does not prevent white slavery, gambling among young boys, violations of the Gay-Shattuck Law, and other evils which destroy the sons and daughters of our community."

In 1914, she supported an effort in the state legislature to close all prostitution districts in Louisiana — not just the legal one in New Orleans but also the unofficial tenderloins in Shreveport, Baton Rouge, and other major cities in the state. A bill was drafted, but thanks to the influence of Representative Tom Anderson and the other Storyville landlords — who were still enjoying comfortable profits, despite the overall decline of the District — the measure was indefinitely tabled. But the woman sometimes called "the Joan of Arc of New Orleans" was nothing if not persistent. The efforts of 1908 and 1914 may both have failed, but the clamor for reform was growing in New Orleans, especially after the start of the world war. The third and most serious effort to take on the city's vice lords — and their enablers in City Hall — would have far wider support.

Reformers weren't the only group in New Orleans undergoing a change in leadership during the second decade of the twentieth century. The ranks of the city's Italian underworld were also turning over — and usually with far more violent consequences. After the rash of killings that had roiled the city around 1910 — when (alleged) capo Vincenzo Moreci answered the unsuccessful attempt on his life by having his two assailants summarily executed — the city's (alleged) Mafia had experienced a few years of relative peace. Occasional Black Hand slayings continued to occur, but Moreci — representing the Morello element in the city, which stood opposed to the more loosely organized Black Handers

— seemed to have matters under control. But then, at two A.M. on the morning of November 19, 1915, another wave of homicidal chaos began. Moreci was walking home alone on Rampart Street when gunfire erupted from an abandoned storefront on the corner of St. Anthony. "They finally got Moreci," the *Times-Picayune* reported: "[And] when they did, they got him all the way. They shot him from the right; they shot him from the left; they went up to him and hit him with a shotgun so hard that they broke the gun. They blasted half his jaw off; they put 11 buckshot in his right arm; they put two balls into his back and two into his chest; they broke his right arm with the butt of their gun and knocked the .38 revolver that he waved desperately 15 feet up the street." It was, in other words, an all-out massacre. This time, their target did not survive.

Only one man was arrested in the shooting — a notorious and much-feared Black Hander by the name of Joseph Monfre (or, variously, Manfre, Mumfre, and Mumphrey). Sometimes known as "Doc" because he dispensed patent medicines as a sideline, he was well known to New Orleans police, having been implicated in Black Hand activities as far back as the Lamana kidnapping in 1907. During that episode, Monfre (who was apparently a relative — perhaps even a brother — of conspirator Stefano Monfre) had been so aggressive in trying to "thrust himself forward" into Lamana's confidence that he was suspected of being a spy for the kidnappers. Several months later, he was arrested for bombing the grocery-saloon of an Italian named Carmello Graffagnini, who had refused to comply with a Black Hand letter demanding $1,000. While out on bail awaiting trial, Monfre was again arrested — for an identical extortion bombing, this time of a grocery owned by a man named Joseph Serio. Convicted in July 1908 for the Graffagnini bombing, Monfre was sentenced to twenty years in the state penitentiary. But even when in jail, Doc Monfre was feared in the Italian community. At the time of the Schiambra murder in May of 1912, for instance, relatives of Monfre were said to be living in the Schiambras' neighborhood — a fact that the murdered man had worried aloud about shortly before his death.

And now, in November of 1915, Monfre had again been arrested, this time for the murder of Vincenzo Moreci. Monfre had apparently been released on parole from the state pen several weeks earlier, after serving just six and a half years of his twenty-year sentence. And it hadn't taken the Black Hand leader very long to settle his score against the Mafia capo, though of course he denied it. "Vincent Moreci was the best friend I had," Monfre insisted to police, claiming that the murdered man had been instrumental in securing his recent release on parole. And although police gave this claim very little credence, they had no concrete evidence against Monfre, and the charges against him were eventually dropped. Despite their strong suspicions that Doc Monfre was one of the most dangerous men in New Orleans, police were forced to set him free.

Meanwhile, the power vacuum left by Moreci's murder soon plunged the city's underworld into another frenzy of tit-for-tat killings on the street. The first half of 1916 saw a virtual orgy of bloodshed in the Italian neighborhoods of New Orleans. On March 20, a stevedore named Joseph Russo was shot and killed by Francesco Paolo Dragna, an in-law of a known family of Black Handers. Four days later, another dockworker — Joseph Matranga, of the Matranga family implicated in the Hennessy assassination — was murdered by one Giuseppe Bonforte. On May 12, three men working for the Matrangas took out Joe Segretta (the saloon owner who had earlier tried to have Henry Ponce killed, and nearly shot Louis Armstrong in the process). Then, a mere twelve hours after Segretta's demise, Vito DiGiorgio and Jake Gileardo were shot in DiGiorgio's grocery-saloon. And finally, on May 15, Pietro Giocona was shot and wounded by two men who turned out to be sons of Joseph Segretta.

Just keeping all of these names straight was no small task for the police department. Superintendent Reynolds was overwhelmed. "Black Hand shootings and murders are going to stop. They are going to end right now!" he told reporters on May 16, pounding his desk to emphasize the point. "I am going to hunt out every criminally inclined Italian in the city, if it takes every moment of time of every man on my force."

Speaking later to an assembly of his officers, Reynolds announced a new campaign to scour the Italian colony and bring the perpetrators to justice. "You men are going to find and bring in the heads of these vendetta organizations," he said. "You are going to find the sources of this Italian crime wave. There is no 'probably' about this order. I am going to give this situation every ounce of my own energy and I expect every man on my force to do his duty and do it to the limit."

Sounding much like Mayor Shakspeare twenty-six years earlier, after the Hennessy shooting, he exhorted his men to make mass arrests of Italians, without much bother over anything like modern probable cause. "I believe you will find that, out of every ten you arrest, nine will have a loaded revolver concealed on his person."

Draconian as these measures were, Reynolds was adamant. "When we get through with our work," he concluded, "New Orleans will be a city in which no agent of the Black Hand will have any desire to operate." It was, of course, a vow that New Orleanians had heard many times.

The final campaign in the war against Storyville began in January of 1917, just months before the United States entered the ongoing war in Europe. On the night of the fifteenth, the Citizens League of Louisiana held a mass meeting at the First Methodist Church on St. Charles Avenue to launch the effort. "We have in the City of New Orleans a Sodom," announced the first speaker, Rev. S. H. Werlein (uncle of Storyville-hater Phillip Werlein). "Last year an expert reformer visited the red-light district and the revelations he made were so repulsive that no decent person could read them without a blush of shame. The cabaret, an institution that is utterly violative of the law, flourishes. We have in the city some fifteen hundred or sixteen hundred saloons —"

"Nineteen hundred and twenty!" Jean Gordon corrected him from the audience.

"Nineteen hundred and twenty," Dr. Werlein repeated ("obviously pleased by the interruption," the *Daily States* observed), "and I don't suppose there is one of them that doesn't violate the law."

At last, the city's upright citizens were fed

up enough to really do something about the situation. And for once they had the full support of the city's newspapers, virtually all of which had now embraced the cause of total prohibition. "We have the *American*, the *Times-Picayune*, the *Item*, and even the *States* with us in this fight," he thundered on. "I have more hope for the press of New Orleans today than I've ever had before."

With the fourth estate now united behind vigorous reform, according to Werlein, the city's elected officials would finally have to take real steps to solve the vice problem. "The mayor and the commissioner of police have the opportunity to immortalize themselves," the reverend said in closing. "They have the law — let them enforce it! They have the police — let them instruct it!"

Then Miss Gordon herself stepped to the pulpit. Now approaching her fiftieth birthday, the city's Joan of Arc was already a seasoned veteran of moral campaigns like this, and she was not one to mince words. "I stand here tonight," she began, "and make the statement — in all solemnness and in full appreciation of what I am saying — that I have been keeping tabs on political and moral conditions in this city for the past 25 years, and never have I seen such open, flagrant violation of all moral laws as under the present commissioner of police and public safety."

Violations were numerous all across the

city, she continued — ranging from the sanctioned gambling on horses at the Fair Grounds racetrack to the blatant disregard of the Sunday Closing Law at the "Dago shop" on her very own street corner. But far more insidious was the grave danger posed to the city's young girls by the ubiquity of vice as practiced in the legal red-light district. "Never in the history of the world," she proclaimed, "has society had to face the problem of making the city a safe place for the young girl to go to and fro in . . . But due to the changed economic conditions in which we find ourselves, girls of fourteen and upwards are leaving their homes every day at 6 or 6:30, not to return until 7 [in the evening] — if then. . . . Being able to earn a little money makes the child of fourteen or fifteen very independent and only too willing to listen to the temptations offered by the advocates of a gay life as against the advice of a mother. Where are the fathers of the girls from whose mothers I receive note after note telling me of the downfall of their daughters?"

The root of the problem, however, was not the girls' mothers and fathers; it was a lack of vigilance among those men who had been entrusted with enforcement of the laws — including those men who posed as reformers. "For the commissioner of public safety [Harold Newman] to say that he does not know that the Gay-Shattuck Law is being violated is to convict him of one of three things — he is either so utterly lacking mentally that he has not a proper perception of his duties, or he is utterly negligent of the affairs of his office, or else he is acting in conjunction with other authorities *not* to see violations." Miss Gordon did not mention those authorities by name, but another speaker obliged. "In the name of God," Rev. William Huddlestone Allen shouted, jumping up from his chair in the audience, "who is the man higher up in this town? Is he Tom Anderson? If it's Tom Anderson, let's take his crown away from him; if it is Martin Behrman, let's shift him!"

The mass meeting stretched on into the night, with speaker after speaker reiterating the new unanimity among the city's righteous citizens to finally demand action of their elected officials. At the end, a vote was taken on whether the Citizens League should submit a full report on vice conditions to District Attorney Luzenberg. It passed without a single negative vote. "Take it to the district attorney," one speaker concluded, "and tell him if he don't do his duty, you'll kick him out!"

Whether Tom Anderson's crown would finally be taken from him remained to be seen. But as one reporter later put it, it was now clear "that the most serious and hopeful reform movement of this generation in New

Orleans had actually begun."

And, miraculously, the city really did respond, and promptly. CITY WILL CONTROL SEGRE-GATED AREA UNDER NEW SYSTEM read the headline in the *Times-Picayune* of January 24. Commissioner Newman, acting with the grudging acquiescence of Mayor Behrman, had announced sweeping new measures to "drop the lid" on Storyville and the adjacent Tango Belt. For one thing, the city imposed a new ban on cribs in the District. No longer would prostitutes be allowed to rent these places (at exorbitant rates) by the hour or day; the women must hereafter actually live in these structures in order to practice their profession from them. Moreover, any prosti-tutes living outside the boundaries of the Tenderloin would immediately be evicted, even if their workplace was within the Dis-trict. As for the cabarets and saloons of Storyville, Newman would refuse to renew their licenses once they expired, so that the places could be closed for good. Until that time, he would revoke their permits for music and for staying open all night. "The cabarets as they have been conducted in the cabaret district, and as legal institutions, are impos-sible," the commissioner announced. A simple sandwich would no longer serve as a way of getting around the Gay-Shattuck Law. In order to operate and serve drinks, a cabaret or dance hall "must have a licensed restaurant attached." And to ensure that these goals were actually accomplished, Newman would take personal command of the city's police department until further notice.

But the edict that would change the culture of Storyville more than any other was Newman's order for the total racial segregation of the District. Going well beyond the requirements of Gay-Shattuck, the order would require all "Negro inmates" to vacate the neighborhood by March 1 and reestablish themselves in the Uptown district that had come to be known as Black Storyville. Even customers would be segregated under the plan. "The appearance of a white man in the Negro district will cause his arrest," Newman decreed, and "should a Negro woman even stroll in the white district, she will be jailed." As for the famous octoroon houses of Basin Street, they would either move or be closed, since the word "Negro" in New Orleans now meant any person with even a trace of African blood, whether self-described as black, Creole, or octoroon.

This was, needless to say, an extreme measure. Until now, Storyville had been more or less an oasis of relative racial tolerance. Granted, the District had not been entirely immune to the prevailing mood of racial regimentation; by 1908, for instance, the listings in the Blue Books, formerly separating prostitutes into "white," "colored," and "octoroon" categories, had begun describing the women only as "white" or "colored." But the attraction of the mixed-race brothels had apparently not diminished significantly. This lingering appeal, in fact, was the source of much of the wrath against Storyville from reformers like Philip Werlein, for whom the idea of interracial contact seemed far more objectionable than that of legalized prostitution. But now, Basin Street as an affront to white racial purity would be a thing of the past. And when in February the city council unanimously passed Ordinance 4118, Newman's edict officially became city law. Beginning on March 1, Storyville — and Basin Street in particular — would become a very different and very segregated place.

For Tom Anderson, the racial segregation of the District would not be particularly onerous. His extensive interests in Storyville brothels were virtually all white-only (and there is some evidence that Anderson, Mayor Behrman, and other Ring politicians allowed Newman to go ahead with his plan because they thought it would mollify reformers without actually closing the legal district). But for important Storyville figures like Lulu White, Willie Piazza, and Emma Johnson — with their large investments in brothels founded on the trafficking of interracial sex — the new law promised to be financially disastrous. White, Piazza, and a score of other madams and prostitutes immediately filed suit against the city, attacking the ordinance on constitutional grounds. They claimed that it denied their rights to equal protection under the law and discriminated against them — not on the basis of where they lived, but rather on their employment outside the home. Surprisingly, the court initially upheld these petitions, and when the March 1 deadline arrived, many were allowed to remain in Storyville pending the outcome of their legal actions (though not without first being arrested).

But events in the greater world would soon render all of these cases moot. On April 6, 1917, the United States officially entered the war in Europe. Mayor Behrman and New Orleans' business leaders, hoping to attract federal dollars and visitors to the city, lobbied to host a military encampment within city limits. Their effort succeeded, and doughboys were soon pouring into Camp Nicholls in City Park. As hoped, this influx proved to be a boon to the local economy — not least of all in Storyville, given the proclivities of young soldiers. But it also put the city at the mercy of the US Department of War. And the federal government in times of war had powers that social reformers could only dream of. Before summer arrived, Congress would pass a law that — more than any local reform effort ever could — would threaten the very existence of the twenty-year-old legalized district, leaving the city little choice but to close its famous tenderloin entirely.

Storyville, in other words, was now truly under siege. But it would not go down without a final fight.

■ ■ ■ ■

PART FOUR:
TWILIGHT OF THE
DEMIMONDE

1917–1920

■ ■ ■ ■

■ ■ ■ ■

CHAPTER 16
EXODUS

■ ■ ■ ■

Louis Armstrong and Joe Oliver **Hogan**
Jazz Archive, Tulane University

Little Louis Armstrong needed money. Ever since the shooting incident at Henry Ponce's honky-tonk, the place had been closed down, meaning that Louis had lost his best and most regular paying gig. The recent reform efforts to suppress the city's cabarets, meanwhile, had made other engagements harder to come by. Armstrong still had his job making deliveries on the coal cart (pulled by an amiable mule named Lucy), and Mayann had started working as a domestic for club owner Henry Matranga, but it wasn't enough. Not long before, one of Mayann's second cousins had died after giving birth to an illegitimate son, Clarence. Louis, though still in his teens, had decided to take financial responsibility for raising the boy (he would later adopt him). So now there were four mouths to feed in their little household, and Louis was feeling the pressure to earn.

So he thought he might try his hand at a slightly different kind of business. "I had noticed that the boys I ran with had prostitutes working for them," he later recalled. "I wanted to be in the swim, so I cut in on a chick." The chick in question was named Nootsy, and although she was hardly a great beauty — she was "short and nappy-haired and she had buck teeth," according to Armstrong — she made decent money. Of course, it's questionable how much value a shy, peaceable teenager could be to her as a pimp, but Nootsy apparently took to him immediately. One night she even invited him to share her bed. Louis, who admitted being a little afraid of "bad, strong women," demurred. "I wouldn't think of staying away from Mayann and Mama Lucy," he told her, "not even for one night."

"Aw, hell," Nootsy replied. "You are a big boy now. Come in and stay."

But Louis still refused. In a fit of pique, Nootsy grabbed a pocket-knife and plunged it into her new pimp's left shoulder. He retreated in a panic, planning to say nothing about the incident. But when he got home, Mayann saw the blood on his shirt and coaxed the story out of him. Enraged, she pushed her son aside and marched right over to Nootsy's crib, with Louis and several of his neighborhood friends following behind. She pounded on the door, and the moment Nootsy opened it, Mayann grabbed the prostitute by the throat. "What you stab my son for?" she shouted.

Fortunately, Black Benny was among the witnesses to this spectacle. "Don't kill her, Mayann," the drummer pleaded, pulling her off the traumatized woman. "She won't do it again."

"Don't ever bother my boy again," Mayann spat, still furious. "You are too old for him. He did not want to hurt your feelings, but he don't want no more of you."

So much for that experiment in income supplementation. But Louis still had his music to fall back on, though even on the bandstand he was not invariably successful. He was still a relative beginner on the cornet, and despite his substantial raw talent, his repertoire was limited. This fact became painfully clear when he was asked to sit in for his mentor on a gig. Joe Oliver, it seems, had taken up with a woman named Mary Mack and only had the opportunity to visit with her from eight to eleven in the evenings. Oliver asked violinist Manuel Manetta and trombonist Kid Ory, whose band he was playing with, whether Louis could substitute for him during those hours. They agreed, but discovered that the protégé did not have the drawing power of his mentor. According to Manetta, Louis knew how to play only three tunes at this time, which the group would have to play over and over again, to an almost empty house. "People lined up outside,"

Manetta recalled, "but not a soul came in the hall" — until, that is, Oliver returned from his tryst at eleven P.M., and the crowd flooded in like the Mississippi River rushing through a levee breach.

Part of the problem could have been Armstrong's style, which may have been a little too advanced for these early jazz audiences. Louis played in a freer, highly improvisational manner, tracing a complex melodic line more like a clarinet's obbligato than the lead cornet's usual, relatively straightforward, statement of the tune. ("I'd play eight bars and be gone," he later admitted. "Clarinet things, nothing but figurations and things like that . . . running all over a horn.") Oliver once even criticized the boy for this. "Where's that lead?" he asked Louis one night after hearing him perform in a honky-tonk band. "You play some lead on that horn, let people know what you're playing." But Armstrong was already taking the sound pioneered by Bolden and moving it in new directions. Audiences — not to mention his fellow jazzmen — would eventually catch up.

The increasingly oppressive atmosphere in New Orleans, however, was making some of Armstrong's colleagues — like Sidney Bechet — yearn to get out of the Crescent City and try their luck elsewhere. Certainly Bechet wasn't hurting for work; in recent years — making good on the astounding versatility he'd displayed as a child at Piron's barber-shop — he'd been developing his skills on other instruments. He'd learned to play the cornet (to pick up work with marching bands) as well as the saxophone (a relatively new instrument that had yet to make much impact in New Orleans). Even so, he was still impressing audiences primarily as a clarinet-ist. For his occasional gigs at Pete Lala's, he'd learned George Baquet's old trick of taking his clarinet apart as he was playing it. When-ever he'd perform the stunt, gradually disas-sembling the instrument until he was tooling away on the mouthpiece alone, the crowds would respond with enthusiastic glee. "Mr. Basha [*sic*] is screaming 'em every night with his sensational playing," one black newspaper wrote, about a series of performances at New Orleans' Lincoln Theatre. "Basha says, look out, Louis Nelson, I am coming."

But when an opportunity arose to play outside the city, Bechet grabbed it. In late 1916, pianist Clarence Williams put together a traveling vaudeville troupe; Bechet signed on to play in a quartet that would accompany comedy and vocal routines (with the musi-cians sometimes doubling as actors in the skits). The company set out with hopes of touring widely throughout the country, but ran out of bookings once they reached Galveston, Texas. Bechet and pianist Louis Wade, still eager to see the world beyond

New Orleans, joined a traveling carnival for a time — until one day they woke up in a town called Plantersville and discovered that the whole company had moved on without them. "When we went down to the carnival ground in the morning, it was just an empty field," Bechet recalled. "I learned later there had been some sheriff who had come around and told them they had to clear out. And so there we were."

A few nights later, Sidney was asked to play for a dance in town. He was reluctant at first; the dance would end late, and walking back to his lodgings after midnight would be a dangerous thing for a black stranger to do in a small Southern town. But one of the organizers promised to find someone local to walk him home, so Sidney agreed to do it. Unfortunately, however, his escort proved to be a drunken white man whose idea of a joke was taunting his young companion and scaring him half to death. As they were passing through a dark and lonely rail yard, the man disappeared into the blackness and then jumped out at Sidney from behind a pile of railroad ties. Sidney, who had picked up a slab of wood for protection, swung it at him before he could think twice. "I felt that stick hit and I knew I'd fixed him good," Bechet wrote. "He made a grab at me and I swung that stick again, and then I didn't know what I was doing." Panicking, Bechet started running away along the dark railroad tracks as fast as he could. "I kept running for a mile, maybe a mile and a half, until I had to catch my breath."

Now he was truly frightened. In these parts, he knew, a black man who assaulted a white man could not expect to live long, no matter how justified his action. So he hopped on the first freight train that passed, hoping it would take him back to Galveston, where one of his older brothers was living at the time. But his trouble didn't end there. A brakeman who had seen him board came over the top of one of the boxcars and began swinging his club at Bechet, trying to knock him off the ladder he clung to. But Sidney would not let go. "He could have killed me," he recalled, "but I'd have died holding on to that bar."

Eventually — perhaps after seeing how young Bechet was — the brakeman gave up trying to dislodge him from the ladder. He came down between the cars and made the young man climb to the top of the ladder. Then he marched him back along the swaying boxcar roofs to the caboose. Sidney was expecting trouble, but the brakeman had turned friendly now; he and the other crewmen in the caboose talked about having Bechet arrested at the next stop, but he could tell that they were just teasing. He also found out that the train was headed straight to Galveston, just as he'd hoped. "That kind of changing around, the way luck goes faster than you can figure it," he later wrote, "it just won't be understood."

When the brakeman saw the clarinet case tucked into Sidney's waistband, he asked to hear him play, and Sidney complied. "If I had any doubt before [about the brakeman's good intentions], I knew it was gone when I saw him sitting there listening to the music. It was noisy in that caboose, but the clarinet had a tone that cut through those train sounds, and I could tell that these men, they were enjoying the music real good."

And so he played for them all the way to Galveston, rocking along in the caboose through the chilly Texas night. When they finally reached the station, the brakeman even pulled him aside and told him how to get away from the train yards without running into the resident detective, who would be on the lookout for tramps.

For the next several weeks, Sidney lived with his brother Joe in Galveston. They'd play some engagements together at local joints, returning home early every night. But Sidney, being Sidney, could behave only for so long. One night when his brother wasn't with him, he stayed out late, hopping from saloon to saloon as the hours passed unnoticed. In one place he met a Mexican guitarist who spoke little English but "could play the hell out of that guitar." They jammed together for a time, and then, at the end of the night, when Sidney learned that the man had no money and no place to stay, he decided to take him home to his brother's house.

It was apparently time for Sidney's luck to change again. As they made their way down M Street in the early hours of the morning, they were stopped by two policemen who asked them where they were going. Sidney tried to explain that they were going to his brother's house, which was tucked away on an alley he knew only as "M and a Half Street." The cops just laughed, claiming that there was no such place, and carted them off to jail as suspicious characters.

It quickly turned into a nightmare. One of the detectives at the station, who had lost a hand in a shooting incident in Galveston's Mexican ghetto, apparently held all Mexicans responsible for his misfortune and proceeded to beat Sidney's friend until his face was an unrecognizable bloody pulp. Sidney could only watch in terror. "I was just standing there," he recalled, "frozen up with fear, thinking they'd be doing the same to me . . . that it would be me lying on the floor with my face kicked in."

In the end, they merely threw him into a cell with several other men and slammed the door behind him. They hadn't hurt him physically. They'd even let him keep his clarinet. And that was what he turned to for comfort. "It was while I was in jail there," he wrote, "that I played the first blues I ever played with a lot of guys singing and no other instruments, just the singing. And, oh my God, what singing that was."

With Sidney playing along, the other men in the cell just started chanting about the hard times they'd seen. "This blues was different from anything I ever heard. Someone's woman left town, or someone's man, he'd gone around to another door . . . I could *taste* how it felt . . . I was seeing the chains and that gallows, feeling the tears on my own face, rejoicing in the Angel the Lord sent down for that sinner. Oh my God, that was a blues."

For Bechet, it was a lesson about where the blues — and the blues impulse behind jazz — really came from. The singer or player of blues, he realized, "was more than just a man. He was like every man that's been done a wrong. Inside him he's got the memory of all the wrong that's been done to my people . . . You just can't ever forget it. There's nothing about that night I could ever forget."

The next morning, his brother explained to the police that there really was an M and a Half Street, and got him released from jail. (Sidney would never know what happened to his Mexican friend.) As they walked home, Joe told him that he'd just gotten a job offer to play in New Orleans again, and he wanted Sidney to come back and play with him.

Sidney agreed immediately. "I hadn't been out of New Orleans long," he wrote, "but there never was anyone who could have been readier to go back." Before the week was out, he was home again.

But Bechet would soon have other opportunities to escape the oppressive environment of his Southern home. Many of the jazzmen who had already left New Orleans were finding enthusiastic audiences elsewhere in the country. Freddie Keppard, for one, kept sending home newspaper clippings from the road, full of praise from critics in places like San Francisco, New York, and Chicago. And it wasn't just musicians who were making good elsewhere. With the economy gearing up for the coming war effort and factories losing many of their workers to the armed forces, jobs were increasingly plentiful in the industrialized cities of the North; some companies were even sending labor agents through the South to recruit black workers for their factories. The first wave of the Great Migration of African Americans had begun, and its pull would be felt by blacks across the South for decades to come.

Those who went north, moreover, now had a little money in their pockets to spend on entertainment. And spend they did, in numerous new clubs and theaters, some owned and operated by black entrepreneurs. In Northern cities, jazz could be performed with far less fear of police raids and reform efforts aimed at suppressing the music in the name of morality and white supremacy. The new sound, in fact, was exciting admiration even among certain white audiences. In 1917, a white ensemble called the Original Dixieland Jazz Band (ODJB) — made up of New Orleanians Nick LaRocca, Larry Shields, and some other players from Jack Laine's old Reliance Brass Bands — made the first jazz recordings for Victor in New York. Some black musicians disparaged the work of these white interlopers, who were admittedly less skilled technically and who played virtually everything so fast that they drained all of the soul out of it. Sidney Bechet, for one, didn't think white musicians could really play jazz. "I don't care what you say," he wrote in his autobiography, "it's awful hard for a man who isn't black to play a melody that's come deep out of black people. It's a question of feeling . . . Take a number like *Livery Stable Blues*. We'd played that before they could remember; it was something we knew about a long way back. But theirs, it was a burlesque of the blues. There wasn't nothing serious in it anymore."

But for white audiences, the music of the ODJB was a sensation. Their recording of "Livery Stable Blues" became wildly popular. And soon many black bands were reaping the benefits of that success. Some black groups changed up the composition of their ensembles, eliminating the violin to emulate the ODJB lineup. They also adopted the neologism "jazz" — sometimes spelled "jass" or even "jasz" in these early years — for the music they had informally been calling "ragtime" for twenty years. Before long, black bands were recording as well, to wide popular acclaim. And 1917 was the turning point. As one historian put it: "By 1917 jazz, the Southern folk music, had emerged as jazz, the profitable commodity." Whatever its reception among the elites of its place of birth, Bolden's new sound now belonged to the world.

In New Orleans, however, the American entry into the war — and the simultaneous reinvigoration of local reform efforts against vice — was making the situation for local jazzmen increasingly dire. Not least of the troubles was the fact that many musicians now had to worry about being conscripted into the military. In July, the federal government instituted a draft lottery for all men twenty-one to thirty-one years of age. Louis Armstrong and some of the other rising players were still too young to worry, but most of the other musicians fit squarely into that age bracket, and few were enthusiastic about serving. One night, after a gig attended by Mayor Behrman's secretary, Manuel Manetta asked him whether his and Ory's band would have to be broken up. The secretary told him not to worry, that any band members who were married would be exempt from the draft. As Manetta later recalled: "A lot of these guys were running wild" at the time, neglecting their marriages. "Well," Manetta admitted, "they [soon] made up with their wives."

The more serious problem was collateral damage from the other war — the one between reformers and the forces of vice in the city. Commissioner Newman's moves to close the cribs, segregate Storyville, and enforce the requirements of Gay-Shattuck had taken their toll, forcing substantial layoffs of musicians, waiters, bartenders, and prostitutes. Emboldened by these successes (and by his growing approval among the reform element), Newman next turned his sights on a zealous enforcement of the Sunday Closing Law, ordering a detail of patrolmen to adopt plainclothes and visit saloons on the Sabbath to root out violators. For Mayor Behrman, this was going too far. Using plainclothes police to "spy on business people," he announced, was contrary to good public policy, an inducement to distrust and an invitation to graft. Newman disagreed. "You might just as well telephone to a burglar that you are coming to arrest him as to expect policemen in uniform to catch violations of the Sunday law," he insisted.

But Behrman drew the line on this issue. The mayor instructed Superintendent Reynolds to discontinue the practice; Newman, who had nominal authority over the police force, issued orders for the practice to continue. After one Sunday when police had no idea whether to don their bluecoats or not, the conflict came to a head — and Behrman won. In a highly sanctimonious statement to the press, Newman announced his resignation as commissioner of public safety. "I do not believe I could have slept another night with this thing hanging over me," he said. "It was a violation of all my principles and moral convictions." But he warned the Ring that public sentiment had changed in the city: "The people of New Orleans have seen that the Sunday law can be enforced, and the brewery interests have made a bad move for themselves in this effort to reopen the city. The sentiment here is for law enforcement."

Reformers soon had the federal government behind them as well. The war effort had raised concerns nationwide about the fitness of the country's fighting forces; the feds were now insisting on strict enforcement of all vice laws designed to keep soldiers and sailors away from the evils of indulgence. "Men must live straight to shoot straight," as Navy secretary Josephus Daniels put it. That meant keeping temptation out of their path. "Keeping Fit to Fight," a pamphlet written by the American Social Hygiene Association and distributed to all soldiers, put the matter in no uncertain terms: "The greatest menace to the vitality and fighting vigor of any army is venereal diseases (clap and syphilis) . . . [and] the escape from this danger is up to the patriotism and good sense of soldiers like yourself . . . WOMEN WHO SOLICIT SOLDIERS FOR IMMORAL PURPOSES ARE USUALLY DISEASE SPREADERS AND FRIENDS OF THE ENEMY."

While the War Department did stop short of some extreme measures of enforcing chastity (like that of one letter writer who proposed that they "shoot the lewd women as you would the worst German spy"), they did declare all tenderloin and other entertainment districts off-limits for members of the armed forces. But such edicts proved difficult to enforce, especially in New Orleans. Reports abounded of soldiers and sailors sneaking into Storyville — often in civilian clothing helpfully rented to them by District entrepreneurs. And if the soldiers couldn't get to Storyville, Storyville obligingly came to them. One investigation of conditions around Camp Nicholls revealed that numerous women from the District were flocking to the vicinity and "accosting soldiers as they enter or leave camp grounds." Makeshift houses of prostitution were set up along

418

Bayou St. John near the camp, and "large numbers of girls 14 to 17 years old remain in City Park after nightfall visiting with guardsmen in secluded places."

On May 18, however, Congress took a decisive step, passing the Selective Service Act of 1917. Section 13 of the act, designed to prevent venereal disease among the troops, explicitly outlawed prostitution within a ten-mile radius of any military encampment; at the same time, it set a penalty of $1,000 or twelve months in jail for anyone guilty of selling alcohol to soldiers. DISTRICT OR TROOPS MUST GO ran the headline in the *Daily Item* of July 1, 1917. Unless Storyville was closed, the paper reported, "there could be no post, barracks, or cantonment in — nor even any movement of troops through — the city of New Orleans."

Even so, Mayor Behrman delayed taking any immediate action, and this did not go unnoticed. "Situation here not substantially improved," one local reformer telegraphed to Raymond Fosdick, chairman of the Commission on Training Camp Activities. "Recent regulations largely disregarded. District frequented by men in uniform in spite of police orders to keep them out." Other local reform groups, from the Citizens League and the Louisiana chapter of the Women's Christian Temperance Union, also stepped up the pressure on Fosdick and other federal authorities: "Must the Louisiana boys be sacrificed to the brewers of the state while the mothers who have borne these sons, and reared them to young manhood, beg and implore the government to protect them?"

Finally, in August, a representative of the Fosdick Commission showed up at City Hall, claiming to have orders to officially close the restricted district once and for all. Mayor Behrman refused to comply, insisting that the man had no authority to issue the order and urging him to consult with local military commanders before doing anything. Then, in a hastily organized junket, the mayor took a train to Washington, DC, to put the matter before Secretary of War Newton Baker. In their face-to-face meeting, Behrman laid out the rationale for keeping Storyville open, pointing out that closing the District would merely scatter prostitution and vice around the city. The mayor also insisted that military and municipal police patrols could effectively keep the soldiers out of trouble. Secretary Baker, a former mayor of Cleveland, had his own opinions on the topic, but ultimately conceded that he "would not require anything to be done about [the] district unless [he] was told that soldiers were admitted to it, in which case it would have to be closed." Behrman left DC convinced that he had saved Storyville, at least temporarily.

But when local reformers got word of the

mayor's successful mission, they were outraged. Kate Gordon in particular railed against Behrman's alleged high-handedness, accusing him of making secret deals on behalf of his powerful friends and playing politics in a time of war. Behrman vehemently denied the charges. "I am at a loss to know just how Miss Gordon acquired her knowledge of what occurred at an interview at which she was not present," he remarked acidly. "How any sane person can attribute politics to anything connected with this whole matter is beyond me."

In the end, however, the old Ring warrior lost this battle. By late September, Navy Secretary Daniels had made the decision his superior would not. He sent a letter to Louisiana governor Ruffin G. Pleasant (and copied it to Mayor Behrman) expressing the secretary's "intense desire that immediate action be taken" in the matter. Knowing he could delay no longer, Behrman quickly drafted an ordinance requiring that the Storyville District be shut down, effective midnight of November 12. "Our city government has believed that the [vice] situation could be administered more easily and satisfactorily by confining it within a prescribed area," the mayor observed when presenting the ordinance. "Our experience has taught us that the reasons for this are unanswerable, but the Navy Department of the federal government has decided otherwise."

Even after unanimous passage of the ordinance by the city council, however, most people in Storyville believed that Tom Anderson would somehow save the day and keep the District open. And he certainly tried. In recent years, he had taken up with a madam named Gertrude Dix, a "witty, pretty, and natty" young transplant from Ohio who ran the brothel next door to the Annex at 209 Basin Street. Hoping to create a legal obstacle to the District's closing, he persuaded Dix to file a writ of injunction against the city, citing her substantial investment in the Basin Street brothel, including a $3,000-a-year lease running until 1919. Dix's attorney argued that the closing ordinance was not only unconstitutional and void, but that it would also subject his client to "irreparable injury and damage" by making it impossible for her to do business. Given the partial success of the Willie Piazza and Lulu White suits earlier that year, it was at least reasonable to think that Dix's suit might give the District at least a few more months of life.

Even so, desperation was setting in among the denizens of Storyville. In October, rumors began circulating that some of the Basin Street landlords were conspiring to burn their buildings to the ground in order to collect insurance on properties that were bound to lose much of their value should the ordinance be enforced. A police investigation found no evidence of any conspiracy; but insurance companies soon began canceling policies on properties within the District's boundaries. As the November deadline approached, special police details were sent into Storyville to put down threatened riots and demonstrations by the affected residents, though none ever developed. All hope of saving the District, it seemed, was pinned on Tom Anderson and the Dix court challenge.

On November 11, just one day before the scheduled closing, Judge F. D. King of the Civil District Court ruled that the city was within its rights in enforcing the new ordinance, and Dix's request for an injunction was denied. A hasty appeal to the Louisiana Supreme Court was likewise denied a few hours later. STORYVILLE DYING WITH FEW MOURNERS read the headline on a *Daily Item* story, which described how the atmosphere in all of the District's establishments — even Tom Anderson's — had become downright funereal in these last days: "Storyville was unusually quiet last night. . . . Men stood at the bars and discussed the situation in low voices. They told each other sad, sad stories, dolefully drank their drinks, and abjectly gazed out into the quiet streets."

As midnight approached on November 12, moving vans appeared on the streets of Storyville to start hauling furniture and brica-brac from the former pleasure palaces. Some secondhand dealers were looking to pick up a few bargains from the distressed prostitutes and madams. "Many were the eloquent arguments on why several occupants of huts should sell furniture worth $200 for $20," the *States* reported. "Words were passed, but little furniture changed hands." One exception was Willie Piazza's legendary white piano. According to Storyville legend, the magnificent instrument — once played by the likes of Tony Jackson and Jelly Roll Morton — was sold under duress for the sum of $1.25.

"As late as 11:30," according to the *States,* "a stream of women, Negro maids, and porters [wended] their way toward Rampart Street with furniture and cut glass on their backs." Louis Armstrong was there to witness the exodus. "It sure was a sad scene to watch the law run all those people out of Storyville," he wrote years later. "They reminded me of refugees. Some of them had spent the best part of their lives there. Others had never known any other kind of life."

And thus did Storyville become history. According to an editorial in the next day's *States,* New Orleans had finally "put itself in line with the enlightened moral sentiment of the country. The effect will not be to destroy the social evil. It will never be completely destroyed. But it has come to be against sound public policy to legally sanction the vice, and by enacting the [closing] law, New Orleans relieves herself of an advertisement which did her infinite harm abroad."

Certainly the *States* was right about one thing — prostitution would not end in New Orleans after the closing of the District. Despite federal efforts to keep an eye on the neighborhood, despite regular police raids to make sure the laws against prostitution were observed, despite even an attempt by local club women to create a program to retrain former prostitutes for worthier professions (a program for which, apparently, there were very few applicants), the practice of selling sex did not die in New Orleans. As Armstrong later observed: "After Storyville closed down — the people of that section spreaded out all over the city . . . so we turned out nice and reformed."

For Tom Anderson, however, the end of legalized prostitution in New Orleans was disastrous. Now almost sixty years old, a grandfather twice over, and suffering from high blood pressure, he was no longer the tireless empire builder he had been twenty years earlier, his young mistress notwithstanding. For a time after the District's demise, he tried to keep his old empire of vice intact, but it just became harder and harder. In the summer of 1918, the Fosdick Commission, still concerned about the corruption of soldiers, forbade dancing and the playing of any kind of music in cabarets. The order was enforced with particular energy at the Annex. In July, Anderson wrote a letter of protest to the new superintendent of police, Frank T. Mooney, complaining that he was being singled out by law enforcement. "As a citizen and taxpayer, and the operator of a licensed legal business," he wrote, "I do not intend to allow myself to be unfairly treated while the other fellow continues operating, and if necessary I will take the matter into the courts . . . I pay the largest license of any establishment in New Orleans. We have in every way complied with the law. Orders have been issued that no woman may eat in my place without an escort, and not even with an escort if she is a woman of questionable character. Yet she can go right next door or to any other restaurant in the city and eat. This is discrimination and can't stand in law."

The irony was humiliating. Tom Anderson, the man who in 1913 was seemingly exempt from legal restrictions imposed on other cabaret owners, was now the one hit hardest by them. Eventually, he turned the Annex over to his old lieutenant, Billy Struve, in order to focus on his Rampart Street place, the Arlington Restaurant. But even this establishment would soon be untenable as a business proposition. With Prohibition almost certain to pass in the near future, grand restaurants like the Arlington would face difficult times. By September, the *Times-Picayune* was gloating: "Tom Anderson's place in Rampart Street may be turned into a coffee-house when Uncle Sam puts the ban on other liquids next July," the paper reported. The writer thought it might actually do better business as an ice-cream parlor.

At least the erstwhile mayor of Storyville still had his legislative career in Baton Rouge to keep him busy, though now he had fewer vested interests to lobby for in the House. And his oil-company business, bolstered by the growing success of that industry in the Pelican State, was still thriving. So Tom Anderson was not quite out of the picture yet. He put day-to-day control of the Arlington into the hands of his son-in-law, George Delsa, and began spending much of his time with Gertrude Dix at his new summer home in Waveland, Mississippi. And who could tell what the future would bring? Perhaps after the war was over and the federal government got out of the purity business, there would be opportunities again in New Orleans. As the *States* had pointed out, the social evil could never be completely destroyed.

And so New Orleans in 1918 became a much tamer, more virtuous place than it had been just a few years earlier. Even Mardi Gras that year proved to be a decidedly subdued affair. Because of the war, the traditional

Carnival parades and balls were discontinued. Even masking was forbidden, because Mayor Behrman thought that "it might give the nation's enemies an opportunity to work mischief while disguised." The Spanish flu epidemic just made matters worse, closing down theaters and other places of congregation. Then, in the summer of 1918, Louisiana became the fourteenth state to pass the Prohibition Amendment to the Constitution. Soon it would be illegal even to drink a beer in the Great Southern Babylon.

Piling on in a time of difficulty, the *Times-Picayune* took the opportunity to perpetrate an assault on the city's own homegrown style of music. In a now-legendary editorial entitled "Jass and Jassism," published on June 20, 1918, the paper finally took notice of the phenomenon that had been thriving in its ghettos and entertainment districts for almost two decades now. "Why is the jass music?" the editorial (somewhat awkwardly) asked. "As well ask why is the dime novel, or the grease-dripping doughnut? All are manifestations of a low streak in man's tastes that has not yet come out in civilization's wash."

The editorial went on to pontificate on the differences between "truly great music" and its lesser, rhythm-based illegitimate cousins — to wit, "the hum of the Indian dance, the throb of the Oriental tambourines and kettledrums, the clatter of the clogs, the click of

Slavic heels, the thumpty-tumpty of the Negro banjo . . ." (Translation: music not created by privileged white people of Northern European heritage.) "On certain natures," the writer continued, "loud and meaningless sound has an exciting, almost an intoxicating effect, like crude colors and strong perfumes, the sight of flesh, or the sadic [*sic*] pleasure in blood. To such as those the jass music is a delight."

But respectable New Orleanians should not stand for the outrage: "In the matter of jass, New Orleans is particularly interested, since it has been widely suggested that this particular form of musical vice had its birth in this city — that it came, in fact, from doubtful surroundings in our slums. We do not recognize the honor of parenthood, but with such a story in circulation, it behooves us to be last to accept the atrocity in polite society, and where it has crept in we should make it a point of civic honor to suppress it. Its musical value is nil, and its possibilities of harm are great."

So much, it would seem, for the music that would eventually be regarded as the first truly American art form. The *Times-Picayune* did not approve of it. Nor — judging from the unusually large number of letters to the editor inspired by the editorial — did much of the paper's readership; even the correspondent most sympathetic to jazz referred to it as "a departure from the proper in music." But the editorial's reference to the new music as "musical vice" was telling. For the city's privileged white elite, jazz and vice were of a piece, along with blackness generally and, for that matter, Italianness, too. All were forms of contamination — blots on the city's escutcheon that found expression in crime, depravity, drunkenness, lewdness, corruption, and disease. These were the ills that reformers had first taken arms against almost thirty years earlier, with the lynchings at the Orleans Parish Prison. And now, in 1918, it seemed that perhaps the reformers had won. Storyville was closed, the Italian underworld was subdued, Jim Crow reigned supreme, and even jazz was under attack. Granted, the Ring was still in power, but the city seemed finally under some semblance of control. New Orleans' thirty-year civil war, like the Great War in Europe, appeared to be nearing an end, and the city was poised to become the kind of "normal," orderly, and businesslike place that the reformers wanted it to be.

Until, that is, the appearance of a mysterious figure with an ax in his hands.

■ ■ ■ ■

CHAPTER 17
A KILLER IN THE
NIGHT

■ ■ ■ ■

Diagram of an Axman crime scene
NOLA.com/The Times-Picayune

In the same manner in which Joseph Maggio and his wife, Italians, were chopped to death with a hatchet as they slept behind their grocery store at Upperline and Magnolia Streets a month ago, Louis Besumer and his wife were chopped with a hatchet early Thursday morning as they slept in their quarters back of their grocery store at Dorgenois and Laharpe Streets.

Police believe the hatchet user in both crimes was the same man.

The latest hatchet victims are in the Charity Hospital in a critical condition.

— *New Orleans Times-Picayune,*
June 28, 1918

First the Maggios and now the Besumers. Two similar crimes, two pairs of married grocers, two points on a grid that could be connected with a straight line of causality. Or not. Superintendent Frank T. Mooney couldn't be sure. His detectives were uncertain too, though some of them clearly wanted to believe that the two events were unrelated. There were, after all, a lot of corner groceries in New Orleans, and a lot of reasons why a married couple might be brutally attacked in one of them. The two crimes didn't *have* to be related. But it was impossible not to wonder: *Mrs. Maggio is going to sit up tonight just like Mrs. Toney.*

Certainly there were important differences between the two attacks. For one thing, they happened on entirely different sides of the city. The Besumer assault occurred over near Esplanade Ridge, in an established, densely settled part of town; it was more than four miles away from the sparsely populated edge of Uptown, where the Maggios had been killed. And Besumer, far from being Italian, was an Eastern European Jew — a Pole, he claimed — which made no sense if the attack was Black Hand–related. That organization preyed only on other Italians. Or at least that was what Mooney's senior detectives had always believed.

Another difference: the Besumers had actually survived their attack. They were now in Charity Hospital, both gravely injured, but Louis Besumer was expected to recover quickly. So Mooney had potential witnesses to this crime. But he hadn't been able to get much sense from either of them in their current state. The extreme trauma of the ax attacks, which had left both victims with apparent skull fractures, had disoriented them, and they claimed to know nothing about what had happened. It might be days before they could remember any details about the attacks.

And there were no other witnesses. No one in the neighborhood had seen or heard anything — at least not until John Zanca, the driver of a bakery van, had shown up at the Besumer grocery with a delivery of bread shortly before seven on Thursday morning. Zanca had been surprised to find the grocery door closed and locked; the store was usually open at that hour. So he'd pounded on the door, and, when he got no answer there, at a side door leading to the residence behind the grocery. Finally, Zanca heard a voice inside. Someone came around to the front door and unlocked it. And when it opened, he saw Louis Besumer standing unsteadily on the threshold. The grocer was holding a damp sponge to his face and blood was streaming from a deep wound over his right eye.

"My God," Zanca cried. "What happened?"

Besumer said he wasn't sure — that he was attacked in the night, but that it was nothing to worry about. Nonetheless, Zanca pushed past him into the store to reach the telephone. Besumer tried to stop him: He said that he didn't want the police or an ambulance, that he would see a private doctor instead. But

435

Zanca immediately telephoned the Fifth Precinct police station. "There's been a murder or something here," he shouted into the receiver, over Besumer's continuing objections.

Minutes later, when police arrived and entered the residence behind the store, they found a scene in gory disarray. In the first bedroom, a sheet-less bed with bloodstained pillows stood amid piles of clothing and other effects strewn over the floor. This was apparently where Besumer had been attacked. But in the back bedroom, under a sopping sheet, they found Mrs. Harriet Besumer, unconscious and bloodied, with gaping wounds over her left ear and on the top of her head. A smudged trail of bloody footprints led from the bedroom, out through the hall, to a screened-in gallery overlooking the backyard. Here police found a hank of hair sitting in a pool of gore. Leaning against the screen nearby was a rusty ax head separated from its wooden handle.

The pair were immediately transported to Charity Hospital, where Superintendent Mooney, apparently worried that he might lose his only witnesses, rushed to question them. He found Louis Besumer conscious but dazed. The grocer — fifty-nine years old, bespectacled, and somewhat scholarly in appearance — claimed to remember nothing of the attack, or of anything at all that happened the night before.

"I felt like I was going to faint," he told the superintendent from his hospital bed, describing the moment he awoke, "and remember getting up and finding my wife in bed covered with blood. I put a sheet on her. I also recall having washed my face with a sponge and going to the door when the baker knocked. I found the door was not locked and that the wrong key was in the lock."

This struck the superintendent as strange — Zanca had said that the grocery door was locked when he first tried it — and Mooney's first suspicion was that Besumer was dissembling, that he had attacked his wife himself, perhaps cutting his own head in the struggle. That would explain his insistence that Zanca call a private physician rather than an ambulance and the police. When Mrs. Besumer regained consciousness, however, she categorically denied that there had been a quarrel with her husband. But she could remember nothing else.

Over the next few hours, Louis Besumer became more talkative. For a man who had just been attacked with an ax, he soon grew remarkably expansive, even boastful. He was rich and well educated, he said, and he spoke many languages. Two years ago, he'd met and married Harriet Anna Lowe in Fort Lauderdale and the two had moved to New Orleans for a rest. He'd bought the grocery store for

437

$300 and was running it for a change of pace, almost as a hobby. His doctor, he said, had recommended that he do something like that — to buy and run a small, undemanding business — to help him recover from overwork.

"Have you any enemies?" Mooney asked him.

"Not that I know of."

"Any business competition?"

"Yes," Besumer replied, "some Italian grocers. I've been selling things pretty cheap."

Mooney made a note of it but didn't pursue that line of questioning any further.

Eventually, Mrs. Besumer became more lucid as well. When Mooney asked her whether she remembered being attacked on the gallery, she paused a moment and then said she thought she did. She remembered finding someone in the grocery early that morning. It was a mulatto man, she said, and he asked her for a package of tobacco. When she told the man that the grocery didn't carry tobacco, he chased her. He pursued her back through the grocery, across the hall of the living quarters, to the screened-in gallery, where he struck her with an ax. That, she said, was all she remembered.

Here, finally, was something tangible to work with. Mooney alerted his detectives on the crime scene, and by afternoon they had a suspect in custody. He was Lewis Obichon, a forty-one-year-old, light-skinned black man who had apparently done a few odd jobs for Besumer earlier that week. Found at his mother's home near the grocery, he'd been questioned about his whereabouts that morning. Obichon claimed that he'd been at the Poydras Market since one A.M. the night before. But when several witnesses denied this, Obichon admitted that he had lied and was evasive about why. He was arrested and taken to the Fifth Precinct station for further questioning.

But there were reasons for Mooney to doubt Mrs. Besumer's story. Why, for instance, would Mrs. Besumer be tending the open grocery in her nightclothes? Why wouldn't she have screamed while being pursued through the building by an ax-wielding assailant? And why would no one in the populous neighborhood have seen or heard anything at an hour when businesses up and down the street were opening for the day? All in all, Mooney was not satisfied with her account of the crime. And when he questioned Mrs. Besumer again a short time later, she turned vague and confused. No black man had attacked her, she insisted. "If I said so formerly, I didn't know what I was saying."

For Mooney, of course, this was maddening. He could see the Besumer case unraveling in the same way the Maggio investigation had come apart several weeks earlier. In that case, the evidence against Andrew Maggio, the victim's brother, had virtually evaporated under closer examination in the days after his arrest. The murder weapon that had been identified by a witness as Andrew's razor was not, after all, the one the barber had brought home from his shop "to hone a nick from the blade"; *that* razor had subsequently been found in Andrew's apartment, and the witness had been forced to admit his mistake. The alleged bloodstains on Andrew's shirt, moreover, had proved to be red wine stains.

Faced with these embarrassing blunders, Mooney had been obliged to release Andrew Maggio immediately. "The case has taken a peculiar turn," the superintendent had announced to the press, hoping to put a better face on the fiasco. "It has become more interesting from the standpoint of investigators. . . . Tomorrow we will take up another phase."

More "interesting" or not, the second phase of the Maggio investigation had yielded precisely nothing, and the case remained unsolved.

And now Mooney might have to release another man arrested on the mistaken testimony of a witness, with no alternative suspect. Hoping to put the case under tighter control, Mooney decided to deny reporters access to the confused and loose-tongued victims. But this did little to quiet the rampant speculation in the press. MYSTERY GROWS IN ORLEANS AX CASE, the *States* reported after a few days of fruitless investigation. The *Item*'s headline was more probing: MOTIVE OF AX MYSTERY PUZZLES POLICE: WHAT WAS BEHIND OUTRAGE? WHO DID IT?

By the weekend, the case had taken another bizarre turn. "My husband is a German," Mrs. Besumer blurted during one of her rambling monologues. "He claims he is not. I don't know where he got the money to buy his store." In July of 1918, with the United States actively at war with the Germans in Europe, this was an electrifying revelation, full of insidious possibilities. And when police turned up several suitcases in the Besumer home stuffed with hundreds of letters and pamphlets in Russian, Yiddish, and German, speculation rose to new heights. SPY PLOT MAY BE AT BOTTOM OF AX MYSTERY, the *Item* announced. Stories were soon circulating about hidden code books, suspiciously expensive clothing, and a foot locker fitted with a homemade secret compartment. If Besumer was indeed a German spy, the *Item* wondered, could this explain the violence that had occurred on Thursday morning? "Did the woman discover Besumer's supposed German connections and attack him? Did he have cause to distrust her loyalty and attack *her*? . . . Did the two have a fearful silent struggle on the gallery?"

Clearly Mooney, the neophyte police superintendent, was out of his depth. When agents from the Department of Justice arrived to question the Besumers, he was more than willing to turn at least this part of the investigation over to the feds. They began to have Besumer's letters translated and sent agents to Fort Lauderdale to pursue inquiries into the man's alleged business interests there.

All of this convinced detectives that the attacks were the result of something other than a crazed ax murderer, but Mooney just wasn't sure. Much as he would have liked to see the Besumer and Maggio cases as unrelated, he was convinced that the same assailant — crazed or not — was responsible for both crimes, and he wasn't afraid to say as much to the newspapers. The fact that Besumer was not Italian did not faze him. Besumer himself admitted that his business practices had upset his Italian competitors, and a neighbor had once even warned the grocer that his rivals might "burn him down" for his insistence on underselling them. And something else that Mrs. Besumer said was suggestive. On Monday morning, when she seemed to be getting some of her memory back, detectives had questioned her again about the events preceding the attacks.

"The last I remember," she said, "was the

evening before, about six o'clock, when I saw my husband counting his money at the safe in the grocery store. The door was open, and I said to him, 'Oh, you oughtn't to do that; anyone can see you and you will get us both killed one of these days.' But he didn't say anything, and I went back through the hall into the little screened gallery at the end. I don't remember anything more. I don't remember leaving the veranda. I don't remember doing anything there. I don't remember undressing, and they say I was found in my nightgown, in bed. Oh, my poor head!"

On Tuesday morning, five days after the attack, Louis Besumer was deemed healthy enough to be released from Charity Hospital. He was transported directly to police headquarters, where he spent three hours talking to Superintendent Mooney and several agents from the Department of Justice. Faced with an attentive audience, the ever-pompous Besumer again waxed grandiloquent, claiming that he was a student of criminology and a "born investigator." He would not rest, he said, until he had helped clear up the mystery, and was willing to borrow against his considerable assets — he could easily raise several hundred thousand dollars, he claimed — in order to get to the bottom of it.

Asked further questions about his history, he insisted on correcting a few "misunderstandings." First of all, he said, the woman identified as Mrs. Harriet Lowe Besumer was not his wife; she was instead his "traveling companion," toward whom he felt as toward a sister, which was why they slept in separate bedrooms. His actual wife was an invalid residing in Cincinnati. He also insisted that he was a Pole, not a German, and that he knew not nine foreign languages, as had been reported in the press, but thirteen. And although he still had no recollection of the attack, he was going to consult with physicians at Charity Hospital to recapture the memory "psychopathically."

Mooney and the federal agents were now uncertain how to proceed. There was clearly not enough evidence to hold Besumer in custody. Possessing letters written in German was no crime, even in wartime (unless, of course, the ongoing translations of them proved otherwise). And while it might be suspicious for a well-traveled, well-educated business tycoon to be running a corner grocery in New Orleans, it wasn't illegal. In the end, they agreed to release Besumer on his own recognizance. But Superintendent Mooney did assign two of his men — Detectives Balser and Baradot — to stay with Besumer, ostensibly to assist him in his investigations, but also to keep an eye on the man, whom no one was prepared to trust fully.

That afternoon, Mooney returned to Charity Hospital to speak to the woman calling herself Mrs. Besumer. When asked if she really was married to the grocer, she grew agitated. "If I am not, he is the greatest deceiver yet," she said. "He was married to me by a Jewish rabbi in New York two years ago and promised to turn Catholic and marry me with a priest. But he never did it."

"Did you have a license?"

"He said so."

"Did you see it?"

"No."

When asked why they slept in separate bedrooms, she claimed it was because he insisted on sleeping with an electric fan running in the room. She didn't like the noise it made, so she had moved to the back bedroom to sleep.

Trying a different tack, Mooney then asked her: "Mr. Besumer read the newspapers a great deal, didn't he?"

"Yes, oh yes," she replied.

"Did he read about the Maggio case?"

"The what?"

"The Maggio case — those Italians who were found murdered in bed with an ax and a razor."

"Oh yes. [It was] like our case, wasn't it?"

"And you never before saw the ax with which you were apparently struck?"

"No. We didn't have an ax in the house even."

Mooney left Charity Hospital that afternoon as confused as ever. Was it possible that Besumer, wishing to kill the woman who passed as his wife, struck her with an ax in order to make it look like the work of the Maggio assailant, whose crime he took such an interest in? Could he actually have inflicted his own head wound as a way of allaying suspicion? Granted, his injury was far less grave than the woman's, but it was serious enough to cast doubt on any such notion.

It was now a week since the attacks at the Besumer grocery, and New Orleanians were clamoring for some — for any — explanation from the city's law enforcement authorities. Mooney had supposedly reformed the notoriously corrupt and incompetent police department — the latest in a long series of attempts to improve the force. But as in the Maggio case in May, results of any kind in this investigation were distressingly thin. In fact, the two detectives he'd assigned to watch Louis Besumer had proved to be an all-too-familiar embarrassment to the force. One afternoon when they were supposed to be surveilling their prime suspect, the two were found at the Milneburg resort on Lake Pontchartrain, enjoying an afternoon excursion. Mooney had been forced to demote both of them — something that hadn't happened on the force in more than twenty years. Needless to say, this kind of story did not inspire public confidence in the police department *or* its new superintendent.

When speaking to the press, however, Mooney tried to seem confident and in control of the situation. He did admit that the case was "one of the most baffling mysteries" ever to confront the department, but he assured the public that all avenues of investigation were being vigorously pursued. "We are making progress," he temporized, "and I feel sure that, before we are through, the mystery will have been solved."

It's doubtful that New Orleanians found much comfort in these anodynes, but public concern about the crime was apparently on the wane. Many people seemed to have come to the same conclusion as Mooney's detectives — that the attack was the result of some strange domestic quarrel that the Besumers were determined not to talk about. As such, the case was likely unrelated to the Maggio case, which itself could just have been the result of some obscure Italian feud. Maybe there *was* no mysterious axman haunting the streets of New Orleans after all.

But then — on July 7 — something happened that immediately changed the complexion of the case. After eleven days of confusion, Mrs. Besumer apparently got her memory back for real.

"Along toward dawn," she told police from her hospital bed, recalling the morning of June 27, "I awoke from sleep. I don't know what caused me to wake, but I opened my eyes and in the light I saw a man standing above me, making some sort of motion with his hands. . . ."

She said she told the man to go away, but he remained, still making strange gestures that she couldn't decipher. She said she felt dazed, perhaps because he had already struck her with the ax. But she *could* describe him: He was tall, heavyset, a white man with rumpled, dark brown hair. He wore a heavily soiled white shirt open at the collar.

The next thing she remembered was waking up outside on the gallery, her face in a pool of blood. "I couldn't breathe," she said. "I was strangling. I tried to get up, but each time I would fall back. There were feet scuffling about me . . . the feet of a man, clad in shoes that were black and heavy and laced — the kind of shoe a laborer might wear." But then she blacked out again, and remembered nothing else before waking up in the hospital, hours later.

Hearing this, Superintendent Mooney was inclined to be cautious, aware that this latest recollection of Harriet Lowe Besumer, if that was her name, might be another fantasy, like her account of being attacked by a mulatto. But for many in New Orleans, the story was credible enough. And it led to a chilling conclusion: the axman was real, and he apparently was still at large.

■ ■ ■ ■

CHAPTER 18
"ALMOST AS IF HE
HAD WINGS"

■ ■ ■ ■

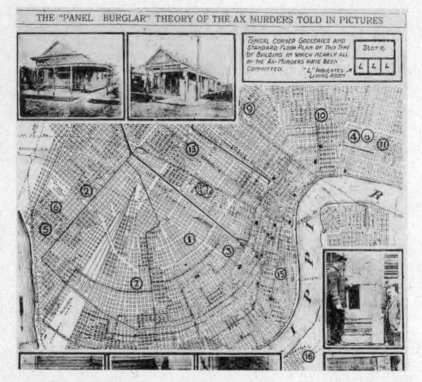

The Times-Picayune *'s attempt to make sense of the ax attacks* **NOLA.com/The Times-Picayune**

It was two A.M. when a woman's scream pierced the silence of the soggy August night. Kate Gonzales, lying in bed with her husband, bolted awake at the sound. She was confused at first. Had she really heard something, or had she just dreamt it? But then another scream erupted from the darkness, and the sounds of scuffling, a shattering of glass. The commotion seemed to be coming from next door, in the other half of their duplex Elmira Street cottage. This was where Kate's sister lived with her husband and their three young children. Mary Schneider, she knew, was alone with the children that night, since her husband was working a night shift.

Kate shook her husband awake. When he also heard the screams, the two of them jumped out of bed and rushed into the street. Several other neighbors were already standing on the banquette, staring at the front door of the Schneider home, which stood wide open like a gaping mouth.

Gonzales and the neighbors entered the cottage, which was quiet now. In the middle room they found Mary Schneider, nine months pregnant, sprawled across the bed in a state of semiconsciousness. Bloody gashes lacerated her scalp and mouth. Several broken teeth lay scattered on the bedclothes, which were stained with oil from a broken glass lamp that lay on the floor beside the bed. Mary muttered something about being attacked by a tall, heavyset man, but then fainted before she could say more.

Police and an ambulance were called, and Mary Schneider was rushed to Charity Hospital, directly to the maternity ward because of her "delicate condition."

Toward morning, when Edward Schneider returned from his job at the Southern Pacific wharf, he found his entire household in an uproar. Police were combing through the cottage and yard for clues, and other officers were searching the surrounding neighborhood. Superintendent Mooney, personally overseeing the investigation with Chief of Detectives George Long, asked Schneider to check the house to see if anything had been taken. A wardrobe in the bedroom had been broken open, and six or seven dollars had apparently been taken from the top shelf. But a box containing $102 of Schneider's back pay had been left untouched in plain sight on the bottom shelf. Nothing else was missing.

The newspaper reporters wanted to know immediately whether Mooney regarded this as another axman attack. The superintendent was cautious at first. Mrs. Schneider's head wound, he pointed out, was quite possibly caused by the broken oil lamp that had been found beside the bed; in fact, several strands of the victim's hair had been found on the lamp, snagged on the metal prongs that held the lamp's glass chimney to its base. But the wound to Mrs. Schneider's mouth was another matter, obviously caused by something heavier than the lamp.

By late Monday, an even more disturbing piece of evidence was found. Mooney's investigators turned up a discarded hatchet in one of the yards neighboring the cottage. Edward Schneider, on examining the premises more carefully, discovered that his own ax was missing from a backyard shed. But did this necessarily point to an axman? Or could the intruder have seen the ax and carried it away, hoping to make his aborted burglary look like an axman assault?

"At the present time," Mooney told reporters on the day after the attack, "I am unable to say if it was the axman who struck Mrs. Schneider. But the finding of the hatchet and the disappearance of the ax is puzzling."

Puzzling indeed, though Mooney's reference to "the" axman reveals his suspicions that a single perpetrator was responsible for at least some of the crimes. Mary Schneider's was the fourth such assault to occur in the city since Mooney became superintendent less than a year ago. Only one had been fatal — the slaughter of the Maggios back in May. Since the perpetration of that bloody crime, Mooney had learned of an earlier incident back in December 1917, when a sleeping Italian grocer named Epifania Andollina was attacked by a hatchet-wielding man standing over his bed. Andollina had survived, and the story hadn't even made most of the daily papers at the time. But its resemblance to the Maggio incident was eerie — the panel chiseled out of the back door, the lack of any fingerprints or significant robbery, the discarding of the weapon in a neighboring yard.

The Besumer and Schneider cases, though, were somewhat different. The victims in those crimes were not Italian, and only Louis Besumer was a grocer. As for Mary Schneider, her head wound had proved to be relatively minor, and in fact she would successfully give birth to a baby girl within twenty-four hours of being attacked. It was possible that Mrs. Schneider, who now claimed to have no memory of the incident, had merely been awakened by a common burglar rifling through the wardrobe, and that the thief had struck her with a convenient object — the oil lamp — when she saw him and screamed. But what, then, of the allegedly missing ax, and the hatchet in the yard next door? All in all, despite the dissonant elements in both the Schneider and Besumer attacks, Mooney was regarding both — for the time being, at least — as part of the axman pattern.

His veteran detectives disagreed. "Members of the [detective] squad detailed by Superintendent Mooney to investigate the attack upon Mrs. Schneider," the *Daily States* reported on August 7, "have not for a moment entertained the notion that the person who attacked Mrs. Schneider bore the brand of 'the axman.' . . . They assert there is no such person as the axman going about committing these assaults. They believe that each of the so-called ax cases was separate and distinct." The officers were not mentioned by name, but they were identified as "men who have many years' experience in the handling of criminals of all types." That these veteran detectives would publicly ridicule the whole idea of a serial ax murderer — when their chief and other police officials were on the record as believing that one existed — indicates just how disordered and undisciplined the investigation had become.

Certainly the people of New Orleans seemed to believe the axman was real. ARMED MEN GUARD SLEEPING FAMILIES FROM AXMAN, the *Item* announced on the day after the Schneider assault, reporting on "all-night vigils" kept by shotgun-toting fathers over their sleeping families. The *Times-Picayune* and the *Item,* at least, seemed totally convinced that "some insane beast" was at large in the city. The *Item* even went so far as to link the current ax attacks with those that had been committed back in 1910–12. "More than 12 victims have fallen under the dreadful blows of the weapon within the past few years," the paper reported, alluding to the Crutti, Davi, and Schiambra outrages, attributed at the time to the Black Hand. One recalled detail of the 1910 Crutti attack seemed especially haunting: A witness had watched as the perpetrator — who had just chopped grocer Crutti with a meat cleaver — exited the residence by the back door carrying the weapon, his shoes, and the Cruttis' pet mockingbird in a cage. After tossing the cleaver away, he scaled a fence, walked to the street, and sat down on someone's front stoop. There he rolled himself a cigarette and smoked it. Then he calmly released the mockingbird from its cage, put on his shoes, and walked away — all while Mrs. Crutti was screaming for help in the house he had just left.

If that was the man who was active again now, eight years later, New Orleans had reason to be in a panic.

Superintendent Mooney, meanwhile, was coping as best he could, assigning as many patrolmen as could be spared from his inadequate force to the thinly settled parts of town that the axman seemed to prefer. Mooney had been receiving anonymous letters from an alleged forensics expert who claimed to have made a "study of criminals, especially perverts," and who was apparently brimming with all sorts of tips and useful advice about apprehending the perpetrator. Modern FBI profilers might speculate that such unsigned missives could very possibly have come from the axman himself, but the neophyte superintendent seemed — or pretended to seem — not at all suspicious. He merely appealed to the letter writer through the newspapers, urging him to present himself in person to discuss his ideas. "The man seems to know considerable [information] about criminals," Mooney told a reporter, "and if he comes to headquarters I'll be glad to talk to him. He has given much study to the axman, it appears from his writings."

What Mooney's more skeptical detectives thought of this anonymous expert can be imagined. But then the city was jolted by yet another crime — one that seemed to banish any doubt that an axman was at large in the city, and that he seemed strangely drawn to Italian-owned grocery stores. At three A.M. on Saturday morning, August 10, Pauline and Mary Bruno, two teenage girls living in the residence attached to their mother's grocery on Gravier Street, were awakened by the sound of a scuffle in the bedroom next to theirs. "I've been nervous about this axman for weeks," Pauline told police. "I couldn't sleep well last night, and haven't slept well for a long time." As she was dozing in bed, the commotion brought her wide-awake, and she sat up. "There at the foot of the bed was this big, heavyset man," she said. "I screamed. My little sister screamed. We were horribly scared. Then he ran."

The figure — which she thought was that of a white man, but couldn't be sure — disappeared "almost as if he had wings."

Their uncle Joseph Romano, who slept in the room next door, had stumbled into the bedroom a few moments later, holding his head with blood-smeared hands. "I've been hit," he shouted. "Call an ambulance." Then he fell into a chair, fatally wounded, and lost consciousness.

Superintendent Mooney and his detectives were on the scene within an hour, piecing together what had happened. The intruder, armed with the household's own ax from a rear shed, had entered the residence via a broken slat in the kitchen window. He'd apparently gathered Joseph Romano's clothes in the bedroom and carried them into the kitchen, where he rifled through the pockets and found a wallet, which was now missing. Then he had returned to the bedroom and begun hacking at the sleeping form in the bed, fracturing the base of Romano's skull. The assailant may have intended to attack the girls next door as well, but their screams, much louder than their uncle's groans, presumably forced him to retreat, discarding the ax in the rear yard as he fled.

Here again, the question of a robbery motive remained unclear. As in so many of the earlier attacks, the perpetrator had obviously ransacked the premises, and some small amount of money was taken. But much more was left behind — in Romano's case, a gold watch on the mantelpiece and the victim's own diamond ring. If the axman was indeed a thief, he was a curiously incompetent one, especially considering his ability to escape from the scenes of his crimes without leaving any tangible clues behind.

"I'm convinced that the Romano murder is the work of a madman," Mooney told reporters later that day, "an ax-wielding degenerate who has no robbery motive but who is taking small sums to throw the police off the track." But the superintendent again tried to reassure the public. "Take this as the gospel. We're going to get him yet! I'm doing everything in human power to run down this murderous maniac." He described his decision to consult with expert criminologists and private detective agencies to aid in the investigation. "This series of ax outrages is the biggest thing in New Orleans police history," he announced.

"We are not stopping with the facilities of my own department. I can't tell all of the steps we've taken, but I can tell this much: we've called in outside help."

But the public seemed hardly reassured. WHO WILL BE NEXT, IS QUESTION ITALIANS ASKING, read one headline in the *Times-Picayune,* over an article about elaborate precautions being taken among the city's Sicilians. "A literal reign of terror has swept through many quarters in New Orleans," the *Item* reported. In some Italian households, "members of the family divide the night into regular watches and stand guard over their sleeping kin, armed with buckshot-loaded shotguns." A kind of hysteria seemed to grip the city as reports of alleged axman sightings came in from all over town. Numerous people called police to report unfamiliar axes found in their yards, or missing hatchets, or panels chiseled out of their doors. Everyone seemed to have a different theory about the killer's identity. And — significantly — the suspected culprit always seemed to be a member of one of those groups targeted by reformers in the struggles of the past three decades. Many thought the axman was an Italian belonging to the Mafia or the Black Hand. Others thought he must be a crazed black man like Robert Charles. A few gullible souls, impressed by Pauline Bruno's statement about the axman's having wings, thought he might be some kind of supernatural being. (One wonders, in fact, why no one thought to suspect a disgruntled prostitute, or perhaps Tom Anderson himself.)

Even so, given the preponderance of Italians among the axman's victims, suspicion fell most commonly on the city's Sicilian underworld. Perhaps for this reason, New Orleans' chief Italian detective, John Dantonio, sought to deflect criticism from the community he had served for so long. "Although practically all of the victims were Italian," he told the *Times-Picayune* in an interview published on August 13, "I do not believe the Black Hand had anything to do with any of them. I have never known the Black Hand to kill women."

Dantonio instead proposed another theory. "I am convinced the man is of a dual personality," he said. "And it is very probable he is the man we tried so hard to get 10 years ago, when a series of ax and butcher-knife murders were committed within a few months. . . . Students of crime have established that a criminal of the dual-personality type may be a respectable, law-abiding citizen when [he is] his normal self. Then suddenly the impulse to kill comes upon him, and he must obey it."

Dantonio pointed out that this serial ax murderer — like Jack the Ripper in London some years earlier — would be "cunning and hard to catch." He would work methodically, making his plans well in advance to ensure that he wouldn't be caught. But he would have a weakness: "This sort of criminal is easily frightened," the detective claimed. "He fears a dog more than he does ten watchmen. My advice to the public is to put dogs in their yards."

Just how many New Orleanians took Dantonio's advice is impossible to say, but the axman hysteria did not dissipate quickly. People were now shooting at suspicious figures lurking in their neighbors' backyards, and every character encountered on the streets at night was seen as a potential axman. In one incident, a man named Charles Cardajal insisted he saw the axman dressed as a woman, hiding behind a tree on Dupre Street. As Cardajal approached, the figure jumped out from its hiding place and ran away, and Cardajal himself did likewise. The figure later turned out to be "a badly frightened Negro woman" who had actually thought that *Cardajal* was the axman.

Superintendent Mooney was, if anything, just stoking this paranoia, insisting that any and all suspicious incidents should be reported immediately. "I believe it is criminal for citizens to withhold such cases from police," he announced. "To withhold information means to assist the axman in his murderous work." Confronted with "scathing criticism" for the absence of any arrest in the crimes, Mooney was eager to seem in command of the situation. But he clearly was not, and his repeated confident statements that the perpetrator would be caught were sounding increasingly desperate.

On August 19, however, a development in the Besumer case allowed Mooney to at least make an arrest. Mrs. Lowe (who had finally admitted that she was not married to Besumer after all) had recovered sufficiently from her head wound to be released from the hospital, and she had been living again with Besumer for several weeks in the grocery/residence on Dorgenois Street. On that Monday morning, she stopped a passing patrolman and asked him to summon the superintendent. When Mooney arrived shortly thereafter, she told him that she had "recovered from the trance that had followed the attack on her," and that all of the details of that night had come rushing back to her.

On the night I was assaulted, I asked Mr. Besumer for money due me. He had promised to pay me $10 a week. It was around 7:30 and the store had just been closed. He was writing on a blueprint. I asked him again for the money and he turned upon me with the most furious expression I ever saw on a man's face.

I became frightened and turned around. Hardly had I taken two steps when I was struck from behind and felled. I heard Mr. Besumer say: "I am going to make fire for you in the bottom of the ocean."

I have a recollection then of being dragged over the floor, and next I was in the hallway where there was a light. Oh, how I tried to call out to him that I had done nothing, and how I tried to raise my arm for protection. But I could not speak nor move. Then I felt the stinging pain on the right side of my face.

What happened from then to the time I found myself in bed — it seemed like morning then — I don't know.

It's doubtful that Mooney put much credence in Mrs. Lowe's sudden recollection; this was the fourth or fifth time she had revised her account of the crime. But the new accusation was enough to have Louis Besumer arrested on a charge of assault with intent to commit murder. Other revelations by Mrs. Lowe also reignited the Justice Department's interest in the case. Besumer, she claimed, had gone by several different names in the time they had been together. He told her several times that he was a German Jew, not a Pole, and he had a secret compartment in one of his trunks where he kept blueprints and documents in German. Police and federal agents confirmed this last claim, and that Besumer had sewn secret pockets into many of his clothes.

Besumer, of course, had explanations for everything. He adopted different names for each of his separate commercial ventures, he said. The secret compartment in the trunk was where he kept his wills, and the hidden pockets in his clothing were for hiding the ample sums of money he handled in his various business endeavors. He also continued to deny that he was anything but a Pole. "Mrs. Lowe is a good woman," he insisted to investigators, but she was "changeable," and she was for some reason telling them lies. "[She] knows who assaulted us. I just want to get to the bottom of this case and solve the mystery."

If so, he would have to do it from prison. Worried about Besumer's ability to pay the bail on a simple assault charge, Mooney had him charged as a "dangerous and suspicious character" — a "crime" that in the New Orleans of this day did not require any bail to be set. In the meantime, according to the *Daily States,* police and federal authorities were giving "some weight to the theory that Besumer may be an enemy agent," and were investigating the matter closely again.

Whether or not Louis Besumer was actually the ax-wielder in the attack on Harriet Lowe, few people believed he could be the man responsible for the other ax attacks in the city. And so concern about the dreaded axman continued, though alleged sightings of the monster occurred with less frequency as more time elapsed since the Romano murder. By late August, some were even confident enough to see some humor in the situation: ATTENTION MR. MOONEY AND ALL CITIZENS OF NEW ORLEANS! read one notice in the *Daily Item.* THE AXMAN WILL APPEAR IN THE CITY ON SATURDAY, AUGUST 24. It turned out to be an advertisement for a chain of grocery stores. "He will ruthlessly use the Piggly Wiggly Ax in Cutting off the Heads of All High-Priced Groceries," the ad continued. "His weapon is wonderful, and his system is unique. DON'T MISS SEEING HIM!"

By the time autumn arrived, the city had settled down into something like its normal self. The all-night axman vigils ended, and impressionable New Orleanians stopped scaring one another on the streets at night. Mooney and his overextended police department, relieved of the intense pressure to produce an axman suspect, could turn back to the task of clamping down on the city's vice industry. Not that this was so difficult in 1918. Thanks to heavy-handed War Department strictures and the cresting of the Spanish flu epidemic, which at times required the closing of many public spaces, nightlife in the city remained relatively subdued. Music was still played around town, but aside from the great number of funerals caused by the raging epidemic, gigs were few and far between.

Meanwhile, the diaspora of jazzmen to cities north and west continued, and soon claimed some of New Orleans' giants. Sidney Bechet, who had managed to avoid the military draft by claiming that he was supporting his parents, was still suffering from what he called "itchy feet," hearing tales of the better life to be had beyond his hometown. "A whole lot of musicianers started to leave New Orleans for up North," he wrote in his autobiography. "They was all writing back to New Orleans that work was plentiful, telling the New Orleans musicianers to come up. . . . It was a real excitement there." Eager to get away, he joined another vaudeville troupe — the Bruce and Bruce Company — and toured throughout the country. When the troupe played in Chicago in May 1918, Bechet decided to stay on. He joined the band led by Lawrence Duhe (a fellow clarinetist who had been one of Kid Ory's early bandmates in LaPlace). Bechet soon became their "featured hot man," and apparently didn't look back. He would never live in New Orleans again.

The city lost yet another important player before the year was out. On June 19, a dance at the Winter Garden played by the Ory-Oliver Band was raided by police. Paddy wagons were backed up to the doors at around eleven forty-five P.M. — when the night had barely started — and the frightened patrons were herded into them. "What about the band?" a patrolman asked the sergeant on the scene. "Oh," he said, "I guess you better run them in too." Any band members who couldn't come up with $2.50 in bail money thus had to spend the night in jail. According to Ory, Joe Oliver was furious at this indignity, and totally fed up with the place New Orleans had become. When Ory saw that there was no other way to appease the man, he told him about an opportunity in Chicago — an offer he had recently received to bring his band to the Second City. Ory himself didn't want to go, and although he was reluctant to lose the services of one of the best soloists working in New Orleans, he felt he had to offer it to Oliver. The cornetist didn't hesitate to accept the job, and even persuaded clarinetist Jimmy Noone to go with him.

This was devastating news for Oliver's young protégé, Louis Armstrong. But as with his stint at the Waif's Home, it turned out to be a lucky misfortune. Armstrong later described the day he saw Oliver and Noone off at the station: "I was back on my job driving a coal cart," he wrote, "but I took time off to go to the train with them. Kid Ory was at the station, and so were the rest of the Ory-Oliver jazz band. It was a rather sad parting.

They really didn't want to leave New Orleans, and I felt the old gang was breaking up. But in show business you always keep thinking something better is coming along."

And something better came along for Louis that day. After the train had departed, Ory called him over. "You still blowin' that cornet?" he asked. Louis said that he was. So Ory invited him to come play with the band that night in Oliver's stead. "What a thrill that was!" Armstrong wrote. "To think I was considered up to taking Joe Oliver's place in the best band in town!"

Ory wasn't entirely sure the boy *was* up to it. He remembered the time Louis had subbed for Oliver and could play only a handful of tunes. But Louis had apparently learned a lot from his mentor in the meantime, and Ory saw the boy's potential. So he told him to put on a pair of long trousers and show up for the gig that night at Economy Hall.

It became a legendary night in jazz history. Louis showed up looking like a miniature version of Joe Oliver, right down to the bath towel draped around his neck. And, by his own account, he managed to "blow up a storm." "After that first gig with the Kid I was in," he wrote. "I began to get real popular with the dance fans as well as the musicians." But the music scene in New Orleans remained depressed, and Armstrong still had to work various jobs as a saloon bellboy, carpenter, coal-cart driver, and (at least until the day he saw a huge rat on the wharves and quit) as a stevedore. He was still delivering coal on his old cart (with Lady the mule) on the day the war ended — on November 11, 1918, when the Armistice was signed. "I was carrying the coal inside [Fabacher's restaurant] and sweating like mad," he later recalled, "when I heard several automobiles going down St. Charles Street with great big tin cans tied to them, dragging on the ground and making all kinds of noise." When he asked a bystander what was going on, the man told him that the war in Europe was over. The news hit him, he said, like "a bolt of lightning." He realized that the end of the war would likely mean a resurgence of jobs for musicians. "I immediately dropped that shovel," he wrote, "slowly put on my jacket, looked at Lady and said: 'So long, my dear. I don't think I'll ever see you again.' And I cut out, leaving mule cart, load of coal, and everything connected with it. I haven't seen them since."

But Armstrong's optimism about a revival of New Orleans nightlife proved misplaced. Though the lights did go on in some previously closed clubs, the jazz scene would never return to its old glories. Thanks to the coming of nationwide Prohibition (the Eighteenth Amendment was ratified just two months after the Armistice), the forces of reform would retain the upper hand in New Orleans for years to come. As one music writer has put it: "The freewheeling days of the honky-tonks and cabarets were over."

And so the atmosphere in New Orleans remained muted. The Mardi Gras celebration in early 1919 proved to be another subdued affair. With little time after Armistice Day to design and assemble any elaborate parade floats, the processions were canceled again, and the few spontaneous street celebrations that did occur were relatively tepid. Even the axman seemed to go into hibernation. With Louis Besumer in jail (now on a murder charge, since Harriet Lowe had finally succumbed to her head injury in September 1918), some may have speculated that the axman was silent because the actual perpetrator was behind bars. But Mooney and his detectives never seriously entertained the idea that Besumer was responsible for the other ax attacks. They were convinced that he had killed his housekeeper and then injured himself to make it *look* like an axman attack.

The calm, however, proved short-lived. Early on the morning of March 10, 1919, an Italian grocer in Gretna — a town on the other side of the Mississippi — heard screams coming from the grocery across the street from his own store. He ran over and discovered Charles Cortimiglia, bloody and unconscious on the floor, and his wife standing over him, screaming, with a bloody child in her arms. It was clearly an attack like the others; the telltale signs were all there — the missing door panel, the bloody ax left in the yard, no sign of burglary. After a seven-month lull, the axman was back.

■ ■ ■ ■

CHAPTER 19
THE AXMAN'S JAZZ

■ ■ ■ ■

The cartoon on the cover of Davilla's sheet music *Hogan Jazz Archive, Tulane University*

Who is the axman, and what is his motive? Is the fiend who committed the Gretna butchery the same man who executed the Maggio and Romano murders and who made similar attempts on other families? If so, is he madman, robber, vendetta agent, or sadist?

— *New Orleans Daily States,*
March 11, 1919

It was, in many respects, the most brutal assault so far: a two-year-old child killed instantly by a single blow to the skull; her critically injured parents rendered senseless by multiple head traumas. Clotted gore soaked the bed where they all lay. Across the walls and curtains around them, blood spatters radiated like birdshot. And yet, despite this evidence of what must have been a savage frenzy of violence, no one in the neighborhood had heard a thing. The perpetrator had been able to escape without a single witness to the crime, and with hours to spare before his deed was detected. The axman was apparently becoming even more adept at his trade with time.

The crime had been discovered at about seven o'clock on a Sunday morning. Several neighbors had made earlier visits to the grocery, which usually opened at five A.M., and had merely walked away when they found it closed. But one little girl named Hazel Johnson was more persistent. After getting no response at the front door, she decided to try around back. In the alley leading to the rear of the building, she found a chair set up below a side window. She climbed up on the chair and peered inside, but couldn't see anything in the murky morning light. So she continued down the alley to the backyard. There she found the back door closed, but with one of its lower panels missing. Puzzled, she called a passerby into the yard, and he persuaded her to go inside, perhaps because she was small enough to fit through the missing panel. She crawled in — and moments later burst out the back door, screaming.

Aroused by this clamor, a young neighbor named Frank Jordano ran over with his aging father, Iorlando. They found Charles Cortimiglia half-conscious on the floor, and Rose Cortimiglia clutching her lifeless toddler and sobbing inarticulately. Her husband,

Charles, roused out of his stupor by the younger Jordano, sat up on the floor. "Frank," he said. "I'm dying. Go for my brother-in-law." It was the last thing he would say for several days.

Since the town of Gretna was in Jefferson Parish, Peter Leson, chief of the Gretna police, and Jefferson sheriff Louis Marrero would conduct the investigation of the Cortimiglia case, with Superintendent Mooney's force merely assisting from afar. What Leson and Marrero found at the scene, however, indicated that the crime was clearly related to the previous year's cases across the river. The axman's signature modus operandi was obvious — from chiseled door panel to rummaged belongings, with little sign of anything of value actually being taken. This time, a box containing money and jewelry was found undisturbed in the bedroom, along with $129 in cash hidden under the Cortimiglias' mattress. But two trunks and a dresser had been practically torn apart in some kind of frenzied search; even the face of the mantelpiece clock had been pried open and examined. As in the other axman cases, however, no fingerprints were found anywhere, and any footprints in the yard had unfortunately been trampled by the curious crowd of neighbors that had gathered at the scene after hearing Hazel Johnson's screams.

The discovery of two axes on the premises

— one bloody and obviously the murder weapon, another covered with fresh mud — led Leson to believe that two men might have been responsible for this attack. Perhaps one had stood on the chair in the alley to keep an eye on the victims — and simultaneously on the street — while his partner worked on the back-door panel to gain entrance. This two-perpetrator idea could even illuminate one nagging aspect of the earlier attacks. Having an accomplice could explain how the axman was so successful at eluding detection, even while chiseling away at a back door — an activity that must have been noisy enough to be heard by anyone lying awake in bed or passing on the street. In other words, the axman may not have had wings (as the impressionable Bruno girl had speculated), but he could have had a second set of eyes — keeping a lookout while he performed his grim duties inside.

But Leson and Marrero were not interested in solving the earlier crimes; they were concerned only with the one in their own jurisdiction, and they pursued their investigation with an aggressive single-mindedness that they would later come to regret. While interviewing the Cortimiglias' neighbors, they gleaned hints that the Jordanos might not be the Good Samaritans they at first had seemed. According to the neighbors, the two families had been feuding for some time, ever since the Cortimiglias had taken over the languishing Jordano grocery in 1916 and turned it into a success. The Jordanos had taken back the business just a few months ago, forcing the Cortimiglias to find a shop elsewhere in Gretna. But recently the Cortimiglias had come back, setting up a brand-new grocery on the lot adjoining that of the Jordano store. And now, just two weeks later, the Cortimiglias were lying near death after being brutally attacked in the night. When asked about the situation, the Jordanos insisted that they had made peace with the Cortimiglias and were now good friends, but Marrero had his doubts.

Back on the other side of the river, Superintendent Mooney continued to insist that all of the ax attacks (except, perhaps, for the Harriet Lowe murder) had been committed by a "degenerate madman," and that "he ransacked the places he enters to create the impression that robbery is his motive." The superintendent's desk was now covered with maps, police reports, and photos of all of the ax cases in the city, and he was reportedly poring over them night and day. According to the *Times-Picayune,* his collection also included "the opinions of some of the South's best recognized scientists, placing the axman in the same class as Catherine de' Medici, the French author Sade, and other historic degenerates."

But the Gretna authorities had a far more mundane perpetrator in mind for the Cortimiglia attack. So sure were they of Frank Jordano's guilt that they kept asking the Cortimiglias again and again whether he was the man who assaulted them. The victims were still barely coherent and could do little more than nod or whisper in reply. But while Charles Cortimiglia (by some accounts) continued to insist that he did not recognize his assailant, his twenty-one-year-old, highly traumatized wife apparently indicated an affirmative to the question. This was enough for Chief Leson. He promptly had the younger Jordano arrested, despite the fact that the Cortimiglias' doctor refused to "vouch for the condition of their minds." "Both Charlie Cortimiglia and his wife, Rosie, told me that Frank Jordano had committed the crime," Leson told a skeptical press. "We have worked up a strong case against him and I am satisfied that the circumstances surrounding the case justified the arrest."

Frank Mooney ignored these developments in Gretna, preferring to pursue his own theory of the murders. In a high-profile presentation to the press — including, as a visual aid, a large city map marked with no fewer than sixteen alleged axman incidents — the superintendent outlined what he was now calling his "panel theory." There were common elements, he claimed, not just in the various ax assaults, but also in the numerous attempted ax break-ins that had been reported throughout the city over the past year. And these common elements convinced him that the crimes were all the work of a single man.

The *Times-Picayune* reprinted the commonalities in full:

LOCATION — In nearly all of the cases a corner house with a high board fence at the side and rear has been selected, and in most instances it was a grocery or barroom or a combination of both.

TIME — The hour generally has been about 3 A.M.

METHOD — Entrance has been effected by removing a lower panel of a rear door. The plan of work in each instance has been remarkably similar.

WEAPON — Where the crimes proceeded to the attack, an ax has been used (except in one case where a hatchet was wielded) — sometimes an ax found on the premises, sometimes brought by the murderer, but always an old ax and always left behind.

THE ATTACK — Always on sleeping victims with no apparent choice between men and

481

women, and use of the blade of the weapon as a rule.

PRECAUTIONS — Complete failure to find fingerprints, together with the fact a pair of rubber gloves was left behind in one case, leads to the belief that the murderer uses rubber gloves to protect himself against identification by the fingerprint method.

ROBBERY AS A CAMOUFLAGE — In practically every ax murder, while bureaus, safes, and cabinets have been ransacked, little was stolen, and money and valuables in plain sight were left behind. And in numerous instances of "panel burglaries," the work of the intruder has been so incomplete as to leave strong doubt whether robbery was the real motive.

Mooney did acknowledge that each assault and break-in could conceivably be a separate, unrelated incident. He also admitted that they all might be part of a systematic campaign of revenge or terrorism by the Mafia or Black Hand. But he remained convinced that the culprit in all or most of the incidents was a "solo maniac" — "a diabolical, bloodthirsty fiend, cunning and shrewd," as the *Times-Picayune* described him, "a slinking agent of the devil at 3 A.M."

Then, on Sunday, March 16, the city received a kind of confirmation of this macabre description. The *Times-Picayune* reprinted a remarkable document the paper had received in the mail on Friday. It was an open letter to the public purporting to be from the axman himself. Addressed to the newspaper's editor, and written in a hand similar to that of the letters received by Superintendent Mooney from the anonymous criminologist, it began with an attention-getting flourish: "Esteemed Mortal: They have never caught me and they never will. They have never seen me, for I am invisible, even as the ether which surrounds your earth. I am not a human being, but a spirit and a fell demon from hottest hell. I am what you Orleanians and your foolish police called the axman."

The letter went on to ridicule the police for their inept investigation of his crimes. The department's antics had been so "utterly stupid," in fact, that they had amused not only him, but also "His Satanic Majesty" and the recently deceased emperor of Austria, Franz Joseph, among other denizens of hell. "Undoubtedly you Orleanians think of me as a most horrible murderer, which I am," he continued, "but I could be much worse if I wanted to. If I wished to, I could pay a visit to your city every night. At will I could slay thousands of your best citizens, for I am in close relationship with the Angel of Death."

The letter writer followed this with a threat,

specifying the time of his next appearance: "Now, to be exact, at 12:15 o'clock (earthly time) on next Tuesday night, I am going to pass over New Orleans."

But those in fear of their lives had one way to protect themselves:

"I am very fond of jazz," he wrote, "and I swear by all the devils in the nether regions that every person shall be spared in whose house a jazz band is in full swing at the time I just mentioned. If everyone has a jazz band going, well, then so much the better for the people. One thing is certain, and that is [that] some of those persons who do not jazz it on Tuesday night (if there be any) will get the ax." The letter was signed, simply: "The Axman."

The sensation created by this letter — particularly in the poorer ethnic neighborhoods that had been hardest hit by the ax crimes — can only be imagined. Certainly many, if not most, people in the city must have doubted the authenticity of the document. There was something too slick — too ironic and knowing — about the entire exercise to be fully convincing as the ramblings of a crazed maniac. But for a populace traumatized by a bizarre and brutal crime wave, the letter was a shock, hoax or no hoax. After all, *something* was stalking the streets at night with malicious intent. And if the way to appease the demon was to cut loose for a night, then New Orleans, starved of music and conviviality by the forces of reform, would cut loose with abandon.

And indeed, when Tuesday night arrived — the eve of St. Joseph's Day, a major holiday for the city's Italians — New Orleans made sure to mollify its axman. "The tinkle of jazz music coming from dozens of New Orleans homes at 12:15 o'clock Wednesday morning demonstrated that many New Orleanians took the axman letter seriously," the *Times-Picayune* reported on March 19, "and that scores of others who didn't take it seriously found inspiration in it for house parties." Homes and cafés all over town were brightly illuminated and filled with jazz all night long. One group of uptown revelers expressly invited the axman to attend their stag party. "Enter by way of the bathroom at the head of the stairs," their invitation said. "It will not be necessary to remove any panels, for all of the doors will be open."

One enterprising local composer even took the opportunity to do some self-promotion: Joseph John Davilla claimed to have composed "The Mysterious Axman's Jazz" while waiting for the eponymous fiend to make an appearance. By Thursday morning, Davilla was already offering the composition — containing "every known incidental, accidental, syncopation, flat, sharp, and casualty known to man" — for sale to the public.

Dedicated to the New Orleans Police Band, the sheet music was soon being advertised in the daily papers ("Immunity promised all homes wherever played," the ad insisted). Davilla's marketing ploy was so ingenious, in fact, that one wonders whether he himself may have written the axman letter — to create an eager market for his new composition.

Whether it was the jazz being played all around town, or Superintendent Mooney's decision to put the police on high alert, there was no ax attack in New Orleans on that St. Joseph's Eve. Certainly the night had been a boon for the city's jazzmen, suffering from a lack of work under the recent restrictions. And it was apparently just as much a bane for the city's petty thieves ("No burglar," as the *Times-Picayune* pointed out, "likes to enter a home where there is a prospect of receiving the welcome of a sawed-off shotgun"). But in the days and weeks following the big night, the axman seemed to go silent.

Perhaps he, like the rest of New Orleans, was riveted by the spectacle of two court trials of alleged ax criminals that occurred in the city that spring. In the first, which took place in early May, Louis Besumer finally got his day in court. Serving as his own best witness, the loquacious grocer testified for four hours, telling the jury the same story he had been telling police for months — that he was essentially a prominent businessman running a small grocery as a temporary sideline, that Harriet Lowe was his housekeeper and companion, and that the two of them had probably been attacked by the axman responsible for so many other assaults in the city. He reiterated that he had no idea why Mrs. Lowe had accused him of the deed, and suggested that she may have been forced to make that dying declaration by an overzealous district attorney. In the end, the jury believed him — or at least they disbelieved the deceased Harriet Lowe. After deliberating for just seven minutes, they came back with a verdict of not guilty.

Later that same month, Frank Jordano and his father Iorlando (who had been arrested two days after his son) went on trial for the murder of baby Mary Cortimiglia. Here again, the defense attempted to show that the principal evidence against the defendants — the accusation by Rose Cortimiglia — had been coerced from a highly traumatized victim influenced by aggressive and tendentious interrogation techniques. Charles Cortimiglia continued to insist that the man he struggled with in his bedroom that night was not Frank Jordano. But his wife, appearing in court with shorn hair and head bandages still in place, would not be shaken from her testimony. And although the defense tried to put Superintendent Mooney, Louis Besumer, and others on the stand to convince the jury that this was another in the long series of axman cases, the judge ruled their testimony irrelevant. Convinced by a living victim's own testimony, the jury found both Jordanos guilty. The case would eventually be appealed to the state Supreme Court, but in the meantime, Frank was sentenced to death, and his father — perhaps because of his age — was given life in prison. Evincing some agitation after the verdict, Rose Cortimiglia stood up and tried to make an announcement to the court. "You can say what you want, but before God —" she began, but the judge did not allow her to finish.

So at least one axman candidate was convicted, but few New Orleanians thought that it was the true culprit who was headed to the gallows. (No one, in fact, had ever even suggested that Frank Jordano might be responsible for the other axman assaults.) Meanwhile, Superintendent Mooney and his police were coming under increasing criticism for their uselessness. "There is no getting away from the fact that the police department of the city is utterly incompetent," claimed an open letter from the Citizens League printed in the *Daily Item.* Seven unsolved ax murders, a resurgence of prostitution in the city, and a host of police scandals, according to the League, indicated a growing crisis of leadership in New Orleans. Had the hard-won victories of the forces of reform during the war years been in vain? Was New Orleans once again to descend into the chaos, lawlessness, and turpitude of the not-too-distant past?

As if in answer to these questions, the axman soon made his presence felt again. At 3:15 A.M. on Sunday, August 4 — in a house at 2123 Second Street, virtually around the block from the Uptown residence in which Buddy Bolden had lived for much of his life — a scream again rent the silence of a summer night. Sarah Laumann, a nineteen-year-old woman asleep in her parents' house, woke in pain to find someone looming over her in the bedroom. "I felt a stinging of the left ear," she later explained, "[and] I saw a man standing over me under the mosquito bar . . ." That's when she screamed, and the man bolted away, scrambling out an open window. By the time her parents had rushed into her room from their own bedroom next door, the intruder was gone.

But had he been the axman? There was no blood in the bed, and Sarah Laumann didn't even realize she was injured until several hours later, when she found a small but painful laceration behind her left ear. Was this the result of a glancing blow from an ax that had perhaps gotten tangled in the mosquito netting? (One wonders how many ax victims' lives were saved by this ubiquitous New Orleans necessity.) But Laumann had seen no ax held by the man standing above her bed. Hours later, an ax was found under the school building next door, which was under repair, but it had no bloodstains on it. And the Laumanns, unlike so many other victims, were not grocers, Italian or otherwise. And yet Sarah's description of her white assailant matched that of the Bruno girl in the Romano case a year earlier: "He was about five feet and eight inches tall," she told police, "had a dark complexion, weighed about 160 pounds, [and] wore a cap pulled down over his eyes, dark coat and pants, and a white shirt with dark stripes."

Axman attack or not, the Laumann incident set off yet another round of hysteria throughout the city. Less than a week later, a grocer named Steve Boca stumbled to the door of a neighbor on Elysian Fields Avenue with a bloody gash in his head and no idea what had happened to him. Police discovered that his house had been broken into via a chiseled-out panel in the back door. A bloody ax had been left on the kitchen floor. Then, on September 2, a druggist named William Carlson, lying awake reading, heard sounds coming from his back door. Panicking, he called out a warning, but when the noise continued he fired a shot at the closed door with his revolver. When he worked up the courage to open the door, he found that one of its lower panels had been scored with chisel marks.

By now, the people of New Orleans seemed prepared to believe that the axman was everywhere, and that Mooney and his police could do nothing to stop him. This became terrifyingly apparent when, on the night of October 27, Deputy Sheriff Ben Corcoran, returning late to his home on Scott Street in Mid-City, heard yet another scream coming from yet another Italian corner grocery. He ran to the end of the square and found eleven-year-old Rosie Pipitone out on the street, "bellowing that her father was full of blood." When he entered the premises, he found Mrs. Michael Pipitone, whom he knew as a neighbor, distraught and near hysteria. "Mr. Corcoran," she wailed, "it looks like the axman was here and murdered Mike."

The crime scene was by now sickeningly familiar. Mike Pipitone lay in a gore-soaked bed with a fractured skull and the entire left side of his face beaten in. This attack had apparently been particularly savage. Bloodstains spattered the bedroom walls to a height of eight feet. The obvious murder weapon lay on a chair beside the bed. But it was not an ax or a hatchet; it was a foot-long thick iron bar with a large iron nut screwed to its end.

Mike Pipitone, rushed to Charity Hospital, died there at 3:15 A.M. of massive hemorrhaging in the brain. Later, after Superintendent Mooney and Detective Long had arrived on the scene, Mrs. Pipitone explained what

491

had happened. She had been sound asleep until she heard her husband's cries in the darkness beside her. "Someone was calling me," she told them. "The cry seemed to get louder and nearer and suddenly I opened my eyes and I heard my husband say, 'Oh, my God!' That is all he said. And then I saw the forms of two men. I could just see the outlines of their figures as they hurried from our room into the children's room and disappeared in the darkness."

"I turned to my husband," she continued. "What I saw terrified me. Every time he turned his head, blood came from his head and face. It simply poured over the bed." That's when she jumped up, ran into the dining room window, and began to scream for help.

This was another horrifying crime, but again, as in the Laumann case, it seemed questionable whether this was indeed an axman assault, for several reasons. Most obvious of them: the murder weapon was not an ax. The means of entry — through a smashed side window — was another atypical element in the axman repertoire. And Mrs. Pipitone seemed certain that she had seen *two* men, not one, fleeing in the darkness. In fact, if not for her initial remark to the deputy sheriff — not to mention the ongoing serial-killer obsession in the city — one wonders whether the deed would have been considered an axman crime at all.

Mooney's detectives eventually turned up a different intriguing possibility, linking the Pipitone murder to the rash of Mafia killings that had broken out in the years following the Lamana kidnapping in 1907. The 1910 shooting of Paulo Di Christina, after all, had been laid at the door of Mike Pipitone's father, Pietro (at the time, some detectives had even believed that Mike actually did the shooting). Now free on parole for that crime, the senior Pipitone had been in the house when his son was killed. But although the police questioned him and numerous others involved in the Di Christina murder — including all of the attendees at Mike Pipitone's funeral — they could find no connection to the current crime. When asked by a *Times-Picayune* reporter whether Mooney had any theory to explain the apparent coincidence, the superintendent frankly admitted "that the police have not the slightest clue."

It was, in any case, to be the last alleged axman crime. Several suspects were arrested for one or another of the ax crimes over the next weeks, but all eventually had to be released for lack of evidence. And as time passed without another ax attack, the hysteria in the city subsided. Even the Jordanos, convicted in the Cortimiglia case, were ultimately released. Young Rose Cortimiglia apparently had a nighttime visitation from Saint Joseph, who urged her to clear her conscience before she died. She subsequently recanted her testimony against the Jordanos. "Everyone kept saying to me that it was them," she explained, and so she began to believe it. "I was not in my right mind." But now she claimed to understand the seriousness of her false accusation, and she apologized to her erstwhile neighbors. "God, I hope I can sleep now," she told the judge, who, after some procedural difficulties, managed to get the convicted murderers released.

And so even this one "solved" ax crime became unsolved once more. But although there would be no more murders in the night, the shadowy axman would claim one more victim. Superintendent of Police Frank Mooney, under continuing criticism for his inability to solve the murders, was eventually forced to resign in late 1920. He went back to the job he did best — running a railroad, which he did in the wilds of Honduras until his death after a heart attack in August 1923.

But the axman ordeal did have a final chapter. Late in 1921, New Orleans police would learn something that would shed new light on the long series of attacks, pointing to one well-known career criminal who might have been responsible for the mayhem (see Afterword). In the meantime, the case remained unsolved, and the city seemed to forget about its nemesis. Order had been restored to the streets, and the city had returned to its more circumspect postwar self. The ever-conservative *Times-Picayune* seemed positively delighted by the quieter, more respectable atmosphere. After New Year's Day of 1920, the paper could report on an admirably sober observation of the holiday. PUNCTILIOUSNESS, PRIMNESS, AND PRUDERY PREVAIL HERE read the headline in the January 2 issue, over an article about the tameness of the usually raucous celebration. "The first day of the new year was observed, rather than celebrated," the paper reported, "with hushful, Sabbatical ceremony . . . [New Orleanians] paraded with dignity and aplomb, feeling that they looked as virtuous as they felt." Casualties were few, and arrests were "practically nil."

But the reformers — though clearly in the ascendant — were not finished with the city quite yet. There was, after all, still one symbolic figure who had survived this triumph of supposed virtue in New Orleans. Tom Anderson, the erstwhile mayor of Storyville, was still sitting in his seat of power in the state legislature. In order for the reform revolution to be complete, many felt that this situation had to be rectified. Tom Anderson — and the political machine that supported him — would have to be destroyed entirely.

■ ■ ■ ■

CHAPTER 20
THE END OF AN EMPIRE

■ ■ ■ ■

A typical tenderloin saloon **Hogan Jazz Archive, Tulane University**

By 1919, Tom Anderson's Empire was in significant disarray. With the closing of the restricted district and the failure of the resulting lawsuits to overturn the decision, Anderson's business interests were suffering. For a time, he and the other vice lords of New Orleans had hoped that the end of the world war might derail the juggernaut of wartime puritanism, but the hectoring had only grown more insistent over time. Reform groups like the Citizens League had not backed down a bit after the Armistice. In fact, they were now putting so much pressure on city officials that even a police force still largely under Ring control had been forced to respond with aggressive enforcement efforts.

As a result, the vice underworld of the city was not so much collapsing as fragmenting, dispersing, going truly underground. Open brothels were now largely a thing of the past, replaced by discreet assignation houses, call girls with pimps, and temporary cribs that would have to close down the moment some meddling preacher got wind of their existence. Those who tried to operate in the old ways now paid a price, as some of the formerly prominent madams soon found out. Lulu White and Willie Piazza, for instance, were each arrested at least once in the immediate post-Storyville years, and Anderson's consort, Gertrude Dix, even had to spend a short time in jail for trying to operate her brothel. Of course, vice was still alive in the city — as Mayor Behrman once famously remarked, "You can make prostitution illegal in Louisiana, but you can't make it unpopular" — but as a business proposition, it was becoming less and less tenable.

Meanwhile, Tom Anderson's share of even this diminished market was shrinking. He had begun downsizing his vice holdings as early as 1907, when he sold his tony restaurant the Stag to Henry Ramos (already famous as the inventor of the Ramos Gin Fizz). In 1918, disgusted by his failure to save Storyville, he had divested himself of the district's so-called city hall — the Annex on Basin Street, which he turned over to his long-time lieutenant, Billy Struve. Even his stately home on Canal Street was no longer his own; he'd given it to his daughter, Irene Delsa, so that she and her husband could raise his grandchildren in comfort (albeit with the agreement that Anderson could still use it for entertaining and political business). Now he lived modestly in an apartment on Rampart Street, a few doors down from his sole remaining vice headquarters, the Arlington, the establishment with which he had begun his empire in the 1890s. And even here he wasn't left alone, with police pestering him continually for alleged violations of one law or another. Staying in business now required constant vigilance, not to mention an untold number of favors called in to make the violations disappear. For the former mayor of Storyville, the situation was downright humiliating.

But the city's reformers were still far from satisfied. Their ultimate goal was to end the entire era of Ring rule — not just in New Orleans, but at the state level as well. And they knew that the way to do this was to focus their attacks on a symbol of Ring turpitude who could be used as an example to discredit the entire organization as the 1920 elections approached. That symbol, naturally enough, turned out to be Representative Thomas C. Anderson, now serving his fifth term in the state legislature. If they could accomplish the total demolition of Anderson, they reasoned, Martin Behrman and the entire Ring could be toppled — first in the state elections, which were to take place in early 1920, and then in the New Orleans municipal elections at the end of that year.

This new reform offensive began in late

1918. From pulpits and lecture halls around the city, orators tirelessly pounded away at Anderson and his Ring supporters. As they did before the closing of Storyville, Jean Gordon and William Railey of the Citizens League fulminated at length before large crowds, demanding that officials take Anderson to task for his flagrant disregard of the Gay-Shattuck Law. "Why was Anderson never prosecuted for repeated violations of this law?" Railey asked in an open letter to the *Times-Picayune.* "Was the district attorney ignorant of a fact that was well known all over town? . . . The police are not such boneheads as not to know where gambling and prostitution are being carried on when it is well known to the public. [But DA] Luzenberg doesn't act; [Superintendent] Mooney doesn't act; the police board doesn't act and the mayor doesn't act. What is the remedy for this carnival of gambling and law violation that is openly carried on in our city every day?"

The remedy, as Railey well knew, was the one law enforcement agency not subject to Ring manipulation — that is, the US Department of War. Although the Armistice had ended the active fighting in Europe, the world war would not officially be over until a formal peace treaty was signed, so the US government was still tasked with keeping the soldiers and sailors in New Orleans free of sin.

Responding to the local reformers' pressure, the feds launched their own investigation of Tom Anderson and the city's other cabaret owners. In June of 1919, Harold Wilson, southern director of the War Department's Commission on Training Activities, and William Edler, of the US Public Health Service, personally conducted inspections of the city's cabarets. With his impeccable sources of information, Anderson knew all about this supposedly undercover operation, and kept an eye out for the two gentlemen in question. But he couldn't be present at the Arlington every night. And — more important — the prostitutes who frequented his establishment couldn't always be relied upon to lie low when a federal agent walked into the place. Some of them, in fact, just couldn't seem to comprehend that prostitution was no longer legal and that the good old days of open solicitation were long past.

It was on the evening of June 26, 1919, that Wilson and Edler finally appeared at the Arlington and were seated at a small table on the busy main floor. Tom Anderson, talking at the bar with an acquaintance, saw them arrive. "There he is now," Anderson muttered to his companion. "I thought he'd be in here tonight." Then he spoke to the manager. Before long, waiters were streaming through the room, whispering to the women seated at tables all around the floor. "Captain Wilson and Dr. Edler are up there," the waiter told two women at one table (where, unbeknownst to them, they were flirting with one of Wilson's undercover associates, Army sergeant Thomas Pierce). "Don't move around, but keep quiet."

A hush descended over the room, but not all of the women had gotten the message in time. One of them — "a little girl, dressed in black, with very large eyes" — walked over to the table where Wilson and Edler were sitting. "That little fool," a woman at Pierce's table whispered. "She'll queer the whole thing."

And queer it she did. The black-clad woman sat right down beside Wilson and proceeded to proposition him in terms that could not be misinterpreted. When Wilson demurred, she turned to Edler and asked whether he wanted to "have a good time." That's when the Arlington's jazz band began playing. According to Edler's later court testimony: "The girl began wriggling and shaking herself. She looked up in the air and rolled her eyes, and upon inquiry as to what this purported, she said she was 'vamping.' In the meantime, a woman sitting at the next table poked me in the back and winked her eyes. . . ."

It was, in other words, a disaster. For the next half hour, Wilson and Edler watched as numerous other women around the room, apparently unaware of the waiters' warnings, went about their business as usual, propositioning men and then leaving for the upstairs hotel, with their quarry following close behind. Helpless to stop the spectacle, Tom Anderson could only grasp his gray head in despair.

And sure enough, within days of Wilson's visit, the indictments started rolling in. "The Orleans Parish Grand Jury," the *Item* reported on June 29, "shook the foundations of serenity on which the Tango Belt of New Orleans seems long to have rested by returning true bills indicting Tom Anderson, Louisiana state legislator." Anderson, cited along with two other cabaret owners, may not have truly been shaken by this first indictment. After all, he had many friends on the bench of the Criminal District Court, and he was unconcerned enough to quickly pay his $250 bond in order to attend a prizefight on the evening he was arrested. But ten days later, when another indictment followed from the US District Court on a similar charge, he knew that the situation was serious. A federal court judge might not be so amenable to persuasion by Anderson's Ring associates. And the $1,000 bond he had to pay to stay out of jail for this case seemed to promise an entirely different level of determination to see that justice was done.

On the morning of Monday, October 6, 1919 — "Cabaret Day in the court," as the

Item dubbed it — Anderson's case was brought before Judge Landry in the Orleans Parish Criminal District Court. Testifying that day, according to the paper, would be "many of the rollicking dancers who chased away the hours until dawn a couple of years ago at the Balls of the Two Well Known Gentlemen." Tom Anderson would in fact have no fewer than seventy character witnesses pleading on behalf of his defense. That number included a judge, an assistant district attorney, a member of the school board, two bank presidents, and an assortment of businessmen, detectives, and police officers. Tom Anderson may have been in diminished circumstances by 1919, but he still had a lot of friends.

And true friends they proved to be. ANDERSON CAFÉ SPOTLESS, SAY BUSINESSMEN ran the headline in Tuesday's *Item.* Dozens of prominent citizens had testified unanimously, under oath, that "Tom Anderson's cabaret on North Rampart Street — the famous Arlington Cabaret in the heart of New Orleans' Tango Belt — had never to their knowledge been aught but a respectable and high-class restaurant." Not one of these witnesses, moreover, had ever been solicited by a woman in the place: "Did you ever see anything in the conduct of the women there that would cause you to believe them immoral?" the prosecutor asked Thomas J. Hill, former

506

manager of the Tourist and Convention Bureau, who had claimed that he frequented the Arlington for years.

"Absolutely not!" Hill replied, with great earnestness (and to considerable laughter in the courtroom).

Against this wall of adamant denial, the prosecutor could present only two witnesses with a contrary story — Harold Wilson and William Edler. They testified quite vehemently that they had practically been accosted by eager prostitutes the moment they crossed the Arlington's threshold. But Judge Landry, eager to be rid of a case that undoubtedly subjected him to intense pressure from all sides, had heard enough. Weighing the balance of the evidence given, he decided that the state had failed to make its case. "There is no evidence to show that Mr. Anderson . . . knew what was going on at that time [when Wilson and Edler were openly solicited], and none to show that there was any intention on his part to violate the act as charged." The ruling? Case dismissed, and the defendant discharged.

"I will not discuss the case!" William Edler fumed as he left the courtroom. "I might be held for contempt of court if I said what I thought!"

The defendant himself seemed unsurprised by the dismissal. "I conducted a first-class saloon and high-class restaurant," he told reporters afterward, "which was patronized by some of the most prominent and influential business and professional men in New Orleans. Many of these men have brought their families to the restaurant. I have built up a reputation as a businessman in the community during the last 30 years and I would be the last man in the city to try and violate the law."

Harold Wilson, of course, had his own thoughts on this last point, but he did see something positive in the outcome. The results of the trial, he insisted — including "the amazing spectacle of reputable citizens testifying to the good character of a place notorious even to the remotest hamlet in the United States" — would surely serve as a kind of "public irritant." It would enrage the truly respectable people of the city and harden their resolve to complete the ongoing cleansing of New Orleans. "The best element of the citizenry of this town is thoroughly aroused," he said. And he vowed that he would make every effort to ensure that Thomas Anderson would be tried again — this time in a federal court.

Tom Anderson's lawyers, on the other hand, were soon making every effort to ensure the opposite. In a petition to the federal court, they argued that the six counts of the federal indictment were all matters of state law, and that the state court had cleared their client of all of them. Recent US court decisions, in any case, had held that the war was officially ended (the Treaty of Versailles having been signed on June 28); that meant that "the period of emergency [was] past, and legislation intended only for that period [was] no longer operative." In other words, the federal prohibition against prostitution, as an emergency wartime measure, was defunct now that the war was over. The charges against Tom Anderson — even if they could be proved — would thus no longer be violations of US law, and would not be within the purview of a federal court.

The logic behind this argument, if somewhat convoluted, was not entirely specious, and there were rumors circulating in mid-October that the federal government might indeed drop the case. But those rumors just sent local reformers into even greater paroxysms of fury. An appeal sent out by Rev. U. G. Foote, chairman of the New Orleans Ministerial Union, urged local clergymen to speak out from their pulpits and give voice to "the indignation of the best elements." And the preachers responded, even going so far as to threaten the US prosecutor with removal from office.

But while the city's clergymen focused their ire on the former mayor of Storyville himself, their more politically minded brethren were after bigger game as well. Anderson may have won his first day in court, but the publicity generated by the trial provided excellent ammunition to be used against his political allies in the upcoming state elections. Specifically, the Ring-backed candidate for governor, Col. Frank P. Stubbs, was soon being tarred with the Tom Anderson brush in election rallies all over the state, with opponents warning that his election would bring about a "thoroughly Tomandersonized" atmosphere at both the state and city level of government. Soon the reform candidate himself began picking up the anti-Anderson rhetoric. "In this state," John M. Parker intoned at a campaign rally shortly thereafter, "there are two kinds of democracy: the Thomas Anderson Democracy and the Thomas Jefferson Democracy. . . . The Thomas Jefferson Democracy is government of the people and for the people. The Thomas Anderson Democracy is government of the people, by the bosses for private gain. I admit that I have never been a Thomas Anderson Democrat. . . . I have always fought this system, and hope, with your help, to destroy it."

Even an ambitious young railroad commissioner named Huey P. Long (who would eventually become the nemesis of both Parker *and* the New Orleans Ring) took up the cry against Anderson and the machine he represented. "This New Orleans Ring sends to the legislature the men who run the red-light district, and these men make the laws under which the ministers and the boys and girls throughout the state must live," he wrote in a statement published in the newspapers. "Surely the country should make it possible for the citizens of New Orleans to free themselves from this octopus."

Faced with this barrage of attacks, that octopus could do little else but distance itself from its newly noxious tentacle. Anderson was thus dropped as the Ring candidate for a sixth term in the House (causing him to rail against his former friends' "ingratitude" in private conversations). Even so, the barrage of anti-Andersonism went on unabated.

The *Times-Picayune,* firmly in the anti-Ring camp, did its part by running a series of exposé articles in early January, on the eve of national Prohibition (and just before the state primaries). The series, under the title "New Orleans Nights," depicted the adventures of a young couple just looking to have a little naughty fun in the city's demimonde. What they find, however, is an increasingly ugly world of dissipation and lawlessness, of aggressive prostitutes, addicted gamblers, and paid-off cops looking the other way. The series — which of course included a late-night visit to Anderson's Arlington cabaret — culminated in an editorial diatribe against the notorious political machine that continued to let this filth thrive. "Under 20 YEARS

OF RING RULE," the paper complained, "this crawling, fetid, contaminating monster of the UNDERWORLD has grown and grown, poisoning and corrupting all it touches." Every word published in "New Orleans Nights," the paper insisted, was true. "Our prayer is for you mothers and fathers and decent people of New Orleans, that the TRUTH SHALL SET YOU FREE."

For Stubbs and the rest of the Ring-backed candidates, this was the coup de grace. When the Democratic primary was held just a few days later, John M. Parker — the reformer who in his youth had been part of the mob of worthies who perpetrated the Orleans Parish Prison lynchings — defeated his opponent Stubbs by some 12,000 votes and went on to become governor. He vowed that this was not the end: "We are going to finish the destruction of the New Orleans Ring," he told supporters at a rally in Lafayette Square, "[with] a final, smashing, knockout blow in the municipal campaign in September!"

For Tom Anderson, meanwhile, the news just kept getting worse. Despite protracted efforts by his lawyers to have the federal charges against him dismissed, the case in US District Court did go forward. At 11:51 A.M. on Tuesday, February 3, 1920, Judge Foster called to order what the *Times-Picayune* called "the case which has probably attracted more attention than any other cause

lodged in federal courts here in many years."
The official charge against Anderson was for
"knowingly conducting an immoral resort
within 10 miles of a military camp." That
word "knowingly" was going to be the key to
the entire case. Given the evidence, no jury
could possibly doubt that immoral liaisons
were initiated at the Arlington; Anderson's
conscious involvement in those activities,
however, would be harder to prove.

The first witness called was William Edler,
the public health officer whose testimony in
the first trial had been so damaging to
Anderson's cause. Here again he described
the experience of his and Harold Wilson's
visit to the Arlington in June (much of which,
according to the reporter from the *Item*, "was
of such a character that it cannot be admitted to print"). Anderson's lawyers raised
objections of all kinds to this testimony, and
the exchanges between the defense and the
prosecutors became rather heated. But Anderson himself just sat impassively behind his
"screen of lawyers." "Not one single strand
of his thinning, iron-gray hair was out of
place," the *Item* reported, "and the only
evidence of mental disturbance or agitation
that could be remarked in his appearance was
that he sat with his lower jaw sagging just a
trifle, so that his mouth was open."

This aura of equanimity was ruffled only
once, with the testimony of the next witness,

Sergeant Pierce, the undercover Army officer. Pierce had actually been within earshot of Anderson at the bar, and had witnessed the café owner's order to have everyone in the place behave themselves. According to the *Item,* "As the witness recounted this, Mr. Anderson's habitually flushed face turned a few shades redder, and he muttered something under his breath and into his carefully cropped white mustache." As well he might, for Pierce, it would seem, had just provided the evidence required to prove that Anderson had been fully aware of what was going on in his restaurant every night.

On the second day of the trial, Anderson himself was called to testify. Maintaining a cool, unruffled, and affable demeanor, he categorically denied the charges against him. "I was never aware of any women visiting my place for immoral purposes," he said (under oath). "I simply operated a saloon and restaurant. There is no doubt that some sporting women went there, but it was for eating and drinking only. They were never authorized to solicit and, so far as I know, there was no soliciting in any way, shape, or manner."

Too bad for Anderson, then, that his testimony was blatantly contradicted by that of Captain Wilson, who arrived in New Orleans from Washington that morning. Wilson testified next, and his account of his night at the Arlington cabaret was even more lurid than in the first trial. In vivid strokes, he described the "vamping" intruder at his table, and the women sitting around with their skirts hiked up to their knees, "rolling their eyes about, smiling at the men" at other tables. "The orchestra was playing what is commonly called jazz music," the bespectacled captain observed, using a term that by now had become a watchword for dissipation to some New Orleanians. "The women were going from table to table, speaking to men. . . . Many of them were smoking. All of them were contorting their bodies and keeping time to the music with their breasts."

This last image was not one that a jury was likely to forget. And when testimony was finally closed and the jurors were sent into deliberation, the outlook for Tom Anderson seemed grim. But as the minutes and then hours passed without a verdict, his situation began to look more hopeful. Could it be that the mayor of Storyville would escape yet again? And when the jury finally returned on Thursday, the news for Anderson was good. "If it please the court," the foreman announced, "we have failed to reach an agreement."

It did not, in fact, please the court. But after some discussion about whether a unanimous verdict might possibly be reached with further deliberation, Judge Foster was finally forced to declare a mistrial. The unshakable vote of the jurors stood at seven for acquittal and five for conviction.

"I am more glad than I can say," a relieved Tom Anderson told reporters after leaving the courtroom. "The prosecution — and the persecution, for it has been that, too — has been very hard for an old man, for that is what I am. But I feel that it is a vindication that a majority of the jury felt I should be acquitted, and I am doubly glad for the sake of my daughter and my grandchildren."

His principal lawyer was less gracious. "It looks like somebody was trying to frame up on Mr. Anderson," Charles Byne told the press. "It looks like somebody wanted to get him at all costs. . . . Doesn't this look like a deliberate attempt at a frame-up?"

Frame-up or not, the federal government eventually declined to retry Tom Anderson on the charges in the indictment. Local reformers and the newspapers were livid at this outcome; the *Times-Picayune* sarcastically noted that Anderson "must be [one] of those who see no evil, hear no evil, and believe no evil" if he really didn't know of prostitution at the Arlington. Still determined to punish the vice lord, reformers subsequently tried to snare him on other charges — of voter fraud and violations of the Injunction and Abatement Act — all to no avail. But although Anderson had escaped a prison term, he was all but dead as a politician in

Louisiana. The Tom Anderson name, in fact, was now poison — a weapon that could be used against all of his old Ring friends, including Martin Behrman himself.

That weapon was used freely in the municipal elections that fall. "The Tom Andersons, the cabaret keepers, the pimps, the panders of the city — these are the supporters of Behrman and his organization," ran a typical campaign diatribe. Reformers, along with some disaffected members of the Ring, were united under the banner of the Orleans Democratic Association (ODA), and they were determined to consolidate their recent successes and take back the city once and for all. In rally after rally, they pounded away at the four-term mayor, decrying his underworld associations, his repeated failures to reform the police department, his support of vice, and his now-notorious trip to Washington, DC, to try to save the restricted district. At times, their crusade took on an almost apocalyptic tone: "Our city is at a parting of the ways," one ODA spokesman said at a large rally shortly before the primary. "It is for our people to decide which way they will go. One way — the way of the Ring — leads to death, to political, financial, moral, and civic death. But the other way — the way against the Ring — leads to life; to a prosperous future for our city; to a successful business administration; to political freedom; to civic decency; to a higher and more honorable public service; and to a better citizenship for all of our people. It is for our people to choose, for them to decide whether they will remain in bonds or whether they will become free."

In the end, the people of New Orleans decided to become free, at least by the reformers' definition. The election was closely fought, but Behrman's efforts were hampered by an illness that kept him convalescing in Biloxi for much of the campaign. In a close race, he lost by a mere 1,450 votes to reformer Andrew McShane; the ODA slate also captured four of the five seats on the city council. THE RING IS SMASHED! the *Times-Picayune* exalted. "Ring's Control of Orleans Is Utterly Shattered All Down Line."

It was the final victory in the thirty-year war for the soul of the Crescent City. For the first time in a generation, New Orleans' city government was in the hands of the reformers.

And so the city of New Orleans entered the new decade of the 1920s a very different — and, in many ways, a much less colorful — place than it had been just thirty years earlier. The city's unique atmosphere of open, legally sanctioned vice was now a thing of the past, eviscerated not just by local reform efforts but by national measures as well. Prohibition and female suffrage — both of which, according to moral crusaders like Jean Gordon, would usher in a time of greater virtue and political accountability — were the law of the land by 1920. Jim Crow, now as firmly established in New Orleans as in the rest of the South, would ensure the maintenance of white privilege for decades to come. And while crime would remain a problem in the city, the old days of the Black Hand and the so-called Mafia vendettas were definitely past.

The age of Tom Anderson, in other words, was over, symbolized by the decline of Anderson himself. Out of his job in the statehouse after twenty years of dominance over the Fourth Ward, he would soon be out of the vice business as well. By 1921, he would divest himself of the last major holding of his vice empire, selling the Arlington on Rampart Street to his son-in-law, George Delsa, the longtime manager of the place. Anderson would still be a rich man; his Liberty Oil Company had done quite well over the years, and it was to this legitimate business that he would devote the rest of his life. But he would never again be a force in the New Orleans underworld he had ruled for so long.

The *Times-Picayune* took note of the salubrious atmosphere in the city in July 1921. Reporting on an initiative by New Orleans' new police superintendent, Guy Maloney, the paper described the police department's unprecedented resolve to control vice with beefed-up police patrols and more stringent arrest and parole protocols: "The police, it is said, recognize gamblers, lottery shop operators, and proprietors of immoral houses as organized law violators, and are determined to keep so hot behind them that their illegal trade will become unprofitable." The results so far had been promising indeed. "You could shoot a cannonball down Royal or North Rampart Streets," one police captain told the paper, "and you wouldn't have hit [a single] undesirable."

How different from the heyday years of vice in New Orleans, when that same projectile would have winged any number of pimps, prostitutes, cardsharps, and other miscreants. It may have taken thirty years, but reformers finally had the cleaned-up city they wanted. "Gambling and immorality," the paper concluded, were now "on their way to the high timbers."

But they would not stay there for long.

■ ■ ■ ■

CHAPTER 21
THE SOILED
PHOENIX

■ ■ ■ ■

A celebration in Lafayette Square **Louisiana Division, New Orleans Public Library**

There are no last chapters in history, and the triumph of reform in New Orleans at the end of 1920 — while it may have warmed the hearts of the city's long-suffering "better half" — did not spell the end of vice and lawlessness in this irrepressibly unruly place. For no matter what the *Times-Picayune* might have liked to think, New Orleans had not really been cleaned up. The vice that had been practiced openly in the city in the early 1900s had merely gone underground with the advent of the 1920s, festering in speakeasies, illegal gambling dens, and secret assignation houses. As in other cities around the country, a visitor to New Orleans would now have to look slightly harder for a drink, a woman, or a poker game — and deal with the legal consequences if caught in the act.

The "normalization" of the city's racial atmosphere was also more theoretical than actual. True, interracial contacts of all kinds were now strictly controlled, and the racial ambiguities of the city's past had been eliminated (at least legally) by the rigid two-tiered system of Jim Crow. But Creoles of Color and octoroons did not suddenly change their racial identity. And what went on between the races behind closed doors was controllable only to the extent that policemen were diligent and above taking bribes.

Still, for better or worse, the thirty-year reform effort had been at least a partial success, papering over some of the Crescent City's flagrant sinfulness and creating a more businesslike, temperate, and racially regimented urban environment like that of the other large cities of the South. Meanwhile, reformers — often acting in cooperation with machine politicians like Martin Behrman and, yes, even Thomas C. Anderson — had made substantial strides in improving the city's infrastructure and its educational and public health facilities. These changes were unambiguously positive (even if the benefits accrued unevenly to whites, blacks, and immigrants). So the New Orleans of the 1920s was not the backward, unhealthy, and openly sinful place it had been at the end of the nineteenth century, and city officials were eager to make the world aware of that fact. Even local tourism officials started changing their strategies in the '20s and '30s, aiming their pitches at conventioneers and businessmen rather than leisure travelers seeking nightlife, sexual adventure, and a romantic "foreign" experience. As one historian has put it, "The Crescent City, according to the ad campaign organizers [of the '20s], was an economic powerhouse devoted to prosperity, not frivolity. Industrial and commercial interests were paramount." Emblematic of this more serious and practical image was the city's response to the burning of its beloved French Opera House in 1919. After a decade of debate, it was decided that what a modern metropolis needed was not an opera house but a convention center. The result was the new Municipal Auditorium, inaugurated with great ceremony in 1930 — "as a monument to the business community."

And certainly most of the main players of the city's legendary underworlds were gone now — either dead, moved away, out of the business, or else merely operating in the shadows. Many prostitutes and madams simply left town — such as Emma Johnson, who decamped shortly after the closing of Storyville, taking her sexual circus with her. Others, like Countess Willie Piazza, appear to have left the demimonde entirely and entered legitimate businesses. Although Storyville legend has her moving to Europe, marrying a French nobleman, and spending the rest of her life in a luxurious villa on the Riviera, her fate was actually far more mundane. Piazza merely remained at her former brothel at 317

North Basin Street, buying and selling real estate and other property (including at least one yacht). Her business acumen seems to have translated well to her new endeavors; when she died in 1932, she left behind a substantial estate, including two properties on Basin Street, an impressive collection of jewelry, and a deluxe 1926 Chrysler touring car — an astonishing accomplishment for an unmarried non-white woman in 1930s New Orleans.

Lulu White, on the other hand, had no such happy ending. She also continued living in her old Basin Street brothel, but kept it operating as a clandestine house of prostitution. She tried to pass off the new establishment as a transient hotel, but no one was fooled, and her place was subjected to numerous raids by the McShane administration's newly conscientious police department. "I could not do anything wrong [even] if I wanted to," she later complained to a judge. "The police would come in and wake up the boarders and ask them their names and where they came from; Captain Johnson gave his men instructions to go into my house every five minutes, and if the door was not opened right away, to break open the door."

Despite her protestations of innocence, she was arrested no fewer than eleven times for violations of the ordinance that had abolished Storyville. One arrest in 1919 on federal prostitution charges, however, proved more serious. Found guilty, she actually was sent away to the federal penitentiary in Oklahoma to serve a term of a year and a day. Lawyers petitioned for an early release because of her ill health, but were unsuccessful. Finally, she herself wrote a letter to Attorney General A. Mitchell Palmer in Washington: "I am suffering dearly every day," she wrote. "I am full of fistroyer [fistula], rheumatism, and the doctor says I have two or three tumors in my abdomen — [I] can hardly walk and it is a matter of a short time I believe I will die. For God sake do not let me die in this place!"

Palmer proved surprisingly sympathetic, and he passed her letter on to President Woodrow Wilson. He — perhaps just as surprisingly — agreed to commute White's sentence. She was released on June 16, 1919, after serving just three and a half months.

Her health now apparently improved, she turned Mahogany Hall over to a real estate agent on a ten-year lease and moved into the saloon next door, which she had bought in 1912. Here she opened up an alleged soft-drink company — but of course it was just another brothel. She was arrested again in November 1920 for operating a house of prostitution, and four more times during the 1920s for possessing and selling alcohol. Her last arrest came in February 1931, for running a disorderly house on North Franklin

Street. By now, she truly was in ill health; she had grown to "Amazon proportions" and was reduced to panhandling on the street. Lulu White died just before her case came to trial — on August 20, 1931, the year that so many of the old Storyville figures would end up passing from the scene.

New Orleans' jazz culture, meanwhile, was not faring much better than its vice industry. There were still plenty of musicians in town during the 1920s, and many of them still found work, though not enough to keep them playing full-time. Guitarist Danny Barker described what it was like being a young New Orleans jazzman at this time: "So many musicians stopped playing, died, left town — I heard of them but never saw them in person. And many halls were demolished for newer buildings." Some extreme reformers were even discussing the idea of prohibiting jazz entirely, just like alcohol.

The attrition of jazz greats, moreover, just continued throughout the decade, with dominant figures like Kid Ory and Bunk Johnson joining the likes of Bechet, Keppard, and Lorenzo Tio in the search for better opportunities elsewhere. ("With the nightmare of constant raids staring in my face," Ory later wrote, explaining his departure for Los Angeles in August of 1919, "I knew I'd never make it and decided not to operate [in New

Orleans] anymore.") By now, the age of true jazz innovation was all but finished in New Orleans anyway, and its nightlife scene was just a shadow of its former self. When Jelly Roll Morton returned to the city in 1923, after years of successful ventures in Chicago, California, and elsewhere, he pronounced the town "dead" and didn't linger long before moving on.

By that time, of course, even little Louis Armstrong had left the Crescent City — though not before experiencing his share of adolescent adventure and tribulation. Still a teenager when Tom Anderson's empire was toppled, he had continued playing around town through the good times and bad. But he couldn't seem to stay out of trouble, especially after crossing paths with a woman named Daisy Parker — the "prettiest and badest [sic] whore in Gretna Louisiana," as he himself put it. He first saw her while he was playing a date at the Brick House, a honky-tonk on the other side of the river. "Daisy kept on flitting across the floor in front of the bandstand where I was blowing the blues," he later wrote, "giving me the wink with the stuff in her eyes." During a break, he went up to her and said, "Lookheah' Babes — Suppose you wrap it up for the night? And — spend the rest of the night with me upstairs?" Daisy agreed, and they were soon infatuated with each other.

In May of 1918, Louis and Daisy married and moved in together (with Louis's adopted son, Clarence) in a two-room flat on Melpomene Street. But the relationship was stormy from the start. "All she knew how to do was fuss and fight," Armstrong later recalled. Daisy was jealous, unstable, and quick to resort to razors or bread knives when angered. After one particularly ugly fight that ended with the two of them shying bricks at each other on the street, Armstrong realized that the marriage was doomed and began looking for some kind of exit.

That exit presented itself in the form of an offer to play on one of the Streckfus Brothers' excursion riverboats, the SS *Sydney*, under bandleader Fate Marable. For young Louis, this would prove to be a learning experience as important as his time at the Waif's Home. Marable insisted that all of his players be able to read music on sight, so Louis would gain much-needed technical training on the boat. But the job would also provide him with his first glimpse of the world beyond Louisiana and the city of his birth. ("What are all those tall buildings? Colleges?" Louis asked when he first saw the St. Louis skyline.) He ended up playing with Marable for only two seasons, returning to New Orleans during the winter, but his experience on the *Sydney* was crucial to his development as a musician. It also reinforced his growing conviction that there could conceivably be a life for him beyond the hostile confines of his native New Orleans.

Back home, Armstrong, unlike some other jazzmen, continued to find work without much trouble. Kid Ory had already left by this time, so Louis began playing with a small ensemble led by violinist Paul Dominguez at Tom Anderson's cabaret on Rampart Street. He also joined the prestigious Tuxedo Brass Band under trumpeter Oscar "Papa" Celestin. But already he was hearing the siren call of opportunity elsewhere. Ory had tried to persuade Armstrong to come to California, but he had demurred. "I had made up my mind that I would not leave New Orleans unless the King [Joe Oliver] sent for me," he later wrote. "I would not risk leaving for anyone else." And that day finally arrived. In the summer of 1922, Oliver sent him a telegram, offering him the job of second cornet with his Creole Jazz Band at Lincoln Gardens in Chicago (for $52 a week — a princely sum). "I jumped sky-high with joy," Louis said, and prepared to leave immediately — and to end his "four years of torture and bliss" with Daisy Parker.

On the day his train was to leave — August 8, 1922 — Armstrong played a last gig with the Tuxedo band at a funeral in Algiers. Afterward, he crossed the river and headed to the station. "It seemed like all New Orleans had gathered at the train to give me a little luck," he later wrote. His musician friends, the "old sisters" from his neighborhood, and of course his family were all there to see him off, Mayann with a pair of woolen long johns and a trout-loaf sandwich to sustain him on his trip to the frigid North. Many tears were shed, but Armstrong was determined to leave. He didn't want to be "Little Louis" anymore, and he was eager to try his luck in a place where a hardworking black musician could conceivably win "a *living, a plain* life — the *respect*" that he deserved. The reformed New Orleans of 1922 was not that place.

And so Louis got on that train bound for Chicago. "My boyhood dream had come true at last," he would later say. He would not return to New Orleans, even for a visit, until nine years later, when the world had already given him the fame and respect that his hometown had never afforded hm.

But the victory of reform in the Crescent City, which had seemed so commanding after the 1920 elections, would eventually prove fleeting. The new administration of Mayor McShane did keep a lid on sin in the city for a time. By 1922, the city's clergymen were praising him for his successful efforts, which, according to one Pastor L. T. Hastings, gave heart to "all decent, self-respecting citizens of New Orleans." Hard-line reformers like Jean

Gordon were still not satisfied and did not rest, maintaining pressure on the new administration to keep all of its promises on vice suppression. (Miss Gordon also didn't rest on the eugenics issue, advocating to her dying day for a state law to sterilize inmates at institutions for the insane and feebleminded. As her sister Kate said after Jean's death in 1931, "When Jean was convinced that the thing was right, it did not matter what it cost her; she would brave public opinion, no matter how unpopular, in its behalf.") But McShane proved to be an inept politician, and his ODA coalition of reformers and Ring apostates soon fell apart. When the next municipal elections came around, the winner was none other than Martin Behrman, the old Ring standard-bearer, rising like a soiled phoenix from the ashes of his 1920 defeat. McShane's administration had proven so incompetent that even the *Times-Picayune,* the nemesis of the old Ring, had supported the return of the mayor it had despised just a few years earlier.

For Behrman's old friend Thomas Anderson, there was to be no such rehabilitation. Tom had decided to stay out of politics — and out of the vice business — for good. He contented himself with living in sin with his concubine, Gertrude Dix, and looking after his oil company. At Christmastime in 1927, while vacationing at his luxurious weekend house in Waveland, he suffered a stroke so serious that a priest was called in to give him last rites. Tom eventually recovered, but the stroke left him with a weak arm and a pronounced limp. More important, his brush with death brought the old vice lord to religion. He became a devout Catholic, attending Mass every day and even bringing Dix into the Church. But though he made a promise to his priest to mend his ways, he did not marry his longtime concubine, at least not yet. After three marriages, none of which had lasted more than a year or two, he was apparently not eager to take on a fourth.

Another consequence of his stroke was an order from his doctor to move out of his current apartment on Rampart Street, which was on the third floor and required more climbing of stairs than Tom could handle. So Anderson decided to build a one-story home for himself and Dix on Canal Street, on the lot next door to the home he'd given his daughter back in 1907. But this proposed move would prove to be the undoing of his family. Irene, now a widow and living with her four children, was appalled when she heard of her father's plan. One day in April or May of 1928, she went to him at the offices of Liberty Oil on St. Charles Avenue.

"Daddy," she asked him, "is it true that you intend to build next door to me and my family?"

"I was thinking about it."

Irene launched into a vehement tirade against this plan, which would inevitably bring her respectable family into close proximity with a notorious ex-prostitute. Did Anderson not have any respect for her or for his own grandchildren, she asked. Tom seemed taken aback by her reaction, and told her he would think it over. But he was definitely upset. "It's a pretty condition when your own flesh and blood go against you," he complained to his old friend Billy Struve.

Sometime later, Irene repented her harshness, and wrote her father to apologize. "As your daughter, I am sorry for speaking as I did to you," she wrote. "I was so vexed to know that you have chosen such a person [Gertrude Dix] to guide you. You have completely forgotten the respect you owe the good name of your mother and mine, and the promise you made on your dying bed, to the Almighty God, to live a better life if God spared you. I will always pray to God to help you, and someday reunite us with the same love I have always had for you."

Rather than pacifying her father, this apology just ended up enraging him. He wrote a lengthy letter back to her (addressed simply to "Mrs. George Delsa"), bitterly resenting Irene's characterization of Dix as "such a person" and insisting that Irene's mother, Emma Schwartz, had been "such a person" herself. He vigorously defended Dix, noting that she had nursed him selflessly through his recent illness, and told Irene that he intended to marry his concubine before the week was out. He closed by warning Irene that he would someday tell her more about her own history — something that might make her reconsider her sanctimonious attitude toward Dix.

Still fuming, Anderson then went to his lawyer to rewrite his existing will, which split his estate evenly between Irene and Gertrude Dix. "I want to disinherit my daughter Irene," he told P. S. Benedict, the lawyer who had represented his interests for years.

Surprised, Benedict informed him that under the Civil Code of Louisiana, a son or daughter could only be written out of a parent's will if certain conditions were met. "First," Benedict said, "did she marry without your consent?"

"Oh, no," Anderson replied. "She married with my consent."

Benedict proceeded to enumerate the other allowable reasons for disinheriting a child — striking a parent, for instance, or refusing to bail a parent out of jail, or being guilty of cruelty to a parent.

"No, none of those things apply," Anderson said.

"Then I think you cannot disinherit your daughter."

Anderson pondered this for a while. Then he seemed to decide something. "Friend Benedict," he said finally, "I am going to tell you something you don't know. [Irene] is not my legal daughter. I was never married to her mother."

This, of course, seemed like an awfully convenient revelation, given the circumstances. Whether Benedict actually believed it or not is unclear, but he did agree to rewrite Anderson's will, leaving all of his estate to the new Mrs. Gertrude Anderson. But just to make certain that his wishes would be carried out, Anderson also wrote a letter to three of his closest associates, to be opened after his death and only if Irene contested the will. "To whom it may concern," it began. "I am not the father of Mrs. George Delsa, known as Irene Anderson. While I called her my daughter, [this] was for her benefit and protection. I was never married to her mother, Miss Emma Schwartz, [n]or was I her seducer. I met her like all young men meet such women. When she took sick and gave birth to her child, I took charge of her at her mother's request. . . ."

This was spite carried to an almost obscene level of bitterness. Tom Anderson, the man who had built an empire by being loyal to his friends and helpful to everyone, was ending his life with an act of utter betrayal toward his own daughter and grandchildren. That

Irene was in fact the issue of a legal marriage between Anderson and Emma Schwartz is certain. The evidence — as it emerged in the inevitable and ugly trial that resulted when Irene contested the will — was all but indisputable. Even the judge at the trial remarked on the startling resemblance between Irene Delsa and the deceased man. Ultimately, in fact, all of Anderson's written denials were thrown out of evidence as obviously fraudulent, and Irene inherited one-third of her father's $120,000 estate.

But thanks to the dispute between them, Anderson and his daughter were never reconciled during his lifetime. Instead of moving next door to her on Canal Street, Anderson bought a palatial $35,000 mansion on upper St. Charles Avenue and moved there with his new wife — about as far away from Irene and his grandchildren as he could get.

Late on the night of December 9, 1931, Tom and Gertrude Anderson were home alone at the St. Charles Street house when Tom began complaining of shortness of breath. This was not particularly unusual — Tom was now seventy-three years old and had been sickly for some years. So he merely went to bed, hoping to feel better in the morning. But he awoke a few hours later in considerable distress and called for Gertrude. He discouraged her when she proposed calling the doctor at that hour (it was one A.M.), but she insisted. Tom scoffed. "I'll be all right before the doctor even gets here," he said.

He died of a massive heart attack a few minutes later.

The front-page obituaries the next day were effusive. "Mr. Anderson," the *Daily States* wrote, "was widely known. He was beloved by hundreds who had known and enjoyed his bounties." The papers extolled him for his long service as a state legislator, as a political leader in the Fourth Ward, as a prominent businessman in the oil industry, and as a philanthropist to many charities. No reference was made to his other career as a vice lord, racing and boxing entrepreneur, cabaret owner, and restaurateur. Even two of his four marriages (to the prostitutes Catherine Turnbull and Olive Noble) were conveniently forgotten. The closest anyone came to suggesting his other life, in fact, was the comment by the *States* writer that Anderson's favorite quote was the biblical injunction "Let not thy left hand know what thy right hand doeth." These official obituaries were clearly for Tom Anderson's right hand alone. It was as if the left — the hand of the old mayor of Storyville — had never even existed.

But although Tom Anderson's death had made the front pages of the newspapers, Anderson and his world had long ago become old news for most people in 1930s New

Orleans. The revival of the Ring in 1925 had proved ephemeral. Martin Behrman had died less than a year after his surprise reelection. His successor was a mediocrity, and the old Ring organization was plunged into disarray once again, leaving a statewide power vacuum. It was soon filled by Huey P. Long, now a rising young politician, who would lead New Orleans and the rest of Louisiana into its next chapter of infamy.

The Crescent City, meanwhile, was not doing well in the new era of economic depression. The reformers' attempt to turn the city into an efficient manufacturing powerhouse in the '20s had not come off. Business was stagnant, and New Orleans had fallen behind other Southern cities — such as Dallas, Atlanta, and Houston — in industrial development. Desperate to revive their sagging fortunes, city fathers in the late '30s tried to reinvent New Orleans yet again as an interesting destination for travelers. And in their efforts to grow the city's tourism industry, they came to a realization — namely, that the city could actually exploit its checkered and exotic past as an enticement to visitors from the rest of the country and around the world.

This realization precipitated a radical change in the city's attitude toward many of its previously suppressed idiosyncrasies. The French Quarter and its Tango Belt, for instance, would no longer be regarded as a run-down immigrant slum embarrassing to businessmen; instead, it would be restored as an intriguing holdover of a romantic foreign past that people might pay to see. The city's jazz culture, rather than something to be suppressed and condemned, became something to be revived and promoted (albeit as a much whiter phenomenon). Before long, even the city's reputation as a den of sin and iniquity was being turned into a plus rather than a minus. The re-creation of wicked old New Orleans on Bourbon Street, complete with strip clubs and raucous dance halls, began to attract fun-seeking masses from all over — and ended up bearing more than a passing resemblance to Storyville in its heyday.

Granted, the city's racial atmosphere would take more time to loosen up. When Louis Armstrong, now an international star, was invited back to his hometown in 1949 to receive the key to the city, that key apparently opened only the doors to black New Orleans; the beloved Satchmo was forced to stay at a "colored hotel." And some journalists of the 1960s were quick to note the stark irony of using African American jazz culture to attract visitors to a place "still shackled by the iron grip of institutionalized racism and apartheid." But the tourist reinvention of the city did at least preserve some of the culture of the past, and a more genuine version of the city's former self did eventually emerge, especially after the demise of Jim Crow. And when the oil bust of the mid-1980s threatened to send the local economy into crisis, it was New Orleans' notoriety as a destination for jazz, sex, alcohol-soaked nightlife, and exotic culture — the very things the old reformers had tried to stamp out — that enabled the city to weather the bad times.

Of course, it remains to be seen how completely the city will rebound from the ravages of Hurricane Katrina in 2005. As of this writing, recovery is still somewhat spotty, and some of the poorer African American neighborhoods may never return to their former vitality. But as the turn-of-the-century reformers could attest (to their vexation), New Orleans' rebellious and free-spirited personality is nothing if not resilient. And so the disruptive energies of the place — its vibrancy and eccentricity, its defiance and nonconformity, and yes, its violence and depravity — are likely to live on.

■ ■ ■ ■

AFTERWORD
WHO WAS THE
AXMAN?

■ ■ ■ ■

The rooftops of old New Orleans **Library of Congress**

And what of the axman, that other disruptive figure who — like the brothel madam, the Ring politician, and the jazzman — seemed to drop from prominence in the new New Orleans of the early 1920s? After the Pipitone murder of October 1919, he had not been heard from again. As the months passed without another ax attack, police began to suspect that their "fell demon from the hottest hell" — whoever he was — had simply left town, like so many other figures from the city's underworld.

That conclusion was given some credence in December 1921, when inquiries came from authorities in Los Angeles about a man from New Orleans named Joseph Monfre, who had been shot dead in L.A. the day before. Monfre's killer was another ex–New Orleanian — one Mrs. Esther Albano, the former Mrs. Esther Pipitone, widow of the man widely regarded as the axman's last victim. According to Mrs. Albano, Monfre had killed her second husband, Angelo Albano — a small-time gangster who had gone missing in L.A. several weeks earlier — after he had refused to pay $500 in extortion money. When Monfre had shown up to collect the money from the widow, claiming that he was willing to kill her as well, Esther Albano was ready for him. "I grabbed my revolver," she told police, "and began to shoot. He tried to run. After one revolver was emptied, I seized another and killed him on the steps of my house."

But Mrs. Albano also claimed (at least once before changing her story) that Joseph Monfre had been one of the killers of her first husband as well. Why she had denied knowing Mike Pipitone's assailant at the time of the initial police investigation in 1919 is impossible to say; perhaps she was afraid of Monfre at the time, or even in some way complicit in the murder of her husband. But New Orleans Police, who knew Monfre well as a convicted dynamiter, suspected mob assassin, and notorious Black Hand extortionist, were inclined to believe her now.

Los Angeles authorities went on to try Esther Albano for the killing of Joseph Monfre, but their counterparts in New Orleans saw in the revelations about Monfre something of greater interest to them — namely, a thread by which they could tie together much of the Italian crime that had plagued the city over

546

the previous fifteen years. Joseph Monfre, after all, had been implicated in everything from the Lamana kidnapping of 1907 (in which he was suspected of aiding his relative Stefano, one of the principal co-conspirators) to the Black Hand grocery bombings of the same year. He was also suspected of involvement in the back-and-forth mob murders of 1915 involving Paolo Di Christina and Vincenzo Moreci (Monfre was arrested, though never charged, in the Moreci assassination). Now Mrs. Albano's implication of him in the 1919 murder of her first husband allowed police to tie him to the most notorious unsolved crimes of all. Since the Pipitone slaying of 1919 was regarded as the last of the axman attacks, could Monfre have been the axman himself, and thus responsible for all of those killings as well? Clearly his description — a tallish, heavyset, dark-complexioned white man — fit the one given by several witnesses to the axman crimes. And in going over Monfre's criminal records, investigators noticed a pattern. Though arrest and prison records in New Orleans at this time were notoriously confused and incomplete, it seemed that the waves and lulls in the axman's reign of terror jibed suspiciously well with Monfre's arrivals and departures from prison for his various deeds — most notably the lull in axman attacks from August 1918 to March 1919, which coincided almost exactly with one of Monfre's stints in prison.

The pattern was, at best, an imperfect fit, but it at least suggested a solution to the ax-man murders. Certainly the *Times-Picayune* seemed to buy the logic of Monfre as the ax-man. The *Daily Item* was more skeptical. In a December 16, 1921, article on the case, the paper ridiculed the theory, pointing out that Monfre had still been in jail when the Andollina and Maggio ax crimes were committed. (They were wrong about the Maggio slaying — Monfre had been released several days before that murder — but they were right about Andollina.) And in any case, even if the pattern of ax attacks had lined up perfectly with Monfre's prison record, this alone would not have been enough even to arrest him, let alone convict him.

But for many New Orleanians eager to put the episode behind them, it was at least a tempting conclusion to jump to. Joseph Monfre could become the last of the city's under-world monsters slain — like the Hennessy as-sassins, like Robert Charles, like Lamana kidnapper Leonardo Gebbia, even like Martin Behrman and Tom Anderson (slain at least symbolically). And much of the litera-ture that has grown up around the axman legend has uncritically embraced that conclu-sion.

But some latter-day writers have questioned the notion that Monfre could have been the axman. The crime writer Keven McQueen, in his book *The Axman Came from Hell,* has pointed out that the only "axman crime" that Monfre was at all convincingly linked to was the Pipitone murder, which may not even have been an axman crime (the murder weapon was an iron bar — a fact conveniently forgotten by the *Times-Picayune* in its later coverage of the incident). McQueen also points to evidence in prison records that seems to indicate that Monfre was still alive as late as 1930 — though McQueen admits that the records are "muddled." The absence of any death certificate for a Joseph Monfre in California in 1921 just confuses things further.

Part of the problem in trying to solve the case a hundred years after the fact is the overall carelessness of record keeping in the early 1900s. Names — particularly "ethnic" names — were misspelled in contemporary newspaper reports and even official records with a recklessness that seems inconceivable to us today. The axman case has also been hopelessly entangled in a skein of misinformation perpetrated by popular writers on the subject over the years. One of the early chroniclers of the case, Robert Tallant, in his book *Ready to Hang: Seven Famous New Orleans Murders,* seems to have invented freely, altering chronology and planting ficti- tious details that seem to have no basis in contemporary newspaper accounts and police reports. These inventions have all too often found their way into accounts of the axman crimes by later writers.

In fact, a close reading of the Police Homicide Reports and the contemporary newspaper reportage leads one to wonder whether more than a few of the so-called axman crimes were really the work of a single perpetrator acting with an unmistakable modus operandi. As we've seen, some of the crimes later attributed to the axman were actually committed with other types of weapons (even, in the Tony Schiambra case, a gun). They did not, moreover, invariably involve a chiseled-out door panel as the means of entry, or an obviously faked robbery motive. But somehow, in the hysteria that prevailed during those months of terror, such dissonant notes were forgotten or glossed over in the public mind. To many in New Orleans, the axman was real, and so every crime that was even remotely similar that occurred in New Orleans during those months was unconsciously tailored to fit the axman pattern.

If I were to hazard a guess — and it would be just that, a guess — I would say that at least some of the 1918–19 attacks on Italian grocers (the Maggio, Romano, and Cortimiglia crimes in particular) were quite likely the work of one or possibly two men, perhaps members of the same Black Hand organization. One of them could very well have been Joseph Monfre. The attacks on non-Italians were probably unrelated. The impossibly muddled Besumer case may have been a domestic crime of passion made to look like an axman crime, while a case like the attack on Sarah Laumann was likely a robbery gone wrong that merely became an ax attack in the fevered imagination of a traumatized public. The Pipitone murder, along with the Crutti, Davi, and Schiambra crimes of 1910–12, bear all the earmarks of Black Hand– or Mafia-related vengeance, but whether they were related to the 1918–19 crimes is impossible to say. As for the axman letter to the *Times-Picayune,* I think it was almost certainly a hoax, and one that must have fooled only the most gullible New Orleanians.

So was there really a deranged serial killer at large in the streets of New Orleans in 1918–19? Perhaps, though I suspect he was more of a brutal underworld enforcer than a textbook sociopath of the Jack the Ripper type. Any definitive answer to that question, however, is probably lost forever in the empty spaces of a flawed and incomplete historical record. The case remains one of the great unsolved mysteries in the serial-killer literature.

BIBLIOGRAPHY

Historical Newspapers

New Orleans: *Harlequin, The Mascot, New Orleans Bee, New Orleans Daily Item* (in the endnotes abbreviated NODI), *New Orleans Item-Tribune, New Orleans Daily States* (NODS), *New Orleans Times-Democrat* (NOTD), *New Orleans Times-Picayune* (NOTP); and, before 1914, *New Orleans Daily Picayune* (NODP). Others: *The Deseret Weekly, The New York Times, The Washington Post, The Atlanta Constitution, The Los Angeles Times, The St. Louis Post-Dispatch.*

Court Transcripts

ORLEANS PARISH CIVIL DISTRICT COURT
- *Mrs. Kate Anderson vs. Thomas C. Anderson, her husband,* Docket No. 48,601, Division E
- *Thomas C. Anderson vs. Mrs. Anna Deubler, wife of John T. Brady, and said Brady,* Docket No. 125,290, Division E
- *Thomas C. Anderson vs. His Wife,* Docket

No. 43,575

• *Mary A. Deubler vs. Merchants Insurance Company of New Orleans,* Docket No. 80,426

• *Morris Marks vs. Kate Anderson and her husband Thomas C. Anderson,* Docket No. 29,385

• *Succession of Mary Deubler,* Docket No. 107,603

• *Succession of Olive E. Noble,* Docket No. 93,226, Division E

ORLEANS PARISH CRIMINAL DISTRICT COURT

• *State of Louisiana vs. Anderson,* Docket No. 48,491

• *State of Louisiana vs. Thomas C. Anderson and Charles G. Prados,* Docket No. 49114

• *State of Louisiana vs. Louis Bessemer* [*sic*], Docket No. 33,902

• *State of Louisiana vs. Joseph Monfre,* Docket No. 35,993

• *State of Louisiana vs. Vincent Moreci,* Docket No. 35,043, Section B

LOUISIANA STATE SUPREME COURT

• *Succession of Mary Deubler,* Docket No. 21,667

• *Succession of Thomas C. Anderson,* Docket No. 32,083

Books and Articles

Adler, Jeffrey S. "Murder, North and South: Violence in Early-Twentieth-Century Chicago and New Orleans." *Journal of Southern History* 74, no. 2 (May 2008): 297–324.

Anderson, Gene. "Johnny Dodds in New Orleans." *American Music* 8, no. 4 (Winter 1990): 405–40.

Anderson, Maureen. "The White Reception of Jazz in America." *African American Review* 38, no. 1 (Spring 2004): 135–45.

Arceneaux, Pamela D. "Guidebooks to Sin: The Blue Books of Storyville." *Louisiana History* 28, no. 4 (Fall 1987): 397–405.

Armstrong, Louis. "Growing Up in New Orleans." In *New Orleans Stories: Great Writers on the City.* Edited by John Miller and Genevieve Anderson. San Francisco: Chronicle Books, 1992 (article originally appeared in *Life* magazine in 1966).

———. *Louis Armstrong, In His Own Words: Selected Writings.* Edited by Thomas Brothers. Oxford: Oxford University Press, 1999.

———. *Satchmo: My Life in New Orleans.* Centennial Edition. Cambridge, MA: Da Capo Press, 1954, 1986.

Asbury, Herbert. *The French Quarter: An Informal History of the New Orleans Underworld.* New York: Knopf, 1936; Capricorn Books, 1968.

Baiamonte, John V. *Spirit of Vengeance: Nativism and Louisiana Justice, 1921–1924.* Baton Rouge: Louisiana State University Press, 1986.

———. " 'Who Killa de Chief' Revisited: The Hennessy Assassination and Its Aftermath, 1890–1891." *Louisiana History* 33, no. 2 (Spring 1992): 117–46.

Barker, Danny. *Buddy Bolden and the Last Days of Storyville.* Edited by Alyn Shipton. New York: Cassell, 1998.

———. *Life in Jazz.* New York: Oxford University Press, 1986.

Barry, John M. *Rising Tide: The Great Mississippi Flood of 1927 and How It Changed America.* New York: Simon & Schuster, 1997.

Baum, Dan. *Nine Lives: Death and Life in New Orleans.* New York: Spiegel and Grau, 2009.

Bechet, Sidney. *Treat It Gentle.* New York: Hill and Wang, 1960.

Behrman, Martin. "A History of Three Great Public Utilities — Sewerage, Water and Drainage — and Their Influence Upon the Health and Progress of a Big City," Paper delivered at the Convention of League of American Municipalities, Milwaukee, WI, September 29, 1914.

———. *Martin Behrman of New Orleans: Memoirs of a City Boss.* Edited by John R. Kemp. Baton Rouge: Louisiana State University Press, 1977.

Berger, Morroe. "Jazz: Resistance to the Diffusion of a Culture-Pattern." *The Journal of Negro History* 32, no. 4 (October 1947): 461–94.

Bergreen, Laurence. *Louis Armstrong: An Extravagant Life.* New York: Broadway Books, 1997.

Berry, Jason. "The Mysteries of Buddy Bolden." *New Orleans,* November 1996, 43–44.

———. "Satchmo." *New Orleans,* July 1986, 38–39.

Bethel, Tom: "The Quest for Buddy Bolden." *New Orleans Music* 13, no. 4 (June 2007), 14–32.

Bindas, Kenneth J., ed. *America's Musical Pulse: Popular Music in Twentieth-Century Society.* Westport, CT: Praeger, 1992.

Blackstone, Orin. "Big Eye Louis." *Jazz Information,* December 29, 1940, 6–9.

Blesh, Rudi. *Shining Trumpets: A History of Jazz.* 2nd edition. New York: Alfred A. Knopf, 1958.

Blessingame, John W. *Black New Orleans, 1860–1880.* Chicago: University of Chicago Press, 1973.

Blount, Roy. *Feet on the Street: Rambles Around New Orleans.* New York: Crown, 2005.

Botein, Barbara. "The Hennessy Case: An

Episode in Anti-Italian Nativism." *Louisiana History* 20, no. 3 (Summer 1979): 261–79.

Boulard, Garry. "Blacks, Italians, and the Making of New Orleans Jazz." *The Journal of Ethnic Studies* 16, no. 1 (Spring 1988): 53–66.

Brothers, Thomas. *Louis Armstrong's New Orleans.* New York: W. W. Norton and Company, 2006.

Brunn, H. O. *The Story of the Original Dixieland Jazz Band.* Baton Rouge: Louisiana State University Press, 1960.

Buckingham, William D. "Louis Armstrong and the Waifs' Home." *The Jazz Archivist* 24 (2011): 2–15.

Buerkle, Jack V., and Danny Barker. *Bourbon Street Black: The New Orleans Black Jazzman.* New York: Oxford University Press, 1973.

Burrows, William E. *Vigilante!* New York: Harcourt Brace Jovanovich, 1976.

Campanella, Richard. *Bienville's Dilemma: A Historical Geography of New Orleans.* Lafayette, LA: Center for Louisiana Studies, 2008.

Carney, Court. "New Orleans and the Creation of Early Jazz." *Popular Music and Society* 29, no. 3 (July 2006): 299–315.

Carrasco, Rebecca S. "The Gift House: Jean M. Gordon and the Making of the Milne Home, 1904–1931." *Louisiana His-*

tory 34, no. 3 (Summer 1993): 309–25.

Carter, Hodding, ed. *The Past as Prelude: New Orleans 1718–1968.* New Orleans: Pelican Publishing, 1968.

Chandler, David Leon. *Brothers in Blood: The Rise of the Criminal Brotherhoods.* New York: E. P. Dutton & Co., 1975.

Charters, Samuel Barclay. "Storyville: 1913." *Jazz Journal* 2, no. 9 (September 1949): 3.

————. *A Trumpet Around the Corner: The Story of New Orleans Jazz.* Jackson: University Press of Mississippi, 2008.

Chilton, John. *Sidney Bechet: The Wizard of Jazz.* New York: Oxford University Press, 1987.

Cohen, Rich. *The Fish That Ate the Whale: The Life and Times of America's Banana King.* New York: Farrar, Straus and Giroux, 2012.

Colton, Craig E. "Basin Street Blues: Drainage and Environmental Equity in New Orleans, 1890–1930." *Journal of Historical Geography* 28, no. 2 (2002): 237-57.

————. *An Unnatural Metropolis: Wrestling New Orleans from Nature.* Baton Rouge: Louisiana State University Press, 2005.

Committee of 15. "An Appeal to the People of Louisiana." Committee of 15 for the Suppression of Commercial Vice in Louisiana, 1913(?).

Committee on Social Hygiene. "Segregation versus Morality." Committee on Social

Hygiene, New Orleans City Federation of Clubs, 1900(?).

Connelly, Mark T. *The Response to Prostitution in the Progressive Era.* Chapel Hill: University of North Carolina Press, 1980.

Craig, Anne O., and Maia Harris. "Storyville." *Louisiana Cultural Vistas,* Spring 1997, pp. 44–51.

Critchley, David. *The Origin of Organized Crime in America: The New York City Mafia, 1891–1931.* New York: Routledge, 2009.

Cunningham, George E. "The Italian, a Hindrance to White Solidarity in Louisiana, 1890–1898." *The Journal of Negro History* 50, no. 1 (January 1965): 22–36.

Dabney, Thomas Ewing. *One Hundred Great Years: The Story of the Times-Picayune from Its Founding to 1940.* Baton Rouge: Louisiana State University Press, 1944.

Dart, H. P., Jr. "William Stirling Parkerson." *The Record of Sigma Alpha Epsilon,* vol. XXI, no. 2 (May 1901), 130–32.

Dash, Mike. *The First Family: Terror, Extortion, Revenge, Murder, and the Birth of the American Mafia.* New York: Random House, 2009.

Davies, Russell. "Calling My Children Home." *The Listener,* 1980.

DeDonder, Jempi. "Big Eye: The Other Louis Nelson." *New Orleans Music* 3, no. 3 (1992): 6–17.

Dethloff, Henry C., and Robert R. Jones. "Race Relations in Louisiana, 1877–98. *Louisiana History* 9, no. 4 (Autumn 1968): 301–23.

Dominguez, Virginia R. *White by Definition: Social Classification in Creole Louisiana.* New Brunswick, NJ: Rutgers University Press, 1986.

Dyer, Isador. "The Municipal Control of Prostitution in the United States." Pamphlet reprinted in *New Orleans Medical and Surgical Journal* (December 1899).

Early, Eleanor. *New Orleans Holiday.* New York: Rinehart, 1947.

Edwards, Wallace. *The Axeman: The Brutal History of the Axeman of New Orleans.* Anaheim, CA: Absolute Crime Books, 2013.

Ellis, Scott S. *Madame Vieux Carre: The French Quarter in the Twentieth Century.* Jackson: University Press of Mississippi, 2010.

Fairclough, Adam. *Race & Democracy: The Civil Rights Struggle in Louisiana, 1915–1972.* Athens: University of Georgia Press, 1995.

Fiehrer, Thomas. "From Quadrille to Stomp: The Creole Origins of Jazz." *Popular Music* 10, no. 1 (1991): 21–38.

Fireside, Harvey. *Separate and Unequal: Homer Plessy and the Supreme Court Decision That Legalized Racism.* New York:

Carroll & Graf, 2004.

Fortier, Alcee. *Louisiana.* Atlanta: Southern Historical Association, 1909.

Foster, Craig L. "Tarnished Angels: Prostitution in Storyville, New Orleans, 1900–1910." *Louisiana History* 31, no. 4 (Winter 1990): 387–97.

Gabbard, Krin. *Hotter Than That: The Trumpet, Jazz, and American Culture.* New York: Faber and Faber, 2008.

Gambino, Richard. *Vendetta: A True Story of the Worst Lynching in America, the Mass Murder of Italian-Americans in New Orleans in 1891, the Vicious Motivations Behind It, and the Tragic Repurcussions That Linger to This Day.* Garden City, NY: Double-day, 1977.

Genthe, Arnold. *Impressions of Old New Orleans: A Book of Pictures.* New York: Doran Co., 1926.

Gibson, Dirk C. *Serial Murder and Media Circuses.* Westport, CT: Praeger, 2006.

Giddins, Gary. *Satchmo: The Genius of Louis Armstrong.* New York: Doubleday, 1988.

Gilley, B. H. "Kate Gordon and Louisiana Suffrage." *Louisiana History* 24, no. 3 (Summer 1983): 289–306.

Green, Elna C. "The Rest of the Story: Kate Gordon and the Opposition to the Nineteenth Amendment in the South." *Louisiana History* 33, no. 2 (Spring 1992): 171–89.

————. *Southern Strategies: Southern Women and the Woman Suffrage Question.* Chapel Hill: University of North Carolina Press, 1997.

Gregg, Rev. John Chandler. *Life in the Army, in the Departments of Virginia, and the Gulf, Including Observations in New Orleans, with an Account of the Author's Life and Experience in the Ministry.* Philadelphia: Perkinpine & Higgins, 1868.

Gushee, Lawrence. *Pioneers of Jazz: The Story of the Creole Band.* New York: Oxford University Press, 2005.

————. "A Preliminary Chronology of the Early Career of Ferd 'Jelly Roll' Morton." *American Music* 3, no. 4 (Winter 1985): 389–412.

Haas, Edward F. *Political Leadership in a Southern City: New Orleans in the Progressive Era, 1896–1902.* Ruston, LA: McGinty Publications (Department of History, Louisiana Tech University), 1988.

Hair, William Ivy. *Carnival of Fury: Robert Charles and the New Orleans Riot of 1900.* Baton Rouge: Louisiana State University Press, 1976.

————. *The Kingfish and His Realm: The Life and Times of Huey P. Long.* Baton Rouge: Louisiana State University Press, 1991.

Hansen, Harry, ed. *Louisiana: A Guide to the State.* Revised edition. Winter Park, FL:

Hastings House, 1971.

Harris, Martha. "Whatever Became of Josie Arlington?" *New Orleans,* May 1971, 36–48.

Hazeldine, Mike. "Buddy Bolden: First Sightings." *New Orleans Music* 13, no. 4 (June 2007): 6–8

Hersch, Charles. *Subversive Sounds: Race and the Birth of Jazz in New Orleans.* Chicago: University of Chicago Press, 2007.

Hirsch, Arnold R., and Joseph Logsdon, eds. *Creole New Orleans: Race and Americanization.* Baton Rouge: Louisiana State University Press, 1992.

Hobson, Barbara Meil. *Uneasy Virtue: The Politics of Prostitution and the American Reform Tradition.* 2nd edition. Chicago: University of Chicago Press, 1990.

Hunt, Belle. "New Orleans, Yesterday and Today." *Frank Leslie's Popular Monthly,* June 1891, 641–65.

Hunt, Thomas, and Martha Macheca Sheldon. *Deep Water: Joseph P. Macheca and the Birth of the American Mafia.* Bloomington, IN: iUniverse, 2007.

The Illustrated American. "Exterminating the Mafia." A Supplement to vol. 6, no. 58, March 28, 1891, 1–16.

———. "New Orleans' War on the Mafia." April 4, 1891, 319–23.

Jackson, Joy J. "Bosses and Businessmen in

Gilded Age New Orleans Politics." *Louisiana History* 5, no. 4 (Autumn 1964): 387–400.

———. "Crime and the Conscience of a City." *Louisiana History* 9, no. 3 (Summer 1968): 229–44.

———. *New Orleans in the Gilded Age: Politics and Urban Progress, 1880–1896.* Baton Rouge: Louisiana State University Press, 1969.

———. "Prohibition in New Orleans: The Unlikeliest Crusade." *Louisiana History* 19, no. 3 (Summer 1978): 261–84.

Johnson, Jerah. "Jim Crow Laws of the 1890s and the Origins of New Orleans Jazz: Correction of an Error." *Popular Music* 19, no. 2 (2000): 243–251.

Junger, Sebastian. "The Pumps of New Orleans." *Invention & Technology Magazine,* Fall 1992, 42–48.

Kane, Harnett T. *Queen New Orleans: City by the River.* New York: William Morrow & Company, 1949.

Katz, Allan. "The Hennessy Affair: A Centennial." *New Orleans,* October 1990, 58–62, 81.

Kelley, Blair L. M. *Right to Ride: Streetcar Boycotts and African American Citizenship in the Era of Plessy v. Ferguson.* Chapel Hill: University of North Carolina Press, 2010.

Kelman, Ari. *A River and Its City: The Nature*

of *Landscape in New Orleans.* Berkeley: University of California Press, 2003.

Kemp, Kathryn W. "Jean and Kate Gordon: New Orleans Social Reformers, 1898–1933." *Louisiana History* 24, no. 4 (Autumn 1983): 389–406.

Kendall, John S. "Blood on the Banquette." *Louisiana Historical Quarterly* 22, no. 3 (July 1939): 19–56.

———. *History of New Orleans.* Chicago: Lewis Publishing, 1922.

King, Grace. "The Higher Life of New Orleans." *Outlook,* April 25, 1896, 756–60.

Kubik, Gerhard. "The Mystery of the Buddy Bolden Photograph." *The Jazz Archivist* 22 (2009): 4–18.

Kurtz, Michael L. "Organized Crime in Louisiana History: Myth and Reality." *Louisiana History* 24, no. 4 (Autumn 1983): 355–76.

Larson, Edward J. *Sex, Race, and Science: Eugenics in the Deep South.* Baltimore: Johns Hopkins University Press, 1995.

Leavitt, Mel. *Great Characters of New Orleans.* San Francisco: Lexikos, 1984.

Leonard, Neil. *Jazz and the White Americans: The Acceptance of a New Art Form.* Chicago: University of Chicago Press, 1962.

Lewis, Peirce F. *New Orleans: The Making of an Urban Landscape.* 2nd edition. Chicago: Center for American Places, 2001.

Lindig, Carmen. *The Path from the Parlor: Louisiana Women 1879–1920.* Lafayette, LA: Center for Louisiana Studies, 1986.

Logsdon, Joseph, and Caryn Cossé Bell. "The Americanization of Black New Orleans." In *Creole New Orleans: Race and Americanization.* Edited by Arnold R. Hirsch and Joseph Logsdon. Baton Rouge: Louisiana State University Press, 1992.

Lomax, Alan. *Mister Jelly Roll: The Fortunes of Jelly Roll Morton, New Orleans Creole and "Inventor of Jazz."* New York: Pantheon Books Edition, 1993.

Long, Alecia P. *The Great Southern Babylon: Sex, Race, and Respectability in New Orleans, 1865–1920.* Baton Rouge: Louisiana State University Press, 2004.

————. "A Notorious Attraction: Sex and Tourism in New Orleans, 1897–1917." In *Southern Journeys: Tourism, History, and Culture in the Modern South.* Edited by Richard D. Starnes. Tuscaloosa: University of Alabama Press, 2003.

————. "Willie Piazza: A Storyville Madam Who Challenged Racial Segregation." *Louisiana Cultural Vistas,* Summer 2000, 8–10.

MacDonald, Robert R., John R. Kemp, and Edward F. Haas, eds. *Louisiana's Black Heritage.* New Orleans: Louisiana State Museum, 1977.

Mackey, Thomas C. *Red Lights Out: A Legal*

History of Prostitution, Disorderly Houses, and Vice Districts, 1870–1917. New York: Garland Publishing, 1987.

Magill, John. "A Conspiracy of Complicity." *Louisiana Cultural Vistas,* Fall 2006, 43.

Marquis, Donald M. "The Bolden-Payton Legend: A Re-Valuation." *Jazz Journal* 30, no. 2 (February 1977), 24–25.

———. *In Search of Buddy Bolden: First Man of Jazz.* Revised edition. Baton Rouge: Louisiana State University Press, 2005.

———. "Lincoln Park, Johnson Park, and Buddy Bolden." *The Second Line,* Fall 1976, 26–28.

Marr, Robert H. "The New Orleans Mafia Case." *The American Law Review* 25 (May/June 1891): 414–31.

Maygarden, Benjamin D. *National Register Evaluation of New Orleans Drainage System, New Orleans Parish, Louisiana.* Washington, DC: US Army Corps of Engineers, November 1999.

McCusker, John. *Creole Trombone: Kid Ory and the Early Years of Jazz.* Jackson: University Press of Mississippi, 2012.

McKinney, Louise. *New Orleans: A Cultural History.* New York: Oxford University Press, 2006.

McLaughlin, Mary Evelyn. "The Burning Busch." *Preservation in Print* 26, no. 9 (November 1998): 38.

McMain, Eleanor. "Behind the Yellow Fever in Little Palermo: Housing Conditions Which New Orleans Should Shake Itself Free From Along with the Summer's Scourges." *Charities and the Commons* 15 (1905): 152–59.

McQueen, Keven. *The Axman Came from Hell and Other Southern True Crime Stories.* Gretna, LA: Pelican Publishing, 2011.

Medley, Keith Weldon. *We as Freemen: Plessy v. Ferguson.* Gretna, LA: Pelican Publishing, 2003.

———. "When Plessy Met Ferguson." *Louisiana Cultural Vistas,* Winter 1996–97, 52–59.

Mitchell, Reid. *All on a Mardi Gras Day: Episodes in the History of New Orleans Carnival.* Cambridge, MA: Harvard University Press, 1995.

Morris, Ronald L. *Wait Until Dark: Jazz and the Underworld, 1880–1940.* Bowling Green, OH: Bowling Green University Popular Press, 1980.

Nelli, Humbert S. *The Business of Crime: Italians and Syndicate Crime in the United States.* New York: Oxford University Press, 1976.

New Orleans Police Department. *History: New Orleans Police, January 1, 1900.* New Orleans: L. Graham & Son, 1900.

Nussbaum, Raymond O. " 'The Ring Is Smashed!': The New Orleans Municipal

Election of 1896." *Louisiana History* 17, no. 3 (Summer 1976): 283–97.

Nystrom, Justin A. *New Orleans After the Civil War: Race, Politics, and a New Birth of Freedom.* Baltimore: Johns Hopkins University Press, 2010.

Oliver, Paul. "That Certain Feeling: Blues and Jazz . . . in 1890?" *Popular Music* 10, no. 1 (1991): 11–19.

Panetta, Vincent J. " 'For Godsake Stop!' Improvised Music in the Streets of New Orleans, ca. 1890." *The Musical Quarterly* 84, no. 1 (Spring 2000): 5–29.

Parker, Joseph B. *The Morrison Era: Reform Politics in New Orleans.* Gretna, LA: Pelican Publishing, 1974

Peterson, S. Marshall. "Reminiscing with Pops Foster." *The Second Line,* May–June 1967, 67–69.

Piazza, Tom. *Why New Orleans Matters.* New York: ReganBooks, 2005.

Pitkin, Thomas Monroe, and Francesco Cordasco. *The Black Hand: A Chapter in Ethnic Crime.* Totowa, NJ: Littlefield, Adams & Co., 1977.

Police Association of New Orleans. *New Orleans Police Department Commemorative Album.* New Orleans: Police Association of New Orleans, 1985.

Powell, Lawrence N. *The Accidental City: Improvising New Orleans.* Cambridge, MA:

Harvard University Press, 2012.

Putnam, Frank. "New Orleans in Transition." *The New England Magazine* 36 (April 1907): 228–29.

Raeburn, Bruce Boyd. *New Orleans Style and the Writing of American Jazz History.* Ann Arbor: University of Michigan Press, 2009.

Ramsey, Frederic. "Baquet and His Mob 'Caved' King Bolden." *Down Beat,* January 1, 1941.

———. "Fred Ramsey Speaks Out." *78 Quarterly* 4 (1989): 31–39.

Ramsey, Frederic, and Charles Edward Smith, eds. *Jazzmen.* New York: Limelight, 1985 (reprint).

Reed, Germaine A. "Race Legislation in Louisiana, 1864–1920." *Louisiana History* 6, no. 4 (Autumn 1965): 379–92.

Reeves, Thurman W. "From the Scarlet Past of Fabulous New Orleans: Souvenir Edition of the World Famous Tenderloin Directory 'The Blue Book.' " New Orleans: Thurman W. Reeves, 1951.

Reich, Howard, and William Gaines. *Jelly's Blues: The Life, Music, and Redemption of Jelly Roll Morton.* Cambridge, MA: Da Capo Press, 2003.

Reid, Ed. *Mafia.* New York: Random House, 1952.

Reppetto, Thomas. *American Mafia: A History of Its Rise to Power.* New York: Holt, 2004.

Reynolds, George M. *Machine Politics in New Orleans, 1897–1926.* New York: Columbia University Press, 1936.

Rose, Al. *I Remember Jazz: Six Decades Among the Great Jazzmen.* Baton Rouge: Louisiana State University Press, 1987.

————. *Storyville, New Orleans: Being an Authentic, Illustrated Account of the Notorious Red-Light District.* Tuscaloosa: University of Alabama Press, 1979.

Rosen, Ruth. *Lost Sisterhood: Prostitution in America, 1900–1918.* Baltimore: Johns Hopkins University Press, 1982.

Schott, Matthew J. "The New Orleans Machine and Progressivism." *Louisiana History* 24, no. 2 (Spring 1983): 141–53.

Shapiro, Nat, and Nat Hentoff, eds. *Hear Me Talkin' to Ya: The Story of Jazz as Told by the Men Who Made It.* New York: Rinehart, 1955.

Shepherd, Samuel C., Jr. "In Pursuit of Louisiana Progressives." *Louisiana History* 46, no. 4 (Autumn 2005): 389–406.

Shugg, Roger Wallace. "The New Orleans General Strike of 1892." *Louisiana Historical Quarterly* 21, no. 2 (April 1938): 547–60.

Sindler, Allan P. *Huey Long's Louisiana: State Politics, 1920–1952.* Westport, CT: Greenwood Press, 1956.

Smith, Charles Edward. "The Bolden Cylinder." *New Orleans Music* 13, no. 4 (June 2007): 9–12.

Smith, Tom. *The Crescent City Lynchings: The Murder of Chief Hennessy, the New Orleans "Mafia" Trials, and the Parish Prison Mob.* Guilford, CT: Lyons Press, 2007.

Somers, Dale A. "Black and White in New Orleans: A Study in Urban Race Relations, 1865–1900." *The Journal of Southern History* 40, no. 1 (February 1974): 19–42.

Souchon, Edmond. "King Oliver: A Very Personal Memoir." *Jazz Review* 3, no. 4 (May 1960): 6–11.

Souther, J. Mark. "Making the 'Birthplace of Jazz': Tourism and Musical Heritage Marketing in New Orleans." *Louisiana History* 44, no. 1 (Winter 2003): 39–73.

————. *New Orleans on Parade: Tourism and the Transformation of the Crescent City.* Baton Rouge: Louisiana State University Press, 2006.

Spain, Daphne. "Race Relations and Residential Segregation in New Orleans: Two Centuries of Paradox." *The Annals of the American Association of Political and Social Science* 441 (January 1979): 82–96.

St. Cyr, Johnny. "Jazz As I Remember It." *Jazz Journal* 19, no. 9 (September 1966): 6–10.

Stanonis, Anthony J. *Creating the Big Easy: New Orleans and the Emergence of Modern*

Tourism, 1918–1945. Athens: University of Georgia Press, 2006.

———. "A Woman of Boundless Energy: Elizebeth Werlein and Her Times." *Louisiana History* 46, no. 1 (2005): 5–26.

Tallant, Robert. *Mardi Gras*. Garden City NY: Doubleday. 1948.

———. *Ready to Hang: Seven Famous New Orleans Murders*. New York: Harper & Brothers, 1952.

Tallant, Robert, and Lyle Saxon. *Gumbo Ya-Ya: A Collection of Louisiana Folk Tales*. Boston: Houghton Mifflin, 1945.

Teachout, Terry. *Pops: A Life of Louis Armstrong*. New York: Houghton Mifflin Harcourt, 2009.

Thomas, Brook, ed. *Plessy v. Ferguson: A Brief History with Documents*. New York: Bedford St. Martin's, 1997.

Thompson, Kay. "First Lady of Storyville: The Fabulous Countess Willie Piazza." *The Record Changer,* February 1951, 5–14.

———. "Louis and the Waif's Home." *The Record Changer,* January 1952, 9-10, 43.

Thompson, Ray Matthew. *Albert Baldwin Wood: The Man Who Made Water Run Uphill*. Revised edition. New Orleans: Sewerage and Water Board of New Orleans, 1999.

Vyhnanek, Louis. *Unorganized Crime: New Orleans in the 1920s*. Lafayette, LA: Center for Louisiana Studies, 1998.

Warmouth, Henry Clay. *War, Politics, and Reconstruction: Stormy Days in Louisiana.* New York: Macmillan, 1930.

Warner, Richard N. "The First Crime Boss of Los Angeles?" *Informer,* July 2010, 4–15.

Wells-Barnett, Ida B. "Mob Rule in New Orleans." Pamphlet published in 1900.

Wilds, John. *Afternoon Story: A Century of the New Orleans States-Item.* Baton Rouge: Louisiana State University Press, 1976.

Williams, Martin. *Jazz Masters of New Orleans.* New York: Da Capo Press, 1978.

Wiltz, Christine. *The Last Madam: A Life in the New Orleans Underworld.* New York: Faber and Faber, 2000.

Winston, Justin, and Clive Wilson. "The Bolden Photograph: A Photographic Examination." *The Jazz Archivist* 22 (2009): 19–24.

Woodward, C. Vann. *The Strange Career of Jim Crow.* 3rd revised edition. New York: Oxford University Press, 1974.

Zink, Harold. *City Bosses in the United States: A Study of Twenty Municipal Bosses.* New York: AMS Press, 1968.

Manuscripts, Theses, Dissertations, Oral Histories, Etc.

Friends of the Cabildo Oral Histories, New Orleans Public Library.

Oral Histories (Hogan Jazz Archive, Tulane University).

Papers of Iris Kelso, A. P. Tureaud, Bezou-Goffin, Josie Arlington Collection (University of New Orleans); Joseph Shakspeare Collection, William Russell Collection, Frederic Ramsey Papers (Historic New Orleans Collection).

Soards City Directories, US Census records, NOPD Reports of Homicide and Arrest Records, Passenger Lists, Passport Applications, Death Records, etc. New Orleans Public Library, Louisiana Division.

Adams, Margaret. "Outline of the Mafia Riots." Thesis, Tulane University, 1924.

Anthony, Arthé Agnes. "The Negro Creole Community in New Orleans, 1880–1920: An Oral History." PhD diss., University of California at Irvine, 1978.

Badger, A. S. Letter to George Denegre of April 21, 1891, Historic New Orleans Collection.

Carney, Courtney Patterson. "Jazz and the Cultural Transformation of America in the 1920s." PhD diss., Louisiana State University and Agricultural and Mechanical College, 2003.

Carroll, Ralph Edward. "The Mafia in New Orleans, 1900–1907." MA thesis, Notre Dame Seminary, 1956.

Carroll, Richard Louis. "The Impact of David C. Hennessey on New Orleans Society and the Consequences of the Assassination of Hennessey." MA thesis, Notre Dame Seminary, 1957.

Collins, Philip R. "The Old Regular Democratic Organization in New Orleans." MA thesis, Georgetown University, 1948.

Landau, Emily Epstein. "Spectacular Wickedness: New Orleans, Prostitution, and the Politics of Sex, 1897–1917." PhD diss., Yale University, 2005.

Leathem, Karen Trahan. "A Carnival According to Their Own Desires: Gender and Mardi Gras in New Orleans, 1870–1941." PhD diss., University of North Carolina, 1994.

Lester, Charlie. "The New Negro of Jazz: New Orleans, Chicago, New York, the First Great Migration, and the Harlem Renaissance, 1890–1930." PhD diss., University of Cincinnati, 2012.

Levy, Russell. "Of Bards and Bawds: New Orleans Sporting Life Before and During the Storyville Era, 1897–1917." MA thesis, Tulane University, 1967.

Mir, Jasmine. "Marketplace of Desire: Storyville and the Making of a Tourist City in New Orleans, 1890–1920." PhD diss., New York University, 2005.

Stall, Buddy. "Buddy Stall's Storyville." Taped lecture, Historic New Orleans Collection.

Various. *Pamphlets on the Mafia Case,* Louisi-

ana Research Collection, Tulane University.
Winston, Donald E. "News Reporting of Jazz,
1890–1907." MA thesis, University of
Oklahoma, 1966.

NOTES

(Note: Newspapers of this era were notoriously cavalier about names, sometimes spelling the same name several different ways in a single article. In quotations I have silently corrected these variations to correspond with what I regard as the most accurate spelling of the name.)

Prologue

Details about the Maggio killing come principally from the police report on the homicide, dated May 23, 1918, and from contemporary news reports, in particular the May 23 and 24, 1918, issues of the NOTP, NODS, and NODI. See also Robert Tallant, *Ready to Hang,* 193–96.

"one of the most gruesome . . ." is from the NOTP of May 24, 1918.
It was a godforsaken neighborhood . . . The description of the Maggios' immediate neighborhood comes from the newspaper

reports, especially the NODS of May 23, 1918. A more general impression of this area, and of New Orleans' 1918 geography overall, can be gleaned from several works: Peirce F. Lewis's *New Orleans: The Making of an Urban Landscape;* Craig E. Colton's *An Unnatural Metropolis* and also his "Basin Street Blues"; and especially Richard Campanella's (highly recommendable) *Bienville's Dilemma* — see in particular the section "Populating the Landscape," and the maps.

Frank Mooney, forty-eight years old . . . Information about Frank T. Mooney comes mainly from newspaper reports at the time of his hiring as superintendent — the NODI and NODS of August 8, 1917, and the NOTP of August 9, 1917.

The intruder had clearly taken . . . Further Maggio case details from the police report and from the May 1918 articles cited above.

"to have a nick honed from the blade" . . . and the chalk message are from the NOTP of May 24, 1918. [NB: Some newspapers first transcribed the chalk scrawl as "Mrs. Joseph Maggio is going to sit up tonight. Just *write* Mrs. Toney," but I've used the version that appears in the NOTP and in most later sources.]

a series of unsolved attacks . . . The daily

papers were somewhat confused about the dates of the earlier Italian grocer murders, perhaps because they relied on the detectives' memory of the cases rather than checking their own newspapers' morgues. The attacks in question, some of which were not fatal, occurred in August and September of 1910 (Crutti and Resetti), June of 1911 (Davi), May of 1912 (Schiambra), August of 1913 (Chetta), and as recently as December of 1917 (Andollina). The Schiambra murder, a shooting, was actually one of the non-hatchet murders.

"As police superintendent, he will be judged . . ." The NOTP's doubts about Mooney's experience were expressed in an article in the August 9, 1917, edition.

openly speculating about a crazed serial killer . . . The NOTP's speculation was in the August 16, 1918, edition.

Chapter 1: Going Respectable

The account of the events of November 29 is based principally on initial newspaper reports about the shooting (NODSs of November 29 and 30, 1890; NODPs of November 30 and December 9 and 10, 1890) and from surprisingly thorough press accounts of Phillip Lobrano's two trials (NODI of January 29, 1892; NOTDs of January 29 and March 31, 1892; NODPs of January 29 and 30, 1892, and March 31, 1892). Little is known for sure about Lobrano, but a comparison of court testimony (which refers to his prominent family and a brother named Emile) and the obituaries of various related Lobranos indicates that he was the wayward son of Jacynthe (aka Jacinto) Lobrano, a hero of the 1815 Battle of New Orleans, to whom Andrew Jackson once presented one of his swords. Phillip was born in 1847, which would make him forty-two or forty-three in 1890, and some sixteen years Mary Deubler/Josie Lobrano's senior. Further background for this scene and the rest of Chapter 1 comes from a variety of other sources, especially the testimony from Mary Deubler's contested-will trial (*Succession of Deubler*); Alecia P. Long, *The Great Southern Babylon,* 148–90; Herbert Asbury, *The French Quarter,* 448–51; and Al Rose, *Storyville,* 47–49.

what had happened on Royal Street . . . The scene in Louis George's saloon is based on testimony in the two trials by Lobrano himself, A. C. Becker (the bartender), and John T. McGreevy (a friend in the bar).

"flock of vultures" . . . as quoted in Asbury, *French Quarter,* 449.

"You bastard, come take a drink" . . . is quoted in the NOTD of January 29, 1892. [NB: The newspapers did not print the two expletives uttered by Peter Deubler; I don't think I could be far wrong in assuming, in both cases, that "bastard" was the omitted word.]

"It looks as if you want to raise hell" and Deubler's response are from Becker's testimony in the second trial.

"I am going to kill that bastard . . ." is quoted in the NOTD of January 29, 1892.

Twenty-six years old . . . Josie Lobrano's appearance as per a well-known 1890s photograph of her in the Josie Arlington Collection (Earl K. Long Library, University of New Orleans).

Driven into prostitution . . . The best sources for details about Josie's life are Long, *Babylon,* and *Succession of Deubler.*

arrested for disorderly conduct several times . . . The Palmyra Street incident is mentioned in the NODP of November 30, 1890.

"staggered from the scene of combat . . ." The Beulah Ripley fight (with quote) is from Asbury, *French Quarter,* 449.

"too drunk to take to the parlor" . . . was from Josie Lobrano's testimony in the second trial.

According to Phillip Lobrano . . . The Lobranos gave significantly conflicting testimony in the trials. I have generally given more credence to Phillip's account, first, because his version apparently convinced all but a few members of two juries, and second, because evidence exists in the newspaper trial accounts that Josie was "anxious to have this man convicted" and had told a witness that she would "swear the accused to the gallows." Moreover, Josie's other brother, Henry Deubler, was alleged to have intimidated defense witnesses after the first trial.

"You've done it, Phil!" . . . as per Josie in the first trial.

"expected a tragedy to take place . . ." Corporal Duffy's experience in the brothel comes mainly from the NODS and NODP of November 30, 1890, and from his court testimony.

he walked into the Central Police Station . . . Lobrano's surrender and Peter Deubler's "very dangerous" wound as per the NODS of November 30, 1890.

"sinking rapidly" . . . Peter Deubler's relapse and death were reported in the NODP of December 9 and 10, 1890, and in the court reports in the same paper's January 29 and March 31, 1892, editions.

she also resolved to change . . . For Josie Lobrano's decision to become respectable, see especially Long, *Babylon,* 153–55, and Asbury, *French Quarter,* 449–50.

"turn over a new leaf" . . . as quoted in Rose, *Storyville,* 48.

Chapter 2: The Sodom of the South

Vice in New Orleans has been the subject of much first-class academic analysis, the very best of it to be found in Alecia P. Long's *The Great Southern Babylon: Sex, Race, and Respectability in New Orleans, 1865–1920* and Emily Epstein Landau's 2005 dissertation, "Spectacular Wickedness: New Orleans, Prostitution, and the Politics of Sex, 1897–1917" (which has since been published as a book, though all references in these notes are to the PhD thesis). Russell Levy's 1967 master's thesis, "Of Bards and Bawds: New Orleans Sporting Life Before and During the Storyville Era, 1897–1917," is also quite useful, and Levy had access to certain sources that seem to have been subsequently lost. The two best-known books on the topic are Herbert Asbury's *The French Quarter: An Informal History of the New Orleans Underworld* and Al Rose's *Storyville, New Orleans: Being an Authentic, Illustrated Account of the Notorious Red-Light District.* Both lack footnotes, however, and sometimes traffic in apocrypha and folklore (though Rose seems more reliable than Asbury); I have tried to use both with caution.

"I doubt if there is a city in the world . . ." is from Olmsted's *A Journey in the Seaboard States, with Remarks on Their Economy,* as

quoted in Campanella, *Bienville's Dilemma,*
170.

"What a mingling of peoples! . . ." as
quoted in Campanella, *Bienville,* 169, is
originally from Ernst von Hesse-Wartegg's
Travels on the Lower Mississippi, 1879–80.

"It is no easy matter to go to heaven . . ."
is a quote from Rev. John Chandler Gregg,
Life in the Army, 156–57.

these goings-on had begun to spread . . .
See especially Long, *Babylon,* 78ff. and
116ff., and Landau, "Spectacular Wickedness," 66ff.

"concert saloons" . . . Long, *Babylon,* 64,
provides the most complete description of
these establishments.

so-called coon music . . . The spread of
"coon music" to Canal Street was reported,
with great condescension, in the *Mascot* of
November 11, 1890.

**brothels and assignation houses had
become impossible to avoid . . .** The
danger of brothels opening up next door to
decent families was a persistent theme in
the press during these years; see, for example, the *Mascot* of June 11, 1892.

"The social evil is rampant . . ." is as
quoted in Rose, *Storyville,* 37.

"At no time since the war . . ." is from
the *Mascot* of March 2, 1888.

"Negro dives" . . . is from the NODP of
October 20, 1888.

"If given our choice between the Negro . . ." is from the *Mascot* of September 7, 1889.

support for "the Ring" . . . A useful source for the local politics in New Orleans during the 1880s and '90s is Joy Jackson's *New Orleans in the Gilded Age.*

civil war and federal occupation . . . Jackson, *Gilded Age,* is also the source for the city's punishing debt (p. 53) and its drop from fourth- to ninth-largest city (p. 6).

the city desperately needed to rebuild . . . Landau, "Spectacular Wickedness," 5, 67, and 73, is best on the need to improve New Orleans' reputation in order to attract Northern capital. See also Jackson, *Gilded Age,* 221.

"The reputation of our city . . ." From an illegibly signed letter to Mayor Shakspeare in the Joseph Shakspeare Collection (MSS96, Folder 3) dated April 20, 1888.

"Its campaign committee . . ." The best source for the YMDA is John S. Kendall's *History of New Orleans,* Chapter 30. See also Jackson, *Gilded Age,* 96ff. (and p. 36 for "a blue book of the city's commercial elite").

"a ticket which is an insult . . ." Kendall, *History,* 469.

"if need be at the point of the bayonet" . . . Kendall, *History,* 471.

"countless questionable devices . . ." as noted in the NOTD of April 20, 1888.

Chapter 3: The First Casualty

The literature on the murder of David Hennessy (often misspelled Hennessey) and its aftermath is as extensive as it is contentious. For my retelling in the next two chapters, I have relied most heavily on newspaper accounts and on three admirably comprehensive books: *Vendetta* by Richard Gambino; *The Crescent City Lynchings* by Tom Smith; and *Deep Water* by Thomas Hunt and Martha Macheca Sheldon (a descendant of one of the defendants), with backup from Humbert Nelli's much shorter account in *The Business of Crime.* However, given the wide range of conclusions drawn — in these and other accounts — about what role was played by anything resembling a New Orleans "Mafia," I have used all sources with a certain amount of caution. (For a short but sensible account of the Hennessy affair and its contentious historiography, see Katz's "The Hennessy Affair: A Centennial," 58–62, 81.)

the disciplinary hearing of two police officers . . . Details of the Police Board meeting come principally from reports in the NODP and NOTD of October 16, 1890, and from Smith, *Crescent City Lynchings,* xxi–xxii, and Hunt and Sheldon, *Deep*

Water, 230ff.

Virtually his first act as mayor . . . For Shakspeare's early appointment of Hennessy and his intent to reorganize the police department, see Kendall, *History,* 469f., and Hunt and Sheldon, *Deep Water,* 198f.

tall, lean, and dourly handsome . . . Particulars about Hennessy's history and appearance come principally from engravings and obituaries in the daily papers of October 16 and 17, 1890.

the country's youngest police chief . . . as per Mike Dash, *First Family,* 72.

"You had threatened me before . . ." is from the NODP of October 16, 1890.

After the police board meeting adjourned . . . The scene in Hennessy's office after the meeting was described by O'Connor (often identified as "Connors" in the literature) in a statement to the newspapers.

accompanying his friend on a semi-official basis . . . For the city's arrangement with the Boylan agency for the chief's protection, see especially Hunt and Sheldon, *Deep Water,* 230.

roiled by a struggle between two rival families . . . The Provenzano/Matranga feud has been ubiquitously covered in the sources, with significant disagreement over whether or not the feud qualified as "Mafia-related."

Inviting representatives of both clans . . .
The NODS of October 17, 1890, is espe-
cially detailed on the meeting at the Red
Light Club.

**he launched an investigation into the
Matranga organization . . .** Hennessy's
alleged discoveries with regard to Matranga
Mafia connections are based almost exclusively on undocumented statements made
to the press by George Vandervoort (Hennessy's secretary) and his friend, the famous
detective Pinkerton, after the chief's murder.

**on this rainy Wednesday night in Octo-
ber . . .** Details about the walk back to Girod Street come mainly from the daily
newspapers, as told by O'Connor. The
quotes are as reported in the NODP of
October 16, 1890.

**Shortly before the chief reached the end
of the first block . . .** The shooting scene
on Girod Street as per newspaper reports
of the next day and testimony from the
subsequent trial, as reported in the newspapers. [NB: As an example of how careless
the daily newspapers could be with names,
the Boylan's man encountered by O'Connor is variously spelled as Carter, Cotter,
Kolter, and one or two other ways.]

"Which way did they run? . . ." This and
all quotations in this scene as per the
NODP of October 16, 1890.

Several men helped carry the wounded Hennessy . . . The scene at the Gillis House is best described in the NOTD of October 16, 1890.

"No! For God's sake . . ." is from Smith, *Crescent City Lynchings,* xiv.

"Scour the whole neighborhood . . ." For the scene at the Central Station, and Shakspeare's quote, see especially the NODP of October 16, 1890.

Chief Hennessy was now lying on the table . . . Details of events at Charity Hospital are culled from various newspaper accounts, with priority given to the NODP report of October 17, 1890.

"Now go home, Mother . . ." The conversation with Mrs. Hennessy as reported in the NODS of October 16, 1890.

"Chief, you know who I am . . ." and Hennessy's reply is from the NODP of the same date.

"Captain, I tell you . . ." The conversation with Beanham (ending with "These people can't kill me") was in the next day's NODP. [NB: Gambino makes much of the fact that one newspaper, the NOTD, reported that Hennessy at one point shook his head when asked whether he had recognized the shooters. Since no other reporter mentioned this, however, I suspect the chief may just have been refusing to answer rather than denying that he knew his assailants.]

"a class of foreigners . . ." was in the NODS of October 16, 1890.

"to assist the officers of the law . . ." For the newspaper notices, see William E. Burrows, *Vigilante!,* 201.

Forty-two Italians had already been arrested . . . as per the NOTD of October 17, 1890.

Makeshift memorials to the chief . . . as cited by the daily papers.

police assembled at Francis Johnson & Sons undertakers . . . Details of the wake at the Girod Street house come principally from the NODP of October 17, 1890.

A detail of police arrived at the Girod Street cottage . . . All of the papers of October 18, 1890, carried extensive reports on the chief's funeral. I have relied mainly on that in the NODP.

"bosom friend" . . . Anderson is described as such in the NODP of October 16.

short but powerfully built figure . . . Description of Anderson as per Rose, *Storyville,* 42.

"David Hennessy, died Oct. 16, 1890" . . . Anderson's role in placing the temporary marker as per the NODP of October 18.

"by the hands of despicable assassins" . . . The special council meeting of Saturday was covered by all of the newspapers. This and all quotes are from the NOPD report of October 19, 1890.

Chapter 4: Retribution

Official records for the Hennessy murder trial were either lost or conveniently destroyed, so I have depended principally, as have the authors of the four books on the subject mentioned in the previous chapter, on the understandably detailed newspaper reports.

In the main courtroom at St. Patrick's Hall . . . Details for the courtroom scene while the jury deliberated come from the NODI of March 13 and 14, 1891.

the jury had supposedly reached its decision very quickly . . . The rumors of an early verdict were from the NODP of March 13, 1891.

the police had ultimately arrested more than a hundred Italians . . . as per the NODI of February 16, 1891. [NB: The newspapers and most of the population of New Orleans at this time seemed certain of the existence of a full-fledged "Mafia" in the city at this time, modeled on its predecessor in Sicily. Many later historians have accepted this belief as fact, without much proof to back it up. Others, like Richard Gambino and Humbert Nelli, disagree vehemently. While I think it is disingenuous to deny that there was any organized crime whatsoever in the city's Italian community, particularly in later years (see Michael L. Kurtz's unconvincing "Organized Crime in

Louisiana History: Myth and Reality"), I tend to agree with Nelli that Italian crime in New Orleans in 1890 was at best loosely organized and decentralized.]

proved to be maddeningly complicated . . . Details of jury selection, witness examination, the bribery allegations, and Polizzi's antics were ubiquitously reported. For Peeler's alleged drunkenness, see Smith, *Crescent City Lynchings,* 176.

evidence from more than 140 witnesses . . . Smith is especially thorough in his presentation of the overabundance of testimony on both sides.

prizefighter John L. Sullivan showed up to watch . . . Gambino, *Vendetta,* 76, writes about Sullivan's visit.

no other outcome . . . The newspapers of the day (see, for instance, the NODI of March 3, 1891) seemed to believe that the prosecution made a strong case, but to me this seems more like wishful thinking than objective analysis. It's worth noting that a federal investigator examining the trial transcripts months afterward found the evidence "exceedingly unsatisfactory" and "not, to my mind, conclusive one way or the other" (see Gambino, *Vendetta,* 192).

At one thirty P.M., a knock . . . The moments before the verdict as described in the NODI of March 13 (which also reports the excitement on the street as comparable to that on the day after the shooting).

"to turn and look at one another . . ."
and the heckling of the jurors are both from
the NODI of March 14.

"Red-handed murder . . ." is from the
NODI of March 14, 1891.

"Alien hands of oath-bound assassins . . ." is from the NODS of the same
date.

**When William S. Parkerson stepped into
his second-floor law office . . .** Much of
the description of Parkerson's activities on
the night of the verdict are from an interview he gave to the *Illustrated American* for
the issue of April 4, 1891.

**Balding, bespectacled, and somewhat
portly . . .** Parkerson's appearance and history from the *Illustrated American* interview;
from his entry in Fortier's *Louisiana,* Vol. 3;
and his obituary in the NOTP of February
15, 1915.

"Southern 'special gentlemen's police' "
is from Giose Rimanelli, as quoted in Hunt
and Sheldon, *Deep Water,* 339.

**at the corner of Royal and Bienville
Streets . . .** The location of Hayne's home
as per the NODP of March 15, 1891.

Many had heard stories of raucous demonstrations . . . For the meeting at
Hayne's, see also Hunt and Sheldon, *Deep
Water,* 337–41. [NB: Some Italian community leaders insisted that the celebra-

tions had to do with King Umberto's birthday and had nothing to do with the acquittals.]

MASS MEETING! . . . Text of the newspaper announcement as per numerous sources (see, for instance, Smith, *Crescent City Lynchings,* 213).

rode a horse-drawn wagon . . . For the trip to Albert Baldwin's hardware store for arms, see Hunt and Sheldon, *Deep Water,* 341.

at eight thirty A.M. he left his office . . . Villere's search for the mayor comes mainly from the *Illustrated American* account and from Hunt and Sheldon, *Deep Water,* 342ff.

heading through the streets in the same direction . . . Corte described his search for the mayor in a letter to Ambassador Francesco Fava dated March 15, 1891, reproduced in various sources (e.g., Gambino, *Vendetta,* 158–60).

Corte and Villere hurried over . . . The Corte letter indicates that the governor was "not far away at a lawyer's office," though other sources, like Gambino, *Vendetta,* 79, say he was at a friend's house on the outskirts of town.

a white-haired former Confederate general . . . The governor's appearance and history as per Gambino, *Vendetta,* 80.

crowds were already gathering . . . The mass meeting at the Clay statue was widely reported in the press.

"People of New Orleans, once before I stood before you . . ." The complete text of Parkerson's speech was reprinted ubiquitously (e.g., in Gambino, *Vendetta,* 157).

made their way down Royal . . . The newspapers disagree slightly on the exact route the mob took to the Orleans Parish Prison.

"The crowd accordingly fell in line . . ." is from the NODI of March 14, 1891.

"like a mighty roaring stream" . . . This and other details in this paragraph are from an account in the *Deseret Weekly,* March 21, 1891.

"It was the most terrible thing . . ." is from the Parkerson interview in the *Illustrated American,* 321.

Two municipal detectives left the park . . . The two municipal detectives and the scene with Lemuel Davis is principally from Hunt and Sheldon, *Deep Water,* 344ff. Other accounts are similar, though there is some disagreement over whether Davis actually gave a set of keys to the prisoners.

"I've done all I can" . . . is from Smith, *Crescent City Lynchings,* 220.

Eventually, Parkerson himself stepped up . . . Here again, the newspaper accounts and secondhand literature disagree somewhat on the exact details of the scenes in the prison, though not substantially.

among them Phillip Lobrano . . . Lobrano's presence in the prison as noted in an article about the Marchesi family's later lawsuit against the city, in the NODP of December 19, 1893.

"The intention had not been to shoot . . ." is from the *Illustrated American* interview.

"There's Scaffidi!" . . . This quote and the rest of this scene primarily from Smith, *Crescent City Lynchings,* 223.

Macheca was the first to be found . . . Hunt and Sheldon are best on the killing of Macheca (*Deep Water,* 352–54).

"Bagnetto, Scaffidi, Polizzi . . ." For the hanging of Polizzi and Bagnetto, and for Parkerson's speech afterward, see the *Illustrated American* article, page 322, and Hunt and Sheldon, *Deep Water,* 35f.

"You have today wiped the stain . . ." is from the NODI of March 15, 1891.

a gruesome tableau . . . Details of the scene back at the Parish Prison mainly as per Gambino, p. 87.

"Of course, it is not a courageous thing . . ." is from the interview in the *Illustrated American,* 322.

virtually unanimous in its approval . . . For the reactions of the business community and the newspapers, see especially Hunt and Sheldon, *Deep Water,* 358f.

"Government powers are delegated . . ." is from the NODP of March 15, 1891.

"When the ordinary means of justice fail . . ." is from the NODI of March 14, 1891.

promised further extralegal means . . . The threat to burn down Little Palermo as per the interview in *Illustrated American,* 322.

Many were forced to leave town . . . For the plight of Seligman and the other jurors, see especially the NYT of March 15, 1891, and the *Deseret Weekly,* March 21, 1891.

As for the lynchers themselves . . . The report of the grand jury about jury bribing and the lynching is reprinted in its entirety in Gambino, *Vendetta,* 163–81.

"the entire people of the parish . . ." Quotes are from the grand jury report as reprinted in Gambino, *Vendetta,* 180–81.

became something of a national celebrity . . . Information about Parkerson in later years from various newspaper reports and his obituary in the NODP.

"a rather good thing" Gambino is best on the aftermath of the lynchings and its effect on US-Italian relations; see *Vendetta,* 97 (for Theodore Roosevelt's comments) and 113–28.

"the able manner in which . . ." Letters to Mayor Shakspeare (including the one quoted) are from the Joseph Shakspeare Collection at the Williams Research Center of the Historic New Orleans Collection

(MSS 96, Folder 7).

"They are quiet, quieter . . ." See Smith, *Crescent City Lynchings*, 277.

the city's Italian underworld — "Mafia" or not . . . The question of whether the defendants in the Hennessy case were guilty or innocent is at this point all but impossible to say. The possibility that non-Italians might have been involved was never even entertained. But as Gambino has pointed out, whether or not Mayor Shakspeare and the city's commercial elite truly believed that the defendants were guilty and that they were tools of the Mafia, it was very much in their interest to reinforce that belief among the general populace.

Chapter 5: A Sporting Man

The best single source on Tom Anderson is the court case that resulted in the wake of his disputed will, *Succession of Anderson* (Louisiana Supreme Court Docket No. 32,083).

dapper and always well groomed . . . Tom Anderson's appearance from various sources. See also photo in Rose, *Storyville,* 42.

a hand in many different ventures . . . Anderson's activities as a business entrepreneur and sporting man as reported in local news reports — for instance, the NODPs of May 7, 1894 (boxing manager) and

October 3, 1895 (horseracing entrepreneur) and the *Mascot* of November 24, 1894 (restaurant owner).

"Only Independent Oil Company . . ." Anderson touts Record Oil in ads collected in the "Thomas C. Anderson Record Oil Company" files at Historic New Orleans Collection.

contemplating that inevitable next step . . . Anderson's growing interest in politics as reflected in the NODP news reports of, for instance, October 21, 1892 (marching with then-Mayor Fitzpatrick in Columbus Day parade) and August 4, 1897 (chosen VP of the Choctaw Club, the base of Ring operations in New Orleans).

a disaster from the beginning . . . For Anderson's contentious second marriage, see Orleans Parish Civil District Court Case 43,575: *Thomas C. Anderson v. His Wife* (Louisiana Division of the New Orleans Public Library).

the product of a bloody-fisted childhood . . . For Anderson's personality and early history, see especially Rose, *Storyville,* 42–43.

a bookkeeper and shipping clerk . . . For details of his apprenticeship at Insurance Oil, see *Succession of Anderson.*

"Well, boys . . ." is from the testimony of William Ulmo in that trial, as are the quotes in the following paragraph.

his childhood sweetheart . . . For Anderson's early marriage to Emma Schwartz, see his succession case and the reports of same in the NODPs of June 2, 8, and 28, 1932.

Emma succumbed to typhoid fever . . . For Emma Schwartz's death, see the NODP of November 23, 1881.

a boondoggle of impressive proportions . . . The most useful source for the Louisiana Lottery is Kendall, *History,* 483–501; $40,000 for Charity Hospital as per Kendall, 485.

No. 110–112 North Rampart Street . . . Tom Anderson's restaurant opening and the establishment's use as a rendezvous point as cited in Rose, *Storyville,* 43; Asbury, *French Quarter,* 434–35; and Long, *Babylon,* 155.

"neutral ground" . . . See Rose, *Storyville,* 43.

"My motto . . ." is from Rose, *Storyville,* 45.

"The Ball of the Two Well Known Gentlemen" . . . A good source for the French balls generally is Rose, *Storyville,* 21–22.

created expressly to bring order . . . For the elite appropriation of Mardi Gras, see Leathem, "Carnival," 3, 18.

"the queen and her court . . ." is from Leathem, "Carnival," 189.

"excesses of cruel treatment and out-

rages . . ." For details of Anderson's marriage to Catherine Turnbull (a marriage that seems to have eluded most of the literature on Anderson), see Orleans Parish Civil District Court Cases 43,575 and 48,601. Quotes here are from the appeal in these court records. For the two-dollar keg of pickles, see the "Inventory of Assets" in the same court record.

Rumors of a romantic relationship . . . Many writers, like Rose and Asbury, seem convinced that there was a romantic relationship between Anderson and Josie Arlington; I side with others, like Long, who have examined the various court records and see no evidence for it.

a businessperson on the rise . . . Details of Josie Arlington's years after breaking with Lobrano come mainly from *Succession of Deubler*.

a new paramour, John Thomas Brady . . . Brady's real surname was Hearn, but like many in New Orleans' sporting world, he used a pseudonym.

a former orphaned child . . . The *Succession of Deubler* case records are best for Josie's orphan years (see also Long, *Babylon,* 150).

"gracious, amiable foreign girls . . ." and quotes from advertisements are from Asbury, *French Quarter,* 450.

"a hoochy-koochy dancer . . ." from Asbury, *French Quarter,* 450.

Josie Arlington sold an interest in the Chateau . . . For the partnership between Anderson and Josie Arlington, see Rose, *Storyville,* 43, and Long, *Babylon,* 155–56.

allowing the genial Tom Brady . . . Brady's ability to quit his job and buy a partnership in a poolroom as per his testimony in *Succession of Deubler.*

to regulate and isolate the trade . . . For Storyville's genesis, see Rose, *Storyville,* 36–39; an interview with Sidney Story in the NODI of December 22, 1902; Long, *Babylon,* 102–06, 110–15.

reputation as a center of sin and perdition . . . Early New Orleans history overview comes principally from Campanella, *Bienville,* and Kendall, *History.*

"to establish, thirty leagues up the river . . ." John Law is quoted in Campanella, *Bienville,* 109.

"Disorderly soldiers . . ." is from Phelps's *Louisiana,* as quoted in Asbury, *French Quarter,* 9–10.

a chronic shortage of women . . . as per Landau, "Spectacular Wickedness," 13, and Hansen, *Louisiana,* 95.

among them eighty-eight inmates . . . The women from La Salpêtrière comes from Asbury, *French Quarter,* 11–12.

"without religion, without justice . . ." is from Asbury, *French Quarter,* 20; see also Rose, *Storyville,* 56, for the city's early history with "sinful women."

the Spaniards sent over few additional colonists . . . according to Hansen, *Louisiana,* 80.

Napoleon sold New Orleans . . . See Asbury, *French Quarter,* 67.

rowdy flatboatmen . . . Hansen, *Louisiana,* 42, is best.

"wholehearted wallowing in the fleshpots" . . . is from Asbury, *French Quarter,* 80.

confidence men and professional riverboat gamblers . . . See Asbury, *French Quarter,* 198.

prosperous Anglo-American planters and merchants . . . New Orleans was the richest metropolis below the Mason-Dixon line according to McKinney, *Cultural History,* 18–21.

downtown "Creoles" . . . For the history of the term, see Campanella, *Bienville,* 161–67, and Anthony, "The Negro Creole Community."

"That vice should be allowed to flaunt . . ." The quotation from Alderman Story is from the interview in the NODI of December 22, 1902.

widely applauded by the city's business

reformers . . . For the motivating need to attract Northern capital, see Landau, "Spectacular Wickedness," 5.

"obscure neighborhoods . . ." is from the NODP of January 1, 1898 (as quoted in Landau, "Spectacular Wickedness," 84).

a mixed-race working-class neighborhood . . . For more on the makeup of Storyville, see Long, *Babylon,* 128.

notices of eviction . . . See Landau, "Spectacular Wickedness," 78.

on the first day of 1898 . . . Storyville's opening as per Rose, *Storyville,* 38.

a choice property in Storyville-to-be . . . Anderson's purchase of the Fair Play Saloon per Rose, *Storyville,* 43.

Chapter 6: New Sounds

The origins and genealogy of jazz have been the subject of considerable contention among music critics and historians (see Bruce Boyd Raeburn's *New Orleans Style* for an account of the controversies over the years). For the development of jazz in New Orleans and Buddy Bolden's role in it, I have relied mostly on Charles Hersch, *Subversive Sounds;* Donald M. Marquis, *In Search of Buddy Bolden;* Samuel Barclay Charters, *A Trumpet Around the Corner;* Vincent J. Panetta, " 'For Godsake Stop!' "; and Court Carney, "New Orleans and the Creation of Early Jazz," all of which do a good job of clearing away the vast mythology that has grown up around the topic.

poor Uptown neighborhood . . . For the neighborhoods and venues where the new sound emerged, see Hersch, *Subversive Sounds*, 13 and 31–32, and Marquis, *Bolden*, 49.

"the good-time, earthy people" . . . The description of early jazz fans as such is from Isidore Barbarin, as quoted in Barker, *Life in Jazz*, 28.

"That boy could make women jump . . ." is from Bill Matthews, as quoted in Marquis, *Bolden*, 100.

"I'd never heard anything like that . . ." is from George Baquet, as quoted in Shapiro and Hentoff, *Hear Me Talkin' to Ya*, 38.

The grandson of slaves . . . For Bolden's early childhood, see especially Carney, "Creation of Early Jazz," 303; and Marquis, *Bolden*, 13–15, 18, and 23. [NB: The house at 385 First Street still stands, though today the address is #2309.]

not a very healthy place to live . . . For the character of the neighborhood in Bolden's day, see Marquis, *Bolden*, 22, and Hersch, *Subversive Sounds*, 36.

Music was everywhere around him . . . Hersch, *Subversive Sounds*, 15–16, is especially good on young Bolden's rich musical environment.

"The city was full of the sounds of music . . ." is from Danny Barker, as quoted in Shapiro and Hentoff, *Hear Me Talkin' to Ya,* 3.

cornet lessons from a neighbor . . . For Bolden's early lessons with Manuel Hall, see the oral history of Louis Jones, January 19, 1959, in the Hogan Jazz Archive; also Marquis, *Bolden,* 38.

plenty of opportunities to play . . . Marquis, *Bolden,* 32, talks about the young musicians filling in for older band members.

Excelsior, Onward, and Eureka . . . Panetta, " 'For Godsake Stop!,' " 29, enumerates the black brass ensembles active in the 1890s.

"ragging the hymns . . ." is from Marquis, *Bolden,* 43.

hot, wide-open, low-down . . . Descriptions of Bolden's sound as per Marquis, *Bolden,* 43; Hersch, *Subversive Sounds,* 1–2, 16; and Chilton, *Bechet,* 5.

"ratty . . ." is from Barker, *Life in Jazz,* 27.

"He could go and hear a band playing . . ." is from Louis Jones's oral history of January 19, 1959, in the Hogan Jazz Archive.

"Buddy, he stole lots of things . . ." is from Kid Ory's oral history of April 20, 1957, in the Hogan Jazz Archive.

"Bolden would blow so hard . . ." is from

Zue Robertson, as quoted in Marquis, *Bolden,* 43–44.

the Bolden persona . . . Marquis, *Bolden,* 7, 40–41, dispels many of the Bolden legends.

the Bolden Band . . . Marquis, *Bolden,* 46, makes the interesting point that Bolden was one of the only leaders who named his band after himself.

"Buddy was the first . . ." is from McCusker, *Creole Trombone,* 54.

improvised solos, or "rides" . . . See Winston, "News Reporting of Jazz," 17.

"With all those notes he'd throw in . . ." is from Albert Glenny, as quoted in Marquis, *Bolden,* 101.

Critics would argue for decades . . . Where jazz came from is a question that few critics seem to agree on. Carney, "Creation of Early Jazz," 300ff., does a pretty good job of summing up the various sources proposed by different critics.

"That's where jazz came from . . ." is from Peter Bocage's oral history of January 29, 1959, in the Hogan Jazz Archive.

"Who cared if you read music? . . ." is from Barker, *Life in Jazz,* 7.

"He wasn't really a musician . . ." is from Kid Ory's oral history of April 20, 1957, in the Hogan Jazz Archive.

bringing the soloist — that is, himself — to the fore . . . For Bolden's new emphasis on the soloist, see Carney, "Creation of Early Jazz," 303, and Marquis, *Bolden,* xvi.

"sort of Maori look about him" . . . as per Berry, "The Mysteries of Buddy Bolden," 43.

a harem of female admirers . . . Marquis, *Bolden,* 45–46; this is also the source for Bolden's relationship with Hattie Oliver.

"Oh, he was crazy about womens" . . . is from Ramsey's interview with John Joseph (Frederick Ramsey Papers, Folder 282).

"whipping heads . . ." Cutting contests described by Bechet, *Treat It Gentle,* 111.

the new sound was dangerous . . . The best sources for the early (white) reception of jazz are Leonard's *Jazz and the White Americans* and Anderson's "The White Reception of Jazz in America."

"Here male and female . . ." in the *Mascot* and the NODP's "demoralizing and degrading" quote are cited in Hersch, *Subversive Sounds,* 5.

"Jazz was musical miscegenation" . . . Hersch himself is the source of this quote (Ibid.).

some dismaying changes in the city . . . The most helpful sources for changing race relations in New Orleans in the latter nineteenth century are Blessingame's *Black New Orleans,* Dethloff and Jones's "Race Relations in Louisiana," Somers's "Black and White in New Orleans," and Reed's "Race Legislation in Louisiana."

a relatively accommodating place . . . For the environment of the 1870s, see also Anthony, "Negro Creole Community," 41–43, and Medley, *We as Freemen,* 25.

"For at least two decades . . ." is from Somers, "Black and White," 30.

a long tradition of interracial fraternity . . . Medley, *We as Freemen,* 20, describes the immigration from Haiti, Cuba, and Martinique.

Creoles of Color often took up trades . . . For the occupations of Creoles, see Kelley, *Right to Ride,* 53.

some of them even owned slaves . . . Fairclough, *Race & Democracy,* 15, points out that many free blacks owned black slaves.

a widely accepted system known as *placage* . . . *Placage* and the Quadroon Balls are ubiquitously described. See especially Long, *Babylon,* 7–12, and Landau, "Spectacular Wickedness," 18ff.

the racial dynamics of the city . . . For social and geographical differences between African Americans and Creoles in New Orleans, see especially Anthony, "Negro Creole Community"; Blessingame, *Black New Orleans;* Dethloff and Jones, "Race Relations"; Woodward, *The Strange Career* *of Jim Crow;* and Reed, "Race Legislation."

All of this had begun to change in the late 1870s . . . Post-Reconstruction changes as per Somers, "Black and White," 27, and Reed, "Race Legislation," 382–85.

Fearing a return of federal military intervention . . . See Somers, "Black and White," 36.

"White and colored people mingled freely . . ." Warner is cited in Somers, "Black and White," 33.

time to reassert old racial hierarchies . . . Somers, "Black and White," 36–39, and Reed, "Race Legislation," 383, describe the changes starting around 1890.

a young man named Homer Plessy . . . Numerous books have been written about *Plessy v. Ferguson* and its implications. From a narrative perspective (details about Plessy's life, etc.), I found Medley's *We as Freemen* most useful.

new laws were passed to suppress the status . . . For the tightening of racial restrictions in the mid-1890s, see Somers, "Black and White," 37–40, and Reed, "Race Legislation," passim.

the music challenged the spirit of Jim Crow . . . Hersch, *Subversive Sounds* (especially 56–58), is best on jazz as a perceived challenge to Jim Crow.

close the notorious "Negro dives" . . . For the effort to close the Franklin Street dives for health reasons, see Long, *Babylon,* 102.

kept within boundaries . . . Landau, "Spectacular Wickedness," 68, is best on the perceived importance of clear racial boundaries to the attraction of Northern capital investment.

"I'm telling you, that was it . . ." The "Home, Sweet Home" story, with quote, is from Frederick Ramsey's interview with Raymond Lopez of August 30, 1958 (Ramsey Papers, Folder 430).

another young black man . . . For Robert Charles's arrival in New Orleans, see Hair, *Carnival of Fury,* p. 67.

Chapter 7: Desperado

By far the most thorough and authoritative treatment of the Robert Charles Riot is William Ivy Hair's excellent *Carnival of Fury: Robert Charles and the New Orleans Riot of 1900.* In the following account, I have relied most heavily on that book, on Ida B. Wells-Barnett's "Mob Rule in New Orleans," and on contemporary newspaper accounts.

a dark, tropical Monday evening . . . Details in this first paragraph come from Hair, *Carnival,* 114–19, and the NODP of July 26, 1900.

"air of elegance" . . . This and other characteristics as per the NODP of July 25,

1900. For other details, see Hair, *Carnival*, 107.

Born just after the Civil War . . . For specifics about Charles's early life, see Hair, *Carnival*, 3–7, 27–34.

during a dispute about a stolen pistol . . . For the shooting incident in Vicksburg, see Hair, *Carnival*, 36, 55–56.

By late 1894, he had found his way . . . Charles's move to New Orleans and his activities with the International Migration Society are from Hair, *Carnival*, 67–68, 96–97.

the timing of Charles's application . . . Charles's resentment of disenfranchisement as per Hair, *Carnival*, 107.

the night of July 23, 1900 . . . The details of the incident on Dryades Street as per Hair, *Carnival*, 19–20, and reports in the NODPs and NODIs of July 25 and 26, 1900.

An hour later, Lenard Pierce was sitting . . . Details mainly from Hair, *Carnival*, 112ff., and the newspaper reports cited above. "I know where I can get that nigger now" is quoted by Hair, *Carnival*, 123.

The captain's instinct was right I have relied on Hair's careful account of the incident at Charles's Fourth Street home, supplemented by the same newspaper reports cited above. All quotes from Hair, *Carnival*, 125–30.

"Do you need any assistance . . ." is from Hair, *Carnival,* 128.

the three officers ran away . . . Details of Perrier's actions come mainly from the report in the NODP of July 25, 1900.

At five A.M. . . . The actions of Aucoin and Trenchard as per Hair, *Carnival,* 126ff.

"In a moment, a hundred or more . . ." and the outhouse incident are from the NODI of July 24, 1900.

Charles's cache of migration literature . . . See Hair, *Carnival,* 132.

"evil toward the white man . . ." The quotes in this paragraph are from the NODP of July 25, 1900.

largest manhunt in the history of New Orleans . . . as per Hair, *Carnival,* 135.

"one of the most formidable monsters . . ." is from the NOTD of July 26, 1900.

even one white visitor from New York . . . See Hair, *Carnival,* 143. Page 145 of the same source cites the rumors of Charles's capture in Kenner.

"as a class" . . . The editorial in the NOTD of July 25, 1900, blames blacks as such.

"We know not, it seems . . ." Quotes from Hearsey's editorial are from the NODS of July 25, 1900.

"Unable to vent its vindictiveness . . ." is from Ida B. Wells-Barnett (as quoted in Lester, "New Negro of Jazz," 45).

"Negroes fled terror-stricken . . ." is from the NOTD of July 26, 1900.

some three thousand men and boys . . . The scene at the parish prison as per Hair, *Carnival,* 152f.

"The angry men swayed . . ." is from the NOTD of July 26, 1900.

"The red-light district was all excitement . . ." and "Out went the lights . . ." are from the NODP of July 26, 1900.

"Aah, we never had nothing like that . . ." There is some confusion in various sources as to whether Peyton, Bolden, Nelson, and the others were playing at Big 25 or Club 28, both clubs on Franklin Street, though the version quoted here says the former. The description of the scene by Nelson is quoted from Lomax, *Mister Jelly Roll,* 111–12.

"The supreme sentiment was to kill Negroes . . ." is from the NODP of July 26, 1900.

By morning, three blacks had been brutally killed . . . For the aftermath of the night of rioting, see Hair, *Carnival,* 152–55.

"The better element of the white citizens . . ." is from Wells-Barnett, "Mob Rule in New Orleans," 33.

"bloodthirsty champion . . ." as quoted in Hair, *Carnival,* 2.

In a small room in the rear annex . . . The scene in the Saratoga Street annex comes mainly from Hair, *Carnival,* 156–74, and from contemporary newspaper accounts.

instrumental in turning away the mob . . . Porteus's actions at the Orleans Parish Prison as reported in the NODI of July 26, 1900. See also Hair, *Carnival,* 152, 159–60.

"his brother Robert Charles . . ." and "Robert Charles was no relation" are as quoted in Hair, *Carnival,* 161–62.

One off-duty police officer . . . Officer Fenny's description of the scene as per "Testimony of Officer Fenny" in the NODP of May 15, 1901.

"For God's sake, don't shoot!" as quoted in Hair, *Carnival,* 166.

a Turkish bath at the St. Charles Hotel . . . See Hair, *Carnival,* 167.

dozens of answering reports . . . According to the NODP of July 28, 1900, some five thousand shots hit the annex building in which Charles was holed up.

the standoff was not to go on indefinitely . . . Charles's last stand was covered extensively in all of the local papers; see also Hair, *Carnival,* 172–74. [NB: The NODP of July 28, 1900, claims that Noiret was alone in the room at the time Charles entered.]

"Now who says . . ." Trenchard's moment of absurdity was reported in the NODI and

NODP of July 28, 1900.

one more night of terror . . . For the second wave of rioting after the death of Charles, see mainly Hair, *Carnival,* 176–78.

"Robert Charles was the boldest . . ." is from the NODP of July 28, 1900.

"Never before was such a display . . ." is from the NODS of the same date.

the inevitable conviction of absolutely no one . . . The judicial aftermath of the case as per Hair, *Carnival,* 198–89.

"The nigger's all right . . ." The quote from *Outlook* is from the May 17, 1902, edition (No. LXXI).

more outright suppression . . . For the uptick in harassment at black music venues after the riot, see Lester, "New Negro of Jazz," 65.

"Nobody knew him . . ." The scene with Louis Nelson's father, and the quotes, are from Lomax, *Mister Jelly Roll,* 112–13.

"This song was squashed . . ." For the Robert Charles rumors, and for Jelly Roll Morton's quote, see Lomax, *Mister Jelly Roll,* 69–70.

Chapter 8: Storyville Rising

The literature on Storyville is extensive, though of varying reliability, much of it compromised by large amounts of folklore masquerading as history. Rose (*Storyville, New Orleans*) is the most complete account, and he spoke to many eyewitnesses from the District's heyday, but his book lacks endnotes and so must be approached with some caution. The latter-day academic accounts by Long (*Great Southern Babylon*), Landau ("Spectacular Wickedness"), Leathem ("Carnival"), and Levy ("Bards and Bawds") are all excellent sources.

"We didn't have no sunglasses . . ." and the one hundred lights are from Rose, *Storyville*, 75.

"most modernly equipped . . ." and the quote about opening night are from an interview with Struve in the *New Orleans Item-Tribune* of August 2, 1931.

a former reporter . . . as per *Succession of Anderson.*

"the man who wants to be a thoroughbred bounder . . ." and other instructions are from Kane, *Queen New Orleans,* 269.

ads, photos, and descriptions . . . The most thorough coverage of the Blue Books is Arceneaux, "Guidebooks to Sin."

"Anyone who knows to-day from yesterday . . ." is from Arceneaux, "Guidebooks to Sin," 401.

"Mr. Anderson had a little white, waxed mustache . . ." For the description of Anderson, see Early, *New Orleans Holiday,* 253 and 270.

an ever-growing domain . . . Anderson's various businesses at this time as per Rose, *Storyville,* 43.

"that Nero himself . . ." Quote from the NODI of December 31, 1901.

"mayor of Storyville" . . . Anderson is referred to often in the press as such, as in, for instance, the NODP of April 16, 1900.

Representative Anderson . . . Many sources incorrectly say that Anderson served in the state legislature from 1904 to 1920. He was actually first elected in 1900.

"Mr. Anderson . . ." and quotes in the following paragraph from the NODP are from the edition of March 13, 1900.

full-throated opposition . . . For the actions of the State Democratic Committee, see the NODP of March 17, 1900.

allegiance to no one . . . For Anderson's vow to be a reformer, see the *Harlequin* of May 26, 1900.

"certain saloon influences . . ." See the *Harlequin* of June 23, 1900.

petition to open up the palatial new establishment . . . See the NODP of November 28, 1900.

a pesky arrest in March of 1901 . . . The arrest for violating the Sunday Closing Law as per the NODP of March 18, 1901.

elected, some said, expressly to overturn . . . as per the NODP of April 15, 1900.

to suffer the depredations of bigger fish . . . is from *Succession of Anderson.* Anderson struggled against the strong-arm tactics of the Standard Oil conglomerate for most of his business life.

paid off for their genial blindness . . . For the payoffs to police in the Tenderloin, see Rose, *Storyville,* 35–36.

laid out almost as rationally . . . An excellent hand-drawn map of Storyville and its various establishments is in the collection of the Historic New Orleans Collection (1950.57.17).

mostly white women . . . Rose, *Storyville,* 96, is the source for the claim about the race of the crib women on Liberty and Marais versus those of Villere and Robertson.

a campaign to eliminate the vice establishments . . . See especially Landau, "Spectacular Wickedness," 85.

doing very well indeed . . . Long, *Babylon,* and Landau, "Spectacular Wickedness," are the best sources on Josie Arlington.

225 Basin Street . . . For a picture of the Arlington brothel, see Rose, *Storyville,* 74.

"oriental statuary" . . . Brothel descriptions as per Landau, "Spectacular Wickedness," 101, and Long, *Babylon,* 162–63.

"absolutely and unquestionably . . ." is quoted in Rose, *Storyville,* 48.

"These places were really something . . ." is from Shapiro and Hentoff, *Hear Me*

Talkin' to Ya, 11.

the most racially integrated square mile . . . See Long, *Babylon,* 6.

Often in trouble with the law . . . For White's arrests, see, for instance, the NODPs of May 10, 1888, and August 12, 1891.

The furniture alone . . . $2,000 value of furniture as per Kane, *Queen New Orleans,*

"the lights of the St. Louis Exposition . . ." Rose, *Storyville,* 40–42, describes Mahogany Hall and cites the Louis Armstrong quote.

the madam who played the role most convincingly . . . For Willie Piazza, see especially Long, *Babylon,* 199, 206–07, and Rose, *Storyville,* 158.

"the most handsome and intelligent . . ." is quoted in Long, *Babylon,* 208. See also Long's article, "Willie Piazza."

an estimated 1,500 prostitutes . . . For the statistics on number of prostitutes, see Long, *Babylon,* 169.

landlords of property in the District . . . See Long, *Babylon,* 145, for the silk stockings who owned property in Storyville.

Even the Storyville mayor's personal life . . . Virtually the entire literature on Storyville — following the erroneous NOTP obituary for Anderson, which cites his "two" marriages — misses the fact that Anderson in fact had four wives in his lifetime.

woman from Kansas named Olive Noble . . . Sources on Olive Noble include *Succession of Olive Noble, Anderson v. Anderson* (the source of the pistol incident), and her death notice in the NODP of December 28, 1907.

"I'll never have a girl ruined . . ." is cited in Kane, *Queen New Orleans,* 272.

Josie's relationship to Anna . . . Long devotes an entire chapter of *The Great Southern Babylon* to Josie Arlington/Mary Deubler and her niece.

"in love with Anna . . ." and all subsequent quotes and details to the end of this chapter are from testimony in *Succession of Deubler.*

Chapter 9: Jazzmen

"The Knights of Pleasure Club . . ." Invitation as cited in the Bolden chronology, page 3, in the Buddy Bolden Vertical File at Hogan Jazz Archive.

a member of the Ladies' Providence Society . . . as per Marquis, *Bolden,* 69.

"Tell all yo' friends! . . ." as cited in Bezou article typescript, Bezou-Goffin Collection (MSS 17, Folder 17–1, University of New Orleans).

"The main topic of talk . . ." is from Ramsey's interview with Danny Barker (Ramsey Papers, Folder 310, Historic New

Orleans Collection).

"All over New Orleans on Saturday night . . ." is from Foster, "Tarnished Angels," 16.

"The picnics at the lake . . ." is from St. Cyr, "Jazz As I Remember It," 6.

playing regularly at Storyville clubs . . . Bolden at Nancy Hank's and Pete Lala's as per Marquis, *Bolden,* 58–59.

began by hiring a string trio . . . and Willie Piazza as first madam to hire musicians, as per Ramsey and Smith, *Jazzmen,* 32.

a single piano "professor" . . . as per Shapiro and Hentoff, *Hear Me Talkin' to Ya,* 54.

Lincoln and Johnson Parks . . . For the new black parks, see especially Marquis, "Lincoln Park," 26–28.

picnics, prizefights, and other entertainments . . . The description of Lincoln Park also relies on Marquis, *Bolden,* 66.

the weekly hot-air-balloon ascensions . . . For Buddy Bartley's ascensions, see also McCusker, *Creole Trombone,* 65–66, and Marquis, *Bolden,* 61.

"One Sunday, he drifted too far . . ." is from McCusker, *Creole Trombone,* 66.

"That's where Buddy used to say . . ." is from the Louis Jones oral history of January 19, 1959, in the Hogan Jazz Archive.

"Old King Bolden . . ." is from Lomax, *Mister Jelly Roll,* 74n.

"I thought I heard Buddy Bolden say . . ." For the lyrics to "Funky Butt," see Marquis, *Bolden*, 109–10.

"When the settled Creole folks . . ." is from Leonard Bechet in Lomax, *Mister Jelly Roll*, 120.

trades traditionally pursued by Creoles . . . See Lester, "New Negro of Jazz," 32.

George Baquet, a Creole clarinetist . . . Baquet in Robichaux's band per Marquis, *Bolden*, 79.

"George, why did you do it?" The incident of the cutting contest is described in several places, including Ramsey in *Downbeat*, December 15, 1940, and January 1, 1941. Also, Marquis, *Bolden*, 81.

"Bolden cause all that . . ." is from Paul Dominguez in the Buddy Bolden Vertical File, Beg.-1999, Hogan Jazz Archive.

"I came to New Orleans in 1906 . . ." is quoted in Shapiro and Hentoff, *Hear Me Talkin' to Ya*, 31–32.

Edward "Kid" Ory . . . The best source for Ory is McCusker's *Creole Trombone*.

"Sometimes the guys would put the horns down . . ." For Ory's early life and the quote, see McCusker, *Creole Trombone*, 30–31.

straight hair, light skin, and Anglo features . . . For Ory's appearance, see Mc-

Cusker, *Creole Trombone,* 22.

"It was dark and no one could see us . . ."
is from McCusker, *Creole Trombone,* 37.

made their own musical instruments . . .
McCusker describes the homemade musical instruments in *Creole Trombone,* 38–39.

"After finishing the three instruments . . ." is from McCusker, *Creole Trombone,* 38–39.

"an old beat-up valve tombone" . . . and Ory's difficulties after his parents' deaths are from McCusker, *Creole Trombone,* 50.

"Then we had some real rehearsing . . ." is from McCusker, *Creole Trombone,* 51.

"Young man, are you blowing the trombone? . . ." The Ory-Bolden incident is cited in several places. Quotes here as per McCusker, *Creole Trombone,* 53–56.

Robichaux, from whom Ory learned . . . McCusker, *Creole Trombone,* 61–62, is the source for Ory's modeling his polished style on Robichaux.

perhaps the greatest jazz clarinetist . . . The best sources on Bechet are his own autobiography, *Treat It Gentle,* and Chilton's *Sidney Bechet: The Wizard of Jazz.*

first heard Bolden playing on the street . . . For Bechet's first hearing of Bolden, see Chilton, *Bechet,* 5.

trying to blow the nozzle of her douche . . . See Chilton, *Bechet,* 4.

"[It] was down there around Canal Street

somewheres . . ." is from Bechet, *Treat It Gentle,* 62–63.

"**Us Creole musicians always did . . .**" is quoted in Chilton, *Bechet,* 5.

"**No, no, no . . .**" The Papa Tio incident as per Bechet, *Treat It Gentle,* 79.

"**Some musicians played the tune prettily . . .**" Chilton, *Bechet,* 7, discusses Bechet's modeling himself on Louis Nelson's playing style, and is the source for the quote.

birthday party in April 1907 . . . Leonard's birthday party as per Chilton, *Bechet,* 5–6, and Bechet, *Treat It Gentle,* 70–72.

"**I knew I was too young for them . . .**" is from Bechet, *Treat It Gentle,* 71.

"**He kept me there all evening . . .**" is from Chilton, *Bechet,* 6.

"**I used to see Sidney around . . .**" is quoted in Lomax, *Mister Jelly Roll,* 115.

"**When Baquet wanted to lay off . . .**" is quoted in Lomax, *Mister Jelly Roll,* 116–17.

Ferdinand Joseph La Menthe . . . Valuable sources for Jelly Roll Morton are Lomax's *Mister Jelly Roll* and Reich and Gaines's *Jelly's Blues.*

"**Uptown Negroes**" . . . For Morton's disdain of Uptown black music, see, for instance, Carney, "Creation of Early Jazz," 301–03.

"**didn't want to be called Frenchy**" . . . is

quoted in Lomax, *Mister Jelly Roll,* 4.

a three-piece string band . . . For Morton playing in the band, see Gushee, "Chronology," 392.

"a very good piece of ragtime" . . . as per Lomax, *Mister Jelly Roll,* 7.

"I was so frightened . . ." is from Lomax, *Mister Jelly Roll,* 30.

"The streets were crowded with men . . ." is quoted in Lomax, *Mister Jelly Roll,* 30–31.

"more money than I ever heard of . . ." is from Lomax, *Mister Jelly Roll,* 31.

"no matter how much his Diamond Sparkled . . ." is from Armstrong, *In His Own Words,* 24.

Laine had a few musicians in his fold . . . For the interest of the white musicians from Laine's band, see Carney, "Creation of Early Jazz," 303, Charters, *Trumpet Around the Corner,* 68, and Shapiro and Hentoff, *Hear Me Talkin' to Ya,* 42.

"Whites who played jazz . . ." is from Hersch, *Subversive Sounds,* 111.

When Giarolamo LaRocca discovered . . . The incident with LaRocca's father as per Charters, *Trumpet Around the Corner,* 128, and Brunn, *Original Dixieland Jazz Band,* 1–5.

"the citadel of white caste privileges" . . . Edmond Souchon's story is from Souchon's *Jazz Review* article, 8–9.

"Most saloons had two sides . . ." is from Foster, "Tarnished Angels," 64.

a rise in cocaine use . . . See the *Chicago Tribune* of July 13, 1903.

"The orchestra consisted of a clarinet . . ." is from the NODI, as quoted in Winston, "News Reporting of Jazz," 33. (NODIs from this year are missing from library microfilms.)

A short, ill-tempered man . . . Morton's description of the shooting at a Bolden performance, including quotations, as per Lomax, *Mister Jelly Roll,* 71–72. [NB: Marquis believes Morton may be conflating two separate incidents in this story.]

"I've often wondered why . . ." is from Lomax, *Mister Jelly Roll,* 72.

"When we started off playing Buddy's theme song . . ." is quoted in Marquis, *Bolden,* 111.

"manifestations of cultural resistance . . ." is from Lester, "New Negro of Jazz," 50.

"These guys wouldn't wear . . ." is quoted in Lomax, *Mister Jelly Roll,* 23.

"just the sight of the famous cornetist . . ." is Bob Lyons as quoted in the Ramsey Papers, Folder 319, Historic New Orleans Collection.

"King Bolden! . . ." as per Marquis, *Bolden,* 96.

Nora Bass, a twenty-two-year-old . . . For Nora and their daughter, see Marquis, *Bolden,* 96–98.

"Sometimes he would have to run away . . ." is Albert Glennie as quoted in the Ramsey Papers, Folder 765, Historic New Orleans Collection.

severe headaches . . . see Marquis, *Bolden,* 112.

Other symptoms appeared . . . For his failure to recognize friends and talking to strangers, see Ramsey Papers, Folder 304.

send Buddy's friend Louis Jones . . . For Jones having to bring Bolden home, see Ramsey Papers, Folder 286.

a fear of his own cornet . . . Marquis, *Bolden,* 112.

Some said he drank too much . . . Louis Armstrong thought Bolden's madness stemmed from excessive drinking per Shapiro and Hentoff, *Hear Me Talkin' to Ya,* 39.

an untreated ear infection . . . Louis Jones on the ear infection is from his oral history of January 19, 1959, in the Hogan Jazz Archive.

he just played too loud . . . Paul Barbarin's mother's theory is cited in Marquis, *Bolden,* 70.

"You can go back home . . ." The incident with Dusen is cited in Ramsey and Smith, *Jazzmen,* 17–18. [NB: The black Masonic and Odd Fellows Halls were the same building on the corner of Rampart and Perdido.]

attacked Mrs. Bass with a water pitcher . . . The incident in which Bolden attacked his mother-in-law is from Marquis, *Bolden,* 112–13.

threw a neighbor's baby out of a window . . . is from Ramsey, "Ramsey Speaks Out," 37.

"He's nuts, you know" . . . as cited in Marquis, *Bolden,* 118.

"Character of Disease: Insanity . . ." Bolden's final decline as per Marquis, *Bolden,* 118–22, which reproduces the commitment document in full.

"Before the dance . . ." is from Armstrong, "Growing Up in New Orleans," originally in *Life* magazine, reprinted in Miller and Anderson, eds., *New Orleans Stories,* 23.

Chapter 10: The Sin Factory

"Representative Anderson of the Fourth Ward . . ." The opening quote, as indicated in the text, is from the NODP of June 20, 1902.

as lucrative and efficient as any lumber mill . . . According to Leavitt, *Great Characters,* 29, prostitution had become the second-largest industry in New Orleans at this time. 230 brothels, etc., as per Long, *Babylon,* 158.

"I'll tell you, five minutes . . ." is from Rose, *Storyville,* 162.

"This Tenderloin District . . ." is quoted in Shapiro and Hentoff, *Hear Me Talkin' to Ya,* 6.

"A lot of the prostitutes lived in different sections . . ." is quoted in Shapiro and Hentoff, *Hear Me Talkin' to Ya,* 5.

"Those places were organized . . ." is quoted in Rose, *Storyville,* 160.

a lagniappe — a little bonus . . . as per Rose, *Storyville,* 162.

"the king of the district" . . . is from Rose, *Storyville,* 114.

a quick delivery of the really good Champagne . . . Details about Champagne sales at Lulu White's come from *State of Louisiana vs. Lulu White,* Docket No. 15,896, as cited in Landau, "Spectacular Wickedness," 176.

"From time to time . . ." is from Danny Barker, *Buddy Bolden,* 54–55.

the corner of Basin and Iberville . . . For renaming of Customhouse Street (in 1904), see Rose, *Storyville,* 219.

"Tom Anderson overtops the restricted district . . ." The excerpt from *Collier's* as cited in Rose, *Storyville,* 46.

"below whore scale" . . . For Sarah Bernhardt's visit, see Rose, *Storyville,* 78.

host to some of the greatest sports fig-

ures . . . as per Levy, "Bards and Bawds," 126.

When George M. Cohan showed up . . . The George M. Cohan and John L. Sullivan incidents as reported by Billy Struve in the *New Orleans Item-Tribune* of August 2, 1931.

"immaculate, cool-headed, and calm" . . . as per Barker, *Buddy Bolden,* 56.

"He listened to their love problems . . ." is from Barker, *Buddy Bolden,* 57.

"characteristically humorous . . ." is from the NODP of June 22, 1904.

a fairly effective representative . . . For Anderson's bills supporting the asylum, and for his gift of oil during the yellow fever epidemic, see the NODP of August 11, 1905, and July 28, 1905.

when President Theodore Roosevelt came to New Orleans . . . See Behrman, *Martin Behrman of New Orleans,* 149.

named to the honorary committee . . . as per the NODPs of October 8 and 27, 1905.

A picture of the two of them . . . is mentioned by Struve in the *New Orleans Item-Tribune* of August 2, 1931.

bills to raise the salaries . . . Proposals regarding police and stenographers were reported in the NODPs of May 18, 1904, and June 21, 1906.

arrested, tried, and convicted . . . Ander-

son's initial conviction on the Sunday Closing Law charge as per the NODP of February 18, 1905.

a large supply of liquor and cigars . . .
Gifts to Judge Skinner as reported in the
NODP of January 4, 1906.

**a Ring stalwart named Martin Behr-
man . . .** Useful sources for Behrman are
his own autobiography, *Martin Behrman of
New Orleans* (hereafter *Memoirs*), and Zink,
City Bosses in the United States.

**"always knew what [had] led to the fall
of the Roman Empire . . ."** Behrman's
definition of a silk-stocking is from Behrman, *Memoirs,* 108.

"uncouth" . . . Behrman's discussion of the
Times-Democrat's calling him this is from
Memoirs, 89.

"Mr. Behrman does not rise . . ." is
quoted in Behrman, *Memoirs,* 81n.

Parkerson accused Behrman . . . For
Parkerson's grafting accusations, see Behrman, *Memoirs,* 91.

"I would rather be a maggot . . ." is
quoted in in Behrman, *Memoirs,* 100.

Steel Arm Johnny, Mary Meathouse . . .
The list of Storyville characters is selected
from a roundup in Rose, *Storyville,* 55.

**rate of violent crime was actually rela-
tively low . . .** See Rose, *Storyville,* 64, for
this claim. For the comparison of per capita
murder rates of New Orleans and Chicago,

see Adler, "Murder," 297ff.

"no doubt the most heartless . . ." is quoted in Rose, *Storyville,* 55.

"Lulu dashed into the room . . ." is from the NODP of November 14, 1904. The ultimate charge against her as per Landau, "Spectacular Wickedness," 83ff.

a discount book of fifteen tickets . . . as per Levy, "Bards and Bawds," 63.

Olivia the Oyster Queen . . . is from Rose, *Storyville,* 85.

"sex circuses" . . . Rose, *Storyville,* 50, describes the goings-on at Emma Johnson's brothel.

"They did a lot of things . . ." is quoted in Rose, *Storyville,* 50.

"was in dread fear continually . . ." is from the *Succession of Deubler,* Tolliver testimony.

She named the place Anna's Villa . . . is from other testimony in the *Succession of Deubler* case.

on the morning of December 1, 1905 . . . For the fire at Josie Arlington's brothel, see the NODP of December 2, 1905.

"scantily clad" . . . The story of the crying prostitute, with quotes, is from the NODP of December 2, 1905.

she began to speak gloomily . . . For Arlington's attitude change after the fire, see Rose, *Storyville,* 47–48, and Harris, "Whatever Became of Josie Arlington?," 40.

Arlington purchased an imposing white mansion . . . All details about the move to Esplanade Avenue are from testimony in *Succession of Deubler.*

Some of her more presentable Storyville associates . . . Anderson's visits to Esplanade Avenue and Anna's Villa, and other details in this paragraph, are from testimony in *Succession of Deubler.*

some tough times ahead . . . For the coming reform legislation governing poolrooms, racetrack betting, and alcohol, see especially Landau, "Spectacular Wickedness," 202–08.

Chapter 11: The Black Hand

The best source for the Lamana kidnapping remains the daily newspaper reports, though Tallant, *Ready to Hang,* 90–137, does a good job of recounting the story accurately and making sense of the plethora of accusations, false leads, and other peripheral details.

On a warm June evening in 1907 . . . The most complete accounts of the abduction scene are in the NODI of June 14, 1907, and the NODPs of June 15, 1907, and July 7, 1909 (with additional details that emerged in the trials). For the scents of Little Palermo, see, for instance, Morris, *Wait Until Dark,* 85.

Lamana had one of his horses saddled

up . . . For Peter Lamana's trip to West End, see especially the NODI of June 10, 1907.

"sewers, dark alleys . . ." is from the NODI of June 10, 1907.

"Your boy is comfortably housed . . ." The text of the ransom note is from the NODP of June 11, 1907.

"cut up in pieces" . . . The threat was reported in the *St. Louis Dispatch* of June 30, 1907.

"Some twelve years ago . . ." is from the NOTD of August 11, 1903.

a man calling himself Francesco Genova . . . For information on Genova/ Matesi and his arrival in New Orleans, see Critchley, *Origin of Organized Crime,* 58. For his Sicilian history, see also Kendall, "Blood on the Banquette," 819–20.

his supposed accomplice in the Seina murders . . . Reid, *Mafia,* 177–79, is best for Di Christina/Marchese.

One day in early May 1902 . . . The conflict with the Lucianos was reported in the NODI of June 12, 1902.

a brutal interfamily mob war . . . For the murder of Salvatore Luciano, see Kendall, "Blood on the Banquette," 22–23, and the NODI of June 12, 1902.

"I am satisfied . . ." is quoted in Kendall, "Blood on the Banquette," 823. For this scene, see also Reid, *Mafia,* 179, and the

NODI of June 13, 1902.

Espare calmly took a revolver . . . For the killing of Antonio Luciano, see Kendall, "Blood on the Banquette," 824–25; Reid, *Mafia,* 181–82; and the *Chicago Tribune* of August 10, 1903. For Espare's jump onto the Arlington Restaurant's roof, see the NODI of June 16, 1907.

the first time in the city's history . . . The first execution of an Italian for killing another Italian as per Kendall, "Blood on the Banquette," 826.

the city's Italian underworld was reawakening . . . *Chicago Tribune* of June 13, 1902.

a marked increase in so-called Mafia activity . . . A good general source on the Black Hand is Pitkin and Cordasco, *The Black Hand.* For the uptick in activity following Genova's arrival, see the *Washington Post* of May 6, 1906.

"prosperous and worthy" The NODP called Lamana this in an editorial of June 11, 1907.

"The people of New Orleans are easygoing . . ." The mass meeting at the Union Française Hall as reported in the NODP of June 13, 1907.

"From now on, the Italians will be resolved . . ." was quoted in the NODP of June 13, 1907.

"There were also loud calls . . ." and the Wickliffe quote are also as reported in the NODP of June 13, 1907.

"make more history for Congo Square" and the quote on vigilantism are from the NODP of June 13, 1907.

two schoolboys who admitted having seen . . . For the search and discovery of the boy witnesses, see the NODI of June 13, 1907, and Tallant, *Ready to Hang,* 100.

a strange Italian had recently purchased a covered wagon . . . The NODI of June 14, 1907, reported on the Campisciano rumors.

"With tears in my eyes . . ." The text of the Thursday letter is from the NODP of June 14, 1907. [NB: I have changed "Harvey's Canal" to the more accurate "Harvey Canal."]

police had by Friday arrested ten suspects . . . as per the NODI of June 14, 1907, and Tallant, *Ready to Hang,* 103.

Capt. Thomas Capo, the inconveniently named officer in charge . . . See Tallant, *Ready to Hang,* 106.

police were forced to release all except Tony Costa . . . The release of prisoners as per the NODI of June 15, 1907.

persistent rumors that the boy had been killed . . . as reported in the daily newspapers throughout the search.

searched with a team of bloodhounds . . .

For the search, with Campisciano looking on, see Tallant, *Ready to Hang,* 107.

tensions began to surface . . . as noted frequently in the newspaper coverage (see especially the NODI of June 17, 1907).

"That is the man who wrote it!" is quoted in Tallant, *Ready to Hang,* 107.

Patorno sent some detectives out to Pecan Grove . . . The search for Gendusa's mistress as per Tallant, *Ready to Hang,* 108.

soon began to turn up some suggestive connections . . . Tallant, *Ready to Hang,* 108–09, recounts Patorno's success in tying together connections among the suspects Gendusa, Luchesi, and Gebbia.

police staged a raid on the Gebbia home . . . For the raid and Leonardo Gebbia's confession, Tallant, *Ready to Hang,* 109, is best.

the confession of Gebbia's sister, Nicolina . . . Tallant, *Ready to Hang,* 110, reports her confession.

"We put out the headlight . . ." The interview with Mooney (and all quotes) was apparently printed in an issue of the NODP missing from the online database. Fortunately, the entire interview was reprinted in the *St. Louis Post-Dispatch* of June 30, 1907 (and, more briefly, in the *New York Times* of June 24 of that year). Some specifics of Campisciano's confession are from the

NODI of June 24, 1907.

This last macabre detail . . . Coverage of the discovery of the boy's corpse (with the detail about the detached head) was especially thorough in, among others, the *New York Times, San Francisco Chronicle, Atlanta Constitution,* and *Washington Post* of June 24, 1907.

"The mob thronged the yard . . ." The scene at the morgue is from the NODP of June 24, 1907.

other information was emerging from interrogations . . . For the details at Campisciano's farm, see the NODI of June 24, 1907, and Tallant, *Ready to Hang,* 112–13.

Angelo Incarcaterra — allegedly on the order of Leonardo Gebbia . . . For Incarcaterra as the murderer, see the NODP of July 17, 1909. [NB: His name was spelled several different ways in different papers.]

"tall man named Joe" . . . as mentioned in the NODI of June 24, 1907. Mrs. Monfre's testimony as per *St. Louis Post-Dispatch* of June 30, 1907. "Mr. Cristina" is mentioned in the NODI of June 15, 1907.

"The reign of the Black Hand is over . . ." is from the NOTD of June 25, 1907.

sending detectives to Kansas . . . For the posse sent to look for Monfre, see the NODI of June 29, 1907.

"Guilty . . ." Trial proceedings as per wide

newspaper coverage. See also Tallant, *Ready to Hang,* 130–31. Jurors' explanation was reported in the NODI of July 19, 1907.

"We want the Dagos!" . . . For the unrest after the trial, see especially the NODI of July 19, 1907.

"A real verdict . . ." was in the NODI of July 22, 1907.

Friday, July 16, 1909 . . . For Gebbia's execution, see the *New York Times* of July 17, 1909.

"just deserts" . . . Lamana's gratitude is from the *Atlanta Constitution* of July 18, 1909, and Tallant, *Ready to Hang,* 135.

a death sentence for anyone convicted of kidnapping a child . . . See the NOTP of January 4, 1917.

Chapter 12: A Reawakening

For background on reform efforts against vice and prostitution, I have relied most heavily on (in addition to the indispensible Four L's of Long, Landau, Leathem, and Levy) Ruth Rosen's *Lost Sisterhood,* Thomas C. Mackey's *Red Lights Out,* and Mark T. Connelly's *The Response to Prostitution in the Progressive Era.*

part of a speaking tour throughout the American South . . . The details of Carrie Nation's visit to New Orleans come principally from contemporary news reports.

"New Orleans is too tough a place . . ." is from the NODP of December 12, 1907.

"I believe in being everlastingly on the warpath . . ." as per the NODP of December 19, 1907.

"I am nothing but a lump of mud . . ." as per the NODP of December 20, 1907.

"President [Theodore] Roosevelt is a bag of wind . . ." as per the NODP of December 20, 1907.

she made sure to investigate Storyville . . . The visits to Emma Johnson's and Josie Arlington's brothels were reported in the NODP of December 22, 1907.

"as soon as [I get] a little richer" . . . as per the NODP of December 22, 1907.

"Welcome, Mrs. Nation . . ." The scene at Tom Anderson's, with quotes, is from the NODP of December 22, 1907, as well as a latter-day report in the NOTP of October 19, 1958.

an audience of eight hundred at the local YMCA . . . as per the NOTP of February 15, 1987.

The mayor's response is unrecorded . . . Nation's parting interview with Behrman — NODP of December 23, 1907.

rise of the Social Hygiene and other Progressive Era movements . . . The shift from Victorian to Progressive notions of prostitution is discussed in Rosen, *Lost Sisterhood*, 61.

"Frisco depot" . . . The opening of the depot as per Landau, "Spectacular Wickedness," 204.

a gorgeous neoclassical pile . . . The description of the depot is from the NODI of June 1, 1908.

so-called lighthouses . . . See Rosen, *Lost Sisterhood*, 82.

unsuspecting young women wandering off . . . For waving prostitutes and wandering women passengers, see the NODI of December 16, 1909.

"We have no doubt that every person . . ." is quoted in the NODI of August 12, 1908.

"The restricted district was already unfortunately located . . ." per the NODI of August 12, 1908.

the classic Southern anthem . . . The publication of "Dixie" per Stanonis, "Woman," 8.

a blueblood through and through . . . For Philip Werlein's biography, see *American Biography: A New Cyclopedia*.

Werlein proposed to erect a wooden screen . . . Werlein's screening proposal was described in the NODI of January 27, 1910.

the aldermen ended up defeating it soundly . . . The vote on screening in the city council per the NODI of February 1, 1910.

the so-called Gay-Shattuck Bill . . . The best source for Gay-Shattuck is Long, *Babylon,* 181ff.; see also the NODI of July 16, 1908.

barrooms in New Orleans would be forced into bankruptcy . . . *Item*'s prediction of about half of the barrooms going bankrupt per the NODI of June 16, 1908.

"the saloon-men and divekeepers . . ." is from the NODP of January 7, 1909.

"antique sandwich" . . . For the exploitation of loopholes in Gay-Shattuck, see Leathem, "Carnival," 226; Landau, "Spectacular Wickedness," 202; and the NODI of January 5, 1909.

a new enterprise — Liberty Oil . . . Founding of Liberty Oil as per Levy, "Bards and Bawds," 130.

Olive Anderson had become sick . . . as per the NODP of December 28, 1907.

they had another ceremony performed . . . The marriage of Tom and Olive as per *Succession of Anderson.*

Two days later, the funeral was held . . . Attendees at Olive's funeral per the NODI of December 29, 1907.

"If an absolutely truthful man . . ." Quotes from Collins and Smith per the NODP of March 2, 1908.

conducting his own undercover investi-

gation . . . For the investigation of Anderson launched by Reverend Lawrence, see various editions of the NODP from June 28 to September 13, 1910.

no judge or prosecutor . . . For difficulty finding anyone willing to try the case, see Levy, "Bards and Bawds," 128.

a large sign outside the establishment . . . The issue of the sign listing Anderson as proprietor per the NODI of August 8, 1910.

lacking a valid address for the saloon . . . Problem in the affidavits per the NODP of August 16, 1910.

"No good excuse . . ." is from the NODI of August 22, 1910.

Anderson agreed to plead . . . Outcome of the trials per the NODPs of September 12 and 13 and October 18, 1910.

Josie Arlington had retired . . . See Long, *Babylon,* 182, and *Succession of Deubler.*

"Josie Arlington solved the problem . . ." The arrest of respectable women at Anderson's ball is recounted in Rose, *Storyville,* 64.

increasingly morbid and religious . . . Characterization of Josie per *Succession of Deubler.*

an elaborate red-marble tomb . . . See Harris, "Whatever Became of Josie Arlington," 45, and Rose, *Storyville,* 49.

"I am living only for Anna" . . . is per *Succession of Deubler.*

"Because men are dogs" . . . is per *Succession of Deubler.*

"The one thing that all Southerners agree upon . . ." is quoted in the NODI of February 1, 1910.

One pair of brothers from New York . . . For the arrival of the Sapir or Parker brothers, see Levy, "Bards and Bawds," 147, and Rose, *Storyville,* 67.

Chapter 13: An Incident on Franklin Street

Much has been written by and about Louis Armstrong. For the account in this chapter, I have relied most heavily on his own *Satchmo: My Life in New Orleans,* and his collected occasional writings in the book *In His Own Words.* [NB: Armstrong's *Swing That Music* was ghostwritten, and apparently in a way that gives doubt to its accuracy, so I have generally not used it.] Numerous biographies exist, but I have drawn on three in particular — Teachout's *Pops: A Life of Louis Armstrong,* Bergreen's *Louis Armstrong: An Extravagant Life,* and Brothers's *Louis Armstrong's New Orleans.*

A dance craze had been sweeping the country . . . See the NODP of March 30, 1913.

numerous dance halls and cabarets had opened . . . Levy, "Bards and Bawds,"

170–74, gives a good list of the establishments operating in the District in 1910.

Their first target was John "Peg" Anstedt . . . For the incident with Anstedt, see Levy, "Bards and Bawds," 148, and Rose, *Storyville,* 67–8, 72, 92.

Phillips renovated the building and reopened it . . . The opening of the 102 Ranch is from Rose, *Storyville,* 68–70. (For Tom Anderson's occasional retreats to the Ranch, see Rose, *Storyville,* 152.)

they opened the Tuxedo . . . Details about the Tuxedo as per Rose, *Storyville,* 95–96; the NODP of March 24, 1913, and Charters, "Storyville," 3.

"I worked at my trade all week . . ." is from Lomax, *Mister Jelly Roll,* 91.

"a noisy, brawling barn of a place . . ." For Pete Lala's, see Rose, *Storyville,* 88.

"Pete Lala's was the headquarters . . ." is quoted in Shapiro and Hentoff, *Hear Me Talkin' to Ya,* 12.

"all the big-time pimps and hustlers . . ." is from *Hear Me Talkin' to Ya,* 5.

"the most famous nightspot . . ." as per Rose, *Storyville,* 94.

"My first job was in Billy Phillips' place . . ." quoted in Shapiro and Hentoff, *Hear Me Talkin' to Ya,* 41.

"After Buddy died . . ." Bechet, *Treat It Gentle,* 84.

Cornetist Joe Oliver . . . For details on Oliver, see Rose, *Storyville,* 119.

"How he could make it talk!" . . . For Oliver's "freak" style, see Shapiro and Hentoff, *Hear Me Talkin' to Ya,* 41–42.

"Something got into Joe . . ." is quoted in Ramsey and Smith, *Jazzmen,* 62–63 (Rose says the incident was at Abadie's, not Aberdeeen's).

Hoping to discipline their wild child . . . For Bechet's childhood years, see Chilton, *Bechet,* 12–14.

"I'd always catch hell . . ." Bechet, *Treat It Gentle,* 78.

"We could never keep our hands on that Sidney . . ." Chilton, *Bechet,* 16.

pouring Musterol ointment . . . Bechet, *Treat It Gentle,* 73.

"I'm sure I can support a wife . . ." Bechet, *Treat It Gentle,* 75.

"One night we ended up in jail . . ." Chilton, *Bechet,* 18–19.

"more assertive than ever before" . . . See Mitchell, *All on a Mardi Gras Day,* 126.

a melee on Burgundy Street . . . For the 1908 Carnival incident, see Mitchell, *Mardi Gras Day,* 113.

"The objectionable feature . . ." Mitchell, *Mardi Gras Day,* 126–27.

"I went carefully up one side . . ." is quoted in Leathem, "Carnival," 216 (also the NODP of March 6, 1911).

Born on August 4, 1901 . . . Armstrong discovered late in life that his birthday was not, as he always believed, July 4, 1900. His Battlefield birth per Teachout, *Pops*, 29.

"pimps, thieves, [and] prostitutes" . . . Armstrong, *Satchmo*, 8.

"I seen everything . . ." Teachout, *Pops*, 14.

quite likely she worked as a prostitute . . . For Mayann as prostitute, see Teachout, *Pops*, 29.

"busy chasing chippies" . . . Teachout, *Pops*, 28.

"It was my first experience with Jim Crow . . ." Armstrong, *Satchmo*, 14.

"disgustingly segregated . . ." Teachout, *Pops*, 15.

"I realize I have not done what I should . . ." Armstrong, *Satchmo*, 16.

natural laxatives . . . On Armstrong's love of laxatives, see, for instance, Armstrong, *Satchmo*, 20–21.

one even struck her in the face . . . Mayann knocked into old Basin Canal per Armstrong, *Satchmo*, 26.

selling newspapers, running errands . . . Armstrong, *In His Own Words*, 9.

"I got to be a pretty slick player" . . . Armstrong, *Satchmo*, 25.

fearlessness, generosity, and respect . . . For his handling of neighborhood bullies, see Armstrong, *Satchmo,* 30.

"In those days . . ." Armstrong, *Satchmo,* 11.

like a second family . . . For the relationship with the Karnofskys, see especially Armstrong, *In His Own Words,* 11ff.

he formed a vocal quartet . . . Singing for coins in Storyville per Armstrong, *Satchmo,* 32.

The trumpeter liked their sound . . . The Bunk Johnson incident is per Brothers, *Armstrong's New Orleans,* 95.

"I got to like Louis a whole lot . . ." This and following quotes are from Bechet, *Treat It Gentle,* 91–92.

"the Mafia moved in on Storyville" . . . For the Italians in Storyville, see Hersch, *Subversive Sounds,* 112; Boulard, "Blacks, Italians, and the Making of New Orleans Jazz," 56; and Morris, *Wait Until Dark,* 91–92.

finding refuge in the bastion of the vice lords . . . Boulard, "Blacks, Italians, and the Making of New Orleans Jazz," 63, has interesting perspectives on the friendship between black musicians and Italian underworld club owners.

regarded by police as the principal figure . . . For Genova as capo, see Dash, *First Family,* 165.

Paul Di Christina was now in charge . . .

Much of the literature disagrees about who was actually in charge of the New Orleans Mafia at this time. See Chandler, *Brothers in Blood,* 97; Critchley, *Origin of Organized Crime;* and Kendall, "Blood on the Banquette."

the Boss of Bosses traveled to New Orleans . . . For Morello's trip, see the *New York Times* of April 3, 1910 and the *Washington Post* of April 26, 1914.

"Mafia death sign" . . . For Morello's red handkerchief, see Dash, *First Family,* 166.

"Dear Friend . . ." For the letter from Morello to Moreci, see Pitkin and Cordasco, *Black Hand,* 132–33. (I have altered some of the diction in the original letter for clarity's sake.)

a native of Termini Imerese . . . For Moreci's background, see the NODS of March 12, 1910; "banana-checker" as per the Police Homicide Report for Di Martini.

"an Italian of the better class" . . . as per the NODP of August 26, 1913.

But there was more to Moreci . . . A good roundup of the subsequent killings was in the NODS of May 15, 1921; see also Warner.

Moreci was walking down Poydras Street . . . For the assassination attempt on Moreci, see the NODS of March 12, 1910, and the NODI of March 13, 1910.

Di Christina was shot and killed . . . Details of the Di Christina killing are from the Police Homicide Report of the incident and the NOTD and NODI of April 14, 1910.

Giuseppe Di Martini was also fatally shot . . . For the Di Martini killing, see the Police Homicide Report and the NODP of June 7, 1910.

"I'm glad I killed him . . ." Manzella shooting details per the NODI and NODS of July 13, 1910. (Josephine Manzella was quoted in the NODI article.)

a series of more mysterious murders . . . Crutti, Davi killings per the NODI of May 17, 1912.

at two A.M. on the morning of May 16 . . . Schiambra (sometimes spelled Sciambra) killing per the NODS of May 16, 1912, and the NODI of May 17, 1912.

"of the latest and most stylish shape" . . . The shoe quote is from the NODS of May 16, 1912.

"Good morning, Mrs. Tony . . ." The two visitors to the Schiambra grocery per the NODS of May 16, 1912, and the NODP of May 17, 1912.

strangely uncooperative . . . Mrs. Schiambra's attitude toward the DA per the NODI of May 17, 1912.

"The Italians of New Orleans . . ." as per the NODI of May 19, 1912.

"Many theories have been advanced . . ." as per the NODS of May 17, 1912.

two new laws . . . For the new restrictions in Storyville, see Levy, "Bards and Bawds," 75–6.

prohibition against interracial concubinage . . . See Long, *Babylon,* 209.

"No subterfuges [would] be tolerated" . . . Smith's campaign against Anderson's ball per Leathem, "Carnival," 227–29.

"Every lover of decency and morality . . ." as per the NODP of March 6, 1911.

fleeing a potential murder charge in New York . . . For Gyp the Blood's arrival in New Orleans, see the NODP of March 25, 1913.

early-morning hours of Easter Monday 1913 . . . The best account of the Tuxedo shootout is the contemporary newspaper accounts and the Police Homicide Reports for Phillips and Parker. See also Rose, *Storyville,* 68, and Charters, "Storyville," 3.

began verbally abusing the Parkers . . . The argument between Parker and Phillips as per the NODP of March 25, 1913, and the NODS of March 24, 1913.

"Come on, give us a drink . . ." and subsequent eyewitness quotes in this scene per the NODS of March 24, 1913.

no meaningful consensus on who shot

whom . . . Conflicting testimony about the shooting melee (as described in later court testimony) per the NODPs of December 20, 1913, and January 14–17, 1914.

a black porter named Willie Henderson . . . Henderson wounded per Rose, *Storyville,* 68.

"As long as the operators of these resorts . . ." is quoted in the NODP of March 25, 1913.

"You will at once take up all permits . . ." is quoted in the NODS of March 24, 1913.

Chapter 14: Hard Times

a detrimental ripple effect . . . For the depressed climate in Storyville after the Tuxedo shooting, see especially Levy, "Bards and Bawds," 84–5.

"New Orleans seems to have put the kibosh . . ." as per the NODP of March 30, 1913.

an increased police presence . . . Levy, "Bards and Bawds," 85

"It is passing strange . . ." as per the NODP of March 30, 1913.

the number of prostitutes working . . . 700 prostitutes, 8 women at Mahogany Hall, etc., per Rose, *Storyville,* 71.

bands reduced the number of players in their rosters . . . per Levy, "Bards and Bawds," 84.

jazzmen were forced to go back to their day jobs . . . Armstrong, *In His Own Words,* 25.

New Orleans caught the tango fever . . . For the rise of the Tango Belt, see Levy, "Bards and Bawds," 85.

"daylight between the dancers . . ." Leathem, "Carnival," 223–24.

Violators were promptly arrested . . . See the NODI of December 10, 1914.

"had closed down the lid so tight . . ." as per the NODI of March 4, 1915.

a new group called the Original Creole Band . . . Reorganization of Tuxedo band per Rose, *Storyville,* 69 and Gushee, *Pioneers,* 76.

touring the vaudeville circuit . . . Original Creole Band's departure per Charters, *Trumpet Around the Corner,* 104–05.

spending much of his time on the road . . . Jelly Roll Morton on the road per Reich and Gaines, *Jelly's Blues,* 55–56.

"Boy, listen to that music . . ." Frisco and McDermott story as per Charters, *Trumpet Around the Corner,* 112–16 (other versions of the story exist).

the name "jass" or "jazz" . . . For the derivation of the term "jazz," see especially Charters, *Trumpet Around the Corner,* 117 (who attributes it to L.A. sportswriters) and Lester, "New Negro of Jazz."

"ballyhoo bands" . . . Jack Laine's ballyhoo bands per Charters, *Trumpet Around the Corner,* 129.

"pointing his cornet skyward . . ." Brunn, *Original Dixieland Jazz Band,* 43–44.

advised James to go hear LaRocca . . . Stein's Dixie Jass Band story as per Charters, *Trumpet Around the Corner,* 130 (again, other versions exist).

a reshuffling of personnel . . . Bechet and Oliver replacing Keppard and Baquet per Chilton, *Bechet,* 19.

more polished style . . . For the popularity of Ory's jazz among white audiences, see Anderson, "Dodds," 422.

"I like the way you play . . ." McCusker, *Creole Trombone,* 107.

"You're doing a good job . . ." Ory hearing Armstrong at Labor Day parade per McCusker, *Creole Trombone,* 102; see also Ory's oral history of April 20, 1957 in the Hogan Jazz Archive.

run with strict military discipline . . . For the Waif's Home, see especially Buckingham, "Waifs' Home," and Kay Thompson, "Louis and the Waif's Home."

"a bad stamp" . . . Armstrong, "Growing Up," 28.

"Davis didn't like me too much . . ." Thompson, "Louis and the Waif's Home," 9.

First, Davis allowed Louis to play the

tambourine . . . For Louis being trusted with various instruments, see Teachout, *Pops*, 34–35; also Thompson, "Louis."

"some rich white folks" . . . Louis listening to jazz while lying on his bunk per Armstrong, *Satchmo*, 52.

"Me and music got married . . ." Teachout, *Pops*, 36.

"I do believe that my whole success . . ." Teachout, *Pops*, 39.

"that great big room . . ." Teachout, *Pops*, 38.

work hauling coal . . . Teachout, *Pops*, 39–40.

"simple, pimply-faced boys" . . . Thompson, "Louis."

"All you have to do . . ." Teachout, *Pops*, 39.

"better than Bolden . . ." Armstrong, *In His Own Words*, 38.

"I'd just stand there . . ." Rose, *Storyville*, 123.

"As long as [Oliver] was blowing . . ." Armstrong, *In His Own Words*, 14, 38.

"which I *loved*" . . . Early mentorship with Oliver, see especially Armstrong, "Growing Up," 29.

"I always knew . . ." Brothers, *Armstrong's New Orleans*, 129.

"Benny asked me . . ." Black Benny bringing Armstrong to National Park per Mc-

Cusker, *Creole Trombone,* 102–3.

"You think you can play . . ." For Black Benny and Bechet, see Bechet, *Treat It Gentle,* 92–93.

"We went out [afterward] and bought some beer . . ." Bechet and Armstrong advertising gig per Bechet, *Treat It Gentle,* 93.

"For the rest of their lives . . ." Chilton, *Bechet,* 22.

"All the bands wanted Benny . . ." Armstrong, "Growing Up," 32.

"Our bandstand was right by the door . . ." Armstrong, "Growing Up," 33.

One night in 1915 at Pete Lala's . . . Bechet and Oliver witness shooting per Chilton, *Bechet,* 21.

"All of a sudden I saw . . ." Incident at Ponce's per Armstrong, *Satchmo,* 60–61.

police would have to break up parades . . . Lester, "New Negro of Jazz," 65.

"Lots of times the both races . . ." Brothers, *Armstrong's New Orleans,* 16.

"People were hearing a lot of excitement . . ." Lester, "New Negro of Jazz," 88.

"Little girl, how I have been fooling you . . ." For Josie Arlington's illness, and the story of her revelations to Anna Deubler (including all quotes), see *Succession of*

Deubler.

"a line of flower-freighted carriages" For
Mary Deubler/Josie Arlington's death and
funeral, see the NODI of February 17,
1914.

"Though her life had been spent . . ." as
per the NODI of February 17, 1914.

"Take her, Tom . . ." For the Anna Deubler–Thomas Brady marriage, see *Succession of Deubler.*

"done up in this deal" . . . For Anderson
suing the Bradys, see *Anderson vs. Deubler,*
Civil District Court, Docket No. 125,290A.

"Segregation of immoral women . . ."
The "No Necessary Evil" editorial was in
the NODI of February 14, 1914.

Chapter 15: The New Prohibitionists

For background on the Gordon sisters, see
especially Kathryn W. Kemp's "Jean and Kate
Gordon," Rebecca S. Carrasco's "The Gift
House," and Carmen Lindig's *The Path from
the Parlor.*

"I'm tired . . ." The death of W. S. Parkerson is principally drawn from newspaper
accounts, particularly the NODPs of February 11 and 15 (from which come all quotes
in this section).

a new commissioner for public safety . . .
For Harold Newman's appointment, see
the NODP of Semptember 14, 1912; more

background on Newman from Stanonis, 107–08.

Two figures in particular . . . The Gordons' background per Lindig, *Path from the Parlor,* 110, and Kemp, "Jean and Kate."

"because we never cared . . ." Kemp, "Jean and Kate," 389.

"Took Lucille Decoux . . ." Kemp, "Jean and Kate," 398.

"and I declined . . ." Kemp, "Jean and Kate," 393.

"stamp out of His world the unfit" . . . Kemp, "Jean and Kate," 398.

"If you don't want the ballot for yourselves . . ." as per the NODI of January 14, 1914.

to close all prostitution districts . . . See Levy, "Bards and Bawds," 86.

"the Joan of Arc of New Orleans" . . . *Literary Digest,* March 24, 1917.

"They finally got Moreci . . ." as per the NOTP of October 11, 1938.

a notorious and much-feared Black Hander . . . For Doc Monfre, see the NODP of December 7, 1907; also *State of Louisiana v. Joseph Monfre,* Docket No. 35993.

"thrust himself forward" . . . Monfre involvement in Lamana case per the NODP of December 8, 1907; see also the NODPs of January 4, 1907, and of January 4, 1917.

arrested for bombing the grocery-saloon . . . Monfre and the grocery bombings per the NODPs of June 12 and 17, 1908.

living in the Schiambras' neighborhood . . . Mention of Monfre in Schiambra murder per the NODP of May 17, 1912.

"Vincent Moreci was the best friend I had" . . . as per the NODS of November 20, 1915.

a virtual orgy of bloodshed . . . For the killings of early 1916, see Warner, *Informer*, 9, as well as the NODS of May 14, 1916 and the NODIs of May 13 through 15, 1916.

"Black Hand shootings and murders . . ." as per the NODI of May 16, 1916.

"I believe you will find that . . ." as per the NODS of May 17, 1916.

"When we get through with our work . . ." as per the NODI of May 16, 1916.

"We have in the City of New Orleans a Sodom . . ." The scene of the Citizens League meeting, including all quotes are from the NODS of January 16, 1917.

"that the most serious and hopeful reform . . ." *Literary Digest,* March 24, 1917, 821.

"drop the lid" . . . as per the NOTP of January 24, 1917.

"**The cabarets as they have been conducted . . .**" as per the NODS of January 16, 1917.

"**must have a licensed restaurant attached**" . . . *Atlanta Constitution,* January 16, 1917.

"**The appearance of a white man . . .**" is quoted in Long, *Babylon,* 216.

describing the women only as "white" or "colored" . . . For the change in Blue Book classification of race, see Long, *Babylon,* 212.

unanimously passed Ordinance 4118 . . . See Long, *Babylon,* 191, 225.

filed suit against the city . . . For the White and Piazza suits, see Mir, "Marketplace," 159–60; Long, *Babylon,* 192; Landau, "Spectacular Wickedness," 186–87.

lobbied to host a military encampment . . . For the lobbying to get Camp Nicholls, see especially Mir, "Marketplace," 163.

federal government in times of war had powers . . . For provisions of the Selective Service Act of 1917, see Mir, "Marketplace," 164.

Chapter 16: Exodus

Ever since the shooting incident . . . For the closing of Ponce's, see Teachout, *Pops,* 42–43.

Mayann had started working as a domestic . . . Mayann working for Matranga per Brothers, *Armstrong's New Orleans*, 167.

he would later adopt him . . . Teachout, *Pops*, 43–44.

"I had noticed that the boys . . ." and Armstrong's description of Nootsy from Armstrong, *Satchmo*, 86.

"bad, strong women" . . . Teachout, *Pops*, 43.

"I wouldn't think of staying away . . ." This and all quotes from Nootsy knife incident per Armstrong, *Satchmo*, 87–88.

"People lined up outside . . ." The story of Armstrong's replacing Oliver is from the oral history of Manetta and Ory of August 26, 1958, in the Hogan Jazz Archive.

"I'd play eight bars . . ." Brothers, *Armstrong's New Orleans*, 290–91.

developing his skills on other instruments . . . Chilton, *Bechet*, 18, 22–23.

he'd learned George Baquet's old trick . . . Chilton, *Bechet*, 21.

"Mr. Basha . . ." is from the *Chicago Defender* of October 7, 1916, quoted in Chilton, *Bechet*, 23.

Clarence Williams put together a traveling vaudeville troupe . . . Chilton, *Bechet*, 23.

"When we went down to the carnival ground . . ." Bechet, *Treat It Gentle*, 96.

"I felt that stick hit . . ." The story of the white escort per Bechet, *Treat It Gentle,* 99–101.

"could play the hell out of that guitar . . ." The story of Bechet's night in jail per Bechet, *Treat It Gentle,* 96–110 (all quotes); Chilton, *Bechet,* 23–24.

newspaper clippings from the road . . . Keppard sending clippings per Bechet, *Treat It Gentle,* 111.

first jazz recordings for Victor in New York . . . ODJB's first jazz recordings noted in McCusker, *Creole Trombone,* 116.

"I don't care what you say . . ." Bechet on why whites can't play jazz in Bechet, *Treat It Gentle,* 114–15. [NB: Nick LaRocca told Al Rose (see Rose, *I Remember Jazz,* 106) that the ODJB played the music so fast in order to fit it on one side of a 78-rpm record, and that after the recording, audiences demanded that they play at that tempo.]

changed up the composition of their ensembles . . . Black groups changing lineup to match ODJB per McCusker, *Creole Trombone,* 117.

"By 1917 jazz, the Southern folk music . . ." Carney, "Creation of Early Jazz," 311.

"A lot of these guys were running wild . . ." On the drafting of jazzmen, see

665

the oral history of Ory and Manetta of August 26, 1958, in the Hogan Jazz Archive.

forcing substantial layoffs . . . Layoffs due to enforcement of Gay-Shattuck per Long, "Willie Piazza," 9; see also Levy, "Bards and Bawds."

"spy on business people" . . . Newman's plainclothes campaign per the NODI of June 19, 1917.

"You might just as well telephone . . ." as per the NOTP of June 20, 1917.

"I do not believe I could have slept . . ." as per the NOTP of June 20, 1917.

"The people of New Orleans have seen . . ." as per the NOTP of June 20, 1917.

"Men must live straight to shoot straight" . . . Landau, "Spectacular Wickedness," 229.

"The greatest menace to the vitality . . ." Landau, "Spectacular Wickedness," 228–30.

"shoot the lewd women . . ." Landau, "Spectacular Wickedness," 230.

sailors sneaking into Storyville . . . Soldiers in civilian clothes per Long, *Babylon,* 228.

"accosting soldiers as they enter . . ." as per the NODI of July 1, 1917.

a penalty of $1,000 . . . as per the NODI of July 1, 1917.

"Situation here not substantially improved . . ." Landau, "Spectacular Wickedness," 234–35.

orders to officially close the restricted district . . . The meeting between the Fosdick representative and Mayor Behrman per the NODS of November 12, 1917.

hastily organized junket . . . For Behrman's trip to DC, see Landau, "Spectacular Wickedness," 237.

"would not require anything to be done . . ." Landau, "Spectacular Wickedness," 237.

"I am at a loss . . ." as per the NODS of November 12, 1917.

"intense desire that immediate action be taken" . . . For the decision by Daniels and the Storyville closing ordinance, see Long, *Babylon,* 227, and Landau, "Spectacular Wickedness," 238.

"Our city government has believed . . ." Rose, *Storyville,* 183.

Tom Anderson would somehow save the day . . . District pinning hopes on Tom Anderson per Rose, *Storyville,* 47.

he had taken up with a madam . . . For details of Anderson's taking up with Dix, see *Succession of Anderson.*

"witty, pretty, and natty" . . . Kane, *Queen New Orleans,* 47.

"irreparable injury and damage" . . . For Dix's court case, see especially Mir, "Marketplace," 165–66.

conspiring to burn their buildings . . .
For arson rumors in Storyville, see Rose,
Storyville, 167.

**insurance companies soon began cancel-
ing policies . . .** Kane, *Queen New Orleans,*
290.

**Dix's request for an injunction was de-
nied . . .** as per the NODI of November
12, 1917.

"Storyville was unusually quiet . . ." as
per the NODI of November 11, 1917.

"Many were the eloquent arguments . . ."
Closing of Storyville per the NODS of
November 13, 1917.

sold under duress for the sum of $1.25 . . .
Sale of Willie Piazza's white piano per Rose,
Storyville, 168.

"As late as 11:30 . . ." as per the NODS of
November 13, 1917.

"It sure was a sad scene . . ." Armstrong,
Satchmo, 96–97.

"put itself in line . . ." as per the NODS of
November 14, 1917.

**federal efforts to keep an eye on neigh-
borhood . . .** as per the NOTP of November 18, 1917.

regular police raids . . . as per the NOTP
of November 13, 1917.

**program to retrain former prosti-
tutes . . .** as per the NODI of November

15, 1917, and the NODS of November 18, 1917.

"After Storyville closed down . . ." Bergreen, *Extravagant Life,* 110.

a grandfather twice over . . . This and other details per *Succession of Anderson.*

forbade dancing and the playing of any kind of music . . . as per the NOTP of September 18, 1918.

"As a citizen and taxpayer . . ." as per the NOTP of July 9, 1918.

he turned the Annex over . . . Annex to Struve per *Succession of Anderson.*

"Tom Anderson's place in Rampart Street . . ." as per the NOTP of September 18, 1918.

the Arlington into the hands of his son-in-law . . . Day-to-day control of Arlington to Delsa per *Succession of Anderson.*

"it might give the nation's enemies . . ." Tame Mardi Gras of 1918 per Mitchell, *Mardi Gras Day,* 167.

The Spanish flu epidemic . . . Armstrong, *Satchmo,* 92, 113.

"Why is the jass music?" The editorial "Jass and Jassism" was in the NOTP of June 20, 1918.

unusually large number of letters to the editor . . . Letters in the June 22, 23, and 25, 1918, editions of the NOTP.

"a departure from the proper in music" . . . as per the NOTP of June 23, 1918.

Chapter 17: A Killer in the Night

Much unsubstantiated nonsense has been written about the axman incident over the years, starting with Tallant's account in *Ready to Hang* (see my reservations in the Afterword) and continuing all over the Internet. The most accurate secondary source I found is *The Axman Came from Hell* by Keven McQueen, who has done yeoman service in the Louisiana prison records. I have drawn my account mostly from contemporary newspaper reports and, where they exist, the Police Homicide Reports.

"In the same manner . . ." The opening quote is from the NOTP of June 28, 1918.

important differences between the two attacks . . . Details about the Besumer attacks come principally from the NOTP, NODI, and NODS editions of June 27 through 30, 1918. Where the newspaper accounts conflict significantly, the source of specific information is cited below.

"My God . . ." and other quotes from Zanca are from the NODI of June 27, 1918. (Some other newspaper accounts say that Zanca ran to the police station to report the incident.)

"I felt like I was going to faint . . ." as quoted in the NOTP of June 28, 1918.

categorically denied that there had been a quarrel . . . Harriet Besumer's denial that Louis attacked her, and Louis Besumer's boasts (about being rich, well educated, etc.) are from the NODI of June 27, 1918.

moved to New Orleans for a rest . . . The NODI of June 30, 1918, says that it had been two weeks since the Besumers arrived in New Orleans, though other sources give other amounts of time.

"Have you any enemies? . . ." This and the rest of the exchange are from the NODI of June 27, 1918.

It was a mulatto man . . . Harriet Besumer's account of being attacked by a mulatto is principally as reported in the NODI of July 1, 1918. Other details are from the NOTP of June 28, 1918.

"If I said so formerly . . ." Harriet Besumer's retraction of her previous accusation is from the NODI of July 1, 1918.

"The case has taken a peculiar turn . . ." The account of the unraveling of the Maggio case and the quote come from the NODS of May 26, 1918.

rampant speculation in the press . . . The cited headlines are from the NODS of June 28 and the NODI of June 30, both 1918.

"My husband is a German . . ." as quoted in the NODI of June 28, 1918.

SPY PLOT . . . Headline and subsequent quote is from the NODI of June 30, 1918.

agents from the Department of Justice . . . The arrival of federal agents as per the NOTP of June 30, 1918.

convinced that the same assailant . . .
Mooney's discussion of possible explanations of the attacks are outlined in the NOTP of July 1, 1918.

"burn him down" . . . is from the NODS of July 2, 1918.

"The last I remember . . ." Harriet Besumer's long quote is from the NODI of July 1, 1918.

"born investigator" . . . The conversation with Louis Besumer at police headquarters comes principally from the NODI of July 3, 1918. Other details are from the NOTP of July 4, 1918.

"If I am not . . ." The long conversation with Harriet Besumer and all quotes are mainly from the NODI of July 4, 1918.

notoriously corrupt and incompetent . . .
For Mooney's attempts to reform the police department, see the NOTP of September 8, 1917.

found at the Milneburg resort . . . For the incident involving the two detectives demoted for being at Milneburg, see the NOTP of July 7, 1918.

"one of the most baffling mysteries . . ."
Mooney's quotes to the press are from the NOTP of July 7, 1918.

"Along toward dawn . . ." Harriet Besumer's recaptured memory of the man above her bed (with all quotes) is from the NOTP of July 7, 1917.

Chapter 18: "Almost As If He Had Wings"

It was two A.M. . . . For the attack on Mary Schneider, see the NODIs of August 4 and 5, 1918, and the NODS of August 5, 1918.

a broken glass lamp . . . Details about the lamp from the NOTP of August 6, 1918.

"delicate condition" . . . as per the NODI of August 4, 1918.

a box containing $102 . . . as per the NODI of August 4, 1918.

several strands of the victim's hair . . . and the detail about the missing ax per the NODS of August 6, 1918.

"At the present time . . ." as per the NODI of August 5, 1918.

earlier incident back in December 1917 . . . Epifania Andollina attack per McQueen, *Axman,* 23

successfully give birth to a baby girl . . . as per the NODI of August 5, 1918.

"Members of the [detective] squad . . ." as per the NODS of August 7, 1918.

chief and other police officials were on the record . . . as per the NODI of August 5, 1918.

ARMED MEN GUARD SLEEPING FAMI-LIES . . . as per the NODI of August 5, 1918.

"all-night vigils" . . . as per the NODS of

August 7, 1918.

"some insane beast" . . . as per the NODI of August 5, 1918, and the NOTP of August 6, 1918.

"More than 12 victims have fallen . . ." as per the NODI of August 5, 1918.

detail of the 1910 Crutti attack . . . For the mockingbird incident, see the NOTP of August 14, 1910, as reported in McQueen, *Axman,* 11–12.

assigning as many patrolmen as could be spared . . . Mooney sending men to thinly settled areas per the NODI of August 5, 1918.

"study of criminals . . ." Letters from forensic expert per the NODI of August 8, 1918.

"The man seems to know considerable . . ." as per the NOTP of August 9, 1918.

"I've been nervous about this axman . . ." as per the NODI of August 10, 1918.

"There at the foot of the bed . . ." as per the NOTP of August 11, 1918.

"almost as if he had wings" . . . McQueen, *Axman,* 30.

"I've been hit . . ." as per the NODI of August 10, 1918, and the NOTPs of August 11, 1918.

a wallet, which was now missing . . . The NOTP said the wallet had been taken; the NODS (of August 10, 1918) claimed it was not taken.

much more was left behind . . . Gold watch on the mantelpiece, etc., as per the NODI of August 10, 1918.

"I'm convinced that the Romano murder . . ." as per the NODI of August 10, 1918.

decision to consult with expert criminologists . . . as per the NODS of August 11, 1918.

"This series of ax outrages . . ." as per the NODI of August 11, 1918.

WHO WILL BE NEXT . . . as per the NOTP of August 11, 1918.

"A literal reign of terror . . ." as per the NODI of August 10, 1918.

reports of alleged axman sightings . . . as per the NODI and the NODS of August 10, 1918, and the NOTP of August 11 and 12, 1918.

Everyone seemed to have a different theory . . . Speculation about axman identity per the NODI and NODS of August 11, 1918.

"Although practically all the victims . . ." Dantonio interview per the NOTP of August 13, 1918.

shooting at suspicious figures . . . as per the NOTPs of August 12, 1918, and the NODI of August 16, 1918.

"a badly frightened Negro woman" . . . Cardajal incident per the NOTP of August

17 and 19, 1918.

"I believe it is criminal . . ." as per the NODS of August 16, 1918.

"scathing criticism" . . . Public response to the absence of any arrest per the NODI of August 12, 1918.

"recovered from the trance . . ." as per the NODS of August 19, 1918.

"On the night I was assaulted . . ." as per the NOTP of August 20, 1918.

Louis Besumer arrested on a charge of assault . . . as per the NODI of August 19, 1918.

confirmed this last claim . . . Confirmation of Mrs. Lowe's accusations as per the NODI and NODS of August 19, 1918, and the NOTP of August 20, 1918.

"Mrs. Lowe is a good woman . . ." as per the NOTP and NODS of August 20, 1918.

"dangerous and suspicious character" . . . Mooney's grounds for protesting Besumer's bail per the NODI of August 23, 1918.

"some weight to the theory . . ." as per the NODS of August 20, 1918.

ATTENTION MR. MOONEY . . . Text of ad per the NODI of August 22, 1918.

cresting of the Spanish flu epidemic . . . Effects of flu on nightlife per McCusker, *Creole Trombone,* 130.

great number of funerals . . . Brothers, *Armstrong's New Orleans,* 239.

"itchy feet" . . . Chilton, *Bechet*, 24–25.

"A whole lot of musicianers . . ." Bechet, *Treat It Gentle*, 116.

joined the band led by Lawrence Duhe . . . McCusker, *Creole Trombone*, 25.

"featured hot man" . . . Chilton, *Bechet*, 28.

On June 19, a dance . . . Charters, *Trumpet Around the Corner*, 164; McCusker, *Creole Trombone*, 125.

"What about the band? . . ." McCusker, *Creole Trombone*, 125.

"I was back on my job . . ." Armstrong, *Satchmo*, 136.

"You still blowin' that cornet?" . . . Armstrong, *Satchmo*, 137.

"What a thrill that was! . . ." Armstrong, *Satchmo*, 137.

gig that night at Economy Hall . . . McCusker, *Creole Trombone*, 126–27.

"blow up a storm . . ." Armstrong's triumph per Armstrong, *Satchmo*, 138–39.

had to work various jobs . . . Brothers, *Armstrong's New Orleans*, 24; Armstrong, *Satchmo*, 133.

"I was carrying the coal inside . . ." Armstrong, *Satchmo*, 144.

"a bolt of lightning . . ." Armstrong's realization re: meaning of Armistice per Teach-out, *Pops*, 46.

"The freewheeling days . . ." McCusker, *Creole Trombone,* 131.

another subdued affair . . . Mardi Gras of 1919 per Mitchell, *Mardi Gras Day,* 167, and the NOTP of March 5, 1919.

now on a murder charge . . . Harriet Lowe's death per the NOTP of September 17, 1918.

morning of March 10, 1919 . . . Cortimiglia murder reported in the NODI, NODS, and NOTP of March 10, 1919.

Chapter 19: The Axman's Jazz

"Who is the axman . . ." as per the NODS of March 11, 1919.

the most brutal assault so far . . . Details of the Cortimiglia attack are mainly from the NODI, NODS, and NOTP of March 10, 1919.

"Frank, I'm dying . . ." as per the NOTP of March 10, 1919 (apparently the Jordanos' real name was Guagliardo, but they did business under the name Jordano).

$129 in cash . . . Details of "robbery" per the NOTP of March 10, 1919, and the NODI of March 11, 1919.

two axes on the premises . . . as per the NODI of March 10, 1919.

feuding for some time . . . Jordano-Cortimiglia rivalry per the NOTP of March 10, 1919.

"degenerate madman . . ." Mooney's speculations in the NOTP of March 11, 1919.

continued to insist that he did not recognize . . . The NOTP and NODS of March 15, 1919, disagreed over whether Charles Cortimiglia joined his wife in condemning Frank Jordano; certainly the husband claimed later not to have recognized his assailant.

"vouch for the condition of their minds" . . . Doctor's refusal to comment per the NODS of March 15, 1919.

"Both Charlie Cortimiglia and his wife . . ." as per the NODS of March 15, 1919.

a high-profile presentation to the press . . . as per the NOTP of March 16, 1919.

Location — In nearly all of the cases . . . List of common elements in crimes per the NOTP of March 16, 1919.

"Esteemed Mortal . . ." Text of Axman letter per the NOTP of March 16, 1919.

"The tinkle of jazz music . . ." as per the NOTP of March 19, 1919.

"Enter by way of the bathroom . . ." as per the NOTP of March 18, 1919.

"every known incidental . . ." Davilla's composition per the NOTP of March 20, 1919.

"Immunity promised all homes . . ." as

per the NODS of May 10, 1919.

police on high alert . . . as per the NOTP of March 16, 1919.

"No burglar . . ." as per the NOTP of March 16, 1919.

Besumer finally got his day in court . . . For the Besumer trial, see the NOTPs of April 29, May 1 and 2, 1919.

arrested two days after his son . . . Arrest of Iorlando Jordano per the NOTP of March 18, 1919.

trial for the murder of baby Mary Cortimiglia . . . Jordano trial per the NOTP of May 6 and 24, 1919.

jury found both Jordanos guilty . . . as per the NODS of May 27, 1919.

appealed to the state Supreme Court . . . as per the NOTP of August 4, 1919.

"There is no getting away from the fact . . ." as per the NODI of April 28, 1919.

3:15 A.M. on Sunday, August 4 . . . Sarah Laumann attack reported in the NODS, NOTP, and NODI of August 4, 1919.

"I felt a stinging . . ." as per the NODS of August 4, 1919.

"He was about five feet and eight inches . . ." as per the NODS of August 4, 1919.

grocer named Steve Boca . . . McQueen, *Axman,* 40.

a druggist named William Carlson . . .

McQueen, *Axman,* 41.

"bellowing that her father was full of blood . . ." Pipitone murder per Police Report of Homicide and the NOTP of October 27, 1919.

a foot-long thick iron bar . . . Police Report of Homicide.

"Someone was calling me . . ." as per the NODS of October 27, 1919.

linking the Pipitone murder to the rash of Mafia killings . . . as per the NODS of October 27, 1919, and the NOTP of October 28, 1919.

"that the police have not the slightest clue" . . . as per the NOTP of October 29, 1919.

"Everyone kept saying . . ." as per the NODI of February 4, 1920.

"God, I hope I can sleep now . . ." as per the NOTP of February 2, 1920.

continuing criticism for his inability to solve the murders . . . See the NOTP of November 21, 1919, and March 20, May 30, and December 7, 1920.

in the wilds of Honduras . . . Mooney running railroad per the NOTP of January 10, 1921.

PUNCTILIOUSNESS, PRIMNESS, AND PRUDERY . . . as per the NOTP of January 2, 1920.

going truly underground . . . For vice going underground in the '20s, see especially Vyhnanek, *Unorganized Crime,* 130–34.

each arrested at least once . . . For White, Piazza, and Dix arrests, see Vyhnanek, *Unorganized Crime,* 132–33.

"You can make prositituion illegal . . ." cited frequently, as in Long, *Babylon,* 156.

sold his tony restaurant the Stag to Henry Ramos . . . as per the NOTP of October 18, 1907.

turned over to his longtime lieutenant . . . Annex to Struve per *Succession of Anderson.*

stately home on Canal Street . . . Canal Street house to Irene Delsa, move to Rampart Street apartment per *Succession of Anderson.*

"Why was Anderson never prosecuted . . ." as per the NOTP of October 13, 1918.

US government was still tasked . . . Continuation of War Department measures after Armistice per the NOTP of June 29, 1919. [NB: Since Republicans had been all but eliminated as a political force with the disenfranchisement of blacks in the 1898 Constitution, the Democratic primary was the key vote in any Louisiana election at this time, with the nominee virtually assured of winning in the general election that followed.]

inspections of the city's cabarets . . . Wilson and Edler investigation per the NOTP of June 29, 1919.

evening of June 26, 1919 . . . The scene at the Arlington comes principally from testimony in the later trial, reported in the NODIs of February 3 and 4, 1920, and the NOTP of February 4, 1920.

"There he is now . . ." as per the NODI of February 3, 1920.

"That little fool . . ." as per the NOTP of February 4, 1920.

"The girl began wriggling . . ." as per the NODI of February 4, 1920.

"The Orleans Parish Grand Jury . . ." as per the NODI of June 29, 1919.

another indictment followed . . . US District Court indictment per the NODS of July 15, 1919.

"Cabaret Day in the court . . ." The Criminal District Court trial per the NODI of October 2, 1919.

ANDERSON CAFÉ SPOTLESS . . . as per the NODI of October 7, 1919.

"There is no evidence to show . . ." as per the NOTP of October 8, 1919.

"I will not discuss the case! . . ." as per the NOTP of October 8, 1919.

"I conducted a first-class saloon . . ." as

per the NOTP of October 8, 1919.

"the amazing spectacle . . ." as per the NOTP of October 11, 1919.

"The best element of the citizenry . . ." as per the NOTP of October 9, 1919.

matters of state law . . . Anderson lawyers trying to get federal charges dismissed per the NODS of October 8, 1919.

"the period of emergency . . ." as per the NOTP of October 17, 1919.

"the indignation of the best elements" . . . as per the NOTP of October 13, 1919.

threaten the US prosecutor with removal . . . Preachers' threats per the NOTP of October 12, 1919.

"thoroughly Tomandersonized" . . . as per the NOTP of October 19, 1919.

"In this state . . ." as per the NODI of October 24, 1919.

"This New Orleans Ring sends . . ." as per the NOTP of October 26, 1919.

"ingratitude" . . . Anderson railing against friends for being dropped per the NOTP of October 19, 1919.

"New Orleans Nights" . . . The series ran in the NOTPs of January 11–18, 1920.

"Under 20 YEARS OF RING RULE . . ." as per the NOTP of January 15, 1920 [emphasis in original].

defeated his opponent Stubbs . . . Parker defeats Stubbs by 12,000 votes per Behrman, *Memoirs,* 289.

"**We are going to finish . . .**" as per the NOTP of January 28, 1920.

"**the case which has probably attracted . . .**" as per the NOTP of February 3, 1920.

"**knowingly conducting an immoral resort . . .**" Official federal charge against Anderson per Vyhnanek, *Unorganized Crime,* 131.

"**was of such a character . . .**" Edler's testimony per the NODI of February 3, 1920, and the NOTP of February 4, 1920.

"**As the witness recounted this . . .**" as per the NODI of February 3, 1920.

"**I was never aware of any women . . .**" as per the NODI of February 4, 1920.

"**rolling their eyes about . . .**" Wilson's testimony per the NODI of February 4, 1920.

"**If it please the court . . .**" Verdict per the NODI of February 5, 1920.

"**I am more glad than I can say . . .**" as per the NODI of February 5, 1920.

"**It looks like somebody was trying to frame up . . .**" as per the NODI of February 5, 1920.

federal government eventually declined to retry . . . as per the NOTP of June 12, 1920.

"**must be [one] of those who see no**

685

evil . . ." Vhynanek, *Unorganized Crime*, 132.

voter fraud and violations of the Injunction and Abatement Act . . . as per the NODI of February 11 and April 3, 1920.

"The Tom Andersons . . ." as per the NOTP of August 5, 1920.

they pounded away at the four-term mayor . . . There is a particularly good discussion of the conflict between Behrman and the reformers in Schott's "The New Orleans Machine and Progressivism."

"Our city is at a parting of the ways . . ." as per the NOTP of August 5, 1920.

hampered by an illness . . . Reynolds, *Machine Politics,* 109–14.

he lost by a mere 1,450 votes . . . Behrman, *Memoirs,* 314n.

THE RING IS SMASHED! . . . as per the NOTP of September 16, 1920.

divest himself of the last major holding . . . Anderson sells the Arlington to Delsa per the NOTP of July 13, 1921.

"The police, it is said . . ." as per the NOTP of July 13, 1921.

Chapter 21: The Soiled Phoenix

speakeasies, illegal gambling dens . . . For the wide availability of liquor in New Orleans during Prohibition, see Joy Jackson's "Prohibition in New Orleans: The

Unlikeliest Crusade." For other vice post-1920, see especially Vyhnanek's *Unorganized Crime.*

improving the city's infrastructure . . . A good source for the civic improvements in New Orleans and Louisiana generally is Samuel C. Shepherd Jr.'s "In Pursuit of Louisiana Progressives"; see also Hair, *Kingfish,* 110.

pitches at conventioneers and businessmen . . . Change in strategy for tourism officials per Stanonis, *Creating the Big Easy,* 46.

"The Crescent City, according to . . ." Stanonis, *Creating the Big Easy,* 28–29.

"as a monument to the business community" . . . Stanonis, *Creating the Big Easy,* 50–51.

decamped shortly after the closing of Storyville . . . Emma Johnson's departure per Rose, *Storyville,* 50.

Storyville legend has her moving to Europe . . . Willie Piazza's later history per Long, *Babylon,* 2, 213, 223.

"I could not do anything wrong . . ." Landau, "Spectacular Wickedness," 189.

"I am suffering dearly . . ." Lulu White's later history per Landau, "Spectacular Wickedness," 191–93.

the saloon next door . . . White's 1912 purchase of saloon per Landau, "Spectacu-

"What are all those tall buildings? . . ." Armstrong, *Satchmo,* 191.

began playing with a small ensemble . . . Armstrong playing at Anderson's per Brothers, *Armstrong's New Orleans,* 261.

"I had made up my mind . . ." Armstrong, *Satchmo,* 226.

Oliver sent him a telegram . . . invitation to play Lincoln Gardens gig per Teachout, *Pops,* 60.

"I jumped sky-high . . ." Shapiro and Hentoff, *Hear Me Talkin' to Ya,* 103.

"four years of torture and bliss" . . . Teachout, *Pops,* 47.

a funeral in Algiers . . . Teachout, *Pops,* 62.

"It seemed like all New Orleans . . ." Armstrong, *Satchmo,* 228.

"a *living,* a *plain* life . . ." Teachout, *Pops,* 62.

"My boyhood dream . . ." Armstrong, *Satchmo,* 240.

nine years later . . . Armstrong's return visit per Teachout, *Pops,* 62.

"all decent, self-respecting citizens . . ." Stanonis, *Creating the Big Easy,* 106.

maintaining pressure on the new administration . . . Stanonis, *Creating the Big Easy,* 112.

didn't rest on the eugenics issue . . . Gordon advocating for state sterilization law per Carrasco, "Gift House," 323.

"When Jean was convinced . . ." Carrasco, "Gift House," 311.

proved to be an inept politician . . . McShane and ODA coalition collapse per Reynolds, *Machine Politics,* 216.

winner was none other than Martin Behrman . . . Martin Behrman's return per Reynolds, *Machine Politics,* 216–23.

out of politics — and out of the vice business . . . Details of Tom Anderson's later history (including all quotes) are mainly from *Succession of Anderson.*

Irene was in fact the issue of a legal marriage . . . The 1880 US Census lists Thomas and Emma Anderson living together at 253 St. Louis Street.

remarked on the startling resemblance . . . Judge's remarks on family resemblance per *Succession of Anderson.*

the night of December 9, 1931 . . . For story of Anderson's death, see the NODS and NODI of December 10, 1931.

"Mr. Anderson . . ." Quotes from obituaries in the NOTP, NODI, and NODS editions of December 10 and 11, 1931.

tried to reinvent New Orleans yet again . . . New Orleans troubles in the 1930s per Souther, *Parade,* 3.

restored as an intriguing holdover . . . For the restoration of French Quarter, see Ellis's *Madame Vieux Carre;* also Souther, *Parade,* 7–8.

something to be revived and promoted . . . For the jazz revival, see Stanonis, *Creating the Big Easy,* 195–234;
Souther, "Birthplace," 42–48.

forced to stay at a "colored hotel" . . .
Stanonis, *Creating the Big Easy,* 239.

"still shackled by the iron grip . . ."
Souther, "Birthplace," 66.

Afterword: Who Was the Axman?

**Monfre's killer was another ex–New Or-
leanian . . .** For Esther Albano's slaying of
Joseph Monfre, see the NOTP and NODI
editions of December 15 through 17, 1921.

"I grabbed my revolver . . ." is from the
NOTP of December 16, 1921.

investigators noticed a pattern . . . Police
compare Monfre's prison admissions and
releases to axman crimes per the NOTP of
December 15, 1921, and the NODI of
December 16, 1921.

the paper ridiculed the theory . . . as per
the NODI of December 16, 1921.

records are "muddled" . . . McQueen on
Monfre's prison records in McQueen, *Ax
man,* 51.

If I were to hazard a guess . . . My
speculations at the end are based principally
on the Police Homicide Reports and the
newspaper reportage of the crimes published in the days after they occurred; much

691

misinformation was introduced by reporters (for example, that the Pipitone murder was an ax crime) in later articles about the axman phenomenon.

ACKNOWLEDGMENTS

My family sometimes accuses me of choosing book topics based on where I want to spend time doing research, and in the case of *Empire of Sin,* there's more than a little truth to the charge. New Orleans, as anyone who knows it can attest, has a kind of insouciant charisma that no other American city can replicate, and the prospect of immersing myself in such a place was undeniably appealing. An unexpected bonus was discovering that so many of the caretakers of the city's history — whether native-born New Orleanians or transplants — had an insouciant charisma all their own, not to mention a willingness to share their expertise that made my job a whole lot easier.

I'd first like to thank Irene Wainwright and the staff of the Louisiana Division/City Archives at the New Orleans Public Library. Irene and her crew (including Cheryl Picou, Christina Bryant, Greg Osborn, Nancy Aloisio, Stephen Kuehling, and Yvonne Loiselle)

693

fielded countless questions, unearthed numerous old documents and court transcripts, and resuscitated many a reluctant microfilm printer for me over the years. A special hat-tip goes to Yvonne and to Wayne Everard, former head of the Louisiana Division, for reading and commenting on the finished manuscript.

I had plenty of help Uptown as well. At Tulane, particular thanks go to Bruce Raeburn, director of the rich and valuable Hogan Jazz Archive, as well as the archive's knowledgeable and always companionable staff — Nicole Shibata, Lynn Abbott, and Alaina Hébert. Also at Tulane, Leon C. Miller, Ann E. Smith Case, Sean Benjamin, Jeffrey A. Rubin, and the staff of the university's Louisiana and Special Collections earned my gratitude for numerous acts of kindness and scholarly guidance.

Down in the French Quarter, I owe thanks to the entire staff of the Williams Research Center at the Historic New Orleans Collection, but in particular to Mark Cave, Daniel Hammer, Eric Seifert, Jennifer Navarre, and Bobby Ticknor. Eddie Gonzales, Deputy Clerk of the Louisiana Supreme Court, was instrumental in locating and making available the full transcript of the Anderson succession trial, one of the most critical (and difficult to locate) documents I needed for this project. Meanwhile, up toward Lake Pontchartrain,

Florence M. Jumonville and the staff of Special Collections at the University of New Orleans were also extremely helpful.

For various assistance, guidance, and other favors, I'd also like to thank Sheila Lee of the Louisiana Newspaper Project at LSU; the staff of the library at Notre Dame Seminary in New Orleans; organized-crime expert Richard Warner; Kathy and Kevin Laborde; author Emily Epstein Landau; restaurateur Joanne Clevenger; the staff of the Mormon Family Research Center in Kensington, Maryland; and (for reasons too complicated to outline here) President Wallace D. Loh, Timothy Hackman, and Patricia Steele of the University of Maryland. Special mention must go to Richard Campanella of Tulane, whose brilliant work in the past and present geography of New Orleans greatly enhanced my understanding of the city. And as always, thanks to my pal Lisa Zeidner for her keen editorial eye.

I'd also like to express appreciation to the friends I've made in New Orleans, especially writers Moira Crone and Rodger Kamenetz, historian Judith K. Schafer, and lawyer Tim Schafer (who is a great-grandson of Thomas C. Anderson). And probably my biggest debt is to Alecia Long, author of the superb book *The Great Southern Babylon,* reader of the finished manuscript, and someone I'm now proud to call my friend. How I will miss dinners in New Orleans with Alecia.

At Crown, I feel incredibly lucky in my wonderful new editor, Domenica Alioto, who stepped in when my former editor, the similarly wonderful Sean Desmond, left the company midway through the project. Thanks, too, to Molly Stern, Dyana Messina, Stephanie Knapp, and many others at Crown. A big fist-bump as usual goes to my friend and agent, Eric Simonoff at William Morris Endeavor, and to his assistant, Kate Barry.

Finally, as ever, I owe the deepest thanks to my family — my wife, Elizabeth Cheng Krist; my daughter, Anna Krist; and, yes, even Lily, my constant and delightful canine companion during the long days of writing this book.

ABOUT THE AUTHOR

Gary Krist has written for the *New York Times, Esquire, Salon,* the *Washington Post Book World,* and elsewhere. He is the author of the *New York Times* bestselling *City of Scoundrels* and the acclaimed *The White Cascade,* as well as several works of fiction. He has been the recipient of the Stephen Crane Award, the Sue Kaufman Prize from the American Academy of Arts and Letters, and a Lowell Thomas Gold Medal for Travel Journalism.